URBAN GOVERNMENT AND THE RISE OF THE FRENCH CITY

URBAN GOVERNMENT AND THE RISE OF THE FRENCH CITY

Five Municipalities in the Nineteenth Century

William B. Cohen

St. Martin's Press
New York

ISBN 0-312-17695-3

Library of Congress Cataloging-in-Publication Data
Cohen, William B., 1941-
    Urban government and the rise of the French city : five
    municipalities in the nineteenth century / William B. Cohen.
        p.   cm.
    Includes bibliographical references (p.) and index.
    ISBN 0-312-17695-3
    1. Municipal government—France—History—19th century Case
    studies.   2. Municipal services—France—History—19th century—Case
    studies.   I. Title.
JS4851.C64 1998
320.8'0944'09034—dc21   97-32955
                                                              CIP

Design by Orit Mardkha-Tenzer

First edition: May 1998
10 9 8 7 6 5 4 3 2 1

For Christine

Contents

List of Tables

Acknowledgments

S tarted many years ago, this project was interrupted by other commitments that I allowed to take precedence. I hope, however, that I gained a deeper perspective on what I had learned and that the extra time spent has resulted in a better book on these diverse and fascinating cities .

If time has passed, my gratitude towards the many people who provided help and encouragement at all stages of this project remains as vivid as ever. I would like to thank the many French scholars who graciously gave of their time and advice, in many cases also providing the hospitality for which the provinces are deservedly reputed. In Lyon it was Yves Lequin, then Director of the Centre Pierre Léon of the University of Lyon; in Bordeaux Jean-Pierre Poussou, Pierre Guillaume, Philippe Loupès, and Georges Dupeux; in the Aix-Marseille region the late Pierre Guiral and Yvonne Kniebiehler; in Toulouse Rolande Trempé. Professor Poussou and his wife Michèle extended their hospitality so far as to lodge me for several weeks in a wing of the eighteenth-century Rectoral Palace of Bordeaux. In addition to these scholars, I would like to mention Jean-Luc Pinol now of the University of Tours, whose interest over the years in this project I appreciate.

Various inhabitants of the cities I visited were especially gracious; we shall always remember the warm hospitality and friendship that Dominique and Guy Sfeir of Toulouse extended to us.

Archivists at the municipal and departmental level were helpful. Particularly worthy of mention is Mme. Maillard of the Toulouse city archives who went out of her way to locate and make accessible sources no other archivist had been able to provide. My colleague and friend George Juergens provided constructive criticism and helpful advice on the manuscript; I am grateful to him for his continuing support and encouragement. Kenneth Goodall helped edit an early draft of the manuscript, giving excellent advice on matters of style and length. Michael Berkvam, friend extraordinaire, was always there; he shared his vast knowledge of France with me, while providing enthusiastic moral support.

This project was assisted by a Fulbright post-doctoral research grant and several grants from the Indiana University West European Studies Program. Generous leave provisions from my department provided the needed time. I am grateful to them for their assistance.

No long-term project can be pursued without extensive family support. I want to thank my three daughters—Natalie, Leslie, and Laurel—who, each in her own way, contributed to this work. My wife Christine cheerfully joined me during my various sojourns in the French provinces. Her love and support have sustained this project.

All translations in this book are mine, unless otherwise noted.

Preface

*M*ore than 150 years ago, a French writer observed that "there is another branch of our history with which hardly anyone has concerned himself. . . . That is the history of French cities, that is of those thousand powerful agglomerations of citizens who for fourteen centuries have constituted the most advanced portion of our nation, and among which developed the spirit of French civilization."[1] Perhaps fittingly, this writer, though he published a six-volume work on French cities, remains obscure.

Through the nineteenth century, interest in urban studies was left first to social commentators and later to statisticians, geographers, and sociologists. The situation changed little in the twentieth century. Surveying the status of French urban historical studies, François Bédarida wrote in 1968 that French urban history "remains mostly unexplored."[2] A few years later, Georges Dupeux noted that urban history had enjoyed little popularity among French historians, and two distinguished American students of European urban history, Andrew and Lynn Lees, complained that as a result of this neglect, "There is a real dearth of works in the area of French urban history." That is particularly true for the modern era. While the lion's share of historical work on France has been devoted to the events of the last two centuries, most writings on French urban history until recently have been devoted to the medieval era.[3]

Since those complaints were written, French urban history has seen the appearance of many important works, most significantly the five-volume synthetic *Histoire urbaine de la France,* edited by Georges Duby with contributions from some of France's most distinguished historians. There have been also a large number of individual biographies of cities, as well as examinations of distinctive themes involving a particular city, or several cities.[4]

Urban history is an immense, rather amorphous field with no clear perimeters. Some studies are of a demographic nature, considering rates of immigration, emigration, birth, marriage, and death. Others consider the physical use and application of space in the city. A less familiar form of urban history is the consideration, as S. G. Checkland suggested, of "those who are responsible for taking decisions. . . . What is the form and the strength of their responses to the challenges of the viability, in both social and economic terms, of the city?"—in other words, the urban policies of city governments.[5] As Jean-Paul Brunet remarked, "the municipal dimension" of the nation's history had been essentially overlooked.[6]

In the last quarter-century, though a number of works have provided histories of individual municipalities, a broader, more systematic and comparative study—the type of comparative urban study Maurice Agulhon called for many years ago—has been lacking.[7]

Paris was and still is by far the largest of French cities, but for this comparative study I chose to bypass this metropolis and examine major provincial cities. Paris has its unique problems and a rich tradition of historic works devoted to it. Much of the work done by the French in urban history has centered on the capital; as Andrew Lees remarks, French writers "concentrated on a single urban entity to an extent that would have been unthinkable in Britain, let alone Germany or the United States." John Merriman speaks of the "scanty literature of French provincial cities" and reminds us that "the capital was not and is not France."[8]

My objective here is to provide a study of French municipal government in the largest provincial cities—those that by 1875 already had populations of at least 100,000. While by 1875 only a small proportion of the French were living in large cities, by 1930 half of France's population was urban; by the end of the twentieth century the country was 80 percent urban. Institutions and solutions, developed in response to many of the pressing problems of France's large cities in the nineteenth century, helped shape the twentieth-century urban landscape. Large cities served as models for smaller towns, and by the end of the twentieth century nearly two-thirds of the urban population resided in these large cities, which had been so importantly reconfigured a century earlier.

Much of this book focuses on the actions of municipal governments. In spite of the alleged centralization of France since the ancien régime and the acknowledged growth of state interventionism in the late nineteenth century, French cities retained considerable autonomy.[9] The emphasis on cities as autonomous actors fits, as two recent historiographers of the French city insist, the agenda of "the new urban history."[10]

In the nineteenth century, city governments forged new roles for themselves. By trial and error, municipalities developed agendas for action, thus presaging the development of the state. If the state was becoming more intrusive in the lives of its citizens during the nineteenth century, city government was even more active. Municipalities expanded their range of concerns during the period between the French Revolution and the outbreak of World War I. A French legal scholar at the beginning of the twentieth century wrote of the remarkable activity of French municipal governments. "In every agglomeration," the doctoral candidate wrote, "the most serious attempts are being made to ensure the . . . greater comfort and well-being" of the population.[11] Edouard Herriot, the powerful mayor of Lyon, listed the roles of the city administration:

> To foresee the rational extension of a human agglomeration; provide it with open space and sufficient air; provide for its upkeep, protect it against epidemics of all sorts, provide transportation, provide clean water, remove waste, improve housing, choose the best form of lighting, inspect food and milk, . . . protect infants, modernize the school . . . provide hygiene, social services, fight against infectious diseases, improve our hospitals, shelters, nurseries. . . .[12]

Alfred Picard, an engineer and social reformer, reviewing at the beginning of the twentieth century the physical transformations French cities had undergone over the preceding century, remarked on the new expectations that city dwellers had developed.

> The inhabitants of large cities have the right to expect well-built streets that are well kept up, a network of sewers that are irreproachable from a hygienic point of view, an abundant water distribution system guaranteeing the health of its consumers, a lighting system which amply provides for the security and ease of traffic during the night, a satisfactory organization of public transportation that is speedy and economical, a view of greenery along the boulevards and the avenues, elegant promenades and flowered squares.[13]

Whereas few services were provided at the beginning of the nineteenth century, by its end urban dwellers could believe that access to city services was their "right." A major transformation had occurred in city government. The growing role of city government helped transform the physical environment and quality of life of urban dwellers.

If throughout the nineteenth century much of France remained traditional in its outlook and slow to change, cities—as Aristide Guilbert, the historian cited at the beginning of the preface, noted—were "the most advanced portion of our nation."[14] City governments pioneered new techniques to improve the lives of their citizens. In a good number of cases, municipalities preceded the central government in taking these initiatives. The urban transformation was slow and uneven, and many cities tottered between archaism and modernity. Techniques of urban improvement often existed for decades before they were adopted. While information on new technologies was available, inertia and financial concerns often led to municipal timidity. And yet change occurred, and, however, hesitatingly, municipalities transformed their cities.

Having chosen to study large French provincial municipalities, I recognized that I could not cover them all and decided to limit myself to five. I based my selection on the cities' functions. Two of those selected, Bordeaux and Marseille, are port cities and thus are fairly typical—of the ten French provincial cities with populations over 100,000 in 1911, four were ports. Of the large provincial cities that were mainly administrative centers, three had populations over 100,000; I chose to study Toulouse. In some cases, industrialization suddenly created new centers of population; I studied one of them, Saint-Etienne. Of the older cities that had been important manufacturing centers before industrialization, I chose Lyon. Most of these five cities, of course, served several functions simultaneously; Lyon, for example, was an industrial, administrative, and trade center. Bordeaux, Marseille, and Toulouse were administrative and trading centers. By coincidence, all five cities lie south of that famous line known as the Saint Malo-Geneva Line. I doubt that that is a significant limitation of the study, making it less representative of large French cities than a more varied geographic choice might have been. After lengthy consultations with the leading historians of French urbanization, I was unable to discover an ideal set of representative cities. The social historian Peter McPhee quite rightly observed, "There was and is no archetypal French city."[15]

Comparing these cities will, I hope, provide a broad context often missing in the purely biographical city study. This tale of five cities also can reveal much about the physical environments and social institutions that developed in the nineteenth century, which to a large degree still inform French urban life today.

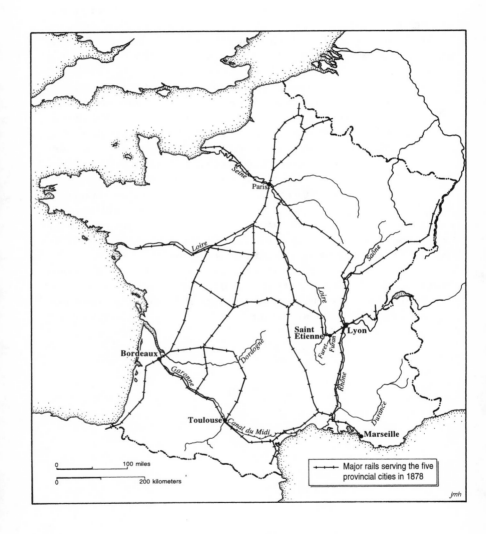

Major rails serving the five
provincial cities in 1878

Paris

Bordeaux

Saint
Etienne

Lyon

Toulouse

Marseille

Seine

Loire

Saône

Loire

Dordogne

Garonne

Furet

Furan

Rhône

Durance

Canal du Midi

0   100 miles
0   200 kilometers

jmh

xiv

Introduction

A Tale of Five Cities

*I*n the nineteenth century, France entered the ranks of urbanized nations. While its over-all population grew by 39 percent, its urban population soared by 300 percent. Except for one generation in the mid-eighteenth century, France had never experienced the rates of urban growth it recorded throughout the nineteenth century.[1]

URBAN GROWTH

Between 1851 and 1911, French census bureau figures show that the number of urban dwellers increased from 25 percent to 44.2 percent of the total population.[2] While growth went on incrementally throughout the century, the most dramatic spurt occurred during the three decades spanning the years 1846-76—an unprecedented period in the growth of French cities.

Beginning in the 1840s many large-scale cities developed. Whereas in 1801 France had only three cities with populations greater than 100,000, by 1851 there were five, and by 1901, sixteen.[3] And it was the largest cities that generally experienced the most exceptional growth. The American sociologist Adna Weber was correct when at the end of the nineteenth century he proclaimed that there was a tendency for large cities to grow faster than small ones: the larger the city, the greater its proportional growth. If the total number of urbanites (persons living in locales with populations over 2,000) increased by 44 percent between 1850 and 1880, the number

1

of people living in large cites grew even faster. Of the five large cities chosen for this study, Bordeaux grew by 76 percent, Lyon by 99 percent, Marseille by 92 percent, Saint-Etienne by 138 percent and Toulouse by 52 percent. While these figures seem to confirm the general rule, they also suggest an exception; thus Saint-Etienne, the smallest of the five cities in 1851, grew the fastest over the next three decades.

The *grandes villes*—cities with populations over 100,000—played important roles as major regional centers for the production, trade, and distribution of goods, services, and culture. Adna Weber described these cities as having an impact not only "beyond their county, but beyond the commonwealth or province, becoming national and even international."[4]

Relative to some of France's neighbors, the country's urbanization was not spectacular. In 1890, when France had 13 cities with populations over 100,000, England had 23 and Germany 26. But in absolute terms, French urbanization was impressive. An increasing number of French citizens experienced life as residents in the *grandes villes:* in 1800, 27 per thousand lived in such cities; in 1850, 44 per thousand; and by 1910, 145 per thousand.[5]

Historians have been struck by the continuity in the French urban hierarchy; with few exceptions, cities that were important in the Middle Ages continued to be so in the nineteenth and twentieth centuries. Many of the largest cities have an ancient lineage and were already major urban sites back in Roman times—some even earlier. Of our cities, Bordeaux, Lyon, Marseille, and Toulouse antedate the Romans.

Particularly striking is the siting of large cities along waterways and coastlines. Accessible to cheap means of transport by boat, foot, and horseback along the river valleys, these locales became sites of commerce and government, or religious centers. Advantageous locations ensured continued prominence; at the end of the nineteenth century, of the 12 *grandes villes,* 8 were situated on either a river or a coastline.[6]

Out of the Countryside

An influx of people from the countryside was the main cause of urban growth in the nineteenth century. Cities were, as Rousseau observed, "the tomb of the human species."[7] Unhealthy urban conditions led to death rates usually outstripping birthrates; only continuing streams of emigration from the countryside contributed to growth.

A variety of economic factors explains the draw of the city. In the first half of the century, industry was not an important stimulant to urbanization; industry was slow in taking off, and factories were often located in rural areas.[8] In many cases, industry actually provided the extra employment that the rural population needed to stay on the land. There were exceptions, of course. Saint-Etienne represents a case of a city that mushroomed as a result of industrialization.

Non-industrial functions, such as the provision of the varied services and goods needed in a city, usually attracted labor from the countryside. Many cities grew without industrializing: Rouen, Nantes, Angers, Montpellier, Orléans, Amiens, Nîmes, and Toulouse, a notable example among our sample of cities.[9] Later, in the second half of the nineteenth century, however, industry contributed to the further development of already growing cities, such as Bordeaux, Lyon and Marseille.

The rural population grew in the first 50 years of the nineteenth century by 30 percent, and by mid-century some areas in the country were overpopulated.[10] Many marginal peasants and day laborers found it increasingly difficult to make a living on the land. Although mechanization was being adopted only slowly, in some regions it reduced the need for farm labor. Artisans and cottage laborers living in rural areas found it increasingly difficult to compete with more efficient manufacturers in the cities, and many had to leave the land. Many of the migrants were temporary and eventually returned home, but others settled permanently in the city. The net emigration to the city in the 1840s was 30,000 persons a year; between 1851 and 1881, 71,000 a year; and between 1881 and 1911, 82,000 persons per year. In the early part of the century, a smaller proportion, approximately a third, of migrants became permanent urban dwellers, while later between one-half and two-thirds did. Competition from North and South America, Australia, and Ukraine forced French agricultural prices down; the price of wheat fell by a third between 1875 and 1900. Also during this time, the wine country was ravaged by phylloxera.[11] Living and staying on the land became less attractive.

To many rural dwellers, cities promised better opportunities than the countryside. In the 1840s, many cities initiated public works programs—straightening and enlarging streets, deepening and widening ports, building rail lines to connect the cities to one another—and such activities were intensified under the Second Empire. These projects employed large numbers of people who needed no specialized skills. And often wages were higher in the cities, ensuring better standards of living.

A writer in the 1860s noted that while countless stories told of peasants who had gone to the city and enriched themselves, no city dweller had ever been enriched by going to the countryside.[12] Migration to urban centers held out the promise of improving one's lot. It was noted that city-living provided various comforts, leisure activities, and institutions—such as schools, hospitals, and local welfare bureaus—that were usually absent in the rural environs.[13]

THE FIVE CITIES

While all five of the cities selected for this study grew during the nineteenth century, they did so at varying rates. Between 1801 and 1911, Bordeaux grew by 187 percent, Toulouse by 210 percent, Lyon by 323 percent, Marseille by 396 percent, and Saint-Etienne by 825 percent.

Our cities lost population during the Revolution and Napoleon, and it took decades to return to their pre-Revolutionary population size. Lyon, Marseille, and Toulouse did so in the 1820s, and Saint-Etienne the following decade; Bordeaux had to wait until the 1840s—fifty years after the Revolution—to return to its pre-Revolutionary number of inhabitants.

France's urban growth rate until the 1840s was modest, then it continued to rise in the two decades of the Second Empire. The twelve largest cities grew in the first half-century at an annual rate of 1.25 percent, while the rate for the five cities in this study was somewhat higher—1.64 percent annually. After that the rate picked up considerably. It was 3.1 percent a year for the twelve largest cities between 1851 and 1872; the cities in this study grew at a similar rate, 3.16 percent annually. From 1872 to 1891, the twelve largest cities grew less rapidly, at a rate of 1.37 percent a year; our five cities by 1.38 percent. And then in the next two decades there was a further slowing down, with these five cities growing by only .58 percent annually.[14]

To understand the experience of the five cities in the nineteenth century, we shall explore briefly their geographic and historic settings.

Bordeaux

Bordeaux is located in the Aquitaine basin, near the mouth of the Garonne River (which also waters Toulouse). The city has been a strategic post on two major routes of communication, sited as it is between the Atlantic and the Mediterranean and on a main route between Paris and Spain. Sitting in a crescent of the Garonne River, protected from storms and located at a particularly wide point in the river, it was an ideal harbor. By the fifth century B.C., the Gallic town of Burdiglia had been established at this location. In 56 B.C. the Romans conquered the city and made it an important post. In the third century A.D., its estimated population was 60,000. It was an important port through the Middle Ages, and the expansion of commerce and navigation that began in the sixteenth century served the city well. As a seaport it connected France with England, Northern Europe, Africa, and the Americas. In the eighteenth century, it was France's principal slaving city. In the next century, rails improved connections with the inland. The Paris-Bordeaux line was built in 1844, and thereafter the city became the railhead for other lines, too.

Bordeaux's economy took off in the eighteenth century, with slaving and the wine trade. The wealth of that era marked the city permanently, and more than two centuries later the opulent private and public buildings of that age still distinguish the city. The American poet Henry Wadsworth Longfellow, after visiting Bordeaux in 1827, remarked, "It is the most beautiful city I saw in France." The literary critic Théophile Gautier, struck by the physical aspects of the city, described it in the mid-nineteenth century as "having been built for an opera stage set." Bordeaux, more than any other provincial city, wrote a commentator early in this century, "resembles a small capital."[15]

But Bordeaux could not hold on to the preeminent position it had in the eighteenth century. During the Second Empire, the port was modernized, but it lacked the large docks and cranes of Marseille. It had been an ideal port, well protected from the sea, but it was not on the ocean and could not be approached directly by the larger trans-Atlantic ships built in the latter part of the nineteenth century.[16] At low tide, the river was 3.5 meters deep, but the ships' holds were 7 meters deep. While Marseille's port increased its tonnage of shipping by 50 percent between 1885 and 1900, that of Bordeaux increased by less than 10 percent. Bordeaux's share of the French maritime business declined in the years 1880-1913. After having been France's largest port in the eighteenth century, it fell to third position, remaining throughout the nineteenth century behind Marseille and Le Havre.[17]

Even with its port in relative decline, Bordeaux failed to diversify and instead continued to count on trade and shipping to provide its economic well-being. The powerful local chamber of commerce proclaimed that "we are not like Rouen, an industrial city,"[18] and observers noted that the city failed to industrialize to any significant degree.[19] One historian of Bordeaux sees it as symptomatic that the rail line connecting the city to Paris was not pioneered by local capital. And while Lyon was the site of a famous national bank, that was not the case with Bordeaux.[20]

The workforce reflected the city's traditional economy. Of the estimated 25,000 workers in the city, 10,000 were employed in the building trades. Most industrial establishments employed but a handful of employees: only 5 percent of them had 100 or more employees.[21] The city witnessed prosperity from trade and the public works programs of the Second Empire, then went into relative decline, beginning in 1873.[22] One historian describes the city as having fallen into "somnolence." Henry James, on his visit to the city in 1884, remarked that it labored in "the smokeless industry of the wonderful country which produces above all the agreeable things of life. . . ."[23]

Nevertheless, contrary to these and subsequent descriptions, it would be a mistake to describe Bordeaux in the latter part of the nineteenth century as bereft of industry; several industries were founded. A government report of the mid-1850s noted that "Bordeaux is not only a port city, receiving from and sending products in all directions of the world; it is today a center in which many of these products are being manufactured."[24] Biscuit manufacturing, food canning, oil extraction, ship-building, barrel making, chemical production, and soap manufacture were thriving in the city, while the building trades represented a reduced proportion of the workforce.[25]

Some of the new industries were quite impressive, but they were never of sufficient magnitude to transform the nature of the Bordeaux economy. The 1891 census revealed that 78,000 Bordeaux residents depended upon industry, much of it artisanal, for a living, while persons employed in commerce or transportation and their dependents numbered 89,000.[26]

The city under the ancien régime had been a major administrative center; it was the site of the intendancy and of a prestigious *parlement* (including at different times Montaigne and Montesquieu among its members). It had a university and was the seat of an archbishopric. While the Revolution stripped Bordeaux of its function as capital of the large province of the Aquitaine, it was the site of the prefecture of the smaller department of the Gironde. And whatever the changes in administrative borders, it continued to play a large role within the region as a university center, a military garrison, and the site of law courts and other governmental functions.

Bordeaux's population did not grow as a result of natural increase; between 1851 and 1872 there were 97,759 deaths as compared with 89,442 births.[27] In the following quarter-century, there was a population deficit of 4,000 as the death rate kept ahead of the birthrate. Immigration helped populate the city. In the first half of the century, prospering commercial classes attracted immigrants who came as domestics, shopkeepers, and clerks; thereafter, there were also industrial opportunities in the city. Because no other city in the region could attract so many people, Bordeaux was very much a primate city in the Aquitaine. It drew migrants not only from nearby in the Aquitaine basin but beyond that from the Massif Central and Brittany. But the building of rail lines redirected migration patterns; many of the migrants now went to Paris, and Bordeaux migrants thereafter came from the Aquitaine and the Pyrenées.[28] Increasingly, the city was marked by the inflow of immigrants; whereas in 1831 60 percent of the city's inhabitants had been born within its walls, by 1906, only 42 percent had been.[29]

A commercial and administrative center, Bordeaux in the nineteenth century was a city that already had put its most dynamic years behind it and had a highly developed consciousness of its past. While the rate of economic growth was disappointing in the nineteenth century, Bordeaux maintained throughout the century its position as France's fourth largest city.

Lyon

Located where two major rivers, the Rhône River and the Saône River meet, Lyon was an ideal location for a Roman outpost. After being a military and administrative center, it later became the site of a major bishopric. The archbishop of Lyon is still primate of France. The river valleys provided convenient transportation by water and land, and Lyon became an important cross-point for people and goods. Trade and manufacture flourished in the city. Later, in the age of railways, the city continued to enjoy a major role as a crossroad. Lyon was provided with a rail connection to Paris in 1845, and the city became a vital link in the French rail system. By the end of the nineteenth century, eight different lines connected the city to the rest of the country.

Many industries prospered in the city from early on. The printing industry was started in the sixteenth century, shortly after Gutenberg's invention of printing from movable type. In the following century, a silk industry was founded, providing the city with prosperity for two hundred years; in the eighteenth century, Lyon was the largest textile town on the continent. Silk production reached its height in the 1870s, then started falling. Other industries came to the fore—metals and chemicals, which after the 1880s represented a large share of the wealth produced in the city.[30] An apparel industry was founded in the last part of the century and ready-made men's clothing manufacturers employed 8,000 persons. A shoe industry also was established.

With nearby coalfields, Lyon developed a thriving metal and machine industry. By the 1830s, machinery was being produced in the city, and by the 1860s some 9,000 workers were employed as boilermakers.[31] Toward the end of the century, several automobile manufacturers started up in Lyon; best known among them was the Berliet company, which in 1913 manufactured two-thirds of all French trucks. The city was at the forefront of France's "second industrial revolution": in the 1890s, electrical industries were established; then the photography industry took off and, by 1900, two thirds of the photographic plates manufactured in France came from Lyon.[32]

The city employed many workers in the tertiary sector. The wealth of the city and its strategic location on major routes across France had made it a regional banking center since the thirteenth century. While most banks of national importance were founded in Paris, in 1863 the Lyonnais Henri Germain established the Crédit Lyonnais, destined to become one of France's most important banks. In 1881, 15,000 persons, or 4.3 percent of Lyon's population, were employed in some aspect of finance. Other service industries also provided work for large numbers: 14,000 Lyon residents were employed in the transportation industry in 1881; 43,000 were shopkeepers or their employees; and another 43,000 worked in hotel, café, and restaurant businesses.

Throughout the nineteenth century, the vigorous commercial and industrial activities of the Lyonnais struck visitors. The German playwright August von Kotzebue, visiting Lyon in 1805, remarked that he had hardly seen a house where something was not being sold. Jules Michelet saw the city as a "laboring anthill." Proudly a Lyonnais called his city "an intelligent beehive. . . . Lyon is always and everywhere the city of work." Hippolyte Taine, struck by the city's philistinism, remarked that the only thing its inhabitants were interested in was making money.[33]

During the ancien régime, the only major governmental presence in Lyon was the government general's seat and a large military garrison. Lyon had neither a *parlement,* a local aristocracy, nor a university. The Revolution divided the *généralité* into two departments, leaving Lyon the administrative capital of the department of the Rhône, the smallest department in France except for the Seine. The city was endowed with law courts and a university. The added administrative offices confirmed rather than created Lyon's importance.

During most of the nineteenth century, Lyon's population was unable to replenish itself naturally; death rates outstripped birthrates. In the second half of the 1870s, for instance, birthrates were 24.6 per thousand, while the death rate was 26.51 per thousand.

Immigration was responsible for the city's growth. The 1886 census shows that, of a total population of 402,000, 41.5 percent—or 166,000 people—were born in the city; 8.8 percent were born outside the city but within the department or a nearby department.[34] The pull of Lyon was powerful; the city attracted migrants from nearby and far away. Relatively few migrants came from the city's department, the Rhône, which was well off and even attracted persons who moved from the city to the countryside. Rather, Lyon's immigrants came from adjacent departments and from afar, from places such as the Creuse, which sent its renowned masons not only to Paris but also to Lyon. Immigrants also came from other poor, mountainous areas, such as the *Limousin* and the Jura.[35]

The city tried to accommodate growing numbers of people within the tight confines between the right bank of the Rhône and the Saône. As a result of the limited space available, Lyonnais built upward. The city was known for its narrow streets lined with crowded five- or six-story houses. In the eighteenth century, the city crossed the Rhône to its left bank, but the center was to remain on the right and retain its densely settled character until some of the urban-renewal projects were implemented in the nineteenth century. In an attempt to control the unruly suburbs—the sites of workers' revolts and protest—the prefect of the Rhône annexed the suburbs in 1852, giving the city a larger population and surface area. Thereafter, however, annexation appeared to be an unattractive option. In the final analysis, the bourgeois of Lyon did not want to engage in the added expenses that annexing ill-equipped suburbs represented. Nor did they want to see the city's working class grow, a development that would only add electoral strength to socialist-minded movements. So Lyon remained a tight, compact city; it was the most densely populated of the five cities in this study.

Marseille

Marseille prides itself on having been founded in the sixth century B.C. by the Phoceans, who came from a Greek colony in Asia Minor. Later it was a Roman city. It became the port through which flowed France's trade with the Mediterranean world and, after the opening of the Suez Canal in 1867, with the East. Throughout the nineteenth century, it was France's largest port. Beginning in the 1840s, the port was enlarged and received impressive increases in shipping. The city was connected with the inland by the Marseille-Paris railroad in 1856.

Industries sprang up to treat imported primary products. Ground nuts from West Africa, for example, were transformed into soap and vegetable oils; sugar from the West Indies was refined. Special industries, such as light hardware and candle manufacturing, supplied the colonies in turn. Regional and foreign markets were supplied by the clothing and food industries—especially sugar refineries—the largest industrial employers in the city. Toward the end of the century, heavy industry was established. The labor force nevertheless still had a predominance of artisans.[36]

In the ancien régime, Marseille had not been an important administrative center. Aix, as the capital of Provence, was the site of the intendant, the courts, the university, and the archbishopric. The Revolution also proclaimed it the capital of the Bouches-du-Rhône department, although the capital was shifted to Marseille in 1804. Slowly, other administrative offices followed, and Marseille gradually acquired various other institutions: in 1818, a school of medicine was founded (but not yet recognized as a faculty);

in the 1850s, the prefecture was expanded, a school of fine arts was founded, and many new churches were built.

Industry, trade, transportation, and service establishments in this large city attracted immigrants from near and far. From many small towns they came to work in Marseille's stores, workshops, shipping and trading houses, and government offices. And immigration was crucial, for Marseille's population barely replenished itself. In a whole century, from 1811 to 1911, the natural surplus of population was but 10,000. From 1870 to 1911, the birthrate decreased from 32 per thousand to 21 per thousand, while mortality fell from 29 per thousand to 21 per thousand.[37]

The first important immigration wave occurred during the Second Empire, when 100,000 persons moved into the city. The largest phase occurred between 1872 and 1911, when 250,000 persons moved into the city. Both in absolute numbers and proportionate to its population, Marseille experienced the largest influx of immigrants of the five cities in our study. The large immigration meant that few Marseillais were natives; in 1886 only 43 percent were born in the commune. Before 1900, the immigrants were equally divided between French and foreign. Marseille's French immigrants came from fairly close by: the 1901 census revealed that 17 percent came from the Midi, 9 percent from Provence, and 13 percent from the Alpine region—places where people had difficulty making a living.[38] The influx of foreign migrants, especially Italians, was significant. In 1851, 10 percent of the city's population was foreign, and 90 percent of the foreign-born were Italians. In 1906, a quarter of the city's population was foreign-born.

While lower-class immigrants were particularly numerous, the middle classes and even the upper classes were also stocked by immigrants. The elite class was fairly unstable; old families were replaced by new ones. Marseille was a city in flux. Old monuments and buildings frequently came down to make way for new ones. The port and its activities made the city truly international, and regionally it was a giant of economic activity. Through most of the nineteenth century, Marseille's population made it France's second largest city. In surface it was the largest, covering 150 square kilometers—although half of it was uninhabitable mountain terrain.

Saint-Etienne

While local historians tried to give Saint-Etienne a prestigious pedigree, suggesting that it was founded by the Romans or by King Childebert or Queen Clothilde, the prosaic reality is that the city was born as the site for some metal workshops in the tenth or eleventh century.[39]

Topography dictated the fortunes of Saint-Etienne. From the Middle Ages on, it was home to varied forms of manufacture, including ribbons and steel, most of which developed as a result of the propitious combination of locally available natural resources. The area had streams, rivers, and rich coal deposits; the waterways drove machines and facilitated the transport of manufactured goods. Nearby was a major center waiting to consume much of Saint-Etienne's production: Lyon and the Lyonnais region. Saint-Etienne had an abundant regional labor supply of rural people with limited land holdings who engaged in thriving cottage industries in mining, textiles, and cutlery manufacture.

Certain forms of manufacture, existing from early on, were later considerably expanded, providing the city's wealth. Beginning in the tenth or eleventh century, the village contained several smiths and weaponsmakers. The weapons industry diversified into cutlery and lock manufacture. With the start of industrialization, coal mining boomed. The Saint-Etienne basin became the greatest coal producer in France: in 1824, half a million tons were excavated; and in 1855, 2.24 millions tons. Production reached its nineteenth-century zenith in 1873, with 4 million tons. Not until the 1860s, with the rise of the Nord, which was closer to Paris and its industries, did Saint-Etienne lose its position as the principal supplier of French coal. But even then, mining employed 15,000 workers in the Saint-Etienne region.

Cloth was manufactured in Saint-Etienne in the later Middle Ages, and in the sixteenth century a new specialty, ribbon-making, was introduced. By the early nineteenth century, the combination of very active mining, metallurgy, and textile industries made Saint-Etienne the prime industrial region in France. The town increased the number of its steam engines from 12 to 122 in the quarter century between 1812 and 1836; in the latter year, 11 percent of all steam engines in France were located in the department of the Loire.[40] A third of France's steel was produced in Saint-Etienne and its environs.

Early in the nineteenth century, observers noted that Saint-Etienne was destined to become "a French Birmingham or Manchester."[41] After 1830, the Saint-Etienne steel works were quick to adopt modern techniques, such as the Bessemer and Martin methods of production. But again by the 1880's, competition from the Nord, had reduced local steel output.

The arms industry burgeoned in the Napoleonic era, but declined with European peace. Later, international conflict fed huge orders; at its height around 1870, the arms industry manufactured between 225,000 and 250,000 chassepots. Between 1864 and 1900, 50,000 cannons were poured in Saint-Etienne. At the end of the nineteenth century, 1,600 Lebel rifles were produced daily in the city. The arms industry spawned other specialized industries, among them bicycle manufacturing, started in the 1880s. That same decade, 10,000 persons were working in the weapons industry and 13,000 in various metal industries.[42]

Saint-Etienne's most significant industry, the one that ensured the city's mid-century wealth, was silk ribbon manufacture. In the 1840s, Saint-Etienne was the preeminent ribbon manufacturer in Europe, providing ribbon for the hats and dresses that were then in style. But this industry, dependent as it was on the vagaries of fashion, also experienced decline. In the 1870s, 40,000 persons worked in the ribbon industry; the next decade, there were only 30,000. Still, in the 1870s it remained the largest employer in Saint-Etienne.[43]

The city's economy was much enhanced by railways. The first rails in France, laid down in 1823, hauled coal from Saint-Etienne to Andrézieux, twenty kilometers away. Then a line was built connecting Saint-Etienne to Lyon in 1827. The first rail cars were horse drawn; the first steam engine, an adaptation of Stephenson's invention, was introduced in 1829. Soon thereafter, Saint-Etienne was also connected by rail to Roanne. The lines brought in all kinds of raw materials to Saint-Etienne and helped in expediting manufactured goods to markets.

While industry fueled the city's growth, Saint-Etienne also had an active retail trade that provided many jobs. In 1900, with 150,000 inhabitants, Saint-Etienne had 4,500 stores, of which a little more than half were grocery stores.[44]

The city was not an important administrative center. Under the ancien régime it had been the locale for a *subdélegué* under the authority of the intendant of the Lyonnais, Forez, and Beaujolais region. The Convention refused Saint-Etienne's bid to become the site of the new prefecture of the Loire (that was given to Montbrison—less important in both its economy and population), and Saint-Etienne was provided with just a subprefecture. Given the continuing growth of the city and its burgeoning economic importance, the prefecture was finally moved in 1856 to Saint-Etienne.

Population was shaped by the local economy and, until the 1880s, Saint-Etienne was to grow dynamically. The economic good fortune of the city was a result of the simultaneous development of three industries: metallurgy, mining, and textiles. But all three sectors of the economy had gone into decline by the 1880s, and the city's population growth then slowed significantly.[45]

Unlike most other nineteenth-century European cities, Saint-Etienne's births outstripped its deaths; workers found it profitable to have children who could readily find employment in expanding industries. In the 1820s, the city experienced 41-per-thousand births versus 27-per-thousand mortality; at the turn of the twentieth century natality was 23 per thousand while mortality was 20 per thousand. About half the population increase occurred as a result of natural increase.[46]

The other half of the city's growth came from immigration, usually from nearby. In the second half of the eighteenth century, 89 percent of the population came from the Saint-Etienne urban agglomeration; by the mid-nineteenth century, the percentage had fallen to 63 percent. Relatively few people were drawn from outside the department of the Loire; in 1872, 79.1 percent of the city's population came from the department in which the city was located, and over half were born in the city; in 1911 73 percent were born in the department, and still over half were born in the city.[47] Two dramatic population additions occurred in 1822 and 1852—when the city was enlarged—as in Lyon by annexing unruly suburbs. In the latter year, the city gained an additional 20,000 inhabitants.

With a natural increase, immigration, and annexation of suburbs, Saint-Etienne's population blossomed. According to official figures, from 16,000 in 1801, Saint-Etienne's population increased ninefold by 1911, reaching 149,000 inhabitants.[48]

Contemporaries compared Saint-Etienne to mushroom cities like Manchester and Chicago, which had suddenly sprung up as a result of intense economic activity. The chamber of commerce of Saint-Etienne proudly proclaimed with only slight exaggeration that "there is no city—not only in France but in Europe—which has grown so rapidly."[49] Most French cities that were large at the end of the nineteenth century had been so at its beginning, but Saint-Etienne's spectacular growth upset the rank order of French cities. Whereas in 1801 the town was not listed among France's thirty most populous cities, in 1851 it ranked thirteenth, and in 1872 it reached seventh place—a position it was to maintain until the 1930s.

The rapid industrialization of Saint-Etienne led to dramatic transformations. Buildings were hastily erected with little style or charm, as noted by Aristide Guilbert, historian of French cities.[50] Smoke from belching stacks and dust from nearby mines filled the atmosphere with "a thick coal dust which forms a floating dome over the city," Guilbert complained. "When it rains this dust becomes a thick, black mud like ink." The city, wrote Armand Audiganne in a survey in the 1860s, was "sooty, badly paved, monotonous and sad. . . ." At the turn of the century Saint-Etienne's air reminded one observer of "the heavy fogs of England."[51]

Saint-Etienne was a hard-working city. It was, Audiganne noted, a "city of workers; all men, rich or not, work by their hands; there is no bourgeoisie, no leisure class." There were millionaires, observed Guilbert, but "no society." Hard work had catapulted some workers into the class of managers and even factory owners (typically of smaller workshops), but this ascension meant that the elite was often uncultured, making it, a local paper admitted, "nearly a barbarian city."[52] Much of the so called industrial production in Saint-Etienne remained artisanal and traditional—unlike the factories of Manchester, the city to which Saint-Etienne was often compared. But in French terms, it was a bustling, industrial center—a boom town.

Toulouse

The Garonne River, coming from the south, bends northwest at Toulouse to end up in the Atlantic; thus the Garonne Valley is a highway both to the west and the southwest. The Romans recognized the value of the site, and since their time it has been an important urban location. Waterways and roads along the valley made Toulouse an important cross-point for trade and transportation. With the seventeenth-century construction of the Canal du Midi, which joined the Garonne River to the Mediterranean, the city also linked the Atlantic to the southeast. Toulouse has for centuries been an *entrepôt* for the agricultural areas surrounding it. With no other large city nearby (Marseille is 451 kilometers away, Bordeaux 251 kilometers) the city dominated the region. When rails were built in the mid-nineteenth century, the importance of the site was confirmed: it became a major railhead for the southwestern region.

When the Languedoc fell under Capetian control in the thirteenth century, Toulouse became the regional capital of the province. To combat the Albigensian heresy in the province, the Church strengthened its position in Toulouse with an enlarged monastic and clerical presence and a university. Being on the route to Santiago de Compostal, the alleged site of the tomb of the apostle James, in northwest Spain, Toulouse became an important stopping place for pilgrims from all over Europe headed toward the holy shrine.

Toulouse, at the crossroads of important trade routes and in the midst of rich agricultural land, won economic prominence in the Middle Ages. At the end of the twelfth century, it had the largest millworks in Europe, and in the late fifteenth century, its trade in pastel, the valuable blue-dye plant, made it one of the most active commercial centers on the continent. Thereafter, however, Toulouse lost some of its economic dynamism, becoming instead a major administrative city, the capital of the Languedoc and the site of a major university, a bishopric, the intendancy, a military garrison, and a *parlement*.[53] Beginning in the fourteenth century, Toulouse was the site of the prestigious *jeux floraux,* a poetry contest that has occurred annually for six centuries—an unrivalled distinction in the Western world that confirms Toulousains' view of their city as a major cultural capital.

The city's regional importance was underscored by its political influence; after 1848 Toulouse became one of the strongholds of Radicalism. Unlike other cities that espoused advanced political ideals in isolation from the nearby countryside, Toulouse was able to shape the surrounding region politically. During the Third Republic, no other city newspaper had as large a subscription list outside its walls as the influential *Dépêche de Toulouse*, the leading national voice of Radicalism. The newspaper, another regional organ remarked, "made it rain or shine in Toulouse, in the Haute-Garonne and other départements of the Languedoc region."[54]

The economic needs of the city and the surrounding area were met by artisan manufacture. There was little concentrated manufacture; the two major industries were state run—a gunpowder and a tobacco factory. Through the nineteenth century, small artisanal firms predominated; in the 1860s, there were eight hundred different establishments providing ninety types of goods. A Toulousain described the city's "industry" as consisting of "160 workshops building coaches and making harnesses; 150 furniture makers, 11 decorative wallpaper manufacturers, 8 weavers, 34 artificial flower-making shops, 25 church ornament makers, and 180 locksmiths." By 1914, only 5 percent of the population was employed in industrial manufacture. The city's banking system seemed to confirm the city's economic archaism; in population the city ranked fourth or fifth, but its branch of the Banque de France was but the sixteenth largest in the nation.[55]

The lack of entrepreneurship in the city was widely noted. The economist Michel Chevalier noted in 1848 that, unlike Marseille and Lyon, Toulouse did not "sacrifice to Mamon." The city, its mayor noted in the 1870s, was neither commercial nor industrial; rather, it was a city with a cultural and administrative vocation: the site of several university faculties, a prestigious theater, a museum, a Court of Appeals, a prefecture, and the headquarters of the tenth military division. Henry James observed in 1884 that Toulouse was a town "which produces nothing whatever that I can discover."[56]

The city's elite was distinctly non-industrial. For the Toulaisain, one of the city's inhabitants wrote, "the professor and the judge were more important than the banker; the scientist was less honored than the poet." And there was a landowning class, comfortably settled in the city. Many landowners in the surrounding regions preferred living in the city, with all its amenities, to living on their land; the census of 1872 revealed that 117 per thousand persons living in the city were in agriculture.[57]

The professional and commercial classes consumed luxuries, providing employment for the less fortunate. They also employed large domestic staffs-more than double those of Paris or Lille throughout the nineteenth century. In 1851, there were 168 domestics per thousand people and in 1872, 123 per thousand.[58]

The city's population depended for its growth upon immigration; birthrates usually could not keep up with death rates. In 1850, the death rate was 28.7 per thousand, and the rate remained remarkably stable, standing at 24.3 in 1913. In the meantime, birthrates had fallen dramatically from 25.7 per thousand in 1850 to 16 per thousand in 1913. Thus the gap between mortality and natality actually increased with the passage of time. The immigration that helped prevent the population from declining was mostly local: a large proportion of people was born within the department: in 1861, the percentage was 80 percent and in 1872, 72.[59]

Most of the immigrants were burgers and artisans from nearby smaller towns nearby who saw greater opportunities in Toulouse. Their immigration did little to change the city's social makeup, which remained mostly artisanal; in 1851, 33 of every thousand persons were in the liberal professions and 445 in the artisan professions. By 1872, the liberal professions' share had increased to 43 per thousand and that of artisans had declined to 277; the decline in the artisanal class was compensated by an increase in the number of manufacturing employees, which rose from 54 to 180 per thousand.[60]

The city in which the immigrants settled was vast in surface area. With less than half the population of Lyon, Toulouse had a surface area 2.5 times greater. Among the five cities selected for this study, only Marseille covered more ground. But Toulouse, never very populous, was the least densely inhabited of the five cities.

URBAN IDENTITIES

In the midst of France's burgeoning urbanization, these five cities, each with its own history and particular conditions based on locale, economy, and population, adapted existing institutions and created new ones in efforts to meet developing needs of their residents and clients. The cities' inhabitants and officials often thought of themselves as living in communities. To them, Bordeaux, Lyon, Marseille, Saint-Etienne, and Toulouse were not mere urban locales. They were rather living realities, and, like organisms, they often were engaged in contention with each other. As Jean Bouvier remarked, the city was the center of struggle—between classes within its walls, between it and the countryside, and between it and other cities.[61]

Beginning in the seventeenth century, cities and towns vied to be designated the seat of a court, or of some other royal administration. The Revolution destroyed the old network of administration and courts; a whole new system was established, and again towns and cities scrambled to be designated as seats of government, regional courts, and other offices. Winning a law court, a tax office, or a prefecture lifted a town's status and provided economic benefits.[62] Political rivalries between French cities were particularly severe during the Revolution, though they certainly had always been present. These rivalries reflected but also created the strong sense of corporate interest with which inhabitants of a particular city were imbued.

Local patriotisms were powerful. One revolutionary leader complained that the Marseillais thought only of themselves: "They only see Marseille. Marseille is their *patrie*, France is nothing." A couple years later, a Prussian traveler remarked that both the Lyonnais and the Marseillais "enthusiastically worshiped their *patrie*, praising their buildings, quais, art, museums. . . ." And in the mid-nineteenth century, a journalist reported that the Lyonnais "see only Lyon, understand only Lyon, admire and esteem but Lyon. For them, outside Lyon, there is no salvation." Local patriotism was far stronger than national sentiment; one of the city's mid-nineteenth-century historians wrote that, "one can be a Lyonnais without being French." And one of the city's historians, reflecting local sentiment, titled his book, *La patrie Lyonnaise*, the Lyonnais fatherland.[63]

Rivalries between cities for preeminence were sharp and frequent, and many of them were economic. In the 1850s, Lyon petitioned that the rail line to Avignon be built on the left bank of the Rhône so as to bypass Saint-Etienne. Later, when the Route Nationale from Roanne to the Rhône was to be built, Lyon lobbied actively—again, to deprive Saint-Etienne of economic opportunities.[64]

People were proud of their cities, often pointing to the cities' illustrious histories, or comparing them to particularly prestigious places. The inhabitants of Bordeaux, Lyon, Marseille, and Toulouse were proud of their cities' pre-Roman or Roman founding, while the Saint Stéphanois, the inhabitants of Saint-Etienne, embraced myths of an ancient founding for their city. In Marseille, a city councilman boasted that his city in antiquity had been "the sister of Athens." A German traveler, who in 1792 had observed Lyonnnais and Marseillais "patriotism," reported that they boasted of being culturally better endowed than Paris. At midcentury, a Lyonnais wrote that his city was really "the first French city"—ahead of the capital—as a result of its spiritual and industrial contributions to French society. The early twentieth-century mayor of Lyon, Edouard Herriot, crowed that in "the realm of ideas, Lyon always has been ahead of Paris." Pride over one's locale and contempt for the capital was not unusual; Adolphe Thiers, born in Marseille, wrote that "Marseille of all the cities of France is the one in which is most often repeated 'In Paris they don't know this or that.'" The local poet Joseph Méry, friend of Alexandre Dumas, boasted if Paris had a Canebière—the major Marseille thoroughfare—then it would be "a small Marseille."[65]

Cities eagerly competed with each other for institutions and facilities to confirm their preeminence. Lyon, beginning in the 1830s, demanded that its medical establishment be recognized as a faculty of medicine; such an establishment, a city councilman announced in 1873, would "continue the traditions which have ensured the glory of the city." Cities proudly pointed to their theaters, investing heavily in them for fear that they would be overshadowed by other municipalities. Tapping into the competitive spirit of the municipalities, a Toulouse architect, urging the establishment of a new cemetery in 1826, utilized the ultimate argument: how can Toulouse lack a "public building as useful and as moral as those of Bordeaux, Lille, Lyon?" In establishing the need for municipal theaters, an official queried "can the great city of Marseille do less than Bordeaux and Lyon, its rivals?"[66]

While Paris was and would clearly remain France's largest city, both Lyon and Marseille, with populations similar in size, were in a position to compete for the honor of being the nation's second largest city. One motive for Lyon's annexation of some of its suburbs in the 1850s was allegedly to protect the city's position as the second most populous city in the country. The competition was so keen that after the turn of the century, both cities falsified census data, creating lists of fictive inhabitants.[67]

Other cities competed for the title of "second city." Although Bordeaux was less populated, one of its city councilmen claimed that as a result of its annexation of suburbs, the city occupied "the first rank after Paris, as to surface." If one judged according to how closely a city resembled a capital, then too, a Bordeaux newspaper claimed, the Atlantic port city ought to be called France's second city.[68]

If cities were rivals, they also knew how much they could learn from one another. Correspondence moved continuously between municipalities asking for information on how they had resolved such problems as water shortages, lack of sewers and gas lines, and narrow streets. The acquired knowledge was used to improve services to fellow citizens, but it was also intended to increase the prestige of the city and distinguish it from its rivals.

In a country noted for its centralization and early nationalism, this localism may strike some as quaint, but it was strongly developed, and is still present today. In fact, paradoxically, the center could be used to legitimate the locale. When Paris granted a city the right to upgrade its school of medicine to a faculty of medicine, both the local medical elite and the city were honored; the act symbolized the city's superiority over its neighbors. And so did other favors, such as the provision of major subsidies and rail connections, and the establishment of a regional branch of the central bureaucracy.

Local elites developed a sense of pride in their cities; while they wished to endow a city with institutions and services that would serve the inhabitants well, they also instituted such improvements to give the city distinction, to make it stand out from its rivals. This local patriotism provided an ideological underpinning for urban government, explaining its drive, independent of the central government, to play an increasing role in the life of its citizens.

Table I.1: Population of Five Major French Cities (in Thousands)

	Bordeaux	Lyon	Marseille	Saint-Etienne	Toulouse
1801	91	110	111	16	50
1806	94	100	99	18	51
1811	88	110	96	18	65
1816		125	107		52
1821	89	131	109	19	52
1826	94	150	116	37*	56
1831	99	134	132	33	60
1836	99	157	149	42	77
1841	105	161	156	49	90
1846	126	178	183	50	94
1851	131	177	195	56	93
1856	150	256*	224	94*	103
1861	163	297	260	92	113
1866	194*	301	300	96	130
1872	194	301	313	111	125
1876	215	322	319	126	132
1881	221	352	360	124	140
1886	241	378	376	118	148
1891	252	416	407	133	150
1896	257	448	447	136	150
1901	257	442	499	147	150
1906	252	456†	522	147	150
1911	262	466†	551	148	155^

* Census subsequent to annexation of suburbs.
† Corrected downward in 1966.
^Adjusted upward in 1921.

1

From City Republic to Republican Cities: The Struggle for Municipal Democracy

*T*he Revolution created uniform municipal institutions, charged with governing their communes. As these institutions developed, their power increased; some of it based on changes in the law, the rest on informal arrangements. Even when regimes in Paris were wedded to central control, municipalities carved out for themselves considerable space for maneuver and were the principal actors responsible for transforming their cities.

The five cities in this study, except for Saint-Etienne, had strong traditions of local rule. Marseille had been an independent republic, and Bordeaux and Toulouse were centers of important *parlements* that throughout much of the ancien régime resisted royal authority. During the Revolution, Bordeaux, Lyon, and Marseille took up arms against the Revolutionary government; Toulouse was only maintained in the fold by vigorous actions of the local Jacobin Club and government officials sent by Paris.[1]

Municipalities took pride in their tradition of self-rule. The Marseille *cahier de doléance* in 1789 protested centralization, asserting its age-old municipal privileges; Marseille, the petition to the National Assembly declared, was unique: "it must not be confused with the other cities of the kingdom. It is a free city, a separate state, a city that was neither conquered nor amalgamated." Several decades later, the Marseille municipality declared that, "there is no city in France whose municipal traditions go further back and are the object of as much pride." Lyonnais insisted on their

21

autonomy—reinforced by memories. As one historian writes, "They remembered not without pride that their city had been a 'free city,'" a "republic of sorts," that had always enjoyed municipal privileges. In 1820, the prefect of the Rhône complained of Lyon's attempts to elude centralized control. The city council's actions, he complained, were "not those of a city of the Kingdom, but rather . . . of Geneva." In the late nineteenth century, the Lyonnnais elite liked to compare its city to Renaissance Florence and other independent Italian republics.[2]

Toulouse was insistent on its historic rights; a police commissioner in 1894 observed that Toulouse "is essentially opposed to centralization. . . . Toulouse has lived its own life . . . Hence, its independence." Given its strong independent streak, it was not a city to which prefects enjoyed being posted; it was a "real hornets' nest." Bordeaux also jealously guarded its prerogatives. During the Revolution, in its petition to the Estates General, it asked for "the reestablishment of its municipal privileges . . . of the jurisdiction, rights, and prerogatives of municipal officers."[3] During Napoleon's rule, in the face of the decline of trade, the city opposed the emperor and his continuous waging of war.

All of the selected cities, except Bordeaux, expressed a desire for municipal autonomy in 1870-71, declaring themselves to be independent communes. Lyon and Marseille, even before Paris, announced themselves as sovereign communes in the fall of 1870—although they were immediately suppressed. And in March 1871, also before Paris declared its Commune, Lyon, Marseille, Saint-Etienne, and Toulouse declared theirs. These attempts to create independent municipalities, which at most were to be linked to each other in a loose federation of communes, was crushed in the late spring of 1871 by the new Conservative Republic, headed by Adolphe Thiers. While the main motivation for these communes was an effort to create social justice locally, their existence also was testimony to the continuing force of municipalism.[4]

Municipalities often physically expressed claims to local authority with impressive city halls. The city hall, the mayor of Marseille declared "symbolizes in stone" the principles of municipal rights. Three of our five cities' buildings were old and impressive, dating back to the seventeenth century. Lyon's city hall, sumptuous and huge enough to continue serving the city's needs for over three hundred years, was considered "the most beautiful of its monuments . . . the most elegant of Europe, after that of Amsterdam." Toulouse's city hall, the *Capitole,* was imposing by its grandeur; it dominated and defined the center of town. That of Marseille, also built in the seventeenth century, dominated the port, which was the city's source of wealth. Its baroque facade and rich internal decoration made it "an authentic jewel." In 1835, Bordeaux created its city hall from what until the Revolution had been the Archbishop's Palace—one of the city's most elegant buildings, situated on the largest plot of ground within the city. The gardens surrounding the Palais Rohan, enclosed by a large iron railing and imposing gates, gave the Bordeaux city hall an added sense of dignity. Saint Etienne's lack of any strong municipal tradition and the modesty of its budget prevented it at first from having a city hall; the municipal offices and the subprefecture were instead housed in the same building, which originally had been a warehouse. A new building, erected in the 1820s, and then remodeled in the 1850s, hardly struck a note of splendor.[5]

RULES OF THE GAME

During the ancien régime, city governments varied in the manner of selecting municipal councils and chief magistrates; their functions and powers were distinctive, developed independently over hundreds of years—except for Saint-Etienne, which had more recent institutions. They were as varied as the titles that members of municipalities bore: in Bordeaux it was *jurats;* in Toulouse *capitouls;* in Lyon and Marseille *consuls;* and in Saint-Etienne, *échevins.*[6]

While, toward the end of the ancien régime, efforts were made to standardize the selection of these councils and their prerogatives, it was as a result of the Revolution that national rules were first imposed upon all communes. The Constituent Assembly provided that each of France's 40,000 or so communes—regardless of size—was to have an elected communal council with a popularly elected mayor. During the Directorate, the stipulation providing for the popularly elected mayor was dropped and never thereafter reestablished. Until 1882, mayors (especially of larger towns) were consistently appointed.

In the late eighteenth century, opponents of royal absolutism had supported local rights, but once the Revolution succeeded, their commitment to local self-government waned; as Mirabeau declared, "Privileges are useful against kings, but they are hateful against the nation." In the face of mass unrest and internal and external threats to the unity of the republic, the mood was to centralize more and more power in Paris. The word *centralisation* was born in 1794 in the midst of deep turmoil.[7]

Rarely in France has commitment to a centralized or decentralized system of government been founded on principle; rather, it has been based on calculations of political interest. Under Napoleon's rule, Royalists favored strengthened regional and local government, believing them to be promising bases from which to challenge Bonaparte. Once the ultra-Royalists had established their power in 1822, they forgot their previous allegiances and became staunch proponents of centralized government. When the July Monarchy and, thereafter, the Second Empire marginalized the ultras, the ultras reverted to embracing localism. In the early 1870s, temporarily at the helm again, Conservatives rediscovered the advantages of centralization.[8]

The Left, on the other hand, was equally calculating, alternately supporting centralization and decentralization as each in turn seemed to hold out the promise of political advantage. During the Second Empire, prominent Republicans, such as Jules Ferry, participated in drawing up an important document, the Nancy Program (1865), which advocated decentralization. Once in power, Republicans were willing to broaden municipal powers beyond their scope under the Empire, but nevertheless they now intended to maintain ultimate power in the central government. Like their predecessors, they were haunted by fears of sedition.

The legal, formal powers given to municipal councils changed with France's regimes. In the early years of the Revolution, municipalities enjoyed considerable powers, but they soon saw their authority reduced. Napoleon only reinforced centralizing tendencies. The Restoration saw centralized control as a safe means to retain mastery over a nation that had witnessed revolutionary agitation for a generation.

Succeeding regimes varied in the intensity with which they maintained central control. Under Napoleon, the city councils and mayors were appointed—an arrangement that lasted until the end of the Restoration. The July Monarchy liberalized municipal administration; laws passed in 1831 and 1833 provided for elected city councils, with limited male suffrage, and for a mayor appointed from among the council members.[9]

The Second Republic provided in 1848 that the municipal council was to be elected by universal male suffrage, an act that enlarged the electorate substantially. In Bordeaux, the electorate increased that year from 2,100 electors to 27,400 voters; and in Toulouse it grew from 2,000 to 20,000.[10] For all its liberalism, however, the Second Republic did not trust mayors enough to allow for their election. Only councils of communes with fewer than 6,000 inhabitants could elect their own mayors; the larger towns had appointed mayors—appointed, as they had been under the July Monarchy, from among the council membership.

Louis Napoleon strengthened his appointive powers over mayors; the constitution of 1852 gave the head of state the right to name as mayor even non-city council members.

On the other side, some liberals and democrats, opposed to the authoritarian rule of Napoleon III, wanted more extensive powers for municipal councils. Adolphe Thiers, one of the Orléanist opponents of the Second Empire, sneered that appointing mayors reduced the holder of the office to a "sous-sous préfet."[11] Municipal councils also registered protests. To ensure local autonomy and the preservation of republican principles, the Toulouse city council demanded an elected mayor.[12] Wanting to curry favor with the liberal opposition, the Second Empire in the late 1860s surrendered its right to name mayors from outside the council, but retained the right to appoint them.

The replacement of the centralizing Second Empire by a liberal Republic in 1870 seemed to hold out the promise of increased local autonomy. But that was not the case. In April 1871, the National Assembly favored granting municipal councils the right to choose their mayors. Thiers, chief minister of the new régime, ignoring his previous position, opposed this measure and threatened to resign if it were enacted. He argued that the preservation of order required the central government to control the mayors, especially of the large cities, which had been the haunts of rebellion. Since France had just undergone military defeat and occupation, the Commune in Paris, and similar rebellions in several provincial cities, Thiers's plea fell on receptive ears. Cowed by Thiers, the assembly agreed that the government would appoint mayors in cities whose populations were greater than 20,000 (city councils in communes under 20,000 could elect their mayors from among their members).

Deprived of the right to elect their mayors, some city councils protested.[13] Such protests, and the increasing presence in Parliament of liberals who had opposed earlier centralizing tendencies, led Parliament in 1882 to allow even large cities to elect their own mayors. The election would not be by popular vote but rather by the elected city councilmen, who elected the mayor from among themselves. The Republicans, controlling the legislature, voted for this liberal law less as a matter of principle than as a calculation of advantage—they did so only after they had been assured by the minister of interior that under this system, within a brief time, a majority of municipalities would be headed by Republican mayors.[14] The provisions of 1882 were included in a general charter on communal government, voted by Parliament in 1884, embodying the powers of municipal councils for a century; it was not replaced until 1982.

Two of France's largest cities, Lyon and Paris were treated as exceptional cases and not covered by the general municipal governance laws—Lyon until 1882 and Paris until the 1970s. The Paris municipality during the Revolution had played the role of a kind of counter government, and the capital had of course been the site of dramatic acts of violence. In reaction, the Consulate in 1800 adopted a law by which Paris was deprived of an elected municipality: the capital was administered by an appointed prefect and council. The 1834 municipal law provided for an elected council. Napoleon III reduced the Paris council again to being appointive. In 1871, the new Republic made the Paris council elective, but it staunchly opposed the establishment of a Paris mayoralty. The prefect continued to run the city. Not until 1975 was Paris allowed to have an elected mayor.[15]

Lyon, the second city to be deprived of municipal governance, was viewed with suspicion in the mid-nineteenth century by the central government. It had been the site of rebellion against the Revolutionary regime in 1793, then of social uprisings in 1831 and 1834. In 1848, revolution had broken out there. Along the Parisian model, the Second Empire established in 1852 an exceptional system for Lyon. The city was run by an appointed municipal commission, and there was no mayor. The prefect of the Rhône served also as the city's chief executive. In 1870, Lyon continued its radical tradition; it declared a commune even before Paris did. This event confirmed the view the Conservatives—who ruled in the early years of the new Republic—had of Lyon "as the nest of radicalism."[16] Though it had a mayor immediately after the fall of Napoleon III, the city was deprived of this office in 1873, and a prefect again ran the city, along with an elected council. The prefect continued to administer the city until 1881; then Lyon was allowed to have its own mayor—as with all other cities, to be elected from among council members.

Local government in France thus has operated under a paradox—the powers of localities since the Revolution have been decided by the center. While in the ancien régime the power, authority, and functioning of municipal councils varied by region and town, the Revolution established a tradition maintained until this day of uniformly legislating municipal power. The municipal charter of 1884, like its predecessors, was a national law specifying the powers of local government, and, like all preceding laws, it essentially provided the same liberties to every commune, regardless of its size and capacity for self-government.

CENTER AND PERIPHERY

Examining the flow of power in a legal, formal sense, one is struck by the limited power of French municipalities and the extensive powers of the seemingly ever-present prefect. The prefect chose the mayors in large cities until 1882, and even beyond that he had to approve municipal legislation and budgets before they became law. Until the end of the Second Empire, he could suspend councils and mayors and replace them with a hand-picked group. Thereafter, he could suspend an elected council and mayor for one-month periods.

Instances of prefects' suspending and replacing of mayors and city councils were numerous. In the July Monarchy, between 1835 and 1847, the terms of 543 mayors and assistant mayors were revoked. Purges were even higher between 1849 and 1851, when 877 mayors and assistant mayors were suspended by the authoritarian regime of Louis Napoleon.[17] Much has been made of these figures; but since there were more than 37,000 communes at the time, each with a mayor and several assistant mayors, the purges actually hit a tiny proportion of the total.

Certainly there are examples of prefectural powers' being exercised at the cost of municipal autonomy. When the central government deprived Lyon of a municipal administration in 1852, the prefect ran the city for the next 30 years. During the Second Empire, the prefect repeatedly suspended mayors of Bordeaux, Marseille, and Toulouse as a result of conflicts. The *ordre moral* government of Marshal MacMahon dissolved the Republican municipalities of all our cities, except Lyon.[18]

The reasons for dissolution or suspension of municipalities varied. Sometimes such moves were reactions to municipal expressions of political dissent. The Radical municipality of Marseille that decided in 1887 to honor the Commune was promptly dissolved by the prefect serving an Opportunist government, for which the Commune was still anathema.[19] Socialist municipalities that were at loggerheads with the national government were dissolved in 1895 and in 1902. Sometimes other causes led to dissolution. In Toulouse, for instance, the Radical municipalities were dissolved in 1894, 1896, and 1898, after they were found guilty of voter fraud.[20]

The centralized administration's exercise of its power to dissolve or suspend councils and mayors seems to confirm the dominance of the center over local institutions. But it must be noted that these dissolutions were exceptional; they were not the norm and do not reflect the day-to-day functioning of French municipalities, especially those of large cities.

The center's exercise of its powers cowed neither the local municipalities nor their voters. City councils considering whether to commemorate the Commune knew perfectly well that such acts were ill-regarded by the central administration, yet they voted their convictions. In fact the municipalities put the central government to a test, for, once dissolved, the members simply ran for re-election, and the voters usually supported them. Voters reelected dissolved councils in Marseille in 1876, 1877, and 1895; and in Toulouse in 1894, 1895, and 1898.[21]

The national government, of course, had the power to make life difficult for a municipality that it did not favor, and sometimes it did so. In the 1890s, the Opportunist national government was hostile to Socialist municipalities and dissolved the one in Marseille. When, after the turn of the century, the Radicals took over national office, they harassed municipalities of other political stripes.[22]

The centralized features of French government created frustrations at the local level. Most decisions made by a local council had to receive approval from higher-ups—the prefect, the ministry of interior and, if it involved the national budget, Parliament. A Marseille city councilman complained that a local decision, "if it does not get lost en route, after months and years will appear in front of Parliament to be examined, discussed, modified, mutilated by deputies from the Pas-de-Calais, the Finistère, the Creuse, the Ardennes, the Pyrenées, or the Savoie. . . ." Just to change the name of a street, a locality had to win prefectural approval and that could take weeks or months.[23] Many other complaints of the pervasiveness and arbitrariness of central rule can be found throughout the period. They reveal the frustrations over a system in which central government representatives could exercise their prerogatives and sometimes did so in a particularly arbitrary fashion. But such complaints hardly reflect the norm. Most city councils and mayors found a way of cooperating with the higher-ups; some sort of modus vivendi usually reigned.

Vivian Schmidt, in her study of French centralization, warns that one should not be misled by the impression of a centralized power in Paris crushing the provinces. Schmidt correctly insists that behind this image of tight central control was a vast store of informal power exercised by local officials.[24] The record of the Parisian relations of the five city governments in this study certainly confirms this view.

While it is true that the central government appointed mayors until 1882, the mayors were by no means pawns. The prefect who appointed the Marquis Montgrand as mayor of Marseille in 1813 boasted that he "hoped to live in peace with a naive young man who would owe his elevation totally to me." But the appointee soon showed his independence. When Napoleon was toppled, this naive young man welcomed the new régime and served it loyally until 1830. In Bordeaux, although the mayor was supposed to ask the prefect's permission before embarking on certain expenditures, the Napoleonic prefect complained that the mayor blithely expended the money and then asked for permission. Supposed to route all correspondence with government ministers through the prefect, the same city official, Mayor Lynch of Bordeaux, systematically ignored the rule.[25]

Appointive mayors, nearly as much as later elected ones, identified closely with their cities and at times did not hesitate to challenge prefects. They even sued. In Bordeaux, after a dispute broke out between the prefect and the mayor in the 1840s over the city's financial obligations towards the insane asylum, the mayor sued his administrative superior and took the case all the way to the Conseil d'état.[26]

It was perfectly legal to replace mayors, and the latter knew they might be replaced; but that did not necessarily lessen their willingness to assert their independence. In the authoritarian Second Empire, the emperor in 1855 appointed as mayor of Marseille one of the city's prominent business-men, François Honnorat. While owing his appointment to the central government, Honnorat did not hesitate to challenge the prefect's attempts to increase his control over the municipality. He vigorously fought the prefect until he was replaced in 1859.[27] Then, finding his policies stymied by the elected Marseille city council, the prefect dissolved the council, replacing it (as he was entitled to do) with an appointive one. Local pride and interest were such that even this appointed council, jealous of its prerogatives, came into conflict with the prefect and did not hesitate to challenge him.[28]

The central government operated under certain restraints that had the effect of empowering its appointees. It could not appoint just anyone as mayor, especially of a large city. It was useful if the nominee had wealth, held a position of status in the community, and enjoyed the respect of his fellow citizens. Such attributes usually ensured the mayor's effectiveness.[29]

Because mayors served without remuneration and incurred large costs of entertainment, wealth sometimes had to be given priority over other considerations. One prefect, having to choose between a liberal and a monarchist as mayor of Saint-Etienne in 1819, appointed the liberal because his income was higher and he could better afford the onerous responsibilities of the position. He in fact turned out to be an outstanding mayor.[30]

Circumstances sometimes led the national government to appoint as mayors men who were politically at odds with it. In the 1860s, elected municipal councils in the large cities were Republican, and thus in conflict with their appointed Bonapartist mayors. Seeking to reduce the causes of friction, the emperor in some cases appointed mayors who were members of the opposition.[31] This practice continued during the Third Republic. Hoping to appease local citizens, Thiers appointed as Lyon's mayor Jacques Hénon, who had been mayor during the city's short-lived Commune.[32] In Marseille, the Opportunist prefect approved appointing a Radical as mayor in 1881, noting that "M. Brochier is according to general opinion the most respected man in conducting city affairs. . . his Radicalism, like that of his colleagues will not resist the exercise of power with the responsibilities that go with it. . . . "[33]

Indeed, the national government often appointed persons who would have been entrusted with the mayoral position had it been elective. In

1871, the prefect appointed as mayor of Bordeaux one of the city's most prominent merchants and republicans, Emile Fourcand; but the *ordre moral* government fired him and his elected council, replacing them with appointed Conservative personnel. When elections were held in 1876, Fourcand and his list were elected, a tribute to his popularity as well as a probable protest against the arbitrary acts of the *ordre moral* government.

That appointments had been made of mayors who would be in harmony with their city councils can be seen by the number of incumbents retained in 1882 when mayors were first elected by councils. The appointive mayors of Bordeaux, Lyon, Marseille, and Saint-Etienne were, for example, all retained. *Le Temps* noted that the new method of picking mayors was not as revolutionary a move as some thought: "The minister [of interior] has nearly always appointed the man whom the council would have elected; any other choice would risk producing difficulties and conflicts harmful to the administrative interests of the commune and the good harmony between populations and the government."[34]

The national government and its representatives wanted to get along with mayors and city councils, whether appointed or elected. That simply made life easier. Léon Gambetta, upon sending out a new prefect to the Haute-Garonne, advised him to "get along with the existing municipalities."[35] Prefects were often appointed with an eye to their compatibility with local officials, and at times they were recalled to please local power brokers. If at times friction arose between prefects and mayors, their associations usually were governed by routine good relations. Many prefects' careers flourished on the basis of their success in courting local officials.

One reason why relations between prefects and mayors had to be good was that the national government depended in many ways upon local officials. Appointive or elected mayors, especially in large cities, were always more than just agents of the central government—the "sous-sous préfets" that Thiers disdainfully described them to be. One striking area of dependence was politics. Often serving as electoral agents, many could mobilize their fellow citizens on behalf of the government. The national government indirectly recognized this role when, under both the Second Republic and the Empire, it called on local officials to get out the vote. *Le Temps*, writing of the 1863 national elections, remarked that "everywhere it was understood that the mayor and their assistant mayors must be the agents of the government; they have to show the same enthusiasm as the prefects for the triumph of the good candidate and the defeat of the bad one."[36] In the early 1870s, it was generally believed that Republican mayors were major factors in producing large victories for Republicanism in national elections.[37]

After 1848, when universal suffrage was instituted, the mayor controlled the registration of voters and thus could influence the outcome of elections. Manipulation of voter rolls and fraud in vote counting occurred, and could be used to help or damage the national government. In Toulouse, for example, 3,000 votes were fraudulently recorded in 1893. This city, in fact, was notorious for its manipulation of elections; the city's very name, a survey claimed, evoked the idea of "electoral fraud."[38]

The Mayor-Deputy

Under French law, several elective offices could and still can be held simultaneously. Mayors often hold national offices as senators, cabinet ministers, and especially deputies. The mayor-deputy was an increasingly frequent phenomenon after the establishment of the Third Republic.[39]

While there were no constitutional impediments to a mayor's serving in Parliament, the practice appears to have been fairly unusual throughout the first half of the nineteenth century. When the mayor of Bordeaux, J. B. Lynch, was appointed peer of the realm in 1816, he stepped down as mayor, declaring that he could no longer fulfill his municipal duties. Among the five cities in this study, however, there were exceptions. In the 1830s, the mayor of Lyon served as a deputy; the following decade, the mayor of Marseille was also a peer of the realm; and in the late 1840s, the mayor of Saint-Etienne also served as a deputy.

The country's primitive transportation system before the mid-nineteenth century discouraged the simultaneous holding of local and national offices. When the Bordeaux city council protested Lynch's resignation, the minister of interior explained that Lynch could not attend functions in both Paris and Bordeaux.[40] Those few men who served as mayor-deputies before mid-century encountered difficulties and embarrassments. Lyon's mayor-deputy, Jean-François Terme, was in Paris, and not in Lyon's city hall, when his citizens rose up in revolt both in 1831 and 1834. The mayor-deputy of Saint-Etienne was away on parliamentary business and thus not minding his city from October 1849 to August 1850, and again from November 1850 to July 1851.[41]

After mid-century, improvements in transportation facilitated a politician's taking on the two offices of deputy and mayor. Within hours a mayor-deputy could go by rail to Parliament, or return to his city, and hence mayor-deputies became more abundant.

Mayor-deputies found that they could exercise pressure in the capital to gain more resources for their cities. As Lyon's Terme declared upon becoming deputy, his national office would put "new forces at the service of his city." Mayor Honoré Serres of Toulouse decided to seek national office in 1904, he announced, to be "closer to central authority, to be better able to accomplish some large municipal projects which need the intervention of the state."[42] Voters seemed to agree that there was value in having a mayor who was well connected in Paris, rarely resenting the reduced amount of time he would be able to give his city.

The advantages to the cities of having mayor-deputies were clear: as deputies they could lobby the central government and effectively circumvent any prefect who stood in their way as mayor. Even under the supposedly highly centralized regime of the Second Empire, when the legislative branch was weakened, prefects were often no match for elected legislators.[43]

Though many large-city mayors were not deputies, they still had to be considered potential mayor-deputies. Antoine Gailleton and Siméon Flaisières, both popular mayors, respectively of Lyon and Marseille, ran for Parliament at the turn of the century and were strong candidates, though defeated. The central government, in its contacts with these two men and other powerful mayors, who were potential parliamentarians or even cabinet members, had to tread carefully. These mayors wielded considerable power when they confronted the prefects, and the prefects had to be attentive. Prefects had to be particularly attentive to deputies. Prime Minister Aristide Briand observed in 1909, "The prefects and subprefects obey the deputy's orders."[44]

Mayors at times had special clout since they were major political figures. At the turn of the century, Serres, mayor of Toulouse, was a pillar of Radicalism in the southwest and well connected to the Sarraut brothers, publishers of the voice of Radicalism in the region, the *Dépêche de Toulouse*. Mayor Herriot of Lyon rose rapidly within the ranks of the Radical party: in 1907, he drew up the party platform; by 1919, he was party chairman. From 1912 until his death in 1957, he was a senator, eventually becoming France's best known mayor-senator. In 1924, he was also named prime minister. Off and on over the next two years (there were several government changes), when the prefect of the Rhône dealt with Herriot, he faced not only a powerful mayor, but his hierarchical superior. The possibility that a local mayor-deputy could rise to high office had an intimidating effect on some prefects. And just being a deputy and having access to the ministries in Paris gave the mayor-deputy considerable leverage. Through their influence at the national level, mayor-deputies could have an obstreperous prefect removed.

If there was less friction than one might expect, it was because prefects were often appointed after their nomination had been approved by the powerful mayors. This tradition was so powerful that a study of one of the most powerful mayor-deputies in post–World War II France claimed that no prefect of the Gironde was appointed without the approval of the mayor-deputy of Bordeaux, Jacques Chaban-Delmas.[45]

THE CITY COUNCIL

At the municipal level as at the national level, there was a struggle to make the government more representative and accountable. Throughout the nineteenth century, forces within the municipalities labored to make them into genuinely democratic institutions. In looking at the origins of the Third Republic, Philip Nord has recently suggested that a civic society, conducive to a democratic culture, developed within a number of French institutions during the Second Empire. One could add to this list the robust debate over increased representation and accountability that occurred within many of France's municipalities.[46]

Various endeavors led to making municipal councils more representative. While the council's social make up never reflected the citizenry exactly, late-nineteenth-century councilors came from more varied social backgrounds than had earlier council members. To accomplish a better class representation in the five cities in this study, some councils strove to implement a policy of having salaried mayors and, in some cases, salaried council members. To make the councils more accountable, some tried to overcome the national prohibition against publishing council minutes.

Social Make Up

In the first half of the nineteenth century, city councils usually consisted of wealthy men. During the Restoration, the central government relied on men of property and means to run the city. In 1829, for instance, 20 of the 31 appointed members of the Saint-Etienne municipal council were among the richest men of the city. And that was not an unusual makeup for councils. Under the July Monarchy, city councils were elected by a limited suffrage based on property. These voters, like most electors, chose even wealthier men than themselves. In Saint-Etienne in 1837, the elected council contained over four-fifths of those in the highest tax bracket. In 1846, 80 percent of the city councilmen were merchants and industrialists; only 6 percent were artisans. Under the Second Empire, elite membership continued.[47]

In Bordeaux, the owners of large trading houses dominated. The city was governed "mainly by merchants and rich men," and many councilmen came from prominent families that had already been prominent in the city's affairs in the eighteenth century. Twenty-five families, each with property worth more than 750,000 francs, made up the cream of Bordeaux society. During the July Monarchy, half of all the members of the powerful chamber of commerce and all the mayors—with one exception—came from the ranks of these families. In 1830, 23 out of 31 city councilors were merchants; their number later went down, but in 1847, a third of the councilors were still merchants. The rich merchants were Catholic, Protestant, and Jewish. Rather than being divided along religious lines, they shared power among themselves. The council always included its share of Protestants, and there was always at least one Jewish member.[48] After the collapse of the Orléanist regime, the social elite continued to run the city. The Republican regime in 1848 replaced the Bordeaux city council with an appointed council of 43 members. For the first time, men of modest background sat on the city council—five or six master artisans and workers, representative of "small and middling commerce." But the dominant figures appointed by the Revolutionary regime included a banker, the dean of the faculty of letters, and several former city council members. And once there were elections, an Orleanist majority returned to the council; 38 out of the 40 councilors were supported by the Orleanist newspapers, *Courrier de la Gironde* and the *Mémorial Bordelais*.[49] So universal suffrage, ushered in by the Revolution of 1848, led on the local as it did on the national level to the continuation in power of a social and economic elite.

In Lyon and Marseille, the experience was similar. Men enjoying local prestige and wealth sat in the councils in the first half of the century. In Marseille, a large number of ship owners and traders sat on the council; in Lyon, manufacturers and professionals, especially medical doctors. When, in 1848, the Revolutionary Assembly appointed Marseille's city council, its 15 members included many leading businessmen, lawyers, and doctors, along with some republican workers. In the six municipalities following each other in the two decades between 1850 and 1870, economic and professional elites predominated; businessmen made up at least 35 percent of the municipality, and, in one case, 48 percent of the municipality.[50]

By the mid-1860s, Republicans had won control over most councils of large cities. In Toulouse, 33 out of the 36 city councilmen who won their seats in the 1865 elections were Republicans, mostly recruited from among the professional classes—lawyers, notaries, and architects.[51] In Marseille, 26 out of 32 city councilmen elected belonged to the Republican opposition, and they came from a more diverse group than those in the earlier years of the Empire.[52]

In Saint-Etienne after mid-century, the established interests, represented by the wealthiest men in the city, were replaced by less wealthy members, many of whom came from the Masonic Lodge, the center of liberal dissent. The municipal elections of 1865 were seen as a turning point. One councilman called them "a real revolution." Many of the new members continued in power into the 1870s.[53]

Elections in the 1870s led to increasingly democratic councils. Léon Gambetta, the Republican leader, had predicted that the ballot would bring new "couches," or layers of society, into the councils of government. "From day to day," he said, "the people-the petite bourgeoisie, the workers and peasants-see more clearly that politics are closely related to their interests; they want representation that reflects those interests; and soon they will represent themselves. It's a revolution."[54]

The actual changes were not so dramatic, but there was a shift from the upper classes to the middling ones at the municipal level. A Marseille councilor announced in 1871 that "we feel the coming to power of a new force, and we who come from that class-the one under the middle class, we are happy to know that the popular movement is slowly but surely growing." The new politicians knew that they needed to prove themselves. "Let us prove," one councilor said, "that it is not necessary to have an important name in business or in finance to run the affairs of a city successfully. . . ."[55]

In 1871, the government, not trusting the electorate after the Commune, appointed a city commission (when appointed they were called commissions, rather than councils), of Saint-Etienne that was broadly representative of the social makeup of the industrial city. Appointees were manufacturers of weapons, chocolate, and ribbons; professionals, such as engineers, notaries, and lawyers; silk, iron, wine, and textile merchants; and artisans, such as weavers, carpenters, and bakers. When elections were held, the number of industrialists on the council went down in favor of professionals and functionaries.[56]

In Bordeaux, important trading interests continued to dominate the city council. In 1874, 17 merchants sat on the council, and in 1892, 19 did. They were part of the moderate Opportunist stranglehold over the city, which lasted, with one interruption, until 1914. Of the five cities in this study, Bordeaux was the only one where Opportunism dominated after the 1880s. *Le Temps* approvingly noted that Bordeaux's municipal council, "where political adventurers are not in the majority, but men who truly represent the important interests of their city," should be a model for other cities.[57] Bordeaux's interests were bourgeois. Big merchants (*négociants*) and men from the liberal professions dominated the city council in the years 1871-1914. Other categories included small merchants, tradesmen, functionaries, and a few workers—never more than four at a time. A report of 1888 described 19 of the 36 city councilors as "rich." In the council elected in 1912, the largest group was composed of big merchants (ten of them), and two members were ship owners. One of the few Socialist members, the postwar mayor, Adrien Marquet, was a dentist.[58]

Marseille was more Radical and had more representation from the working class. In 1881, 8 out of the 36 council members were workers, but a clear majority came from the middle class—doctors, lawyers, professors, and mid-level employees in industry.[59]

In Lyon, the liberal professions were highly represented. In 1881, 11 of 36 councilors were from these groups. Only seven members were salaried individuals. Even with the victory in 1900 of a Radical-Socialist alliance, more left-wing than any municipal government Lyon had seen since the Commune, a majority of the council was made up of professionals—eight lawyers, five doctors, two pharmacists, three accountants, one architect, and one law graduate. The others were artisans of varying wealth, makers of lemonade, and a horticulturist. No industrial worker sat on the council. Only after 1919 did salaried individuals represent a majority on the council.[60]

In Toulouse, city council members came heavily from the middle class: 90 percent of the candidates for municipal office in 1884, 74 percent in 1892 and 71 percent in 1904. Many were professionals such as doctors, lawyers, and architects—callings widely respected in this administrative city. In 1910, of the Toulouse Radical municipality's 35 members, 21 belonged to the liberal professions.[61]

In the Saint-Etienne municipality, workers, usually artisans, played a greater role than in other cities. By the turn of the century, Saint-Etienne was bringing laborers with limited formal education to the fore. In 1908, the Socialist list running for city council was headed by Petrus Faure, a tailor, who had left school at age 12.

Democratization seemed achieved when the masses in the large cities were represented by Socialist councils, in Lyon (in a coalition) in 1884, Saint-Etienne in 1888, Marseille in 1892, and Toulouse in 1906. But the leaders rarely reflected the social makeup of the voters; the mayors typically were bourgeois, elite citizens, such as Drs. Augagneur and Flaissières of Lyon and Marseille, respectively. An artisan became mayor in Saint-Etienne in 1900 and in Marseille in 1910. No industrial worker headed the administration of Saint-Etienne until after World War I, or of Marseille until 1936.

Salaries

The unrepresentative social makeup of city councils and mayoral offices was due in part to a lack of remuneration. Unless one had an independent income, one could not afford to forego earnings to attend council meetings, which were usually in the daytime. The required expenditure of time was even more onerous for the mayor, who, in addition to attending council meetings, carried out administrative tasks (along with his appointed *maires adjoint,* or assistant mayors). The struggle to institute payment of salaries of elected city officials was part of the effort to expand mayoral and council choices and to make the offices more democratic.

Under the ancien régime, the mayor and other principal municipal officials had been remunerated, but the Revolution abolished this practice. Still, it was recognized that the position entailed expenses that demanded reimbursement. The Revolutionary city council of Bordeaux argued in the Year II that "it is just" that new magistrates, who were *sans culottes,* "whose only fortune is their work and effort" should receive "indemnities," the mayor to receive 12,000 livres and free housing.[62] Lyon, subdivided after the Revolution into three communes, provided 5,000 francs as expense allowances and 15,000 francs for a carriage, a theatre box, and clothes for each of its mayors.[63] In 1814, expense allowances for Lyon's mayors were set at 12,000 francs each. Bordeaux provided its mayor with 12,000 francs a year in expense allowance costs in 1831, although his expenses were then between 15,000 and 20,000 francs. In 1855, the mayor of Marseille had at his disposal an expense allowance budget of 30,000 francs.[64]

Arguments for providing expense allowance costs for mayors usually were based on the need to reimburse them for at least part of their out-of-pocket expenses and the desire to not make the mayor's burden so onerous that no one would be willing to serve. At least once, during the Marseille Commune, it was proposed that the mayor be salaried so that the position would be accessible to all—an expression of democratic sentiment.[65] But usually the issue was not salary but rather proper indemnity. A subsidy to the mayor, one Marseille councilman argued in 1876, would make it possible "for all citizens to accept the office. If it is a necessity to be rich to be a candidate for these functions, they will be the monopoly of the aristocracy of money." True to the argument, Bordeaux's first elected mayor, Alfred Daney, chosen in 1884, resigned six years later because he could not afford to occupy the office. The funds provided for his expenses were insufficient, he declared, to allow him to carry on his functions.[66]

Throughout the Third Republic, mayors were not allowed to receive salaries; they were paid for the first time in 1942. The refusal by the French Parliament to countenance mayoral salaries seemed particularly unfair because the parliamentarians themselves received salaries; in fact quite generous ones of 15,000 francs a year after 1907.

As for city councils, it was illegal for their members to receive remuneration for their services. Elected until the mid-nineteenth century by a suffrage based on property, councilmen were men of means, most of whom could afford unremunerated service to their city. As Auguste Fabre explained in 1842, remunerating councilors would be an attack on their dignity, weakening "the nobility of our disinterestedness and our patriotism."[67] But after the introduction of universal suffrage, especially with the election of members of the *"couches nouvelles"* after the 1870s, the need to salary councilmen became more urgent.

In 1870, inspired by the democratic sentiments that had led to the downfall of the empire and the declaration of several Communes, the Marseille Commune demanded that councilors who asked for an emolument should be given it, while the Lyon Commune voted to make five francs available to every councilor attending a session. A few years later, the Marseille council pointed out that lack of remuneration made it impossible for the poor to serve. In 1881, the newly elected Radical council tried, but failed, to implement its campaign promise to "finally" have salaried councilors "to allow all the workers to be part of the council." Twelve years later, when the Socialists captured city hall, they agitated for paid councilors. The Socialist councilor Cadenat, who later became mayor, declared: "If those with no means are not provided with pay, you will always be administered by the rich. If you want proletarians to participate in municipal affairs, you must pay them." And in 1897, the Socialist council provided ten francs a day for attendance; the council acted out of "Socialist principle," while knowing that higher-ups would annul the decision.[68]

The debate over pay became so widespread in the provinces and in Parliament that *Le Temps* in Paris felt compelled to express its opinion, revealing the reasons for official opposition. If councilmen were paid, the newspaper argued, honor would no longer attach to their position. Payment would reduce councilmen to functionaries, and "we have enough functionaries; it is good to preserve in a democracy certain positions which bring in only public esteem." This attitude dominated the period. Even after the turn of the century, the moderate Bordeaux newspaper *Petite Gironde* opposed paying councilmen, arguing that the honor and sacrifice of the position were worthy of a Frenchman.[69]

Whereas some municipalities argued forthrightly against the 1884 law forbidding payments, Toulouse chose to ignore it. In 1892, the Toulouse council members voted to provide themselves with salaries. The mayor, outraged by the council's challenge to the law, resigned, and the prefect annulled the vote. Other municipal councilors explored ways to get around the law. Some voted to reimburse themselves for expenses incurred while carrying out their city functions. Such expense funds could be quite large: Lyon's was 50,000 francs, and Marseille's was 66,000 francs total for 36 city councilmen for one year. In 1900, the Paris city council decided to reimburse each of its 80 members 500 francs a month for undocumented expenses. Since this was obviously intended as compensation for council service, the Conseil d'état declared the measure illegal. The Paris council then made 6,000 francs a year available for what might be viewed as members' documented expenses.[70] The Cour de comptes, the French general accounting office, concluded in 1901 that Lyon under the guise of reimbursing councilors for expenses was actually providing compensation for lost time. Political opponents of the Marseille and Toulouse municipal councils made the same charge about practices in their cities. In 1913, Marseille tried to provide funding for its city councilmen by voting 300 francs a year to each councilor as reimbursement for "displacement costs."[71]

Attempts to pass a national law allowing city councilors to receive salaries were made in the French Parliament repeatedly, but with no success. As early as 1869, the Socialists had in their national party program a demand that all elected offices be remunerated. At the turn of the century, a Socialist party organ explained that such a measure "would allow elected workers to struggle against the bourgeois without having to fear famine."[72] But Republican parliaments always refused to allow remuneration. Not until 1942, under the Vichy regime, were such measures instituted.

Publishing the Minutes

City council meetings were closed, and it was against the law to print minutes of the proceedings. The rationale for not publishing minutes, a mid-nineteenth-century legal scholar explained, was to ensure that the debates "would be calmer, less passionate, more truly free. . . ." A Second Empire prefect of the Gironde explained that publishing minutes might lead to debates being "influenced by dangerous appeals to passions outside the council chambers" or to the intimidation of "shy, but enlightened men who would shrink from debate because of the publicity that would surround their name. . . ." This prefect's superior, the minister of interior, warned that publication might tempt some councilors into demagogy while keeping others from speaking out.[73]

In spite of such national strictures, councils tried to be accountable to the public. Just as the national government began in the 1820s to publish its budgets, so municipalities began to make public their finances.[74] The Bordeaux city council, for instance, began to publish its budgets in 1835. While councils could not publish the contents of their debates, beginning in 1836 the Marseille city council published summary accounts of its final decisions.

When the Second Republic did an about-face and allowed the publication of city council minutes, the Lyon municipality availed itself of this new right. But in Toulouse the habit of not publicizing minutes was so deeply ingrained that when a councilor suggested printing them in accord with the new law, his proposal was defeated.[75]

In liquidating the Second Republic, Louis Napoleon abolished many of its reforms, including in 1852 the right of municipalities to publish their minutes. An 1855 law, however, allowed the public to consult written summaries of council proceedings. The Bordeaux summaries failed to identify speakers, noting only what "one councilor said" or "another councilor said." In the 1860s, the Bordeaux council and the councils in the four other cities in this study, desiring to increase their members' accountability, tried to include the speakers' names. But the prefects forbade the practice. As the prefect of the Haute-Garonne declared, such a move could not be countenanced "in order to preserve the intended character of council meetings."[76] Not until the late 1860s, as the Second Empire was in its last and liberal phase, were summaries allowed that included the identities of speakers.

Municipalities then became more and more insistent on the need to publish full minutes of their proceedings. The Toulouse city council declared, "Publicity is a good thing. It is important for the council, which is the emanation of the free vote of the people, that all its acts be done in the light of day." No sooner had news of the fall of the Second Empire arrived in Toulouse than the city council declared its meetings open. The following year, it published full proceedings. Publication, the council proclaimed, not only would open its actions to public scrutiny but also serve as a school for democracy. In Marseille, the council allowed local newspapers to reproduce the proceedings starting in December 1870. Although the Lyon Commune published only summaries of council meetings, these accounts were fairly complete.

The policy of openness hardly outlasted the Communes. Once the Communes had been crushed and the central government had reestablished its authority, it reinstated the ban on publication of council minutes. Many of the councils of the cities in this study continued to insist on their right to issue full minutes of their meetings, and, in spite of opposition from the central administration and its representatives, municipalities pushed even further. Published summaries, which were reallowed, indicated whether a measure had passed or not, and the Bordeaux council decided in 1878 to record the votes of those in favor and those opposed. In 1880 and 1881, when the Marseille municipality asked that it be allowed to print minutes, it declared that "city hall should be a glass house and nothing that is done there should be hidden."[77]

The 1884 law opened municipal council meetings to the public and made mandatory the publication of minutes summarizing council sessions. Unlike previous laws, it did not specifically forbid the publication of complete minutes, and many municipalities, taking advantage of this loophole, soon began publishing full stenographic records of council proceedings. An important aspect in the battle for accountability on the municipal level had been won.

The process of democratization, which made city councils more representative and accountable, strengthened the public's view of their municipalities as the embodiment of the city, and sharpened the competition between municipalities of various cities. While universal suffrage was instituted in 1848, its impact was blunted by Napoleon III's rule. Thereafter, however, especially following the municipal charter of 1884, city governments became increasingly accountable to their constituents. A strong reformist impulse dominated many city councils. Idealism, as well as political calculation, led many municipalities to embark on various projects to improve the lives of their citizens.

2

City Financing: The Octrois

*T*he main source of income for French cities under the ancien régime and, with rare exception, until World War II, were the taxes known as *octrois*. The *octrois* provided municipalities with strong financial autonomy, but had the severe disadvantage of being a regressive tax, particularly harsh on the poor. Nearly exclusively dependent upon the *octrois*, municipalities had limited sources of income, which constrained their ability to engage in ambitious projects.

The *octrois* were so named because the right to collect them had been granted, *octroyés,* by royalty. These taxes, of medieval provenance—starting in many cities in the thirteenth century—varied in kind, but by the eighteenth century the only *octrois* remaining were the tolls collected on goods entering a city. Popular opposition manifested itself frequently against what was understood to be an unfair tax; after universal suffrage was adopted in 1848 the *octrois* became the subject of intensive debates within municipalities. The failure to transform this method of city financing reveals the persistence of tradition, bolstered by narrow class interests. While Socialists towards the end of the century dominated several city councils, they were unable in most to abolish the *octrois,* suggesting inertia in a field of direct concern to the working class.

ABOLITION AND RESTORATION

The medieval *octrois* had a very long life and broad impact. The *octrois* shaped the urban landscape. If changes in warfare at the end of the sixteenth century promised to make city walls obsolete, they were retained, for they kept smugglers out and forced all goods to enter through *octrois* barriers. New walls were even built just for such purposes, the best-known example in the eighteenth century being the wall in Paris. The populace did not appreciate this measure, which led to the coining of the alliterative phrase *"le mur murant Paris rend Paris murmurant."* (The wall immuring Paris makes Paris murmur)."

Social thinkers and officials differed in their appreciation of the *octrois*. The advantage of such a tax, as Montesquieu noted, was that it could be collected in such a manner "that the people will nearly ignore that they are paying it."[1] Turgot pointed out that the *octrois* impeded the free movement of goods and people, and encouraged fraud. And because the *octrois* taxed goods produced or extracted from the countryside, some observed that they represented an economic benefit to cities at the cost of the countryside.[2]

Public opposition was reflected in widespread protests against the *octrois* in the *cahiers des doléances*. In 1789, revolutionary mobs in many cities attacked the *octrois* posts as part of the hated fiscal system and the ancien régime itself. In Marseille, protest against a tax on flour precipitated the popular insurrection in 1789. The Lyonnais assaulted their *octrois* barriers, the following year in Bordeaux, hostility to the tax was so pervasive that city employees manning the *octrois* posts ran "the greatest risks to their persons."[3]

The National Assembly, responsive to the arguments of economists who had noted the regressive, unequal nature of the *octrois,* abolished it in 1791. This measure deprived cities of most of their incomes, for the *octrois* provided the lion's share of city revenues; in Lyon, for instance, of the 2.4 million livres in city receipts, 2.2 million, or 90 per cent, originated in the *octrois.*[4] Dependence on the *octrois* as a source for funding city services was so great that Bordeaux, which in February 1791 petitioned the National Assembly to abolish the tax, found itself so short of funds after its request was heeded that in May it asked for the tariff to be reinstituted.[5]

Cities, newly entrusted with functions such as education and welfare that had been the responsibility of the Church, found themselves woefully underfunded. In Marseilles city employees, unpaid for 13 months, threatened in the Year VII to stop working unless they were given their back pay.[6]

The national government authorized levies in the Year VII, and the following year it required all cities that had hospitals with insufficient funds to collect *octrois*. The reinstituted *octrois* provided, as in the ancien régime, an independent base of funding for cities. In large cities, the *octrois* represented the single largest source of income. During the Empire, Paris received between 80 percent and 90 percent of its annual income from the *octrois*. The large provincial cities were equally dependent on this source.

As the Lyon city council declared in the Year XI, *octrois* were "so to speak its sole source [of income]."[7]

Although the Restoration promised to eliminate the *octrois*, it continued the tax in accord with a national policy of increased indirect taxation (benefiting also the central government—for until 1852, the central government collected 10 percent of the *octrois* for its own uses).[8] In 1818, of 1.9 million francs in ordinary revenues, Bordeaux collected 1.3 million, or 68 percent, from the *octrois;* Lyon had no other source of revenue that year, all 1.8 million coming from the *octrois.* In Saint-Etienne, 91 percent of the ordinary city revenue came from *octrois;* in Toulouse, 84.5 percent.

The July Monarchy brought no notable changes in the *octrois* proportion of city incomes. Gradually the rates fell to two-thirds of the ordinary income of a city. The *octrois* were the lifeblood of cities. The acute observer of the life of the capital, Maxime Du Camp, described the tax as the "fortune of Paris,"[9] as it was of the other approximately 1400 communes—among them all of France's large cities and towns.

The *octrois* were collected mainly on food, liquor (which was considered a prime necessity), and fuel; the *octrois* on these items made up nearly 90 percent of the total collected. City income from *octrois* varied between cities and over time. There was no standard rate; each city set its own.

The tax rates were set by city councils and reflected their judgment on which items ought to be considered luxuries and therefore could be heavily taxed. They also reflected the economic and geographic situations of each city. Bordeaux, a city of wine merchants, was not about to impose a heavy *octroi* on wine. Also, it was no accident that port cities such as Bordeaux and Marseille and the river city of Toulouse would have low tariffs on fish, for high rates on goods that were available in large quantities would needlessly increase the temptation to smuggle.

Furthermore, tax rates reflected local sensibilities. In the south, wine was considered a necessity, while beer and malt were viewed as exotic; in the north, it was the opposite. So the cities in this study, all of them in the south, had low taxes on wine, but high taxes on beer and malt. Their *octroi* was low on olive oil, high on butter; the opposite was the case in northwestern cities, which were distant from the southern olive groves but close to dairy farms.[10] The differences also reflected protectionist impulses—the desire to encourage the sale of regional products and to discourage consumption of goods originating from more distant places. Protectionist purposes were furthered by imposing particularly heavy tolls on certain finished goods and thus reducing their competitiveness with those locally produced. The Conseil d'état in 1882 forbade the use of *octrois* for such purposes, but it undoubtedly was difficult to prove that an *octroi* was protectionist.[11]

Changes in *octrois* rates had noticeable effects on the consumption of goods brought into cities. A Paris city councilman contended that increased rates on meat after the Revolution had reduced its consumption by the 1840s.[12] When the rates on meat and exotic fruits were increased in Bordeaux in 1908, consumption went down and so did the city income on these items. Even such a presumed necessity as wine proved subject to fluctuations. When the tax on wine was abolished in Lyon, yearly consumption went up, from 131 liters per inhabitant in 1900 to 150 in 1902.[13]

OPPOSITION AND DEBATE

While the *octrois* proved to be convenient sources of income for cities, the taxes were vigorously contested by various groups. An examination of the *octrois* in Nîmes suggests that opposition to these taxes developed only in the 1880s; that was not the national experience, nor that of our five cities. Popular violence was often directed at the *octrois,* changes of regime being particularly propitious moments to revolt. In Bordeaux and Marseille news in 1814 that Napoleon had been overthrown prompted attacks on the *octrois* posts. In Marseille, "the populace asked with loud outcries for the abolition of the tax on fish, broke the furniture and instruments of the [*octrois*] officials, and threatened to throw them into the sea if they returned." The following year in Bordeaux, during the instability concomitant with the Hundred Days, mobs destroyed an *octrois* post.[14] The 1830 Revolution, like the one in 1789, was accompanied by attacks on the *octrois*. In Bordeaux and Toulouse, some posts were destroyed. The events of 1848 also included attacks on *octrois* posts.

Other types of assaults were surreptitious. Smuggling was frequent enough to be broken down by an official of the Seine prefecture, H. A. Frégier, into four categories: dissimulation under clothing, climbing over barriers, throwing objects over barriers, and tunneling under barriers.[15] In Bordeaux, the prefect claimed that smugglers were so undaunted that they had been known to attack an *octroi* barrier and force the employees to withdraw, overcome "by the superiority in numbers of the smugglers."[16] In 1825, an *octroi* employee in Bordeaux died from "murderous excesses on his person by smugglers." In 1831, also in Bordeaux, an *octroi* employee was run over by a coach galloping at full speed across the toll barrier.[17] In some cities, mobs formed for the purpose of forcibly overrunning the barriers.[18]

Later in the century, the situation had not changed. A study by the Lyon city council in the 1870s revealed that *octroi* revenues were well below what the city had the right to expect.[19] Smugglers equipped themselves with specialized devices, such as double-bottom barrels, loose clothing, and especially, vicious whips with which to attack *octroi* officials standing in their way. There were so many tools of the smugglers' trade that a special museum in Lyon was devoted to exhibiting them.[20]

Even *octroi* employees were caught up in the outlawry. In Toulouse, a city commission complained in the 1890s of "multiple fraud" in the collection of *octrois*. The main city newspaper charged that improper methods of collection cost the city 300,000 francs in revenues and that *octroi* employees, while checking goods entering the city, stole some of them. *Octroi* employees in Marseille formed a smuggling ring that was responsible for a 1.5-million-franc loss in revenue. Bordeaux *octroi* officials, known to appropriate for themselves the best portions of what they were supposed to control, were nicknamed *pêle gigots*, "slicers of legs of lamb."[21]

The *octrois* represented a constant nuisance to city dwellers. A Bordeaux newspaper complained of the *octroi* employees' habits of "rudely inspecting the smallest package . . . and if they are faced with a basket they put their nose in it, thinking they will find a gold mine which will cover the increasing city budget deficits." The employees in Lyon were probably just as rude. A city report speaks of their "indispensable . . . severity" and evidently there was a need to direct them to exercise restraint in inspecting people suspected of smuggling goods under their clothes. A report of an inspector of finance in 1888 described the *octroi* employees of Toulouse as rude and arbitrary.[22]

To collect the taxes, an expensive bureaucracy had to be established, using up sums ranging nationally between 27.8 percent of the funds collected in 1823 to 8.8 percent in 1900.[23] Differences depended upon city size, ease of access, and local predilections about hiring large numbers of employees. In the late 1860s, Bordeaux spent 15.25 percent of the *octroi* income on collecting the toll, Saint-Etienne spent 13.25 percent, and Toulouse 11.75 percent. In 1897, Lyon spent the equivalent of 8.5 percent of the *octrois* on collecting them; Bordeaux and Marseille, far larger in surface, spent respectively 14.8 percent and 11.5 percent, while Toulouse, with the largest surface of area in relation to population and most probably desiring to pad its civil service, spent close to a fifth of the *octrois* on collection.[24]

The *octrois* seems to have driven people out of the city to the suburbs, where without the tax, the cost of living was lower. The reformer Louis Villermé claimed that the *octrois* on wine and meat, imposed in 1822 and 1823 in Lyon, drove workers to leave for suburban Croix Rousse and Brotteaux.[25] Later in the century, Lyon's mayor blamed city unemployment on the advantages workers had in locating outside the city, freed of *octrois*.[26] Although decentralization of labor and industry had many causes, the availability of less expensive goods in the countryside certainly played a role. The *octrois* thus helped shape the settlement of working-class suburbs, often creating rings of working and marginal populations around French cities.[27] Suburbanization was seen as reducing cities' populations and thus their tax base.

The *octrois*—like the rest of the French taxation system—was as the French economic historian Jean Bouvier has noted, remarkably immobile, impermeable to change. Revolution did not affect them, although there was always the hope it would. Nor did their unpopularity and the heavy barrage of criticism aimed against them transform the situation.[28]

The *octroi* debate continued through the nineteenth century. More than half a century after Montesquieu's endorsement, the Napoleonic official Louis Molé saw the tax as having the same benefits. A manual on France's finances proclaimed, "The best tax is the one which best dissimulates its nature and dispenses the payer to make savings, and is identified as completely as possible with necessary expenses which one usually makes without regret."[29] On the other hand, the liberal economist Jean-Baptiste Say argued that the tax was unfair, for it disproportionately hit the poor. But not all liberals shared this viewpoint. Anatole Leroy-Beaulieu observed that since the rich consumed more, they paid more. And the liberal statesman Adolphe Thiers observed, "he who buys most objects is the one who pays most taxes." Other liberals also thought the *octrois* might be more equitable than its critics acknowledged; the liberal *Journal des économistes* calculated that workers spent one-fifth of their family budget on the *octrois* but also benefited most from city services. They relied—more so than other social groups—on welfare services, hospitals, and improved streets.[30]

Attacks on *octroi* posts accompanying the Revolution of 1830 led to some local attempts at reforming the tax. In Bordeaux, especially strong hostility had been expressed against the wine tolls—although they were not particularly high—and they were briefly suspended in 1830. The following year, the Bordeaux city council considered cutting *octroi* rates but mournfully concluded that "it would be difficult to find any [resources] as inevitable and easy to collect." The Marseille city council, more daring, considered abolishing the *octrois* on flour. One proponent of this measure spoke out against a tax that "hits especially the food of first necessity and affects in unequal proportions, relative to differences in fortune, in the number of individuals which make up a family." Such inequality, argued the councilor, led to disorders and was an attack on public order. The city won permission from Paris to abolish the tariff on flour, but it was not allowed to establish other taxes to replace the lost 200,000 francs. So this was a discouraging experience.[31]

The unfairness of the toll was widely recognized. A Lyon journal in 1841 estimated that *octroi* payments represented a substantial proportion of a worker's salary: 25 francs per person a year, 13 percent of a worker's yearly salary, or 153 francs for a family. And it was patently unjust:

> when the tax hits objects of primary necessity, when it hits the poor as much as the rich, when it reduces people's well being rather than taxing superfluous wealth, it is at the same time unjust and harmful, one cannot too soon abolish it.
>
> Is it not in effect unjust to augment the distress of a poor family, to weigh on it a heavy tax on flour which provides its daily bread, on meat and wine which give it strength and help it maintain its vitality, on charcoal and wood which preserve it from cold, on straw which makes its miserable sleeping quarters, on soap which keeps it clean and candles which provides light? To tax in such a manner the primary necessities of life, is it not to force people into indigence?[32]

Many liberals found the *octrois* incompatible with their principles. The system of city tolls was against the very principles of free trade for which large port cities, such as Bordeaux and Marseille, agitated. The *octrois* impeded the free movement of goods, services, and people. "Gentlemen, the *octrois* are for Bordeaux what the tariffs are for France," cried out one councilor. As the mayor of Marseille noted in 1840, the *octrois* were being questioned by many authorities.[33]

Bordeaux attempted in the 1840s to abolish the *octrois* entirely. One proponent of abolition argued that it was not true that cities could not survive without local *octrois*. England and the United States were able to do without them. Other sources of revenue could be found, such as taxes on hotels, horses, carriages, dogs, and insurance companies. Significantly, property taxes were not mentioned as an option; the proposal was sent to a municipal commission for further study, and it died there.[34]

Voices opposed to the toll were also heard on the national level. Minister of Interior Léon Faucher noted that "the *octrois* augment the price of the most essential foods, meat, wine; the *octrois* makes fuel more expensive; it makes life materially difficult." He described the *octrois* as "the principal cause for the misery which afflicts urban populations."[35]

The revolution of 1848 was unable to change much in regard to the *octrois* in spite of its social and egalitarian impulses and its proclaimed intention to abolish the tolls. In April 1848, Paris abolished tolls on meat. But the effects were not as expected: prices did not drop, meat consumption did not rise and the capital lost income. In August 1848, the city council reinstituted the *octrois* on meat. Other cities pointed to this experiment as conclusive evidence of the futility of abolishing the *octrois*. And it is striking that even though the populist elements won representation on various city councils as a result of the introduction of universal suffrage after 1848, municipalities in the provinces did not abolish the *octrois*. In fact, the Marseille city council voted to extend the areas of toll collection.[36]

THE STRUGGLE FOR ABOLITION

After mid-century, the *octrois* were debated even more intensely. Tax rate increases made the *octrois* a more obvious subject for examination; also, after the introduction of universal suffrage, city councils became less oblivious to the needs of the poor and members of the working-class. The political left often included abolition of the *octrois* in its program.

As city councils became radicalized in the 1860s, they considered abolishing the *octrois*. In the Bordeaux city council, the issue was thrashed out in a series of debates. In 1866, a councilor declared "the *octrois* are no longer a plausible tax . . . it is not of our time and century . . . it must be suppressed. . . ." Most men of advanced opinions could agree to such propositions, but those with responsibilities flinched from implementing them. Bordeaux Mayor Emile Fourcand, a man of leftist sympathies, admitted that the toll had against it the manner in which it was collected and its regressive nature, "but this tax is indispensable to the life of municipalities and their autonomy." His assistant mayor expressed a similar view, that "the *octrois* are . . . the only resource of a municipality." Besides, he added, if *octrois* were replaced by other taxes, such an effort would be self-defeating. The taxes would be shifted onto property, and workers would then have to pay higher rents.[37]

Belgium had abolished its *octrois* in 1860, replacing them with direct taxes and an increase in national tariffs, and a number of French municipalities looked to their northern neighbor as a possible model. The Bordeaux mayor wrote to his Brussels counterpart asking for information on the success of the changes. The answer was hardly encouraging for a city executive contemplating change. Brussel's mayor wrote that while the change benefited Belgian citizens, it had its disadvantages.

> It was very convenient, doubtlessly [in the past], to have indirect resources, the weight of which was not felt, and which grew in direct proportion to the prosperity of the city. Direct taxes, on the contrary, lead to the discontent of the taxpayers.

He added that because he had been forced to raise direct taxes, it was unlikely he would be reelected. This part of the letter evidently caught the attention of the mayor of Bordeaux, for a long red line in the margin marks it off.[38] It seemed to confirm hesitations on the wisdom of abolishing the toll.

The many discussions of the *octrois* in the municipalities and the repeated criticisms of liberal economists induced the Second Empire at the end of its reign—as it was attempting to shore up its declining popularity—to consider the possibility of abolishing the *octrois*. While individual cities set the *octroi* rates and collected the tolls, they were not allowed to abolish the tax or replace it without permission from the national government. And that is why Paris became preoccupied with the issue.

In 1867, a parliamentary commission appointed by the emperor studied the matter. It recognized the negative aspects of the tax: it slowed the movement of goods, was regressive in nature, hit agriculture harder than industry, was expensive to collect, encouraged fraud and disrespect for the law, and did not constitute an essential tax, since many countries did well without it. Yet the official report came out against abolition, recommending rather that the rates not be further raised and, if possible, that they be lowered. A member of the commission who was a former mayor explained that experience in city government had taught him "the impossibility of replacing this tax with another one without causing serious discontent." And there seemed empirical evidence proving that the tax was not as harmful as its critics maintained. In spite of the *octrois,* he pointed out, immigrants poured into the cities, and the urban laboring classes consumed more goods and services than their country cousins. "They are better fed, better dressed, better housed, better heated, and not only has their condition not been worsened by the establishment of the *octrois,* but they are not even aware of it."[39]

Napoleon III's minister of interior sent a questionnaire to all the municipalities with *octrois*. Of the 89 prefects, 74 answered, and they unanimously supported continuation of the *octrois*. Of the 1,551 communes with *octrois*, 1,206 took up the issue, of which 1,094 favored retention of the *octrois,* 45 favored modifications, and 67 favored abolition.[40]

All five cities in this study took up the issue and debated how to answer the questionnaire. The city council of Lyon questioned the wisdom of maintaining the toll but then also pointed out that it was a small tariff and could hardly weigh heavily on the workers. If the *octrois* were replaced by national taxes that would be redistributed to cities, abolition would represent a threat to city autonomy. To the minister's question as to whether the population desired abolition, the council answered, "No, the population is accustomed to sustain the tax without complaint or difficulty."[41]

While Bordeaux saw the abolition of the *octrois* as potentially providing more sales for the wine industry, it was also anxious about its finances. If the *octrois* were abolished, how would the city coffers be filled? The city council, perhaps forgetting that rioters a year earlier had demanded the abolition of the *octrois*, maintained there was no popular opposition. Abolishing the *octrois* and replacing it with direct taxes would mean a large increase in discontent. A councilor suggested that the very nature of the Frenchman's character made it necessary to have indirect rather than direct taxes, for "in France people naturally oppose authority, elude its rules, or try to escape taxes which are collected." The councilor doubted that his fellow citizens could be trusted to declare their income. The council was evenly split on the wisdom of recommending abolition of the *octrois* and the recommendation to retain it passed only as the result of a vote by the presiding officer.[42]

There was less ambivalence and debate in the Saint-Etienne city council. In response to the minister's questionnaire, councilors favored retaining the tolls on the grounds that if the *octrois* were abolished, they would have to be replaced by "other taxes which might be even less popular and without doubt would be very difficult to collect."[43]

The Marseille city council nearly unanimously voted a resolution indicating "there can be no question of abolishing the *octrois* without replacing it with another tax." Councilors in Toulouse noted that the toll was unpopular, primarily because the population "finds it a hindrance to free trade." As for the question why, if the tax was unpopular, the council had not replaced it with a new one, it disarmingly responded, "because it did not know how." In response to the question whether the octroi should be abolished, it answered no. These large cities were in tune with overall sentiment: more than 90 percent of the 1,500 or so towns and cities collecting *octrois* favored their retention.[44]

Revolutionary Communes were established in four of the five cities (Bordeaux excepted) in the fall of 1870 and spring of 1871. These new city governments were more radical and more representative of marginalized people than the municipalities that had so recently affirmed the need to maintain the *octrois*. These communes moved against the tax. When the Commune was declared in Lyon, it abolished the *octrois*, replacing it with taxes on movable and real property and a special tax on the rich. In Marseille, a new municipal government, also inspired by Communard ideas, tried to shift the tax burden away from the poor to the rich by instituting a progressive tax on rental property. Toulouse, also with a Radical council, pronounced abolishing the toll, "a duty for all those who wish to improve the lot of the people." All these experiments were nullified once the communes were defeated and the central government reestablished control.[45]

The *octrois* spared property owners from municipal taxes on their homes and businesses; the new Republic, just as its predecessors, protected these interests.

But they were challenged. At the national level in the 1870s and 1880s, political parties considered the question of the *octrois*. Léon Gambetta had called for abolition of the tolls with the Belleville program in 1869, and the Radical party, which contained Gambetta's spiritual heirs, favored the abolition. Beginning in 1878, deputies presented abolition proposals to the Chamber of Deputies, but they failed to pass.

In the late 1890s, as the countryside was suffering from an agricultural depression—the wine country rife with phylloxera—the French Parliament, wishing to encourage wine growers and others, voted to lower by 1899 the *octrois* collected on "hygienic drinks" (wine, beer, malt, and mineral water) and allow cities to impose replacement taxes. While this law was passed to further the interests of the agriculturists, it did signal that the *octrois* were not immutable, and many observers saw it as the first step toward complete abolition.

The push for abolition on the national level came from the political left. Radical and Socialist politicians expressed opposition to the tax, but the Radicals, once in power on the national level beginning in 1902, changed their position to merely advocate reduction of the *octrois* and all other indirect taxes. Georges Clemenceau, while in the national opposition in the 1890s, spoke out against the *octrois,* but, once he became prime minister in 1906, he failed to take up the issue. The Radical party's national congress in 1909 agreed that cities had the right to abolish the *octrois*—a right that had already been granted in two individual cases as early as 1900.[46]

The Socialists took a clear stand on the tolls, denouncing them. At the local level they had done so in the early 1880s; in the municipal elections of 1881, the Socialists in Lyon called for the suppression of the *octrois,* which they termed "an immoral tax." The national party, at its Lyon Congress in 1891, committed itself to the abolition of the *octrois,* and six years later the congress of socialist municipal councilors voted to work for their abolition. Gaining a majority in a number of municipalities in the 1890s, they began to work on changing the *octrois.* In Roubaix and Marseille, the Socialist-dominated councils moved the *octrois* from foodstuffs to luxury goods. The Dijon Socialist municipality tried in 1896 to abolish the *octrois* but could not get national permission to do so. In 1899, after the Radicals took power, the national government became more sympathetic to abolition and granted Dijon the right. But when the Socialists tried to implement the reform, they were swept from office in 1900 on this very issue. Re-elected in 1904, the Socialists abolished the city tolls.[47]

Although municipalities might have argued until 1900 that they were un-able to abolish the *octrois* because of difficulties in gaining national permission, timidity is another important explanation. The fact is, they failed to push aggressively for abolition. Bordeaux in 1888 carried out a full-scale study and rejected a change—"the abolition of the *octrois* would lead to the ruin of all large cities of our country which would be unable to find replacement taxes. . . ." Although the Opportunists in Bordeaux's 1892 municipal elections promised "to study with perseverance the suppression of the *octrois*," they failed to act. The unpopularity of the *octrois* and the political advantage of opposing it was revealed when both the Radicals and their Opportunist opponents promised *octroi* reduction in their electoral program of 1896.[48]

Toulouse made a more determined effort to wrestle with the issue. The Radicals there were strongly committed to abolition. Once they came to power in 1881, they spoke of the desirability of abolishing the toll, and a rather modest and regressive substitute, a straight 5 percent tax on income property, was voted unanimously in 1883. But it was not implemented. By then the Radicals had lost some of their reforming zeal; as one of them complained, "in power, the Radical party has forgotten its program and governs like Opportunists."[49]

Lyon, with a leftist majority in power, voted to abolish the *octrois* in 1884, but the national government nullified the act.[50] Ten years later, when Lyon again considered the possibility of getting rid of the *octrois*, Mayor Gailleton, a Radical known for his strong social concerns, denounced the tax as "profoundly unjust, antidemocratic, and annoying; no person today would defend it and it is destined to disappear in a short period." The toll had "but one advantage: it is easy to collect and the income from it rolls in every day."

In both Bordeaux and Lyon, officials in the 1890s failed to consider local alternatives to the *octrois* but looked to national funding to cover their cities' loss of revenue.[51] Joseph Caillaux, Radical minister of finance in 1899, was sympathetic to such a solution, but the government as a whole was unlikely to endorse it.[52] The rural population still dominated France and while the government, largely dependent upon peasant voters, might allow cities to replace their *octrois* with substitute local taxes, it would not provide national resources to subsidize such reforms. Replacing the *octrois* thus had to be done entirely at the cities' expense; under such conditions, few cities were willing to embark on a course of reforming.

THE LYON EXAMPLE

It was Lyon that took the plunge, becoming the first large city to abolish the *octrois*. As noted, Lyon had made several early stabs at abolishing the toll. By the 1890s, the city was governed by a coalition of Radicals and Socialists who were committed to removing social injustice, including the *octrois*. The national environment also had become more sympathetic; the government in Paris was willing to let Lyon serve as a model and allowed it to impose substitute taxes. The process of abolition was lengthy, starting in 1896 and culminating successfully five years later.

The *octrois* were to be replaced by a series of new taxes: on horses, mules, carriages, bars, property, business buildings, alcohol, and rents. Mayor Herriot, a fervent anticleric, later added a tax on bachelors, thereby striking a blow against the many priests and monks resident in the city.[53] The tax on rents, under pressure from the most "advanced" forces of the council, was to be progressive. But the minister of finance, opposed to anything smacking of a progressive tax, forbade the measure. A compromise worked out in 1900 established a modified version: renters paying less than 150 francs a year paid no tax, while those paying more than that were assessed a straight 9 percent. With the last impediment removed, Lyon was able to abolish the *octrois* in 1901.[54]

The successful outcome was the handiwork of the "Red" mayor of Lyon, Victor Augagneur, a powerful personality who galvanized Radicals and Socialists on the city council into action. The reform, Augagneur claimed, was intended "to free the poor from taxes and instead impose them upon the rich. . . . [W]e acted as Socialists in arranging that the burden be carried by the property owners rather than the proletarians."[55]

The mayor's rhetoric appealed to the small artisans of the city, but he was not speaking to the poorest of the poor. They lived in the suburbs, which, beginning in the 1880s, had deliberately not been annexed in order to avoid the added social costs of a population also deemed to be dangerous. Ironically, it was because the very poor were not included within the city walls that the reform could be envisaged. Had they been in the city, the costs of abolition might not have been so easily offset by property taxes. Thus a policy ostensibly designed to benefit proletarians was possible only because many workers had been walled out of the city.

This daring experiment in Lyon had worked out rather well. Cassandras, such as the deputy of the Rhône, who had predicted bankruptcy if the tolls were abolished, were proven mistaken.[56] The replacement taxes brought in revenues close to those lost by the abolition of the *octrois*. Whereas in 1900 the *octrois* collected had been 11.3 million francs, the replacement taxes in 1903 amounted to 10.6 million francs. It is arguable, however, that the cost of living improved.[57]

Lyon's abolition process was closely followed by other municipalities. Toulouse, also under Radical rule, echoed themes raised in Lyon. While all parties on the left agreed on the desirability of abolishing the tolls, the sticking point was which replacement taxes should be imposed to make up for lost revenues. The Radicals could not make themselves institute a progressive tax on property, and their Socialist allies showed an equal lack of resolve. But after the alliance broke up in 1898, the Socialists, finding the *octroi* issue a convenient one by which to distinguish themselves from their erstwhile allies, charged that the Radicals had hypocritically promised abolition for a generation while failing to act. When the Socialists won control of the municipality in 1906, they voted to abolish the toll and replace it with a set of progressive taxes. They assumed the reform would be approved forthwith by Paris, but the minister of interior, opposed to the heavily progressive features and maybe wishing to undermine the Socialists and help the embattled Radicals, vetoed the reform. While the Radicals previously had at least given lip service to the idea of abolishing the *octrois*, they now described abolition as threatening the financial stability of the city, and charged the Socialists with fiscal irresponsibility. At any rate, the Socialists would have needed far more time to implement the abolition than the two years they held power.[58] The Radicals replaced them in 1908.

In Marseille, reform of the *octroi* was attempted even more half-heartedly than in Toulouse. In 1880, the city abolished the toll on flour, a particularly onerous tax that few cities had (Marseille had introduced it in the late 1840s to pay for its ambitious water supply system). But there was little enthusiasm for abolition of all the tolls. While the Radicals had included abolition in their pre-election program, the new Radical mayor did not even mention this part of the agenda in his inaugural speech in 1881.

After passage of the national law of 1897 that allowed reduction or abolition of the alcohol tax, Marseille dragged its feet, and in fact, to make up for lost revenue, raised tolls on other items. In 1898, the council voted to abolish the *octroi* and substitute other revenue-enhancing measures, mainly taxes on inheritance and property. But it did so fully expecting a veto by the ministry of interior, as the council debates indicate. The Socialist councilors were the ones most strongly committed to abolition, but in spite of their strong national plank opposing the *octrois* and the successful Socialist examples in Lyon and Dijon, they failed to take action in Marseille. The Socialist spokesman declared in 1909, a year before he became mayor, that while Socialists were opposed to the *octroi*, it had to be maintained for the time being since "it is the only resource we have...."[59] Considering the difficulty Socialists had remaining in power (they were successfully challenged by Conservatives in several elections after 1900), they may have felt it necessary to project an image of fiscal prudence.

In Bordeaux, where Socialists were not in a strong political position, they took an ambiguous stand. One Socialist newspaper claimed that the *octrois* were actually a very small tax, hardly noticeable, and promised that if the Socialists were elected in 1911, lower *octroi* employees would be given salary raises—hardly a suggestion to abolish the *octrois*. Two years later, the young firebrand of Bordeaux Socialism, Adrien Marquet, forthrightly attacked the *octrois* as an unfair tax on the poor and called for its abolition.[60] Fifteen years later, after becoming mayor, he oversaw its abolition.

In Saint-Etienne, the *octrois* did not pose a problem of political strategy, since the Socialists were firmly in the saddle. A working-class city, loyal to the Socialists and usually returning Socialist majorities, it could permit its leaders to run a policy unambiguously in tune with its doctrines. Located close to Lyon and accustomed to taking its models of government and municipal action from the larger city, it carefully considered abolishing the toll. In 1888, the Socialists presented a plan for replacing the *octrois* with a tax on property, thus drawing the opposition of the local prefect and the minister of interior, and the law was effectively squelched. That this would happen was, according to the local Conservative newspaper, anticipated by the Socialists. They had only passed the plan for effect.[61]

A poor city, Saint-Etienne could not even afford to abolish its taxes on liquor, as the 1897 law permitted. Rather, it retained the maximum taxes allowed on this product. When, after 1900, the Socialists—as a result of the precedent-setting reforms in Lyon and Dijon—could easily have abolished the *octrois,* they decided not to do so. The *octrois* represented 60 percent of the income of a municipality facing growing expenses; there was no obvious alternative source of revenue. By contrast, Lyon was wealthy. Most of its infrastructure had been built up, and it was filled with bustling commerce and rich mansions that could be taxed. But in Saint-Etienne, the workers' city, real estate was modest, and there was insufficient property to tax. So a basic reform, passionately advocated by Socialists at both the national and the local levels, was not adopted in the "Red" city of Saint-Etienne. Nor was it in other cities that also had gained such a sobriquet, for instance Limoges.[62]

The paradox was evident. As the historian of the Socialist experiment in Saint-Etienne, Jean Lorcin, put it, "a working class city such as Saint-Etienne could not afford the luxury, reserved to an aristocratic Dijon or bourgeois Lyon, of experimenting with 'municipal socialism.'"[63] Lyon could have a Socialist policy because it had limited the size of its working class, while in Saint-Etienne, Socialist policies were not possible because there were too many workers.

Until 1900, city councils could quite rightly claim that reforms were stymied by Paris's intransigence. But cities not only failed to fight for the right to institute these reforms; many also demanded that the national government provide the replacement funds. When cities were free to establish replacement taxes for the *octrois* on alcohol in 1897, few did. Between 1901 and 1908, 248 municipalities abolished the *octrois,* but most cities were small, with modest financial needs. Lyon and Dijon were the only large cities to take the step. In the other large cities, municipalities were unwilling to pay the economic and political price of reform. And so the tolls remained in effect in most cities.

After 1914, the cities were left to their own devices; other sources of taxes became more important than the *octrois* and the impracticality of these tolls, which was already obvious in the age of the railroad, became only more so with the growth of automobile and truck traffic. Bordeaux finally abolished the *octrois* in 1928, the building housing the *octroi* offices became home to the municipal archives. Paris also abolished its *octrois* in the 1920s. Many major cities, however, waited for outside administrative fiat to rid themselves of these tolls. The Marseille, Toulouse, and Saint-Etienne *octrois* ended only with a coup de main from the Vichy regime in 1943.

The delay in abolishing the *octrois* reflects the extent to which the French city still retained features of an earlier era. It was willing to live with a tax system that was heavily based on indirect taxation, and that was for 150 years regularly and clearly denounced as regressive, unjust, and arcane. In many cities, particularly the port cities, the bourgeoisie insisted on the principles of free trade, yet usually supported the local tolls that impeded the free movement of goods and people into their own cities. Principles were less important than economic interests. The dominant elites in French cities preferred to maintain a tax system that spared them from paying more taxes while saddling the less privileged with a burden they were thought to barely feel. Direct taxes, an assistant mayor of Lyon remarked, was like "a pail of water in the face," while the *octrois* had the advantage of being a "fog" that could not be clearly perceived.[64]

The medieval city could live *intro muros* with relative ease, and in fact cities defined themselves as spaces enclosed by walls. The modern city, as a center of manufacture, consumption, and communications, needs to be open and to communicate freely with the outside world. The *octrois*, requiring the examination of goods and persons flowing into the city, impeded this free communication, preventing the city from easily playing the role that a modern city occupies in the national and world economies. French cities of the nineteenth century might have been more dynamic if they had been freed of the artificial constraint that the *octrois* placed on them. With the abolition of the *octrois*, the French city took a major step toward modernization.

3

From Patronage to Civil Service:
The City Employees

*H*istorical studies of France's bureaucracy, in line with the nation's centralized tradition, have emphasized the central bureaucracy, while neglecting the history of municipal civil services. The approximately 38,000 communes at the beginning of the twentieth century had some 118,000 employees.[1] Few in number or maybe even totally absent in small communes, they sometimes exceeded the thousand mark in large cities and shaped the way government delivered services to its local constituents. Through the nineteenth century, there was a movement at the local level toward "a modern civil service," understood according to the criteria that German sociologist Max Weber established: that it consist of personnel recruited according to pre-established standards, with fixed ranks, salaries, pension rights, and employment security. The civil servant, Weber stated, has a career, with promotions according to achievement or seniority; his position is his sole or main occupation. Part of the process of modernization of the state was the separation of the public from the private; in the modern bureaucracy, Weber further posited, "Public monies and equipment are divorced from the private property of the official." The bureaucracy cannot be efficient and hence fully "modern" when its members rely on prebendary rights, collecting monies and personally pocketing them.[2]

The process of creating a modern bureaucracy was gradual, occurring by trial and error and incomplete by the end of the period covered in this book. But the direction of change was irreversible and provided the bases for the modern municipal services that eventually emerged.

PERSISTENCE OF SOME ANCIEN RÉGIME PRACTICES

Aspects of ancien régime administration that survived until the mid-nineteenth century in the national bureaucracy also did so at the municipal level.[3] Salaries were not specified for employees. Rather, a lump sum was given to the head of a bureau, who was free to dispense these funds as he saw fit. In Bordeaux in 1837, the city provided 5,000 francs a year to the treasurer for both salaries and expenses, and he controlled how the sum was spent.[4]

Until 1855, municipalities provided commissioners of police who headed the municipal forces lump sums out of which they took salaries and office expenses; only thereafter was the use of the funds specified.[5] The secretary-general, the highest employee running city hall, exercised prebendary rights reminiscent of the ancien régime. He arbitrarily set the fees for services, such as issuing required birth, death, and marriage certificates, then collected and personally pocketed the money.[6]

Sometimes city offices were set up in officials' homes. In Lyon, the office of the chief commissioner of police changed location with each new chief. As a result, the public often had difficulty finding it. In 1839, the city decided to pay rent for an office separate from the commissioner's home.[7]

The sense of performing civil service, with an appointed official embodying municipal powers, was little developed. In Bordeaux, when two *octroi* employees were not collecting city tolls because of illness, they were nevertheless paid. Their sons did the work.[8] Furthermore, the ancien régime's concept that office ownership could be passed on to heirs coexisted in the first half of the nineteenth century with the more modern notion that merit would determine who occupied the office. The concierge of the Lyon theater, aged 80 and with 50 years of service, requested that his son be appointed to succeed him, since he was "the sole support of his father and mother." The request was granted.[9] In Toulouse, the city architect's nephew succeeded him in 1830. While the young man had trained in Paris and clearly was qualified for the post, city officials must have found it quite natural to keep the position in the family. Lyon's city architects in the first half of the nineteenth century often named their successors. In Bordeaux, the head of the *octroi* service was succeeded by his son, who had been his assistant *(chef de cabinet)* for years and thus had experience—most likely thanks only to nepotism.[10] But when the Marseille city architect requested in 1833 that he be succeeded by his son, the mayor was not receptive, asking sarcastically whether the architect imagined the post was inheritable.[11]

In some services, nepotism was institutionalized. Given the shortage of qualified persons to serve as *octroi* employees, Bordeaux instituted a program in which the sons of employees were brought in as junior clerks, given on-the-job training, then promoted to higher positions. Under this system, most of the junior clerks were children, many as young as 15.[12] In a later period, diplomas and technical abilities were required, but family connections could still be helpful. When the Lyon city archivist retired in 1883, the chief candidate had the required training (he was a graduate of the Ecole des Chartes) but presumably was favored because he was the archivist's son.[13]

A position in city administration was long regarded as a form of sinecure. In the 1790s, a petitioner asked the Marseille city council for a job for his brother, since "he was absolutely destitute, having been prey to a long disease which had left him exhausted." Too fatigued to make a living, he nevertheless was considered apt for city employment as a form of welfare relief.[14] In the 1830s, a Marseille toll employee was hired "as a favor, because of his wretchedness." In 1886, in Marseille, the keeper of the local Arc de Triomphe earned a salary of 300 francs, but performed no visible duty. The mayor explained that he had the office because he was 80 years old.[15] It was not uncommon for cities to employ elderly men. In 1914 in Toulouse, a street-sweeper was still working for the city at age 76. Another, aged 83, had retired the previous year because of his infirmities. One wonders how long he had been in that condition. Infirmity prevented many from doing much work. One Toulouse street-sweeper, 81 years old, was absent from work 81 days in 1914 for reasons of ill health. Such people, having no other means of employment, were kept on. Their pay was meager enough. In Toulouse, an elderly water fountain employee was paid 500 francs yearly in the 1910s. As late as 1931, an 81-year-old street-sweeper was still working, "but of course according to the powers of a man his age."[16] In Bordeaux, street cleaning was also a form of relief, but beginning in 1900, according to a local newspaper, the habit of employing the aged and infirm ended.[17]

AN UNPROFESSIONAL PROFESSION

Municipal employees seemed not to take their functions seriously. In Marseille during the Revolution, the mayor noted that "most office employees do not come to their offices on time." Work hours were from 9 or 10 A.M. to 2 P.M., then from 5 P.M. to 8 P.M. A later regulation required all employees to be at work between 9 A.M. and 5 P.M., with an hour off for lunch. This rule must have been flouted, for a new one required the employees to sign in and reiterated that the lunch period was only one hour.[18] In Lyon the rule was that municipal employees had to be at their desks at 9 A.M. and could not leave until 4 P.M. The rule failed to mention lunch. To make certain employees were at their desks, employers enjoined them to stay sitting and could absent themselves only with the permission of their superiors.[19] Nonetheless, absenteeism was frequent. A Marseille financial committee inspecting the public works in 1885 found only seven employees present at one work site that was supposed to have sixteen.[20]

Even when they showed up, municipal employees appear not to have worked very hard. Throughout the century, their work ethic was the subject of repeated complaints. Several prefects spoke of the desirability of "demanding more work from them."[21] The extent to which municipal employees had grown unaccustomed to hard work may be surmised in the declaration of the new Marseille mayor in 1849 that city employment was not a form of welfare. The city's 1885 inspection of a public works site found that of nine workers present, one was taking a walk and another was holding a broom in one hand, a melon in the other. A city councilman in Marseille described city employees as coming in two groups: "first, the hard working and intelligent ones; second, and unfortunately there are many of them, those whose sole function is to collect their pay at the end of the month, who spend whole days in bars and do everything but work. . . . They are never punctual, except in leaving work."[22] Work habits in the Toulouse city offices are suggested by the local decree reminding employees that it was against the rules "to go from office to office visiting, to read newspapers and other works foreign to the administration . . ." Yet that seems to have done little good. The Toulouse mayor said of his own appointees that many receiving salaries of 1,400 francs "provide only 500 francs' worth of work." And one of his fellow councilors charged that "if one goes to the offices one will see the employees walking around, smoking cigarettes, or having a beer in a nearby café." Some problems were typical of office work anywhere. A 1901 Saint-Etienne regulation forbade "visiting between offices and conversations unrelated to the service."[23]

Some employees' lack of zeal may have been due to their moonlighting. Many *octrois* employees in Bordeaux, exhausted from their side employment, slept while on the city payroll. The 1901 regulation in Saint-Etienne prohibited doing work in the offices that was extraneous to official responsibilities. Moonlighting evidently was so common among city employees that only in 1906, after two of the cities in this study had raised salaries, did they feel they could forbid outside employment. Some highly skilled professionals were allowed even past our period of study to do work outside their city employment. That was the case with city architects in Lyon, who, as late as 1937, were accepting outside employ; when asked why he allowed it, mayor Herriot explained that such an arrangement was necessary to retain highly qualified personnel.[24]

Recruitment of competent individuals was difficult. It was common to use supernumeraries—that is, very low paid or non-paid, bottom-rung flunkies—in the city services. After receiving on-the-job training and being evaluated, they could gain a regular appointment. Yet few standards seem to have been applied. A supernumerary in the mayor's office in Marseille, knowing little French and incapable of writing a report, was given a regular appointment and a raise.[25] Because of its low wages, the Marseille octroi service could not fill its vacancies. Of 40 positions only 9 were filled, and they "[left] much to be desired," the director noted in 1855. But not all services had this type of problem. When a city position opened in Toulouse in 1849, there were 30 applicants.[26] In Bordeaux in 1865, a long list of candidates sought *octrois* positions, although few appeared to have any qualifying skills.[27]

No complete files on municipal employees are extant, so we have little reliable knowledge about their qualities. A record of the performance of the 228 Bordeaux *octroi* employees in 1819 reveals that 35, or 15.4 percent, were unsatisfactory. One was described as "not worthy of confidence," another as "lazy," and yet another as a "good employee when he does not take to wine." In 1827, 39 out of 282 toll employees, or nearly 14 percent, had to be dismissed because of corruption.[28] Paid low wages, Marseille *octroi* employees, according to a city councilman, were in a "shameful pact with the smugglers." Such examples were not just the shortcomings of an administrative service undergoing growing pains. In the 1860s, the director of the Bordeaux *octroi* service complained that many of his subordinates were drunk at work, dishonest, and rude with the public. Yet few were dismissed.[29]

The municipal administrations were remarkably tolerant of their employees, willing to retain many who clearly were unsatisfactory. One Bordeaux employee, in the first year after being appointed, was late for work eight times, drunk twice, and insulting to his superior four times. He was finally fired. One official showed up drunk ten times within one year. He was only demoted. A report of 1870 claimed that it was common for *octroi* employees in Bordeaux to show up drunk.[30]

Octroi employees also tended to extort merchants. It became so much the norm that it was not penalized. Even embezzlement could be treated leniently. When one Bordeaux official was found to have a deficit in his account books of 2,400 francs, his superior dismissed him, but then had second thoughts. After all, the official had served for 15 years, apparently without a previous mishap. His superior reemployed him in a lower position where he would have no occasion to handle money and thus could repay the missing funds. A few years later, the director himself was discovered to be unsatisfactory. Prone to drink, he had given himself over "to pleasures and women" and had "borrowed" money from his subordinates. In

Toulouse, the head of the *octroi* service had to be dismissed in 1891 for embezzlement.[31]

SALARIES

City salaries were low, particularly for employees in the bottom ranks. Municipal workers were so poorly remunerated that "it is not possible for them to survive on their modest pay," a Marseille official wrote during the Revolution. Bordeaux employees in the 1830s earned as little as 400 francs a year.[32]

Pay disparities were great among city employees. In Saint-Etienne in 1817, the head of the secretariate earned seven times more than the lowest functionary in his service. By 1870, the disparity had worsened to ten times more, but by the turn of the century it had improved to a ratio of 6 to 1.[33] Lyon at the turn of the century maintained a pay ratio between top and bottom workers of 4 to 1. In Toulouse, the ratio went from 10 to 1 in 1821, to 5 to 1 at the end of the Second Empire. In Bordeaux, the ratio at the end of the century was 15 to 1, while in Marseille it was 7 to 1. The trend was toward less inequality after 1870, but the pattern is murky. While the cities' ratios varied, they were far closer on the municipal than on the national level, where the ratio in 1800 was a 100 to 1 and in 1900 was still 25 to 1.[34]

Even though the political left demanded higher wages for the lowest-paid municipal workers and when in power often provided raises, that did not significantly change the ratios. The lowest-paid city workers were paid enough to compete with private employers, but it evidently was harder to attract competent higher officials with the wages they were offered. Even leftist mayors agitated for improved wages for top municipal employees to ensure their continued service.[35]

Salaries went up over the century, but the lowest-paid employees remained in dire straits. Before raising employees' wages in 1876, the Bordeaux municipality recognized that 800 francs a year did not constitute a living wage. In Lyon, a report characterized the 1,000 francs wage paid in 1881 as "just above that necessary not to die of hunger." As late as 1912, a Toulouse city councilman claimed that the lowest-paid workers were so poorly remunerated they often had to go on city relief "for their necessary bread." Some cities raised the salaries of the lowest-paid workers; Lyon did so from 1,080 francs in 1880 to 1,440 francs in 1907.[36]

During most of the nineteenth century and in most city services, salary scales were nonexistent. The city provided with little regard for an employee's position or its stated salary. Currying influence might win for an official a salary higher than that provided in the budget. One Marseille official's superior wrote, "good employee. Head of household he needs a raise," thus showing that extraneous reasons might weigh in the balance. Salaries were not necessarily commensurate with rank. In Marseille, for example, low officials sometimes were paid higher than their superiors. The mayor of Saint-Etienne complained to his counterpart in Lyon that his city had "no rule which firmly fixes the classification, salaries, and promotions of municipal employees." A Toulouse commission considering the establishment of a systematic, structured civil service reported in 1910 that "we have been struck by the lack of any regulations in our [city] services. . . . There is no system at city hall except that directed by circumstances, chance, various influences and arbitrariness . . . we have found a situation where employees of about equal abilities started at different salaries, one at 1,400 francs, another at 1,600 francs, yet another at 1,800 francs.[37]

The earliest hierarchies in local administration were established in the *octrois*. Lyon had a hierarchical *octroi* administration with ranks and listed salaries by 1818, but other cities were far slower to act. Not until 1893, on the heel of a corruption scandal, did Toulouse adopt a hierarchical structure with a table of salaries for its *octroi* service.[38]

Marseille adopted a classification system for its civil service with specific salary ranges for each rank in 1884. But this reform seems not to have been very effective, for a quarter century later a Marseille city commission described the civil service as lacking order. "There is no classification system, no hierarchy; here a clerk earns more than his superior, while over there a bureau chief with only a few years' service has a higher salary than his colleague with more than thirty years of service. Two employees entering the administration the same day with identical functions can differ in their salary by as much as 30 percent. There are some employees who have had no raises for twenty years." Lyon, as part of a general reform of its civil services, adopted a sophisticated system of administrative ranks and salary in 1907. The same year, nearby Saint-Etienne adopted a fixed rank and salary system.[39]

RECRUITMENT

Qualifications needed for municipal employment usually were not spelled out. One of the earliest lists of regulations for the Lyon *octroi* service was published in 1818. It stated that candidates for *octroi* positions had to know how to read and write, be at least five feet, two inches tall and "be strong and well constituted." An applicant's first appointment was as a supernumerary, typically earning 300 francs a year. From the supernumerary group, suitable candidates for the lowest ranks of octroi employees were selected. The Lyon *octroi* was the only service that specified that it hired only within its ranks. But Lyon was considerably ahead of other cities in bureaucratizing its *octroi* service and insisting on specific qualifications for being hired and promoted. While Marseille had no specific requirements, it favored former soldiers as *octroi* employees because "we find in this class of candidates a certain guarantee of integrity, discipline, and good bearing." In Bordeaux, entry at the beginning level of the *octroi* service was reserved for sons of employees as late as the 1870s.

Appointments to higher positions did not necessarily come from lower ranks. The Toulouse requirements of 1893 for appointment to the *octroi* service specified that candidates had to be between the ages of 21 and 30 and live in the city; otherwise, there were no specified requirements. Promotions were made partly on the basis of seniority, but more frequently by choice, that is, by decision of the mayor's office.[40]

For general civil service positions, requirements were spelled out later. In 1881, Lyon required a civil service examination for entry-level positions. Saint-Etienne promulgated requirements in 1907, but they were only for entering municipal employees, specifying that candidates had to be under age 30. Promotion within the service was still by choice.[41]

Looking at appointments of city employees in various services in Toulouse, the only city in this study with available employee files, one finds a great diversity in their experience before being appointed.[42] In some cases, lack of appropriate experience probably did not matter—the appointment of a baker and his brother, a carpenter, who were appointed street-sweepers, for instance, or the brewer who was appointed cemetery guard, or the knife sharpener who became an orderly.[43] In other cases, the service may have suffered because its members did not have the necessary experience; for instance, the baker and the peasant who were appointed clerks.[44] To the treasurer's office were appointed, curiously, a former shoemaker and a chair mender-the latter noted as "being poorly educated."[45] But some appointees seemed to have useful backgrounds. A woman who had six children, in seeking the position of overseeing midwives, could plausibly argue, "I am particularly apt for this service."[46] Clerks and accountants who had previously served in private commerce or in the Compagnie du Midi, the railroad company, were probably well prepared for the responsibilities they shouldered in the mayor's office.[47]

Scattered information from other cities confirms similar heterogeneous backgrounds of city employees. Among those hired as *octroi* employees in Bordeaux in 1865, for example, were a former clerk, a farmer, a bootmaker, a wigmaker, a carpenter, a smith, a waiter, a mason, and a day laborer.[48]

The lack of qualifications of most individuals appointed during most of the nineteenth century must have meant that the services they provided were very uneven. But the fact of recruitment being heterogeneous meant that persons from different social classes had access to municipal employment.

THE SPOILS SYSTEM

Recruitment was by the spoils system; the mayor appointed to office whomever he pleased. As the mayor of Marseille put it in 1867, "the mayor alone administers; it is he who organizes the offices of the municipality, who appoints and fires the employees. . . ." The mayor had to account to no one when firing his subordinates. Asked in 1880 why he had fired an official, the Marseille mayor answered, "Because it pleased me." The municipal laws clearly provided the mayor with such prerogatives, the 1884 law declaring in article 88, "The mayor appoints, suspends and revokes municipal employees." And these powers were absolute; as late as 1905 the Council of State declared they could in no way be abrogated or circumscribed.[49]

Regime changes not only affected the employ of central government functionaries[50] but also led to political purges at the local level. In Bordeaux in 1815, 15 employees of the *octroi* collection service were fired for expressing royalist sympathies during Napoleon's Hundred Days. They were reinstated when the king returned, but five of their colleagues were then dismissed for having during that period made "injurious remarks against the royal family."[51] A Toulouse police commissioner appointed by Napoleon was dismissed in 1815 "because of his opinions."[52] As a result of the July Revolution and the change in municipality in Marseille, eight civil servants were fired. In 1849, 14 Bordeaux *octroi* officials were dismissed for political reasons, presumably because of suspected radicalism.[53] In 1870, Marseille's new Republican municipality carried out a thorough purge of imperial appointees, including lowly concierges in city buildings. In 1877, after the MacMahon regime disappeared, the Republicans returned to city hall and dismissed 35 employees. The new municipality in Toulouse also wreaked havoc on imperial appointees in 1870, firing a majority of the personnel, including the watchman of the Jardin de Plantes.[54]

Some officials, regardless of their politics, were indispensable and clung to their posts despite the frequent purges. The secretary-general of the Lyon municipality remained in office continuously through six successive national regimes, from 1800 to 1831. An ambitious man, he was described by his son as working from 5:00 A.M. until 8:00 P.M. He kept most of the information in his head, entrusting little to files. This style of administration may explain how he became irreplaceable, known as "the little mayor of Lyon."[55]

The most frequent reason for mass sweeps of city personnel was not changes in national systems but power shifts at the local level. When a new

Toulouse municipality was elected in 1843, it fired the city architect, who had served the city with distinction for 13 years.[56]

The spoils system became the norm after the introduction of mass politics, and was vigorously defended. It was the custom of old republics to change their administrations with a change in government, argued the mayor of Marseille: "in the United States the entire administration is changed at the same time as the president." When Marseille's Republican mayor, suspended by the MacMahon regime, returned to power in late 1877, he declared his intent to purge his administration of monarchists and retain only "tested Republicans." The central committee of the Radical party called for the dismissal of all city employees "who were not devoted to the Republic," and their replacement with "citizens notable for their attachment to the Republic."[57]

Victories at the polls could repair past injustices. In Lyon, the reactionary municipality appointed by the MacMahon regime refused to appoint as librarian a highly qualified candidate with Republican connections. When the Radicals came to power in 1880, they appointed him to the position.[58]

The seesaw elections led to purges and counterpurges. When the Radicals won control over the Toulouse municipality in 1888, they purged half of the employees of the civil service, who had been appointed by the previous Opportunist municipality. The employees of the municipal school of fine arts, including the instructors, were replaced. Then, in 1896, when an Opportunist municipality was appointed by the national government to replace the Radicals, the Opportunists dismissed three dozen employees as well as the street-sweeping crew. When the Radicals returned to power, their purges led a Conservative newspaper to charge them with treating their political opponents with the same ferocity the English had shown the Boers—eliminating them.[59]

Socialists were no less ferocious in cleaning house. The first of the cities in this study to fall under Socialist control was Saint-Etienne in 1888. The result was a purge of city officials. The city librarian and the heads of the street department and the *octroi* collection services, among others, were dismissed. After being briefly out of power, the Socialists returned in 1900 and a Socialist "committee of vigilance" took it upon itself to control the purging and appointment of officials.[60] At times, large numbers of employees were affected. In Toulouse, Socialists, upon winning office in the elections of 1906, dismissed two-thirds of the city employees, including the concierge of the municipal library, the gravediggers, the registrar of voters, and the city medical hygienist.[61]

Dismissing officials freed places for new political appointees. The Marseille mayor, after dismissing his predecessors' appointees in 1878, added

45 party loyalists to his staff. He conceded that all the appointments were not essential. They were based, he said, not only on the need of the agencies but also on "certain exigencies," political ones no doubt. And according to the moderate *Le Temps,* hostile to the Radical Marseille municipality, the mayor "padded" his administration by, for instance, appointing two employees at 1,500 francs a year as gaslighters in the city slaughterhouse—a task requiring but a few minutes work in the morning and evening. While the Bordeaux municipality enjoyed a less corrupt reputation, it allegedly created a 6,000-franc post for a nephew of the local senator.[62]

Appeals to party bonds frequently secured appointments. An applicant for the position of inspector of the Toulouse funeral services told the mayor that his aptitudes "and my republican sentiments—known to all our friends" made him qualified for the post. A hopeful would-be street-sweeper wrote the Radical mayor of Toulouse that the Radical party headquarters had advised him to apply. In both cases, the appeal to partisanship gained the appointment.[63]

In explaining his appointment policies, the mayor of Marseille was adamant about the need to provide "our political friends . . . the positions which are their due." The mayor explained why he had not appointed a new city archivist: no candidate sharing his political opinions had applied, and "I did not want to entrust archives as important as those of Marseille to the hands of adversaries." The Conservative mayor of the Mediterranean city purged the voter registration bureau of Socialists in 1905, appointing his own men "in whom we can have confidence." In considering applicants for the Lyon welfare office (the Bureau de Bienfaisance), its director took note of their politics and next to their names noted "good Republican," "communard and imprisoned," "good Republican, Freemason." Even if the 60 new employees that Marseille's Socialist municipality had hired in 1911 were not strictly necessary, a Socialist city councilman insisted, it was still a "service to comrades."[64]

The most important official in city government, heading the administration, was the secretary-general. Usually he was well- connected politically. In Marseille, the secretary of city hall between 1877 and 1884 had been subprefect in two departments before his appointment, and he had an impeccable Republican pedigree. Both his father and grandfather had been political deportees under Napoleon III.[65] In Toulouse, the secretary-general from 1888 to 1905 was an important Radical personality who had been the editor of a Radical newspaper and was a member of the regional Radical central committee. Together with the mayor and the local deputy, he was the king-maker. When Honoré Serres, mayor-deputy, died, the secretary-general was elected deputy from the Toulouse region.[66]

City administrations often made extra funds available to loyal employees. When a political party returned to power, it compensated its partisans who had suffered under the previous regime. In Toulouse, nine city officials who had been fired by the reactionary MacMahon-appointed municipality were reappointed in 1879 when the Republicans rewon city hall. They were even given pensions for the period they had not been working for the city. In Marseille, Socialists who had been fired by the Conservative municipality in 1902 were given monetary compensation for their loss of earnings when the Socialists returned to office.[67]

It was common for mayors to provide bonuses to their employees. And since they jealously guarded the lists of those they provided with such emoluments, the totals spent were never fully known. A financial commission friendly to the Marseille municipality observed that it had "never been able to fully discover the amounts expended by the offices." A Bordeaux newspaper accused the departing political coalition in 1900 of having provided its political appointees with 40,000 francs in what were fraudulently claimed to be overtime payments. Such disbursements were so frequently abused that the reform administration elected in Toulouse in 1912 suppressed all overtime pay. Other forms of favoritism, allegedly provided to some employees in Bordeaux, were welfare payments and scholarships for their children—although they qualified for neither.[68]

Officials, even those occupying the most modest positions, were expected to conform politically. In Bordeaux, an *octroi* employee was accused anonymously of not being a "good Republican." An investigation revealed that he was not known to have expressed any political opinions, though he subscribed to a Republican newspaper and "appeared pleased" when Republicans won elections. He was allowed to keep his position. The Socialist mayor of Marseille apologized to the council for appointing an employee who, while being a good Socialist, had a relative who had denounced Socialism. Had the mayor known of this denunciation he would not have made the appointment, he assured the council.[69]

In the midst of anticlerical campaigns around the turn of the century, a city sewer cleaner in Lyon who sent his son to a church school was scolded, and it was made clear that anyone wishing promotion should send his child to the lay public schools. Another Lyon city employee accused of sending his son to a church school explained that he had done so only because it was thought a church school would be less rigorous for the sickly youth. When his mistake had been pointed out, he immediately transferred the boy to the public lay school.[70] In Toulouse, the local Radical newspaper called on city employees to withdraw their children from church schools. In Marseille, a law, supported by Mayor Siméon Flaissières, was presented directing all city employees to withdraw their children from religious schools and send them to lay public schools out of "respect for the Republican government."[71]

Municipalities protected and promoted their partisans. After the head of the Marseille cemeteries was accused of incompetence, the reaction of the Socialist municipality was to declare that "it was impossible for a Socialist municipal council to persecute an honorable citizen and old Republican. . . ." When the municipality was accused of retaining and even promoting officials guilty of fraud, it answered that that was the case with only a few officials.[72]

The spoils system strengthened the mayor, since the power to appoint was reserved for him. It also helped fuel a strong participation rate in the political process, since the hope of winning appointments or preserving one's employment motivated a large army of campaign workers and their families to work for a candidate and help bring out the vote. Toward the end of the Second Empire, in the late 1860s, the Marseille mayor had city firemen distribute election propaganda on his behalf. While technically illegal, the use of government employees for electioneering was common under the Second Empire and by no means ended with the advent of the Third Republic. When the Marseille assistant mayor in charge of public works ran for a seat in Parliament in 1878, he sought to mobilize the staff of the public works office for his campaign. Three employees who refused to help were immediately fired. Two of his campaign workers, who could neither read nor write, were rewarded with promotions as clerks.[73]

Employees could not only help run elections, they could also help fix them. Toulouse city officials fraudulently recorded voters in the 1889 and 1893 elections.[74] Such assistance could be crucial in closely contested elections. The 1904 Marseille elections, for instance, were won by only 500 votes.

THE GROWTH OF THE CIVIL SERVICES

The advent of mass politics after the 1870s put increasing pressure on municipalities to hire more employees. Party workers and constituents expected to be rewarded with jobs. In addition, municipalities provided more and more services, and a greater number of employees were needed to staff new or expanded agencies. It is difficult to separate these twin forces driving toward staff expansion—the growth of patronage and an increasing number of city services.

In the first half of the nineteenth century, the number of city employees did not grow significantly. Marseille in 1789 had a total of 85 employees, including its police; in 1809, it still had 85; and in 1832, it had 116. The

Bordeaux municipality increased its employees from 27 in 1815 to 52 in 1830; nine years later they numbered 66. Lyon city hall had 32 employees in 1811, 41 in 1843. But modest as these increases were, and even though they seem to have a rational relationship to the increase in work that many bureaucracies faced, contemporaries complained about them. A Lyon municipal commission called "The increase in the number of administrative employees," "a malady of our epoch."[75]

Some employees undoubtedly were added to help provide additional services for growing cities. Saint-Etienne, for instance, increased its number of employees from 50 in 1815 to 360 in 1870—a time period during which the city population grew five-fold.[76] Specialization required more and separate offices. Whereas Lyon in 1879 had four directorates, in 1883 it had eight. The number of officials in the city hall's central administration increased by 50 percent to 49 in those four years. Bordeaux's rose from 60 in 1871 to 119 in 1889. Some specific services saw dramatic growth; the street service in Lyon grew from having 2 employees in 1820, to 75 in 1869, and 540 by 1910.

It would be hard to argue, however, that the increases were solely the function of urban growth. At times, municipalities were able to scale back. Marseille reduced its city hall employees from 156 in 1874 to 124 in 1900, and Lyon from 49 in 1883 to 37 in 1895. And even at times when there was little growth, the number of employees could rise significantly. Marseille city hall increased its employees from 91 in 1871 to 156 three years later. While Lyon's population grew by a bare 3 percent between 1900 and 1912, its employees increased by 25 percent, going from 2,500 in 1900 to 3,117.[77] Toulouse's employees increased by two-thirds, from 1,244 to 2,074, with virtually no population growth. It is true that added and expanded social and medical services explain some of the growth, but patronage played a significant role in Toulouse. The number of municipal employees seems to be related to the size of the city; in our sample of cities, the smaller the city, the greater number of employees per population. At the turn of the century, the ratio between city employees and population was 1 for every 614 residents in Toulouse, 1 for every 980 inhabitants in Saint-Etienne, 1 for every 1,947 inhabitants in Bordeaux, 1 for every 3,480 inhabitants in Lyon, and 1 for every 4,090 inhabitants in Marseille. The city with the highest proportion of employees to its population was Toulouse. With 1,244 employees in 1900, the city was the single largest employer except for the state-run Tobacco Manufacturing plant.[78] The city had few other large-scale employers and thus few other sources of employment. Bordeaux and Marseille, large trading centers, could absorb a fairly large number of clerks in the private sector; Marseille, for instance, had 11.5 percent of its workforce as sales employees and clerks in 1869. The sort of day laborers that Toulouse might employ as street-sweepers and other lowly menial tasks could be used on the docks and factories of Bordeaux and Marseille or in the factories and mines of Saint-Etienne. There were few such options in the Languedocian capital. Albert Bedouce, the former Socialist mayor of Toulouse, when speaking for a succeeding Socialist municipality, characterized the function of government employment as providing work for the destitute and saving them from poverty. It may well be that traditions of clientage, particularly strong in the first third of the nineteenth century when the aristocracy dominated the city, persisted thereafter, and municipalities jumped into the breach. The result was a bloated administration.[79]

Both the increase in the number of employees and improved salaries led to significant increases in personnel expenditures. Toulouse personnel costs increased from 285,000 francs in 1875 to 600,000 francs in 1905. At the same time, Lyon's went up from 375,000 francs to 563,000 francs, and Saint-Etienne's from 356,000 francs to 451,000 francs. At the turn of the century, administration expenses varied from city to city. Lyon and Marseille spent 4.4 percent of their regular budgets on administration, Saint-Etienne 11.5 percent, and Toulouse 14.4 percent. Looking at these administrative costs, one might conclude that the higher proportions expended by Toulouse and Saint-Etienne represent costs based on the disadvantages of scale. Since every city, regardless of size, had to have certain services, one can see how the larger cities might have advantages based on scale. Also, of course, Toulouse and Saint-Etienne had smaller overall budgets, and hence the budget for employees, while less in real amounts, represented a larger percentage of the municipal budgets. Yet, not only city size was involved in explaining this phenomenon: while Saint-Etienne was able to keep the proportion of its administrative costs stable, Toulouse was not. The latter's expenditures continued to climb steeply, representing 37.1 percent of the budget by 1914.[80] A well-developed form of patronage in the Languedocian capital explains the difference.

PENSIONS

Gradually through the century, city employees acquired the right to have pensions-a recognition of the employees' corporate existence and interests. While the higher-up national civil servants had established a pension system under Napoleon, a regular pension for the national civil service was not systematically adopted until 1853.[81] In the early part of the nineteenth century, municipal employees had no right to a pension. Pensions were granted as an act of charity. In Paris, the prefect of the Seine in the

Napoleonic years provided pensions for city employees out of his own pocket.[82] Municipalities provided them on a purely ad hoc basis. In Lyon, a city scribe, aged 70, was given a pension in 1819 because "his age and the weakness of his hand do not allow him to write correctly." In Toulouse, it was not his 25 years of service that allowed an employee to receive aid but rather the fact that he was ill. To help the family of a deceased employee, the Marseille city council in 1838 bought six of the family's paintings at 1,000 francs a piece.[83]

Providing pensions was the earliest recognition of municipal employees' rights. The *octroi* collection service was the first to set up a pension system—Bordeaux as early as 1812. Other municipal employees began to gain this right in the 1820s in Lyon and Marseille; Toulousains had to wait until the 1840s. Especially in the early years, pensions were very meager, since joining the system was voluntary. To enlarge the pension funds, Bordeaux in 1844 made the pension system mandatory. All employees had to join. Once a pension system was established, it was not overly generous. To qualify for the highest pension and receive the equivalent of half of one's salary during the last three years of service, Bordeaux employees had to be in active service for 25 years or sedentary service for 30 years. An employee had to serve at least ten years to qualify for any kind of pension, and then it was pro-rated. The pension fund was not self-supporting. Bordeaux's, for example, had to be supported by ever larger subsidies from the municipality: in 1859, it was 33,000 francs a year; in 1890, 237,000 francs.[84] Though the pension system proved to be a growing burden for the cities, it also revealed their growing commitment to their employees, for it recognized that these workers possessed status and had specific rights. It was a giant step on the way to forming a civil service.

TOWARD A CIVIL SERVICE

While the spoils system had clear advantages, it proved to be an inconvenient mechanism by which to hire and promote city employees. It raised high expectations among friends and constituents that could lead to embarrassment. In the mid-1890s, Toulouse's Mayor Serres complained of being overwhelmed by office applicants. He wistfully mentioned the advantages of instituting a civil service examination system that would give him a bona fide way of denying positions to insistent partisans. Pushed by financial exigencies, municipal councilors from both major parties in Toulouse, the Radicals and Socialists, came to a consensus on the need to reduce the number of employees. "It is very difficult to refuse one's friend a job he may need, but the municipal council is not here to conduct the business of its friends; rather it exists to conduct the business of the taxpayers," a councilor stated.[85] Purges of the city administration every time a new group won elections led to even more difficulties. Such frequent changes in personnel brought administrative instability, making continuity in administration nearly impossible and contributing to disarray in many services.

Among partisans, the spoils system created anxiety. It might be fine when one was in office, but when in opposition it seemed palpably unfair. When the royalist MacMahon-appointed city council of Toulouse purged Republican employees in the mid-1870s, a convincing case for competitive examinations was made. A Republican councilor charged that the reactionary municipality had dismissed many "men of merit whose services are obvious; their careers have been broken, their family has had its bread taken away." The councilor suggested that the city emulate many central administrations that had competitive examinations. "In a democratic republic all positions ought to be open to merit alone. . . . the only way of evaluating merit is a competitive examination."[86] With an authoritarian municipality recruiting the civil service, insistence on a competitive examination seemed to ensure an opportunity for Republican access to the local civil service. Once the Republicans won control over the city government, however, they saw no need to change a system that was now serving them and their followers well. A civil service exam might in fact be the means by which royalists could regain influence.

When in 1880 the Lyon city council considered a bill to institute a competitive civil service examination system *(concours)*, the prefect who was presiding over the council argued that recruitment based strictly on ability to pass the competitive examination might provide access to government service for individuals who were not reliable Republicans.[87] (This was also a self-serving remark. Lyon, like Paris, had no mayor but was administered by the prefect. A *concours* would deprive the prefect of the opportunity to control appointments to the city administration.)

Some weak attempts at instituting a regular civil service system with entry by competitive examinations was attempted in the early years of the Third Republic by two municipalities in our study. Bordeaux, seeking in 1876 to provide "the administration with intelligent, able, and devoted employees," introduced competitive examinations. Candidates were required to take a spelling test, writing "rapidly, readably and without mistakes," and to show the ability to write an administrative report and letter and to keep vital records and carry out basic administrative arithmetic. But this measure by no means ended the spoils system, for all high school graduates, *bacheliers,* were exempt from these measures and—a significant and telling exception—all entrants to the public service were exempted when the mayor deemed that "the vacant position requires a different mode of admission." Moreover, if he determined an examination was warranted, the mayor could pick at will from those who passed it.[88] In Lyon, the *concours* adopted in 1881 was solely for entry to the lowest levels of the civil service. The mayor continued to choose whomever he wanted for higher levels of the administration. Several years later, in 1897, Toulouse adopted a requirement that all candidates for city posts must pass a civil service exam, but they had to have the mayor's approval before taking it. And the mayor could still promote employees to bureau chief or subchief positions regardless of their previous rank. As he insisted, only he could judge how much an employee worked and how he should be remunerated. The result was that as late as 1914 Toulouse civil servants were described as occupying their positions solely as a result of "chance, intrigue or favoritism."[89]

Early in the twentieth century, some cities moved in the direction of establishing a civil service statute providing for competitive entrance examinations, promotions within the administration based on seniority or performance, and guarantees of tenure. Local political situations shaped this development.

Paradoxically, both political stability and instability contributed. At the turn of the century, the coalition in Lyon of Radicals and Socialists was confident of staying in power. Providing a regular statute and civil service appeared to bring order to the local administration, regularize and improve recruitment, and ensure retention of capable employees. In 1907 the reform administration of Herriot provided a statute for city employees with fixed salaries for each rank, competitive entrance examinations, criteria for promotion, and guaranteed job security and pensions. The eight-hour-day and paid vacations were also provided.[90]

Cities with unstable political majorities found equally compelling reasons to reform the civil service system. In Marseille, the Socialists had controlled the city in the 1890s. Then, when a Conservative administration won control over city hall, it wreaked revenge on the preceding regime by firing 140 employees. It also appointed men of no experience to important and well-paying positions.[91] The Conservatives were followed by a divided municipality: 18 Opportunists and 18 Socialists. The two sides loathed the Conservatives and feared not only their return but also the specter of victory by the other side. Each side was unsure of the future, uncertain about what the results of the next elections might bring; each side had its partisans in the administration and wanted to protect them from dismissal. Neither side felt confident of its electoral prospects and therefore favored the establishment of a permanent civil service with an entrance examination, a firm rank system with stated salaries, and a guarantee of job tenure. Dismissal could occur only as a result of a grave error and after a hearing in front of a duly constituted commission.[92] In 1912, the Conservatives returned to city hall. Having experienced the fickleness of the electorate, they attempted to perpetuate their appointees and safeguard them from any future purges. And so, just before World War I, the Marseille municipality implemented a civil service statute.

In Toulouse, the civil service was highly politicized. Each party, on coming to power, made a clean sweep of its predecessors' appointees. The Radicals, after winning the elections in 1908, fired 72 Socialist-appointed officials, while arguing that the capital of the Languedoc should emulate other cities and create a more rational and fair system. The real reason behind the Radicals' reforming zeal undoubtedly was the one pinpointed by the Socialists: after purging the civil service of Socialist appointees and replacing them, the Radicals wished to provide their own creatures with job security. The partisan nature of the project led the Socialists to oppose it. Their leader, Jean Rieux, declared "I shall vote the reform when I am mayor."[93] In other words, if the Socialists came to power, they would appoint their partisans and then conveniently decide to provide them with tenure by creating a civil service statute. And in fact when the Socialists returned to power in 1912, they tried to introduce civil service reform. While the administration favored it, some Socialist municipal councilors were adamantly opposed. One old Socialist argued that a Socialist municipality should be able to give work to its own. Why should the party deny itself the right to exercise patronage? Introducing a competitive examination system risked the possibility that some Socialists might fail the exam and hence be barred from city service. This was a real risk, since Socialists may have had less formal education than their rivals. The split in the Socialists' ranks prevented the reform from passing.[94] Of our cities, only Lyon and Marseille had implemented meaningful civil service reform by 1914.

City employees agitated for their rights. At first they organized at the regional level; the Bouches-du-Rhône had its first union of municipal employees in 1899. They also formed national groups and pushed for national legislation that would give them a civil service statute guaranteeing, for instance, the right to be dismissed only for cause. By intervention of Parliament they tried in 1914 to circumvent the practices of most municipalities. Since such a law would limit the powers of mayors, who were well represented in Parliament, it was effectively blocked.[95] After World War I, municipal employees, supported by labor unions and increased sympathy from many municipalities, were able to win parliamentary support for a law granting all municipal workers in communes with a population greater than 5,000 a regular civil service statute, with entrance exams, clearly spelled-out criteria for promotion, a rank system with defined salaries, and security from dismissal except with cause.

Security of employment that came with the civil service statute undoubtedly encouraged qualified persons to enter the local civil service. Abolition of the spoils system meant that civil servants stayed in place and presumably were more experienced and competent. French local government was unable to attract the quality of personnel that beckoned the call of national government, yet clearly toward the end of this period the cities were moving in the direction of forming a cadre of employees who could better do the cities' work.

Max Weber saw bureaucracy as the most efficient means by which to control an environment. To be truly efficient, he thought, the bureaucracy needed to be of "a rational type," meaning run and recruited by preset rules—akin to those of a civil service statute.[96] At times, proponents of civil service reform, especially the adoption of entrance exams, argued that such changes would improve the local administration. But while these reforms created a more efficient administration, the major incentive behind them were calculations of political advantage.

Calculations of self-interest did not always lead toward adoption of a modern, rationally organized bureaucracy. In the end, legislation at the national level broke existing local impediments to reform. But municipalities also played a role; some, such as Lyon and Marseille, had done so even before the national law created a civil service statute. Others had made headway by adopting a structured civil service with rank and set salaries, a pension system, and regularized recruitment through entrance exams. All the municipalities had debated and considered the wisdom of adopting a regular civil service system. And so when it was legislated nationally, they readily adopted it.

4

Police and Fire Services

*U*rban histories have neglected the evolution of police and fire services in French cities, especially outside Paris. Most general histories concentrate on Paris and suggest that there was considerable centralization of these services. While that was the case with the political police, directly under the order of the prefect, it was usually small and of limited significance in the provinces.[1] At least through the nineteenth century, cities controlled the most ubiquitous force of order-the municipal police. Over a long period of time and with considerable trial and error, French municipalities developed something akin to professional police and fire forces.

THE MUNICIPAL POLICE

While the ancien régime tried to impose control over police in the provinces as well as in the capital, it failed to do so in the former, where municipal control was largely maintained. An organizational chart might show formal authority vested partly in the central government, but until World War II most municipalities controlled their own police forces.

Napoleon established for the large cities a system whereby the head of the municipal police force, locally recruited and funded, was directed by a commissioner general (after 1823 called central commissioner), appointed by Paris. The central commissioner had two masters: the prefect, who was his administrative superior; and the mayor, who passed on to him requests to preserve order within the confines of the city. This administrative system engendered continuous conflict between municipalities and the central government.[2]

Resistance to centralized control over the police may be seen in the extent to which municipalities flouted the basic rule requiring under the command of the central commissioner one commissioner for every 10,000 inhabitants. Lyon, which during the Empire had a population of approximately 120,000, had only 9 commissioners. Not until 1833, under pressure, did the city conform and designate the required number. Bordeaux in 1855 had the required 15 commissioners for 150,000 inhabitants, but in 1874, when it should have had 20, it still had but 15. The Lyon police system, which after 1851 was run by the prefect, had 17 instead of the required 32 commissioners in 1875. So here was a representative of the central government flouting its rules.

Though appointed by Paris, the central commissioners and their subordinates, the commissioners, were paid by the municipalities. The municipalities also set the salaries, and salaries varied by city. A commissioner in Bordeaux at the turn of the century was paid, depending upon rank, between 3,000 and 4,000 francs. Marseille paid between 3,000 and 7,000 francs, while Toulouse had a single salary of 4,800 francs. By setting salaries, the municipal authority provided some control over the commissioners, for cities could increase salaries and provide supplements. While there was a national pension system, some cities provided additional pensions, thus exercising additional influence. Municipalities also could appoint subordinates to the commissioners, and thereby help make the commissioners' lives pleasant or unbearable.

While the commissioner's appointment by the national government seemed to suggest centralized power over municipal police forces, the manner in which the commissioner related to and depended upon the municipality meant that local control over the police was sustained. To be successful, commissioners had to get along with local authorities. They had to be in the good graces of the prefect, but, as a Lyonnais paper noted, they also had to win over the councilors general, the city councilors, the mayor, and the mayor's assistants.[3]

Usually the local police served the central state unquestioningly in repressing local political dissidence; and spying on, reporting on, and jailing political opponents of the regime. In such situations, the central administration in Paris was particularly insistent on its prerogatives. Yet, even here, it had to contend with local resistance. In 1841, the procureur du roi wanted the Toulouse police commissioner to crack down on the nascent

Republican movement. The commissioner, backed by the mayor, successfully refused the procureur and the minister of interior. A generation later in Toulouse, the situation remained unchanged; the imperial prosecutor in 1870 complained of the lack of cooperation: "the police do not know anything, or else they do not tell me anything."[4]

Although the commissioners were to report to the prefect and be under his orders, they rarely did or were. While the Second Empire consciously tried to create a central police state, it was stymied in its efforts by the persistence of "local influences." And thereafter the situation remained unchanged; in 1880, the director of the *sureté* complained that while commissioners were recruited and promoted by the central administration, they tended to look to the mayor and do his bidding. Those who tried to be independent of a mayor, a parliamentary report in 1885 noted, would find an aide, appointed by the mayor, who effectively ran the police, or else an assistant mayor did so. The police system was not centralized; it was highly municipalized. The police in each city, a ministry of interior report in 1911 concluded, was run by the municipal authorities. Against the mayors, the central administration was powerless in regards to police affairs.[5]

Nationalization

Effective centralization appeared accomplished when, in the early twentieth century, the central government put local police forces under direct national control, subordinating them to the prefects. This move came to be known as *étatisation,* or "nationalization" of the police force. In the few cases where it actually occurred in the provinces, centralized control remained more apparent than real.

Two cases in which the central government established control over the local police in the nineteenth century, though not called nationalization, set a precedent for the later cases and were substantially similar in operation. The first case was in Paris, where Napoleon installed in 1800 a prefect of police, an official appointed by and responsible to the central government, to run the capital's police operations. The municipality retained no police powers. The second case came at mid-century, when a system similar to that of Paris was established in Lyon, posing the possibility of implementing the Paris model more widely in the provinces. Of the five cities in the study, Lyon in the first half of the nineteenth century appeared as most unruly; silk workers twice revolted in the 1830s, and the city erupted in revolution in 1848. To control the city, Louis Napoleon in 1851 made the prefect of the Rhône also prefect of police for the Lyon region, giving him powers akin to those wielded by the prefect of police in Paris. At first, Lyon and nearby communes under the prefect's authority had to pay total police expenses, but in 1873 a law reduced their contribution to 30 percent. While the arrangement became financially advantageous, Lyonnais still resented their municipality's loss of control over its police. Successive Lyon city councils and mayors protested. Several times the municipality refused to cough up the 30 percent and the prefect had to impose it by decree.[6]

Napoleon III expanded central control to all cities when he gave prefects additional powers to act as prefects of police in cities with populations exceeding 40,000. But within a few years, he liberalized his regime and rescinded the prefects' powers in 1867. Central control over the police in most large cities thus was surrendered, and the situation returned to what it had been in 1851—only the Paris and Lyon police forces were controlled by prefects. Elsewhere, as one student of urban police noted, "the mayor conducts himself as chief of police."[7] At the beginning of the Third Republic, the Conservative government of Duke Albert de Broglie tried to "nationalize" all the police forces, but his plan was effectively resisted by the Republicans, who saw such measures as anti-Republican and as undermining the principle of municipal autonomy.[8]

By the end of the century, considerable dissatisfaction with the police had built up: there were too few of them, they were of poor quality, and their performance left a lot to be desired. A 1911 report from the ministry of interior described the police of large cities as often "lacking in aptitude and morality."[9] The solution to these problems that many observers suggested was centralization. Police officials argued that centralization could bolster the size and quality of the police force, making it less beholden to local powers and thus a more effective instrument of order.[10] A 1911 police report suggested that the national government should recruit and appoint police for all cities with populations over 10,000, and that this force should be specially trained in a police academy.[11] The projected costs of such a program, however, were far too high, and the report was shelved.

Calls for reform of the system reflected anxieties about police shortcomings. While actually the overall crime rate was decreasing after the mid-nineteenth century, property crimes were up; in 1880, the lower correctional courts tried 238 percent more suspects of property crimes than in 1830. Published statistics seemed to suggest that crime was on the rise, especially in cities. Whereas in the 1840s, 59 percent of recorded crimes had occurred in rural communes and 37 percent in urban communes, by 1863 an equal number of people were charged for crime in cities as in rural areas even though the urban population was only a third of the total population. In 1902, 40 percent of prosecuted crimes were in rural communes and 60 percent in urban communes, although the latter made up only 40 percent of the population.[12] While reported crimes against persons were about the same in urban as in rural areas, crimes against property were particularly high in cities.[13] While urban areas had higher crime rates, urbanizing areas were even harder hit than other cities. In the 1880s, an urban department such as the Gironde, where 80 percent of the population was urban had a crime rate of 841 per 100,000, while in the Bouches-du-Rhône, which was 84 percent urban and contained the rapidly growing Marseille, the crime rate was 1,350 per 100,000. A general study of French crime found areas with large percentages of migrants more prone to crime than other cities; William Sewell, Jr. confirmed that finding in his study of Marseille.[14] Helping shape these statistics were circumstances peculiar to the countryside and city. Underreporting probably skewed the countryside figures, as did the fact that the two environs defined deviancy differently. Some departments and cities may have had better mechanisms for reporting crime. Thus we cannot know for sure whether the perception of growing urban criminality was accurate. There is no doubt, however, that the specter haunted contemporaries.[15]

Officials in various cities felt that the urban environment induced and encouraged crime. In 1832, Lyon's mayor told his city council that the city offered many temptations, "From all directions the poor are faced with temptations. . . . In a large city everything appears to suggest that honesty be forgotten. There are a considerable number of objects that can be taken; stolen objects easily find fences; young people are surrounded by poor role models." Fifty years later, a city commission report in Marseille noted that the port city seemed to be a particularly auspicious site for crime, since it had "a population at the same time changing and diverse, so different in habits, views and sentiments, there is as it were a constant ferment of perversity."[16] As cities grew, these problems seemed to accelerate. By the turn of the century, there was a sense that the police were being overwhelmed by criminals. French police in 1896 had 87,000 cases in which the criminal had not been apprehended; ten years later it was 103,000 cases. Residents in several cities, alarmed at what they saw as increasing crime, petitioned for more police.[17]

Marseille was particularly hard hit. Toward the end of the century, with about 1 percent of the nation's population, it had 3.5 percent of the declared crimes. And its police force appeared notably unsuccessful in apprehending criminals. In 1899, it arrested 80 percent of armed robbers, but in 1905, only 36 percent. The following year, of 3,700 thefts, 73 percent were without suspects. Comparing several urbanized departments, a student of European crime found the Bouches-du-Rhône department had a 50 percent higher theft and 300 percent higher homicide rate than the department of the Seine at the turn of the century.[18] Marseille was the scene of spectacular crimes, including murders, by organized bands. Some local policemen, as a series of trials revealed, took full advantage of the outlawry, unscrupulously extorting as much as 1,000 francs a month in protection money. Such police behavior confirmed the general image of the city as particularly corrupt.

Aware it had a crisis, the Marseille municipality wanted to double its police force around the turn of the century. The expense, however, would be considerable, and the municipality could envisage hiring more men only if the national government would provide a substantial subsidy. There were good arguments for such aid. The city was France's largest port, the entryway for much commerce and many foreign visitors, and then felt that the increased burdens ought not be borne solely by the city. But, along with its pleas for help, Marseille refused to give up any control over its police force. The minister of finance just as adamantly refused any subsidy, insisting that police budgets were city responsibilities.[19]

The Marseille municipality, by proclaiming that its police force was insufficient to provide adequate protection, made itself vulnerable to nationalization. Some local groups favored such a step; businessmen and members of the press expressed fear of increased lawlessness and looked to Paris for the solution. The Marseille police, too, demanded nationalization, claiming that local influences hamstrung crime control. Perhaps not incidentally, nationalization also presented the prospect of a better pension and promotion system.[20]

In reacting to calls for nationalization, central authorities may have been concerned by the apparently rising crime rate, but they were also motivated by political concerns. Workers' strikes had increased around the country, and much of the Midi was in rebellion in 1907. Georges Clemenceau, the prime minister and minister of interior, who prided himself on being "*le premier flic de France*" ("France's number one cop,") decided he would establish order, and one way of doing so was to extend his government's control over urban police forces from those in Paris and Lyon to the one in Marseille, which had become France's second largest city. In 1908, the Marseille police was nationalized. The city's Conservative mayor explained that the move was intended to restrain "citizens professing advanced opinions," calling it a "blow against Socialists."[21]

Nationalization did not actually put the Marseille police force under central government control. As in Lyon, it became a creature of the local prefect, who often jealously insisted on local control, strenuously resisting efforts by the Sûreté in Paris to control it and including the mayor and the principle of municipal autonomy in his artillery. Had the Marseille police force been truly nationalized, as a recent student of the French police effectively argued, it would have had a common command with the police of Paris and Lyon. But each police force remained independent and local.[22]

The prefect of the Bouches-du-Rhône, an outsider with little knowledge of Marseille, depended on the mayor for help in staffing the force. The mayor recommended his favorites to the prefect, and the prefect, wishing to please, appointed them. The prefect was sensitive to other pressures, too. As in times past, city hall protected its friends. So while nationalization was intended to create a police force independent of the municipality, things continued much as before.[23]

After Marseille's nationalization, Toulon, La Seyne, and Nice followed suit in 1918-20. In the 1920s, three major Eastern cities (Strasbourg, Mulhouse, and Metz) and the following decade three major Algerian cities (Algiers, Constantine, and Bône) had their police forces nationalized—probably less to control crime than to quash political dissent, which was rife in both regions. In 1941, the Vichy government decreed that police forces in all cities with populations over 10,000 would henceforth be under state control.[24] At that point, the era of municipal control over local police forces may appear to have come to an end. Many police functions, such as criminal investigation and information, were placed in the hands of state-appointed and state-paid officials, but cities could and did maintain municipal forces.

Shaping of Local Forces

In the ancien régime, the police forces were disparate, varying in size and power from one locale to another and from one period to another. Lyon, for example, had a volunteer force consisting of 5,000 men after the mid-fifteenth century. This force, divided into 28 districts known as the *pennonage*, after the *pennons* (pennants, or flags) that designated the different districts.[25] In 1787, a regular police force of 31 horsemen and 100 footmen patrolled Lyon to keep the peace.

Toulouse relied as early as 1222 on bourgeois volunteer guards, each of whom was expected to serve a certain amount of time a year. In the fifteenth century, a paid watch was created. From the end of the sixteenth century to 1665, the watch numbered 40 men. But because of difficulties it had in preserving order, it was increased to 60 men in 1690 and still later to 150 men—a considerable size. This force, consisting mostly of former soldiers, was far from satisfactory; the chief of police complained that the men were "not all good recruits." The historian of the Toulouse watch described the men as being very much like the army of the ancien régime, "the refuge of the reprobate and recidivists." The night watch, according to a commentator in 1771, was so "indifferent" that criminals felt encouraged.[26] The watch was reinforced by a group that was peculiar to but a few cities, called the *dizeniers*, or "block leaders," who helped maintain the peace. In 1788 there were 400 *dizeniers*, but their number declined to 90 in 1817. The *dizeniers* were described as "sentries to observe lawbreaking and carefully observe everything that might interest general public safety and keep the police informed of everything it would be useful for it to know." By the end of the nineteenth century, the office of *dizenier* was honorific, appointed, and unremunerated; 500 persons occupied the position. Evidence indicates that as late as the 1930s individuals still held this office.[27] As for regular police, Toulouse had 20 in 1806, of whom 3 protected the city at night.[28] This force was slow in growing; in the 1820s it had 21 men, doubling by the early 1840s.

Bordeaux, with a population of 60,000 in 1535, had a city watch of 6 men. The force was so insignificant that its captain resigned, protesting that "it was impossible to stand up to school boys and wicked boys." In 1579, the number was increased to 15, and 50 years later the men were equipped with uniforms. In 1759, an enlarged force was established: 50 men on foot and 30 on horseback. In 1786, the city was divided into specific districts, each patrolled by a designated part of the force.[29]

The Revolution in 1789 abolished the old institutions. In Bordeaux, for example, the municipality replaced the watch with the garde soldée, totaling an impressive 181 men in 1793. City finances did not allow such a large force to be maintained, however, and it went into decline. In 1808, the city founded the municipal guard with 80 men, which was reduced to 67 after the July Revolution.[30]

Lyon hired men on an ad hoc basis in 1800 to carry out its night watch, and the success of this program led it to regularize the force the following year. In addition, there was a day force of 67 police agents; by 1840, it had grown to 120.[31]

Saint-Etienne had only four policemen in 1817, and the police commissioner observed this force could not effectively prevent crime. The mayor, noting in 1820 that "attacks on persons and property are infrequent, but none of the thefts committed in the last five or six years has been punished, nor their authors discovered," created a night-watch corps consisting of one inspector, three chiefs of brigade, nine watchmen, and three trainees.[32] The corps remained small; by 1848, the force totaled 32 men for a city of 52,000.

Marseille, with a population size similar to Lyon's, had a police force in the 1840s of only 53 men; by 1850, their number had grown to 172, a still modest total in relation to its needs.[33]

The size of each city's police force did not necessarily correlate with the size of its population. In 1806, Bordeaux had 1 policeman for every 1,160 inhabitants, Lyon 1 for every 1,641, Toulouse 1 for every 2,200 inhabitants, Saint-Etienne 1 for every 4,000 inhabitants. By mid-century, the police forces had grown faster than the populations. In the 1850s, there was 1 policeman for every 1,000 inhabitants in Bordeaux, 1 for every 880 in Lyon, 1 for every 1,147 in Marseille, 1 for every 1,144 in Toulouse, and 1 for every 1,305 inhabitants in Saint-Etienne. Compared with Paris, these provincial cities were seriously underpoliced; the capital's ratio was 1 policeman for every 350 inhabitants.

Further growth in the police forces in the provinces after mid-century was due in part to the pressures that prefects exercised. In 1855, having gained control over the police forces of all large cities, the prefects stepped up police recruitment and imposed the added expenses on often reluctant municipalities. In spite of growing populations, the ratios of police to population continued going down. Even after the 1867 law abolished prefectural control over the local police forces, their size was shaped by continuing prefectural pressures. Lyon's police still remained under its prefect by virtue of the law of 1851, and the prefect continued to build up Lyon's force.

Political developments in the late nineteenth century seemed to argue in favor of increasing the forces of order. After communes were proclaimed in 1870-71 in many large cities (Bordeaux among the five cities in this study was an exception), the traumatized national government tried through the prefects to nudge mayors and city councils to build up their police forces.[34]

Table 4.1: Number of Inhabitants per Policeman in Selected French Cities, 1889-1908

	1889	*1900*	*1908*
Bordeaux	526	500	476
Lyon	531	625	588
Marseille	647	625	370
Saint-Etienne	1,102	833	714
Toulouse	822	830	625

Source: Based on F 17. 12647, A.N.; *Revue municipale,* 16 February 1901; City Budgets.

Bordeaux and Lyon were the best policed cities. While Saint-Etienne increased its police force, improving the police/population ratio, it continued to have the highest ratio. A working-class city, it was hostile to the police and kept its number low. Marseille's ratio seems relatively strong, yet it should be noted that this Mediterranean port was the most sprawling of the subject cities, with five times the surface area of Lyon and twice that of Toulouse; after 1908, when the city's police force was nationalized, the new infusion of funds allowed Marseille to further improve the ratio of police to population, to the most favorable of our five cities. While Toulouse's ratio was better than Saint-Etienne's, the Languedocan capital also had a surface area three times larger than that of the Loire industrial city. The improvements in the provinces in the police force pale in comparison to the very low ratio of the capital, which, after the turn of the century, was 1 policeman to 278 inhabitants.

Ratios, of course, give little sense of how many policemen were actually available to fight crime. The police carried out many functions. In Toulouse in 1830, the police, in addition to collecting information on crimes and trying to apprehend criminals, were entrusted with such daily tasks as visiting the city's 33 inns and lodging houses as well as its many furnished rooms, to copy down names of travelers who arrived or left by the eight daily coaches. Other duties included inspecting the streets for cleanliness, patrolling the three markets, and making official inspections of the 30 houses of prostitution in the northern part of the city.[35] That left few men available for street patrol.

In Marseille in 1840, most of the 53 policemen served as messengers, guards, or market inspectors; only 12 to 14 were available to patrol the streets.[36] In 1877, only one-fifth of the 420 policemen were available for service at night, the time of high crime. Bordeaux in 1901 had 435 policemen; 240 of them served in the stations, and 96 provided various services, leaving 100 officers to patrol the city.[37] The Saint-Etienne city council estimated that of its 125 policemen in 1892, half were taken up with desk jobs, guarding city hall and providing services for the administration. Only 62 were available for patrol. With three shifts of eight hours each, only 20 men were available for street patrol at any given time.[38] The force in Marseille in 1905, after performing all its other obligations, had only 347 men, or about 150 per shift, available for patrol service. That was 1 agent for every 4,500 inhabitants (and every 104 square hectares). The police force, one city councilman observed, was like a small tablecloth on a large table: "When we are informed of the need to police a particular area, we send our men there, but then these men are lacking in another place."[39]

Recruitment

The heads of the police forces—the commissioners—were selected nationally and then sent to the localities. Until late in the nineteenth century, commissioners' appointments depended upon patronage.[40] Since the commissioners were appointed by the central government, they were expected to be sympathetic to the regime. In the 1820s, they were presumed to be royalists and, under the July monarchy, "constitutionalists"—although, Bordeaux, for instance, still had three royalist commissioners in the early 1830s.[41]

After the 1848 Revolution, the minister of interior established basic requirements for persons who were to be appointed as commissioners. They had to be aged 25 to 45, able to draw up a report, and knowledgeable enough about French legislation to be able to enforce laws and regulations. But these requirements did not end the tradition of patronage appointment or the perception of the appointees as political agents. The very circular that established these requirements also announced that the increase in liberties that the Revolution had bestowed upon French citizens made it necessary for the government "to retain in its hands the initiative and incentive which our laws have specified. The commissioners of police depend upon the government and as such are its political agents."[42]

Appointment as police commissioner required neither previous police experience nor any other particular qualification, except advantageous connections. Of the ten commissioners in Bordeaux in 1822, none had previous police experience. Only three had occupied government positions, while three had been merchants (two former planters from Saint Domingue and one a bookseller).[43] In the Second Empire, the only apparent qualifications exhibited by the commissioner for Bordeaux were that his father was a court official in Agen and his mother's family was connected to the Murats.[44] An observer in 1861 noted that the commissioners gained their appointments, preserved them, and won promotion "only by intrigue and charlatanism." In the early years of the Republic, political connections apparently continued to be important. The minister of interior complained that commissioners used relations with important individuals to gain promotions.[45] Commissioners themselves considered their positions to be political. One commissioner, writing in the 1870s, declared that he and his colleagues were mainly "political functionaries," their job being to observe and report on the various political parties and personalities in their district—but with "discretion."[46]

The central government moved in the direction of transforming the position of commissioner to a civil service function when it introduced a competitive entrance examination in 1879 for potential appointees without the high school leaving degree, the *baccalauréat*. But those with the degree were exempted, and the exam was so laxly administered that many incompetent candidates passed who soon after had to be fired.[47] In 1895, schools to train commissioners were founded in Bordeaux and Lyon, but they ceased operating after 11 months. Then a new competitive exam was introduced in 1906 requiring appointees to know how to write an official report and to show knowledge of contemporary history; geography; arithmetic; and penal, criminal, and administrative law. Those passing the exam were put in a pool of candidates available for the choosing by individual municipalities.[48] Observing these reforms, one can regard the older system of patronage as moribund. Also, reform led to an increase in municipal autonomy, for the commissioner was not appointed by the central government, but rather by municipalities, from an approved list.

As for the lower ranks of police, they were recruited by the municipalities—unless, as in Paris, and later Lyon and Marseille—they were nationalized. Each municipality specified requirements for joining its force, but none of them were very demanding. In Bordeaux, a candidate needed to be 30 to 45 years old, have completed his military service, be at least 1.60 meters tall, have good morals, and be able to read and write. All members of the force, even married ones, had to live in barracks, and their contracts were for a ten-year period. In 1858, Bordeaux's only requirement was to be between the age of 25 and 35, be of good health and character, and have completed three years' army service.[49] In Lyon, admission requirements for its two police corps, *agents* and *gardiens,* varied somewhat. To be hired as an agent, one had to be in good health and have proof of "honorability" and the "necessary vigor for active service." The *gardiens* were required to be at least 35 years old, at least 1.70 meters in height, and, unlike the *agents,* able to read and write. Veterans were given preference in hiring; at the turn of the century, by law five-sixths of the policemen were recruited from among ex-soldiers.[50] Rules for the police in Saint-Etienne, spelled out late in the nineteenth century, required a candidate to be between the ages of 24 and 30, at least 1.66 meters tall, and educated enough to write a report. He also needed a certificate of good conduct, and, if he was married, his wife had to be of good morals. As in other municipalities, former military men had priority. These provincial requirements were quite similar to the Parisian ones, which were established in 1854.[51]

Minimum requirements thus meant that a mayor could not appoint a very short person or an illiterate to the police force, but otherwise the patronage system remained in place. In the 1830s, Bordeaux fired policemen who were sympathetic to the recently overthrown dynasty, and Marseille and Toulouse did so in 1870. When the members of the police who had lost their positions in Marseille applied for pensions, one city councilor told them "Bonaparte's police deserves no consideration. Never has any police committed as many abuses."[52] In the 1880s, Socialist municipal councilors in Marseille asked that the police be purged of Bonapartists who allegedly still were on the force.[53] Purging and counter-purging of police forces was not unusual.

Contemporary studies of the French police noted that because of patronage, appointments to the municipal forces were "often unusual." In certain large cities, the policemen were recruited from the underworld; their qualifications thus sometimes included firsthand experience.[54] Descriptions of the backgrounds of three Toulouse policemen are revealing. One, a certain Doumerg, was a "tram conductor who abruptly leaves work on August 6, 1907, taking with him the day's receipts and does not return them until he is named a policeman on January 1, 1909." Another, Costes, was "in prison for four months" before being named policeman on January 15, 1908. The third, Bedouch, was a "waiter at a bar of ill repute," known by the police as "a thief and pimp," and nicknamed Pano Poulous (Chicken Thief) before becoming a police agent on January 1, 1909.[55]

Quality

The quality of the recruited men throughout the century left much to be desired. Low salaries and prestige of the police attracted men of limited abilities. Moreover, conditions of the police forces varied greatly.

For a good while, the force in Lyon was allowed to moonlight, so it was paid modest salaries: the night watchmen earned 300 francs a year, and when they were amalgamated to the rest of the police, 450 francs. Their employment was seen as a way to help the poor supplement limited incomes. At 300 francs the Toulouse night watch's post attracted only the aged and the infirm who could find no alternative employment. It was dissolved in 1843, and the general police took over this duty. The policemen of Bordeaux were paid better: the *sergents de ville* made 600 francs a year in the 1830s, and the salary was raised to 800 in 1842.[56] Presumably they did not need to take on extra employment.

The revolutionary uprisings of 1848 increased concern over the quality of the police. In Lyon, the municipality increased salaries to 600 francs while forbidding the police to take any additional employ—a move that would help them become more efficient, it was hoped.[57] By the end of the century, policeman's salaries had doubled, but that was an insufficient incentive. The number of applicants for the Lyon police had fallen.

Among those who entered the service, few stayed for any length of time; they were tempted to leave for the Paris police, which paid more, or to work in the private sector.[58] In 1908, police salaries varied between 1,284 francs and 1,600 francs in Marseille, 1,300 francs and 1,555 francs in Saint-Etienne, 1,150 francs and 1,250 francs in Toulouse, and 1,200 francs and 1,700 francs in Bordeaux.[59] While Saint-Etienne had eight-hour shifts, Toulouse had fifteen-hour ones. The latter had to wait for the Socialist victory in 1906 to see the work day reduced to nine hours. Many policemen still moonlighted; some were "hairdressers, artisans, [or] market-gardeners."[60]

Policemen were demoralized and thought of their job as "a last resource, a temporary position," while waiting for something better to turn up.[61] In Saint-Etienne in the 1870s, three-fifths of the personnel resigned yearly. As a result, the force consisted almost solely of raw and inexperienced recruits. Toulouse, with similar salary levels, also failed to keep its best men. As soon as better opportunities appeared, they resigned.[62]

The quality of the police, both the commissioners recruited by Paris and the locally recruited, lower level employees, appears to have been poor. In assessing the quality of the commissioners, we must depend in part on what may be prejudiced evaluations. It is hard to know whether the commissioners' conflicts with mayors, prefects, and ministers or their real shortcomings led to various negative assessments of their qualities. But there certainly were plenty of complaints. The Bordeaux mayor described several commissioners in 1810 as "negligent, thoughtless, immoral." Of the ten serving in 1823, the mayor found three to be too harsh, three inattentive to their duties, and three incompetent; that left only one whom he judged satisfactory. The prefect in 1855 found two of Bordeaux's thirteen commissioners lacking in energy.[63] In Lyon, the prefecture complained in the 1830s that one commissioner "had little intelligence and education."[64] A history of the commissioners revealed that until the 1870s their recruitment had not been to the satisfaction of the administration. And even later, that was the conclusion of central authorities. In 1895, the minister of interior reported that "a large number of police commissioners have—in spite of demonstrated good will—shown themselves to be absolutely incompetent."[65]

Until reforms arrived after the turn of the century, professional requirements of the commissioners remained low. The reforms' new entrance requirements to retire less competent older staff members improved the commissioners' quality, according to observers at the time. But since promotion was still based essentially on seniority, the highest-ranked officials were not always the most energetic.[66]

The conditions of employment in most municipalities did not attract the best-qualified police candidates. A history of French police forces describes the Lyon contingent in the 1820s as "often elderly men, recruited from the low class, undisciplined and exercising no moral authority over the population."[67] A general study of the Lyon force, commissioned in the 1830s by the prefect, observed that "laziness, ignorance, brutality, corruption, are common among most agents of this city." In fact, he observed on another occasion that the honesty of the police "was less commendable than those they were supposed to watch."[68] Few policemen had a sense of professionalism; an official in 1854 complained that Lyon's *sergents de ville* were sloppily dressed, had their hands in their pockets, and failed to wear their regulation hats and gloves. They smoked cigars, spoke in a familiar tone with women, and used "indecent language." Judging by the list of actions that the police manual defined as offenses against the police, Lyonnais had little respect for them: "insults of speech such as rude expressions. . . . insults of gesture or threats such as throwing mud, whistling, booing, carrying on a *charivari*, lifting a stick against the policeman. . . . Also an offense . . . is to yell 'Down with Officer X,' or to provoke him to duel."[69]

In Toulouse, where over half of the 12 inspectors of police were over the age of 55, only 7 were active enough to work. Towards the end of the period covered in this study, one city councilman described many of the city's policemen as "friends of pimps and of the worst hooligans."[70]

The mayor of Saint-Etienne described the city's low police salaries early in the century as appealing only to "people of low morals, indebted [and] shunned by all"; he wished many policemen "were more intelligent." And half a century later, in the 1870s, the situation appears not to have changed. According to the prefect of the Loire, the only people applying for the police force were "illiterates, of limited intelligence, and generally lazy who prefer the police to factory work."[71]

Bordeaux officials congratulated themselves on having a satisfactory police force, but whatever their quality, the instructions issued to them suggest that at least some needed reminding of their professional obligations. The *sergents de ville* were told that "they must under all circumstances avoid abusing the force and authority, connected with their functions; they must avoid remarks which are sarcastic, harsh, and humiliating, acts that are oppressive and which would only undermine the confidence that the *sergents de ville* ought to inspire." Of 32 *sergents de ville* in Bordeaux in 1854, 5 were poorly regarded by their superior; among the complaints were that, "he is not very intelligent. . . . he never writes a report, he does not like to issue summons." In the 1880s, the Bordeaux police chief lamented that he knew his force could "not be recruited among well-brought-up people," but a greater effort had to be made to recruit better candidates, for "I have had men who were . . . nothing but pimps."[72]

In Marseille, the *sergents de ville* positions, established in 1832, were abolished two years later, mainly because the occupants' behavior rendered them unpopular. Three of the twenty were illiterate; repeated circulars had to be issued forbidding them from taking bribes. When dissolved, the corps members wanted to seek employment in Paris, for in Marseille "their lives are in danger." The reconstituted force did little better. A rating of the Marseille police force in the late 1860s showed that of 223 men, 34 were rated as satisfactory and about half as unsatisfactory. Of the latter, a quarter had problems related to alcohol abuse. In charge of regulating prostitution, a number of police exploited their situation and were known to consort with prostitutes. Of others, their laziness; lack of intelligence and zeal; and proneness to violence, arbitrariness, and disobeying orders were noted. Toward the end of the century, a Socialist councilor charged that the police of all ranks had limited abilities, and the lower ranks spent their time "smoking, drinking, and playing manilla [a card game]." While such charges might be dismissed as politically motivated, they appear to be corroborated by the commissioner of police, who reported that he had found it necessary to "raise discipline, which left much to be desired, to stimulate the action and zeal of the officers and their men and discourage certain abuses."[73] Individual, anecdotal evidence of this sort seems to illustrate the thesis of a general study published in 1880 that French policemen were uneducated and ill-fit for their positions.[74]

With little success, various proposals were floated to improve the police. In the 1830s, the prefecture of the Rhône suggested that Lyon establish an entrance examination system, admit into the force only men with "proven probity," and create a rank system with increased salaries. Marseille in 1895 introduced an examination system for admission or promotion within the police. Formal training of police was introduced in Paris in 1883, but no such program was established in the provinces, except for the short-lived school for commissioners in Bordeaux and Lyon in the 1890s.[75]

The municipal police changed little in its provenance and quality during the nineteenth century. As late as 1936, a critic wrote that the police "personnel are too often of poor quality, their appointment having been made . . . with no concern for their intellectual or moral qualifications."[76]

There were, however, a few glimmers of modernization. After the turn of the century, the Marseille and Toulouse police replaced horses with bicycles, providing themselves with the means to quietly approach the scene of a crime. The Bordeaux and Lyon police installed a criminology laboratory and telephone service.[77] The Lyon police force was the first in France to convict a criminal on the basis of a fingerprint trace.[78] Prime Minister Clemenceau created a national motorized force in 1907, but local forces did not have access to automobiles until after World War I. Nonetheless as the adoption of modern scientific measures helped make the police forces more efficient; they also gained prestige and respect.[79]

The varying political outlooks of municipalities influenced their attitudes toward policing. Toulouse and Marseille dissolved their police forces in 1870 after the collapse of the Second Empire and established new, smaller ones; Toulouse declared that an army of police was unnecessary and that a smaller force of "honest citizens, of irreproachable morality and knowing their duty" could do the job. A short while after the revolutionary euphoria abated, growing crime and fear of disorders led the councils in these two cities to increase their police forces to pre-1870 levels.[80]

Socialists at times took aim at the police, seeing the forces as prone to violence and arbitrariness. Socialist Saint-Etienne cut the number of its policemen, arguing in 1886 that its crime rate was comparatively low. The Marseillais Socialist Bernard Cadenat entertained the utopian idea that the police could be abolished once Socialists had reached their goal—presumably the abolition of capitalism.[81] When in 1910 he became mayor, the central government was in control of the police, Cadenat had lost some of his revolutionary ardor, and capitalism was still alive and well in the Mediterranean city.

It has been posited that the more bourgeois a city is, the more it will spend on police. Bordeaux, which might be considered the most bourgeois of the five cities in this study, spent 2 francs per inhabitant on its police force in the 1880s, while working-class, Socialist Saint-Etienne spent 1.8 francs—hardly a significant difference. By 1900, though, there was a difference: Bordeaux spent 4 francs per inhabitant, more than double Saint-Etienne's expenditures, which had not changed over the two decades. In terms of the proportion of the municipal budget devoted to policing, a gap was evident between Bordeaux and Saint-Etienne even in the 1870s; Bordeaux spent about 10 percent of its budget on police, Saint-Etienne about 7 percent. But Toulouse, also a bourgeois-dominated city (although perhaps pettier than Bordeaux) had an expenditure record not unlike Saint-Etienne's. In the 1880s, Toulouse spent 1.7 francs per inhabitant (7 percent of its budget) on the police; in 1900, it spent 2.6 francs per inhabitant (9.5 percent of the budget). Marseille, a working-class city, spent 2.7 francs per inhabitant in the 1870s—more than Bordeaux. In 1898, after several years of Socialist rule, the amount had hardly changed: 2.8 francs per inhabitant. On the other hand, the proportion of the budget the police expenditure represented was reduced modestly, from 10.6 percent in 1878 to 8.8 percent in 1898—proportionately less than Bordeaux but more than Toulouse. So while some examples seem to show that a strong bourgeois imprint on a city led to comparatively larger police forces, it certainly was not an iron-clad rule.

OTHER FORCES OF ORDER

One might wonder how the limited manpower available to police forces could uphold order in France's provincial cities. The explanation is that there were additional forces of order, notably volunteer national guards, that sprung up in times of emergency, as well as the army and gendarmerie.

The national guard, a volunteer force of citizens, was formed during the Revolution and went into eclipse soon thereafter. But many citizens still thought that some sort of municipal guard would be useful. The government in 1803 considered a plan to equip every city over 10,000 people with a national guard, but the cost of such a proposal prevented its being adopted.

Some cities, including Bordeaux, Marseille, and Toulouse, re-established national guards in 1813 on their own initiative. Each force was limited by national decree to 1,200 volunteers, who were to be men of property.[82] These guards not only protected property but also performed routine police functions; a report of March 1815 describes three national guardsmen arresting noisy billiard players in Marseille at 1:00 A.M. for disturbing the peace. But the guards were not very successful. In Marseille, this force failed to attract the wealthy. Much of the recruitment took place among people of fairly limited means; instead of depending upon volunteers, the guard had to provide salaries to indemnify members for lost income. Few signed up for service, and of those who served a large number shirked their responsibilities.[83]

Most national guards had virtually been disbanded by 1830, but they came back into action during the 1830 revolution. Lyon acquired an impressive force of 15,000 national guardsmen, but they were not dependable. When an uprising broke out in 1831 only 300 guardsmen showed up to put it down. After the rebellion, this force was disarmed and dissolved, while the military garrison increased to 12,000 men.[84] In Marseille, a ragtag group of 4,500 men formed the national guard in 1830; when an expensive uniform, costing 200 francs, was required, the force became bourgeois. But the bourgeois citizens were not eager for service, and by 1837 the force essentially ceased functioning. Toulouse's guard was dissolved when, in 1841, it participated in a pro-Republican riot.[85]

National guards were formed for brief periods in other revolutionary outbreaks, in 1848 and in 1870-71. Toulouse created a reconstituted National Guard with 4,000 men; Marseille in 1848 raised a huge national guard, purportedly numbering 23,000 men, but half were not armed. Soon thereafter, enthusiasm flagged, and the number enrolled dropped, discipline was shoddy, and some guardsmen did not even know to which unit they belonged. By 1850, the guard was virtually nonexistent.[86] In 1870, again a national guard was formed, and soon it also went into oblivion.[87] The national guard turned out not to be a reliable force of order and in fact often had been a revolutionary force—for example, in the capital, where the Parisian Commune had been formed by the guard. After this experience, the national guard went into permanent oblivion, never to be resurrected.[88]

Several cities had military garrisons. In 1831, Lyon had 2,000 soldiers and Bordeaux 200, and these garrisons were subsequently enlarged. As France increasingly resorted to universal conscription, military garrisons grew in size. At the end of the nineteenth century, all five cities in this study had huge military barracks with thousands of men stationed in each city. Saint-Etienne had more than 3,000 troops; Bordeaux, Marseille, and Toulouse between 5,000 and 6,000 each; while Lyon had 10,000.

The national government maintained a gendarmerie; recruited from among former soldiers, it numbered 18,000 men in 1815. A hundred years later, the total had grown to 23,000 in the provinces and 3,000 in Paris. While this force's mission was to keep the peace by patrolling the countryside, the men were stationed in towns, including large cities.[89] At the end of the century, 799 gendarmes were in Bordeaux, 500 in Lyon, and 799 in Marseille.[90]

Both the military and the gendarmerie were available for large interventions. When Toulouse had a transport strike in 1891 and when violence broke out between young Toulousains and Gypsies in 1895, the military restored order.[91] Gendarmes repeatedly controlled public protests and were used to control acts of collective violence. They were brought into action against the Lyonnais working-class district of the Croix Rousse in the early 1870s. In Saint-Etienne in 1879, and again the following year, they were used to quell rioting by Italian laborers and general labor unrest in 1900. In Marseille, they were used to control a prison mutiny in 1885 and labor unrest the following year.[92]

MUNICIPAL FIREMEN

Cities tried to protect themselves from the danger of fires. In the Middle Ages, particular guilds were required to provide fire control. That was especially the case with the building trades; as early as 1406, such obligations were imposed upon the Bordeaux building guilds.[93] It was assumed that their members, knowing about building structures and materials, would be particularly skilled for such service. Other cities in this study had similar ordinances, except Marseille, where the corporation of *portefaix,* or dock-hands, traditionally provided fire services.

The first firemen organized in Paris around 1700. Shortly thereafter, the city of Soissons supposedly became the first provincial city to organize a corps of firemen. In Bordeaux, a royal ordinance of 1756 required men in the building trades to serve as firemen; that of 1781 in Lyon created a corps of firemen, consisting of 112 men in the building trades. A national decree of 1794 obligated water carriers to help put out fires. In Marseille, the fire service for the port came from among carpenters and caulkers, a force of fifteen men who by rotation every two months were responsible for controlling fires in the port.[94] A service with broader responsibilities for all of Marseille was founded in 1816, again of volunteers from the building trades. A prefectural decision in 1804 in Lyon provided for 74 men, all in the building trades, to serve as firemen. A decree in Bordeaux of 1806 obligated all men in the building trades and water carriers to rush to a fire when one broke out. Two years later, Bordeaux created a corps of firemen and, as in Lyon, only men in the building trades could serve.[95] Though known as volunteers, these men were paid a modest sum. They were not always available; they were part-time firemen, who, when a fire broke out, would drop their work, interrupt their leisure or sleep, and try to put out the blaze.

The evolution of fire services was haphazard. By trial and error, city administrations explored various ways of providing these services. Saint-Etienne in 1806 had but two part-time firemen, who were paid 150 francs each. It also provided reward money for citizens who rushed to a fire and helped them. That turned out to be an ineffective system in view of the growing number of forges, kilns, and furnaces; and Saint-Etienne created a force of 37 part-time firemen in 1808.[96] Toulouse in 1807 had 12 master carpenters "recognized as the most agile, who will transport themselves on the site of the fire armed with their axes, saws, ironbars, and other necessary tools." They were paid 6 francs for every time they arrived at the beginning of a fire; the first one to arrive received 12 francs. The city, still hoping it could depend on civilians, offered a premium of 12 francs to the citizen arriving with water.[97]

The size of the volunteer fire brigades gradually increased. Lyon in 1804 had 74 men in the corps of firemen; by 1819, there were 100; and by 1824, 120. Bordeaux had 31 men in 1806, 59 men in 1828, and 137 in 1830. Saint-Etienne had 37 in 1808, Toulouse had the same number in 1819. These figures were quite low, when compared to Paris, which in 1811 had 576 volunteers.[98]

The firemen were usually paid a small sum, 100 francs a year, to supplement their regular take-home pay.[99] Such supplements, though modest, were still sufficient to attract applicants who were destitute. One candidate appealed to the mayor of Toulouse to be admitted to the fire service so he could "feed his children and his old infirm father, aged seventy-five."[100] But for those already employed, the remuneration for dropping one's work and rushing to a fire was insufficient. A Toulouse municipal committee investigating the issue complained that the volunteers gave up from 2 francs to 2.50 francs a day while being paid for fire duty 1.50 francs a day. As a result, there was constant turnover in manpower, and few firemen were well trained.[101]

Various systems were developed to alert the firemen that a fire had broken out. In Bordeaux, a watchman on a lookout tower was responsible for spotting the fires. If he gave the alert before the commissioner of police did, he was given a 5 francs reward. On spotting a fire, the watchman would ring the city hall bell, the number of rings indicating first in which arrondissement the fire was burning; a minute later, the division of the arrondissement. In Toulouse, where a church served as watchtower, one chime indicated the north canton, two chimes the central canton, and so on. Lyon employed a bugle to indicate the arrondissement.[102] While Marseille recognized that ringing a bell or blowing a trumpet would be a convenient way of alerting firemen, such methods, when used at night, would "throw the population into fright, even for the most insignificant blaze." So instead messengers were dispatched to inform individual firemen of the emergency.[103] In 1823, Bordeaux changed its warning system, placing on permanent standby four horsemen who, when a fire was detected, would alert eight firemen each (the corps consisted of thirty-two men). At least that was how the system was meant to work. In practice, the horsemen did not always know how to find the firemen. Sometimes they were so slow in sending firemen to a blaze that "help would arrive when the fire had made such progress that it was hard to stop it."[104] In 1839, Bordeaux started affixing a sign on firemen's doors that read, "Sapeur-pompier" ("fireman").

Many of the part-time firefighters were of limited worth. In 1886, an evaluation of the Saint-Etienne force showed 120 to be satisfactory, 40 not. Among the latter was an individual noted as being "unworthy; conducts himself poorly." Another was a "drunk and lives with a concubine." One officer was promoted, even though a police report indicated that "his conduct and morality leave much to be desired." Another was said to be "given to drink and was poorly carrying out his duties." Still another "only goes to fires according to his whim [and] has forbidden firemen from waking him up at night in case of a fire."[105] Evidently the shortage of officers was so great that the bad apples were retained.

The obvious disadvantage of depending on part-timers was that these men, living scattered around the city and tired from a full day's work, were not always promptly available. In Bordeaux, a city commission observed that volunteer firemen did not reach blazes fast enough to put them out at the critical moment—at their beginning. In Lyon, a critic noted that relying on volunteers meant that they were at work in the daytime and asleep at night, thus not readily available at any time. Describing the situation in Toulouse, a writer noted that

> Most fires break out at night; it takes some time to wake up the firemen; these people, being tired from work all day, find it difficult to wake up and need some time to dress; it takes . . . a lot of time to wake them up. . . . When the firemen finally arrive, the house is burned down."[106]

Even in as small a town as the Saint-Etienne of 1820, the volunteer firemen could not reach the site of a fire for "they are scattered over town and don't hear the tocsin." In 1828, the fire chief noted that when a particularly severe fire broke out, only half the firemen reached the fire.[107]

The obvious solution was professionalization of the fire service. Paris had some full-time firemen, and this example was often cited by those wishing to reform the provincial system. Marseille was the first of the cities in this study to hire full-time firemen in 1840. But the number was a modest ten. Marseille retained 80 volunteers. In 1849, the city had 31 paid firefighters and 128 volunteers. Officers received between 2 francs and 1.50 francs a day, while a non-officer's pay was 1.50 francs a day.[108] Toulouse followed suit in 1843 and trumped Marseille's card by establishing a paid service of 31 men and 20 trainees. Toulouse thus became the first of the five municipalities to depend entirely on a professional fire service. Ten years later Toulouse's 26 firemen received a rather modest salary of 500 francs; by 1914, the city had but 80 firemen.[109] Marseille in 1871 became the second of the five cities to establish an entirely professional fire service with 71 men; by the turn of the century, the force numbered 140. Both Toulouse and Marseille were poorly staffed, given their large surface areas.[110]

Saint-Etienne, while continuing to depend on volunteers, established a four-man permanent fire squad in 1855.[111] Lyon, surprisingly, did not institute a professional fire service for a long time. In the 1870s, it rejected a plan because of the cost. In 1880, the Célestins Theater provided dramatic evidence of Lyon's unpreparedness when it nearly burned down. The volunteer firemen, the press noted, did not know where to find the fire hydrants, and their hoses were in such bad shape that the firemen were more thoroughly drenched than the theater. The following year, the city voted to institute a professional fire service, with salaries ranging from 8,000 francs for the chief to 1,000 francs for a regular fireman. The professional staff was supposed to number 220 men, but financial considerations led to a more modest reality, and it was not until 1890 that the first full-time firemen were hired—9 of them. By 1908, there were 78 full- timers, supplemented by 300 part-timers. In 1914, the part-time service was disbanded, and Lyon's fire service became completely professionalized.[112]

Bordeaux established a paid corps of firemen in 1864. These men lived in firehouses and had help from part-timers. In emergencies, the professional firefighters proved far superior to the part-timers. A retrospective history of the Bordeaux fire service described part-timers as lacking the will and the technical knowledge to fight fires.[113] In 1889, when Bordeaux discontinued the part-time service, the professional corps consisted of 93; by 1907, it had grown to 114. The professionals were recruited from among part-timers and construction workers.

By 1914, all five municipalities in this study except Saint-Etienne had established totally professional forces. Though these municipalities had fewer firemen, the men were available to the city around the clock. Most lived at the fire station.

Early on, most cities had just one fire station, often located in city hall. This meant that while carriages, pumps, ladders, and hoses could be brought to fires near city hall, areas farther away were at a disadvantage. By 1806, Bordeaux had four fire stations serving different parts of the city, and Marseille added two new stations in 1847. By 1907, it had ten fire houses in various parts of the city. In Lyon at about the same time, there were six companies, each responsible for a different section of the city. Toulouse had eight fire stations at the turn of the century, while Saint-Etienne had four.

To inform the fire stations of emergencies, the telegraph was established in cities such as Lyon and Marseille. In 1881, a critic complained that the telegraph system in Lyon did not function with great precision; the code was so unclear at times that it caused confusion about the nature and site of a blaze. The telephone seemed to improve communications. Phone service was established in Marseille in 1882, and at the turn of the century the Mediterranean city had 3,000 telephones, most of them installed on streets and in cafés or other public places, rarely in homes. They provided quicker means to inform firemen of emergencies. In Lyon, 67 of 175 fires in 1890 were signaled to the fire service by telephone.[114]

Firemen were hired and fired by municipalities and were subject to patronage, though a patronage limit was established in 1903, when a national law guaranteed firemen fifteen-year, rather than five-year, terms. As with the police forces, the national government believed it could improve the quality of fire services by providing some control over the fire companies.

Just as the police commissioners at the beginning of the nineteenth century were appointed by Paris, so fire chiefs in 1900 were appointed by the capital. In 1903, the prefects established control over the financing of fire control. While potentially this law might have increased conflict between Paris and the provincial authorities, that was rarely the case.[115] Again, there seemed ready accommodation of the representatives of the central government to the local situation.

As cities during the nineteenth century became more densely populated, crime and fires increased. If the police and fire services had not been transformed in these years, cities would have been less capable of protecting their inhabitants. Both elements of public safety, but especially the police, were subjects of interest to the central government. Yet, during most of the time, the main actors in shaping responses to urban crime and fires were the city municipalities. And even when the central government arrogated to itself considerable powers, local governments were able to shape how Paris and its representatives exercised their authority. The varying sizes of police and fire services (varying not only in absolute numbers but also in relation to urban population or surface area) and the different times at which these municipalities introduced innovations reveal the degree to which local initiative and local decisionmaking—even in an arena so crucial to the central government as public safety—remained critical.

5

Public Schools

*T*he French Revolution took away the Roman Catholic Church's responsibility for schooling the young and instead entrusted the municipalities with this task. Even though national laws regulated the system of primary schools, considerable leeway remained for each municipal government; and local patterns of education reflected local values, budgets, economies, social structures. Education was a subject of considerable local political controversy; it mattered to the local elites, and in later years it engaged electoral politics. To fully understand the educational experience of Frenchmen in the nineteenth century, one has to look at the rich local variety.[1]

Legally, the primary system was in the hands of the municipality; the secondary and university systems were a national responsibility. A small elite attended the latter two, which were funded mainly by the state. The primary system was intended for the masses; until the 1880s, about 90 percent of the municipal educational budget was expended on primary schools. Public education was education for the poor; the wealthy were supposed to attend private schools. Given these priorities, this chapter limits itself to the primary school system.

PURPOSES

Local officials clearly articulated the purposes of education. From early on, and consistently, they viewed education mainly as a means to uphold the existing political and social order. During the Revolution, the Marseille municipality tried to make school attendance obligatory to instill "Republican principles." Under Napoleon's Empire, the Lyon council saw education as establishing an orderly hierarchy, for without education for the poor "there would be no hope of regeneration, ignorance would establish itself, vice and immorality would spread, and society would groan from the sufferings which would ensue." The mayor of Saint-Etienne reported that his city, having a large proportion of working-class people, was particularly in need of schools, for they provided "a considerable improvement in the morality of the children."[2]

But if education was a force of stability, too much of it could be dangerous. In Marseille, a municipal commission on education made quite clear that education was subordinate to preservation of the social order. Elementary education should not last too long, for then it would be useless to the majority of the population destined to "hard and mechanical labor" and might "discourage them from embracing the condition to which the social order calls them." The prefect of the Haute-Garonne noted that while it was "essential that the less fortunate class know how to read, write, and count. . . . I think there is where free education should stop."[3]

The Napoleonic regime, the Restoration, and the July Monarchy lived under the shadow of revolution. During these periods, city elites, having just witnessed an uprising in which popular participation had been critical to the overthrow of a regime, felt a keen need to socialize the poor. While, during the Napoleonic and Restoration regimes, the inculcation of religion was seen as an important element of education, during the July Monarchy public instruction was viewed as strengthening citizenship. In Bordeaux, the commission on education reported to the city council in 1831 that the purpose of education of the young was to "raise them to become good citizens." Education seemed to be a means of inculcating values of orderliness and hard work while also providing the "seed of all progress in industry and our institutions." The main purpose of education, municipal authorities clearly professed, was to emulate preceding regimes by having education "benefit those in power. Thus during the Empire, children were raised to become good soldiers, and under the Restoration submissive subjects. It is high time that they were raised to become good citizens."[4]

Municipal authorities saw schools as places to teach the working-class children the habits of routine, hard work, obedience, and respect for the hierarchical order. Such habits were taught in religious and "morale" classes. Other classes were added because of their presumed ability to facilitate social control. Thus the Marseille city council educational committee established music classes because appreciation of music "has really softened the habits of the people and raised their soul, has turned them away from pleasures enjoyed in bad company."[5]

Another theme became more insistent in the 1840s: education was an instrument of economic development and well-being. As the Marseille assistant mayor declared in 1839, "Future society will be calm or agitated, hardworking, active, and industrial or lazy, careless, and without industrial capacities and hence backward, depending upon whether in childhood the young were well or badly directed." When the crown prince visited Marseille in 1839, he was told that Marseille saw the role of education as ensuring "the love of work and order; it provides the people general well-being, the nation tranquillity." The Bordeaux mayor described education as "the seed of all industrial progress."[6]

The revolution of 1848 did not change the perceived goals of education. The new Republican municipality in Toulouse urged the introduction of a "republican catechism" in the schools of Toulouse so that the children could learn "the duties of the citizen . . . love of the Fatherland and respect of our institutions."[7] But the short-lived Second Republic was followed by nearly 20 years of the Second Empire. General insecurity led the imperial authorities to favor education as a way of moralizing the masses, ensuring social control and making France economically competitive. While the Second Empire was careful not to give the Church monopoly over education, it encouraged the growth of religious schools.[8]

Opponents of the Second Empire shared many of the official assumptions regarding education. The Republicans, who gained control over the councils of many major cities in the 1860s, were strongly committed to education: it could help wean the country away from the authoritarianism of the Second Empire and guide it peacefully to a Republican form of government. Thus local councils on their initiative and with their own funds attempted to change the nation's regime. A Republican opponent of the Second Empire in Marseille approvingly quoted the Republican leader of universal free education, Jules Simon: "The child is the future. Above all let us concern ourselves with children to educate them and moralize them, and later they will become useful to their country as defenders of its political liberties. . . ."[9]

Once the new Republic was declared in 1870, the Republicans in the city councils saw the need for public education as a means to stabilize the nascent regime. The education commission of the Marseille city council declared that "the future of the Republic" depended upon schooling. "Through education we shall prepare honest and courageous citizens, we shall succeed in reforming the morals and uplift the character of a people crushed by a corrupting tyranny." With universal suffrage, citizens were dependent for their welfare upon each other and therefore, announced the Commune government of Toulouse in a unanimous vote, "ignorance was a kind of social crime." Education should be obligatory. In Bordeaux, the chairman of the city council finance committee declared that "in a democratic society, schooling has to be spread, the people enlightened, taught to govern itself . . . in a word education should be the rule, ignorance the exception." Such ideas were supported in a public petition, signed by 2,697 persons, demanding new schools for Bordeaux: "it is absolutely indispensable in a state in which universal suffrage must be sovereign that each citizen have the necessary instruction to vote with discrimination."[10] Civic education was visually communicated in schools; the Marseille city council set in each of the city's 360 classrooms a plaster bust, 30 centimeters high, representing the Republic and costing but 6 francs each "to accustom the children from early on . . . to know and respect the Government. . . ."[11]

The moderate Republic that had taken root by the late 1870s could, it was thought, be best protected from both right- and left-wing extremism by education. President Sadi Carnot, visiting Toulouse in 1881, pointed to the virtues of public instruction: it provided equality of opportunity and gave the citizen a sense of his worth and the value of liberty. He added that "schooling of the people prevents surprises," and "unmasks those who try to exploit to their benefit either suffering or deceptive promises." In Lyon, schooling was also seen as a guarantee against "communism and socialism." A Toulouse city official said that "educating citizens is to render the fatherland great and glorious, to ensure the triumph of the Republic and the application of its principles." The mayor of Bordeaux declared that "the first responsibility of a Republican municipality was to favor schooling which alone can make good citizens and ensure the future of the Republic."[12]

SUPPORT FOR EDUCATION

Municipalities had the initiative on primary education, and through much of the nineteenth century, they made the real decisions on the pace and quality of local schooling. In 1870, two-thirds of primary education was funded by the commune; only in the 1880s did commune contributions drop as a result of legislation by which the national government assumed the responsibility for teachers' salaries. Subsequently, communal contributions dropped to approximately one-third of total expenses on primary education (see table 5.1).[13]

Table 5.1: Public Expenditures on Primary Education in France, 1870-1905 (in Millions of Francs)

Year	Nationally	By Department	By Commune	Total
1870	10.5	9.3	41.8	61.6
1875	16.4	13.1	48.2	77.7
1880	31.3	19.6	57.3	108.2
1882	88.6	18.0	27.2	133.8
1885	86.6	18.0	66.0	170.6
1889	80.1	17.9	71.9	175.9
1890	120.5	—	56.6	177.1
1895	136.4	—	66.9	203.3
1900	146.9	—	71.0	217.9
1905	182.5	—	86.5	269.0

Source: Patrice Grevet, *Besoins populaires et financement public* (Paris: Editions sociales, 1976), 348.

Until 1889, cities on their own initiative, with little interference from Paris, determined how much to allocate to education. Municipalities fluctuated in the funding they provided, and funding levels between cities varied. It is hard to detect any uniform explanations for the differences in funding. In 1830, for example, Bordeaux and Toulouse in relation to their populations provided dissimilar subsidies to education in 1830. Though Toulouse had two-thirds the population of Bordeaux, its education budget, 13,000 francs a year, was less than half that of the port city (28,000 francs). In 1833, Saint-Etienne, the poorest of the five cities in this study, spent the largest amount on education proportionately to its budget and population: 28,000 francs, or 20 percent of its yearly budget. Bordeaux spent the same amount, but the sum was only 1 percent of its budget. Saint-Etienne with a population one-third that of Bordeaux, spent 40 percent more on education. Whereas in other cities religious orders played a big role in education, in Saint-Etienne the sudden spurt in growth had put the burden nearly entirely on city government.

Education expenditures represented varying proportions of city budgets: 2 percent for Lyon, Marseille and Toulouse in the 1840s, 1 percent for Bordeaux, and approximately 8 percent for Saint-Etienne. The per-student expenditures varied, too; thus Lyon spent 3.78 francs per student, Marseille 8.3 francs, Bordeaux 3.45 francs, and Toulouse 7.5 francs. These variations reflected different educational arrangements. Lyon's relatively low cost per student, for instance, came about because the philanthropic Société de l'instruction publique ran much of the school system.

Education expenditures remained relatively low when compared with other expenditures because, in spite of the rhetoric, cities did not regard education as a principal responsibility until mid-century. They usually spent more on their theaters than on education. Indeed, in 1860 the city of Marseille spent three times its yearly educational budget for a reception honoring the visiting emperor and empress.[14]

Significant growth in education allocations began in the 1850s. Bordeaux's annual outlay rose from 100,000 francs in the 1840s to 160,000 francs 20 years later. Lyon's rose from 160,000 francs to 550,000 francs. But growth was not universal; Toulouse's education budget remained almost stagnant.

Expansion, where it occurred, usually meant not only increased outlays on education in a period of general well-being but, more important, bigger shares of city budgets. Lyon, which had spent 6.3 percent of its budget on education in the 1840s, spent 10 percent in the 1850s and 1860s. In Marseille, in the years 1863-70, the annual primary education budget essentially doubled from 222,000 francs to 437,000 francs, an average yearly growth rate of 12 percent. Lyon increased its education budget in the same period from 400,000 to 600,000 francs, or 7 percent yearly. Toulouse, a hotbed of Republicanism that prided itself on its commitment to education, increased its school budget from 70,000 francs in 1860 to 80,000 in 1870, or a yearly growth rate of only 1.5 percent. Toulouse's neglect of education was due in part to its overall low budget; in addition, social antagonisms there were not so strong as in Saint-Etienne, for example, where a greater need for social control made the ruling elite willing to spend more proportionately on education.

Once the Republic was established in 1870, all five municipalities in this study accompanied their rhetorical flourishes with increases in budgetary education allocations. Marseille's school budget increased from 412,000 francs a year in 1869 to 586,000 francs in 1872, and that of Toulouse from 91,000 francs in 1870 to 231,000 francs in 1875 (representing an important increase in percentage of the total city budget from 4.4 percent to 8.4 percent). The yearly average expenditure on education in Bordeaux for 1866-70 was 193,000 francs, while in the five years following the founding of the Third Republic it was 411,000 francs. Not only did the expenditure more than double, it also represented a doubling of education's proportion of the overall city budget, from 2 percent to 4 percent.

The early years of the Third Republic were marked by an increase in the education budget overall and the amount allocated per student. But it was not a unique rise; during the July Monarchy, for instance, Lyon's educational budget increased eightfold, and Bordeaux's fivefold. So proportionately the rise was not as dramatic in the Third Republic as official histories of the Third Republic might make one think. Furthermore, and this is important, education was on the whole better and earlier funded in cities. Much of the needed schooling was provided early on, so that the unschooled population diminished with time, and the truly dramatic spurts in educational growth that marked the July Monarchy and Second Empire were not (and could not be) repeated during the Third Republic.[15]

Cities also continued to spend varying amounts per inhabitant, per pupil, and in relation to their budgets, as shown in table 5.2. Education also represented varying proportions of each of our cities' budgets, most proportions being close to the 1880 national average of 8.6 percent of communal budgets.[16]

Table 5.2: Expenditures on Primary Education in Selected French Cities, 1880

	Proportion of Budget (Percent)	Per-Inhabitant Expenditure (Francs)	Per-Student Expenditure (Francs)
Lyon	7.99	3.56	62.45
Marseille	8.00	3.40	60.73
Saint-Etienne	14.78	2.67	30.04
Toulouse	9.72	2.65	31.13
Bordeaux	7.32	2.48	35.36

Source: "Tableau comparatif de la situation de l'instruction primaire dans les principales villes de France (année 1880)," Copy in 6D 393, A.M.T.

The lower proportions for Bordeaux and Lyon do not signify lesser school systems. They had strong, older systems, which, though under municipal control, relied in part on philanthropic sponsorship. The higher per-student expenditures of other cities reflect their need to catch up. Thus, there is no necessary correlation between the condition of education and expenditure at a given time.

PUBLIC AND PRIVATE

The Revolution proclaimed the right to free education for all, but the heavy cost this principle represented caused the National Convention to withdraw the law in 1794. As noted, several municipalities recognized the social utility of educating the poor; public instruction was originally intended for them. In Lyon after the uprisings of 1834, which had severely shaken the city, the mayor insisted on the need to provide school access for all children. Saint-Etienne's mayor declared in 1836 that the goal of his administration was to provide schooling for all children so that all would know "how to read, write, and count," thus ensuring "the moral improvement of children of the working class."[17]

Still, none of the cities in this study provided free education for the whole population. Lyon was the first municipality to provide free education for the indigent, but since space was limited, not all who wanted schooling received it.

Most city councils insisted that children of all families above the poverty level attend fee-paying schools; admission to the city subsidized Catholic écoles chrétiennes, as well as Protestant, Jewish, and or lay schools, was permitted only to children whose parents were documented indigents. An exception was Saint-Etienne, which already in 1830 instituted free public education for all. Given the absolute poverty of the population and the small number who could have afforded to pay any kind of tuition, it made sense to abolish income requirements for children attending municipal schools. But in other cities there was a requirement that the better-off children attend private schools.

The requirement that public schooling be limited to the indigent was not, however, always followed to the letter. In the absence of massive funding, failure to enforce the law and exclude those who could pay the fees meant exclusion of the poor from the schools to which they had a right to access. Those who illegally attended public schools helped crowd them out, and many put on waiting lists probably were children of poor parents who lacked the means (in either persuasion skills or personal contacts) to convince school officials their charges should be admitted. The well-off did not seem to shun free communal schools.

At the national level, men of the left agitated for gratuity. Alphonse Lamartine demanded it in 1847, and Louis Blanc insisted that education "be free and obligatory." During the Revolution of 1848, the Lyon Democratic Society demanded "free and obligatory education." The national government born of the revolution of 1848 proposed such a program, but the Conservative National Assembly killed any chances of the bill's passing.[18] The reaction after the June days discouraged experimentation, and city officials opposed gratuity. Paying fees, elected and appointed officials averred, would make students more appreciative of the education they were receiving. And it would, of course, provide more funding for the school system. In Paris, the prefect of the Seine, Baron Georges Haussmann, argued gratuity "weakens family ties, frees parents of part of their duties, diminishes children's gratitude, lowers for all the value of education, and finally gives the false impression that there is a right to education."[19]

In spite of such authoritative opposition, France moved toward free education. In the 1860s, many industrialists and business interests favored gratuity, arguing that to be competitive France needed to have all its children in school. Nationally, gratuity increased after mid-century; 38 percent of all French students in 1861 were attending school free of charge, and 54 percent by 1872.[20] By the end of the Second Empire, and before national legislation mandated it in 1882, all five cities in this study had instituted virtually free schooling for all (except in Toulouse for girls).

To ensure the success of their programs, Republicans favored mandatory education. Minister of Education Victor Duruy argued for compulsory education, but he was overruled by Napoleon III, who bowed to Conservative pressure. After the fall of the Empire, the issue continued to be vigorously debated, both liberals and conservatives maintaining positions in apparent contradiction to their basic values. Republicans, identified with the idea of liberty, wished to coerce every family into sending its children to school, whereas Conservatives, of a generally authoritarian outlook, upheld the principle of freedom of choice. At least rhetorically that was how the case was presented. Support for legalization of universal education, that is for requiring mandatory attendance, was presented as democratizing education, making it available to all; but it also was seen as a means of inculcating Republican ideology and solidifying the new regime. Conservatives may genuinely have worried about the usurpation of parental authority that mandatory school attendance represented, but they also undoubtedly were troubled by its cost and the fear that it would bring the whole population under the sway of Republicanism.[21]

Municipalities did not have the authority to institute mandatory education, and in the end national legislation was passed in 1882 introducing free universal mandatory education. But the cities had been in the forefront, providing free education to all long before it was nationally required.[22]

TEACHERS

Schools had difficulty attracting good teachers. In Marseille, the Revolutionary municipality advertised 228 positions in the lay school system it established to replace the closed church schools; 15 or 20 days later, only 58 candidates had applied, and in the end only half of the posts could be filled. In Bordeaux, the situation was similar, and the snag seems to have been poor wages. A German visitor in 1801 noted that the city teachers were so poorly paid that "they lack the necessities of life, even bread."[23]

Teachers had no special qualifications. In Lyon, two school inspectors described them as "people of all kinds, factory workers dissatisfied with their condition or lacking employment." The official in charge of the national public instruction system in 1809 in a circular described the teaching corps as including individuals "whose great ignorance . . . and vicious habits render them unworthy of this profession."[24]

To staff the schools, the cities turned to the male religious orders, the main male order being the Frères de la doctrine chrétienne, also known as the Frères ignorantins, and to a number of female teaching orders. The frères had been the main order providing teachers during the ancien régime, and in the Napoleonic era were allowed to resume their activities. It was a convenient solution and was ideologically compatible with the Napoleonic era, which saw the dissemination of religious values as providing the support for an orderly hierarchical society.

The religious orders presented several advantages as a source of teachers. Above all, they were cheap. Their members, living in a community, could subsist on modest sums that, if provided to a lay teacher, would have led him "to die of hunger."[25] In 1811, Bordeaux provided the ten Christian brothers teaching for the city a subsidy of 7,200 francs, which included the rent on their lodging.[26] Another advantage was that the religious orders could inculcate desirable values. The mayor and city council of Toulouse explained that the Ignorantins were good models of poverty and modesty to the children of the poor—"they can make their students work and be docile."[27]

National laws during the Restoration gave the Church virtual control over education. While some lay teachers ran their own schools or were hired by municipal schools, they had to be approved by Church authorities. All candidates for teaching posts had to have good morals, support the Bourbons, and be religiously orthodox. To prove they had all these virtues, they had to obtain a certificate for the first and second from the mayor, and for the third from the local priest. Correct political and religious views were valued more highly than competence; a circular by the national commission of public instruction indicated that incompetent teachers who held approved views should not be fired merely to make way for more competent ones.[28]

Salaries were low. In the first half of the century, they ranged from 400 to 800 francs for male lay teachers, half that for women. As an historian of education remarked, teachers were paid no more than domestics.[29] Religious orders received even less. The Soeurs de Saint-Charles, who ran girls' schools in Lyon, were paid between 250 and 400 francs per teacher in the 1830s and 1840s. In the 1830s in Lyon, the Frères chrétiens were paid 349 to 467 francs; in 1850, 550 francs; and in 1872, 638 francs.[30] Salaries were eventually raised, but they were still low, with considerable variation between cities. In the 1870s, a male lay teacher's salary in Marseille was 1,000 francs, in Toulouse 900 francs, in Saint-Etienne between 1,000 and 1,500 francs. In Saint-Etienne, teachers were able to make ends meet, it was claimed, only by moonlighting. Toulouse's low salaries made teachers prefer assignment to the suburbs with their lower cost of living; as a result, the suburbs allegedly attracted the better teachers. In Marseille, the city council in the 1870s calculated that for the average teacher, lodging at a modest *pension* house would cost 65 francs a month and laundry 5 francs, leaving only 10 francs for other expenditures. It seemed unacceptable that the teachers were paid less than other municipal employees, and so the council raised their salary from 1,000 to 1,200 francs a year (for women teachers from 800 to 1,000 francs). But even that was far too low, and it was claimed that higher salaries in Paris were attracting teachers away from the port city.[31]

The male-female salary differential was viewed as quite normal. As one Lyonnais city councilman explained, "man is and should remain the responsible head of family; he has more charges and greater needs than a woman. The male teacher must receive a higher salary for a task which by the way is more serious. . . . [I] don't believe in the equality of the sexes." In Marseille, for all ranks males were provided 300 francs more than women per year in the 1880s. A generation later, in 1903, a Conservative municipality in the Mediterranean port (following a Socialist one, which had not addressed the issue) voted the principle of equal pay for equal work. That meant the city would have to provide a supplement for female teachers, since the national government (which in 1889 had taken over the responsibility of paying teachers' salaries) retained unequal salaries for male and female teachers.[32]

Given the low salaries throughout the period, the schools could not be demanding in the quality of teachers they hired. When Marseille tested candidates for a couple of posts in the communal schools in 1840, it appointed one who had scored "mediocre" or "weak" in four of eight subjects; another who had seven negative evaluations of his competence was hired as a temporary teacher with the hope he would improve.[33]

Teachers had little sense of professionalism. A school inspector, visiting Marseille, reported in 1833 that "most teachers consider their profession but a means of making a living. . . . There are precious few who regard the importance or the dignity of their functions." In Bordeaux, an inspection report in the 1830s noted that most of the teachers "were good for nothing and so became teachers." In 1870, nearly all the teachers of Marseille were over 60 years of age. One was 90 but was not relieved because the post was his only means of livelihood.[34]

The national authorities attempted to improve teacher competency by providing a national diploma, the *brévet de capacité*, which from 1816 on became increasingly demanding. Members of religious orders were exempted from the *brévet* in 1819 and continued to be exempt until the 1880s. Maybe anticipating the demand that they have the *brévet* an increasing number of teachers in religious orders obtained the *brévet*. And, stung by accusations, that they offered an inferior education, many, who did not receive the *brévet*, obtained better teacher training from their religious orders.[35]

By the 1880s, instruction had improved. Standards for recruitment had been raised, and on the whole better prepared individuals were put in the classroom. With rare exception, urban posts were considered desirable; most teachers preferred living in cities to living in small, often primitive villages.

CURRICULUM

The dominant pedagogy until the 1840s was the "individual" method of teaching, by which a student would recite a lesson appropriate to his or her level for a few minutes, then the teacher would turn to the next student, who would read an entirely different text. This method meant the teacher could spend only a few minutes a day with each student, and the rest of the time the student would be bored and likely to engage in activities distracting to the rest of the class. In 1829, the minister of public instruction estimated that four-fifths of the teachers used the individual method.[36]

While religious orders ran most of the municipal schools, an alternative system, mutual schools, developed during the Restoration. The mutual system had its origins in England; it was also known as the Lancasterian system after Joseph Lancaster, who devised it in 1798 to instruct a flood of students at his school in southeast London. It was a cheap and quick way of providing literacy for a large number of youngsters. An adult teacher would train particularly able students who, in addition to doing their own schoolwork, served as monitors for younger or less capable fellow students. Many French, however, were suspicious of an educational system not run by the Church, invented by Protestants, and using a new, seemingly untried method; the mutual schools thus remained a distinct minority.

At about that time a new consensus developed on teaching methods. The individual method was abandoned and replaced by the "simultaneous" method. The latter system, with one teacher teaching the same lesson to all the students in a class at the same time, was practiced by the Frères des *écoles chrétiennes,* and it dominated the French school system after the 1840s. Still, no matter which system was used, teaching varied greatly in quality, depending on the individual school and teacher. No clear standards were established by municipalities—nor attained by schools. A report describes one school in Marseille as, "completely rudimentary... not a single child is learning to read." Of another school the inspector noted that, "writing is not even taught." Half a century after the metric system was adopted, at least one school in Marseille still did not teach it. A government report on Saint-Etienne in 1848 described its primary education as "poorly conducted."[37]

**Table 5.3: Inspectors' Evaluations of
Selected French Urban Schools (by percent)**

	Good	Acceptable	Passable	Poor
Bordeaux Schools				
1860	50	23	17	10
1880	78	—	18	4
Lyon Girls' and Boys' Schools				
1860	38	52	9	1
1885	28	31	—	41
1900	48	30	—	22
1914	56	25	—	19
Marseille Boys' Public Schools				
1844	50	—	—	50
Marseille Boys' Private Schools				
1844	35	—	—	65
Marseille Girls' Schools				
1861	28	38	21	23
Saint-Etienne Boys' Schools				
1860	47	28	8	17

Source: Based on Etat de situation de garçons et des écoles mixtes, académie de Bordeaux, arrondissement de Bordeaux, " 1860, F^{17}10412, A.N.; Académie de Bordeaux," Rapport sur la situation... 1880," 102R 14, A.M.B.; Comité communal d'instruction primaire. Etat de situation des écoles primaires, 1844," 6R2, A.M.M.; "Etat de situation des écoles de garçons, 1860; "Etat de situation des écoles de filles 1860, Etat de situation des ecoles de filles, 1861," F^{17}10417, A.N.; "Etat de situation des écoles de garçons, Saint-Etienne, 1860, A.N.; Maurice Saurat, "Les institutrices et les instituteurs à Lyon de 1870 à 1914," (Unpublished D.E.S., University of Lyon, 1968), 32.

National inspectors' reports give an idea of the relative merits of schools located in the provincial cities in this study. They are, however, only approximate indicators of the situation in the schools, for they are subject to individual inspectors' judgments and may vary according to an inspector's own changing temperament as his inspection tour progressed.

While schools in the five cities were differently evaluated, no city appears to have been better or worse than the national average.[38] Nonetheless, there could be differences between a particular city and its hinterland. A report in 1855 observed that whereas 1 of 28 schools in Lyon was of poor quality, 1 of 7 was poor in the department of the Rhône as a whole.[39]

By the 1880s, inspectors generally found schools to be satisfactory, though their standards continued to be idiosyncratic. In a Toulouse school, the inspector found the teacher uninformed and teaching in an unsatisfactory manner, yet he rated her class as "acceptable."[40]

The trend certainly appeared to be toward improvement. That may have been due to the desire of the educational bureaucracy to show palpable progress, or it may reflect an increased supply of teachers coming out of training schools. As a result of their training, they were better informed in the subject matter and socialized into the methods of teaching that would find favor with the educational inspectors. Still, clear national expectations of which subjects should be taught and by what method were developed relatively late; a national curriculum was not established until the 1880s.[41]

ATTENDANCE

In a number of cities even before the Revolution, a substantial proportion of school-age children attended school. It is estimated that on the eve of the Revolution, half of Lyon's 16,000 to 20,000 children were in school, and two-thirds of the boys attended school. Attendance plummeted during the Revolution but improved under Napoleon and thereafter. Urban school enrollments appear to have grown faster than the national averages, although local as well as nationally reported statistics are not fully reliable.[42]

None of the cities in this study had to await the 1833 Guizot law, which made it mandatory for each commune to establish a primary school; they had done so long before. The cities were way ahead of their country cousins, who needed such a law to establish a school.

Cities answered a demand for schooling that was less pressing in the countryside. City parents, the Bordeaux city council explained, "understand better the need of their children for the knowledge which industrial progress requires." And so the children rushed to the schools. In Bordeaux in 1833, 581 registered for the mutual schools but only 150 could attend because of lack of space; in the Christian schools, 2,032 were attending but 525 could not attend, again because of lack of space. The difficulty of gaining admission was so discouraging to the poor that many did not even bother to register, so that the demand was actually higher than the number registered would suggest. The situation was no different in the other cities in this study.[43]

Many school-age children did not attend school. In Toulouse, the city council estimated that only a third were attending. Of those, two-thirds were from well-off families; half of the children of the poor were not attending school. In Bordeaux, half of the estimated 4,000 males of school age attended school. In Marseille in 1836, 70 percent of school-age boys and 65 percent of school age girls attended school.[44] Proportions attending school varied considerably between cities, depending upon the municipal commitment to education and the city's social structure.[45]

Laws against child labor, passed in 1841, should have taken children out of industry and into schools. But these laws were not enforced. A school inspector in Marseille noted that they were a "dead letter," and "the establishment of a factory usually spells the ruin of all the surrounding schools." An official report of 1848 surveying the lacemakers of Saint-Etienne noted that they pulled their children out of school by age ten, which meant they "have not had the time to learn much." In Toulouse, which was urban but not industrial, school attendance was higher within the city limits than in the outskirts, where, according to a school inspector, "gardening and agriculture are always being developed and require the assistance of children."[46] The lowered attendance in the suburbs was, of course, a result of the increasing urban demand for fresh vegetables and other agricultural products; so here urbanization had a negative impact on the city's surroundings.

The varying wealth of the communities also had a lot to do with schooling. In poor industrial towns, the impoverished families could not afford to send their children to school. They needed the children's earnings to supplement the families' meager incomes. The problem with schooling in Marseille, it was noted, was that no sooner had a child taken his first communion, then he would be pulled out of school. An inspector's report claimed that parents sent their children to school mainly to free themselves from the obligation of supervising them; they had no interest in their children's educational progress.

The poor either did not care about or did not understand the need for sustained education—and of course could not afford to forego the services of their children. A Marseille school inspector noted that children of the poor often missed class or arrived late "because their parents have them do errands." A city councilman saw it as a kind of law that "the more a neighborhood is poor, the less a school is frequented." Parents "use their children from their earliest years," he said; "they cannot spare them."[47]

School attendance varied considerably according to city. Marseille in the 1860s had 10,000 school-age children (one-third of the total) who did not attend school, Bordeaux only 500 (4 percent). In Toulouse, it is estimated, nearly all school-age children attended school. Nationally, nearly a third of the country's youths were not attending school in the mid-1860s.[48] Inspectors' reports on individual schools in Marseille confirm the forces at work in school attendance. In the Saint-André district, only 67 children attended school, since a tile factory "by employing children discourages their [school] enrollment"; in the Capelette, "the floating nature of the population discourages the development of education."[49]

In the 1880s, after schooling became compulsory, students still did not always attend school regularly. In a school in Lyon's Brotteaux neighborhood, nearly half of the students were absent, and the inspector was told that "it was the tradition of the neighborhood" not to go to school on Mondays. In Lyon, of those registered in the public schools, 77 percent attended, while in Marseille the average attendance for the school system was 85 percent. Attendance in cities was lower, it appears, than the national average, which in 1886-87 was 92 percent.[50]

BUILDINGS

Cities had no set standards for their school buildings; usually the school was a rented room, attic, cellar, or other available space.[51] Many schools were severely dilapidated. A school in Toulouse was described by its teacher as "an old ruin we would have left long ago if we could have found space . . . an earthen house, upheld by a few beams, half consumed by worms. . . ." One Toulouse girls' school, it was claimed, was so crowded, so deprived of air and light, so unhealthy, that it led the nuns who taught there to a premature death; the children's condition was not commented on. The assistant mayor in charge of educational affairs, inspecting the schools of Toulouse in 1869 described the school buildings as "a real slum." The city council of Saint-Etienne noted the poor condition of the city's school buildings, describing one of them as "crowded and unhealthy . . . humid, poorly enclosed . . . really unfit for its usage."[52]

The following generation saw improvement, but many schools were still inadequate. In Toulouse, an inspection in 1880 found 37 percent of the schools in physically poor condition. In Saint-Etienne, three-quarters of the schools were found to be physically substandard. An 1880 inspection report of the Lyon schools found that "there are only a dozen schools, recently built, which are completely satisfactory." Half the schools in 1892 were still found to be physically substandard.[53]

An 1878 law required communes to become proprietors of schools. Some cities had already taken the initiative; in Bordeaux, 36 of 50 public schools were municipally owned. But that was not the case in the other cities in this study. Financial imperatives seemed to dictate the need for municipalities to own their school buildings. And so, beginning in the 1880s, municipalities attempted to move schools from rented buildings into their own, newly built ones. Lyon was behind other cities in this regard. In 1874, of 144 primary schools in the city, only 16 were municipally owned, and the city was spending 200,000 francs a year on renting schools. Between 1880 and 1886, Lyon built 15 school buildings, but as late as 1895 the city was signing new leases on rental buildings. Old substandard schools continued to be rented.[54]

The pressure of large numbers of students who had to be quickly accommodated did not allow cities to be very discriminating. In Saint-Etienne, when the authorities needed to find new facilities, "we were in a hurry, we needed locales, we took them where we found them," the educational commission noted. Quality hardly mattered; of the 24 rented buildings, 14 were considered in poor shape. In contrast, of the 18 school buildings owned by the city, 16 were acceptable.[55]

French school buildings were relatively spartan. When French delegates returned from the World's Fair in Philadelphia in 1876, they reported with amazement the sumptuousness of American schools. And while hopes were expressed for improving French school buildings, there also were fears that they might become too lavish. A Bordeaux city councilor insisted that school buildings should represent "rectitude, severity, simplicity." While they should have the necessary sanitary facilities, they should not be so luxurious that children from poorer families would become disdainful of their modest homes and leave prematurely, for a child separated from his family "will later only be a bad citizen."[56]

CROWDING

In the early part of the nineteenth century, school crowding was seldom commented upon, but by the 1830s it was a common refrain. An 1833 report for Bordeaux records classrooms with 125 to 150 students. In Marseille, a classroom that should have had 75 students had 230; an 1858 inspection revealed that one-third of all girls in Marseille were attending overcrowded schools. In Bordeaux a school inspector noted that in one classroom "260 children are piled together like a swarm of bees on the branch of a tree; 80 children would have had difficulty being comfortable." One school in a populous Bordeaux neighborhood had three times the enrollment that ministry of education guidelines specified.[57]

While it was recognized that quality education ideally required classes limited to 30 students, it was also noted that a city such as Lyon had neither enough teachers nor enough funds to live up to this standard. With the growth of the city and the move from congregational to public schools, class sizes increased. In 1885, 8 percent of Lyon teachers taught classes with more than 50 students; in 1900, 28 percent did so; and by 1914, the proportion had increased to 31 percent.[58]

For France as a whole, the mean class enrollment fell from a high of 45 in 1840 to a low of 34 in 1901, then rose to 36 in 1906. In the cities, classes typically were larger. Yet by the end of the nineteenth century, the very large classes of a hundred or more students had disappeared. When, in 1897, the statistician Emile Levasseur came across a statistic of 262 students per teacher in Senegal, he proclaimed it an error. He could not imagine such a situation.[59]

SUPPLIES AND HELP FOR THE NEEDY

Municipalities were slow to decide whether they should provide school supplies. In the 1850s, some city councils debated the issue, and in the following decade some schools began supplying textbooks. At the turn of the century, Lyon, Marseille, and Saint-Etienne provided free texts to all students. Toulouse and Bordeaux supplied them only to the needy. Still, Bordeaux had a generous definition of "needy," and 12,000 of its 18,000 students received free texts. Toulouse teachers, in order not to earn parents' hostility, counted children as needy when "with a little good will they can buy the necessary books."[60] The difference in provisions reflects the strong labor influence in Lyon, Marseille, and Saint-Etienne.

By the late nineteenth century, city councils began to view their responsibilities more broadly—especially socially committed ones. Many observers had tied school truancy to poverty; in particular, lack of food and clothing. With the law on obligatory education, it nearly became imperative that this stumbling block to school attendance be removed. Furthermore, the provision of meals in Church schools made it necessary for the lay ones to compete successfully and provide similar benefits to the destitute. Secular schools often also distributed free shoes and clothes.[61] It should be noted that the monies budgeted for these purposes were extremely modest and could not have come close to meeting students' needs. Assuming that at least 10 percent of the children were indigent in Marseille (a figure based on the number of adults so classified) approximately 3,000 then were needy and they were provided for the whole year with a budget of 50,000 francs; for Lyon, similar modest amounts were available.

SECULARIZATION

Cities acted as pioneers in establishing public lay education, antedating the national government in this field by decades. While religious orders ran the majority of communal schools, the cities also had lay schools. Bordeaux in 1834 had nine communally financed schools: one lay (run by the association for mutual schooling), six Catholic (run by the Ignorantins), and one each that was respectively Jewish and Protestant. In the 1830s, Toulouse had nearly a fifth of its students in lay mutual schools. In Marseille in the 1860s, only 9 percent of the schoolchildren attended lay communal schools, while in Toulouse, a city with a stronger tradition of anticlericalism, 30 percent of the schoolboys attended lay communal schools. Nationally the figure was approximately 40 percent.[62]

In the face of assaults on the lay system by Church authorities, who wanted a monopoly over the primary school system, the municipalities began insisting in the 1830s on the preservation of the lay system. The municipal elites in these cities, while not necessarily hostile to the interests of the Church, also favored pluralism and sustained non-Catholic schools— Protestant, Jewish, and secular. For political reasons, some city councils were hostile to Church schools. In Saint-Etienne, for example, the religious orders were thought of as insufficiently supportive of the July Monarchy, and the use of lay teachers in city schools was proposed in the 1840s.[63] Proponents of laicization of the school system in Toulouse brought up the proposal in 1848.

The Second Empire was favorable to the Church and clerical interests, but it did not wish to see the Church gain a total monopoly on education; thus, it did not discourage educational pluralism. Republicans, when they gained substantial victories in municipal elections in the 1860s, tried to limit the Church's authority, especially its role in education. In Saint-Etienne, where Republicans won in 1866, they founded lay schools, which were immediately flooded. By 1871, equal numbers of students were attending the religious and lay schools.[64]

Secular-minded municipalities tried to reduce the influence of church schools. The Saint-Etienne and Bordeaux city councils in 1868 passed a rule requiring all city teachers to have the *brévet de capacité* teaching diplomas. Since clerical teachers did not usually have these degrees, the law was an attempt to exclude them from city schools. In Saint-Etienne, all new schools opened after 1866 were to be lay. "Religious instruction takes a lot of time in school," the argument went. "Those who want it can give it [to their children] in their homes, churches, or private religious schools."[65]

The cost of laicization, however, gave second thoughts to many of its proponents. In the 1860s, it was estimated that the per-pupil cost of lay schools in Marseille was 33 francs per student per year, as opposed to 22 francs in the congregational schools. It was also estimated that if the whole school system were laicized, the city would have to come up with an extra 100,000 francs a year. Renting the school buildings owned by the Church would cost another 500,000 francs a year.[66]

The prefects of the Second Empire kept anticlericalism under control, but once the Republic was proclaimed in September 1870 and the centralizing power was temporarily paralyzed, municipalities stepped up their attempts to eliminate religious influence in education. In 1870, after revolutionary communes were declared in all the cities in this study except Bordeaux, they eagerly moved against religious influences in education. Even after the Communes were crushed, the municipalities retained their dedication to secular education.

When the Conservative national government of Adolphe Thiers was firmly in the saddle, it ordered the reestablishment of the clerical system and had to force it through against recalcitrant municipalities in Lyon, Marseille, Saint-Etienne, and Toulouse.[67] But opposition continued to clerical education.

Strong anticlerical diatribes often accompanied the skirmishes over religious education. In Marseille, the teachers of the religious orders were denounced for teaching under the influence of the Syllabus of Errors and thus negating "all modern civilization." A councilor in Lyon declared that the religious orders were "vipers and Prussians of the interior." In Toulouse, religious education was blamed for the dictatorship of Napoleon III and the defeat of 1870.[68]

The right wing conservative regime of Marshall MacMahon, installed in May 1873, attempted to make primary education a monopoly of religious orders. In a number of cities, the prefect, or the municipal commissions appointed to replace the elected Republican municipalities, signed long-term contracts handing over primary instruction to religious orders—that was the case, for instance, in Toulouse. Republicans who had seen the Church favored under Napoleon III and again under MacMahon saw the struggle against religiously inspired education as part of their struggle against political reaction. A common argument against clerical education, widespread among Republicans, was the fear that the clergy would make the young into enemies of "liberty and the Republic."[69]

Buoyed by aid from the *ordre moral* government of Marshal MacMahon, religious schools had increased in numbers, threatening the future of lay schools. After the Marshal's fall from power, Republicans mounted an attack on behalf of lay education. In 1881, half of all schoolchildren in France were enrolled in Catholic schools (public and independent) and in the cities in this study, the situation was no different. Toulouse's communal lay system steadily lost enrollments; Bordeaux in 1874 still had 60 percent of its schoolchildren in schools run by clerics.[70]

The municipalities carried on a head-on assault on church schools. Lyon in 1879, Bordeaux and Saint-Etienne in 1881, Marseille between 1881 and 1883—all of them laicized their communal schools. Only Toulouse, prevented by a long-term contract imposed on it during the *ordre moral,* lagged behind, laicizing in 1888. Secularization proved to be expensive. In 1874, the clerical-minded municipality of Marseille estimated that the per-student expenditure in lay schools was double that in the congregational ones. Cities lost access to school buildings owned by the Church orders and had to replace them with new ones at considerable cost. Bordeaux, for instance, spent a million francs in 1880 on new school buildings.[71]

Laicization changed enrollment patterns. Parents who wanted religious education for their children shifted them from public to private schools, ending the downward trend in the proportion of students in private schools. Nationally, private schools provided education to 16 percent of students in 1880, and to 25 percent in 1901. In Lyon in 1874, there were 28,630 students in public schools (lay and religious), while only 8,018 attended private church schools. In 1888, the public schools, now entirely lay, experienced a drop in enrollment, to 20,766 students, while the private religious schools had nearly the same number, 19,609. In Marseille, public schools had never been fully appreciated and a large proportion of children attended private schools, most of them congregational; in 1883, 17,852 attended public schools and 12,191 private schools. A number of the newly built lay schools went unfilled because parents shunned them, preferring to send their children to the newly opened congregational schools. But gradually there was a clear shift to the lay public schools; they received 60 percent of the students in 1883; in 1902, 75 percent. Bordeaux seems to have experienced no shift in enrollments as a result of laicization.[72]

In 1886, Parliament made it mandatory for all public schools to be lay, the major cities had already passed such legislation more than a decade earlier. These local laws and their successful implementation in the various cities undoubtedly contributed to shaping the national legislation.

GIRLS

Over the century, municipalities increased access of females to education. In the early 1800s, girls' education had elicited only minor interest. City statistics on schooling often did not include information on girls' schooling (national statistics were not collected until 1837). City budget allocations for education frequently failed to mention girls. Since they were taught by the sisters of charity as part of their charity work, the budget for girls' education was often subsumed under the assistance budget. Saint Etienne in 1803 voted city funds for boys' schooling, but none for girls', which was supported by private philanthropy. The national minister in charge of education, after issuing circulars on "public instruction," often had to issue another one to remind subordinates that the circular also applied to girls.[73] Not until the early 1830s were city funds explicitly voted for girls' education.

Education of girls was seen mainly as familial, "to make them into subservient girls respectful toward their parents, wise and faithful spouses, tender and vigilant mothers." As a Marseille official put it, "the base of happiness and tranquility is assured by the civilizing influence that a wife, who already has been well trained, has on her husband. . . ." Some educational authorities did not see girls' education apart from that of boys' and in fact insisted that "young girls have the same needs as boys for primary education. . . ." A Marseille official stated in 1839, "We have recognized that an elementary knowledge, reading, writing, and arithmetic, were necessary for even the simplest household chores; for a woman of modest means who might wish to open a small retail store, such knowledge is indispensable." But such opinions tended to be in a minority; more common was the view of the Toulouse city councilman, who in 1845 warned that one could not be too cautious when one considered girls' education, or that of a city reformer who rhetorically asked, "What is the necessity for women from among the people to know how to read and write? Reading and writing serve no purpose; they only need to know how to work; education ought not to be for women."

In the later part of the nineteenth century, women's education was favored, but still not for the woman's personal development. Rather, she was thought of as a relay for boy's education. As a Toulouse city councilor put it, "if you want the man to be educated, start with the mother."[74]

Republicans insisted on the importance of controlling female education. Jules Michelet warned in 1845 that the Republic would not be safe as long as "our wives and our daughters are brought up by our enemies, enemies of the modern spirit, of liberty, and the family." A local echo of this view came from the assistant mayor of Toulouse, who explained that education would ensure that women properly raised their children, not only physically but also politically, thus stymieing the attempt of the Church to establish control. "It is the woman who shapes the man."[75]

Student enrollment figures reveal the varying values that parents put on girls' education. Nationally in 1832, 48 percent of all boys attended school, while only 25 percent of girls did; two-thirds of all schoolchildren were boys. Equal access by the sexes was attained in our cities in the decade of the 1860s, about a decade before it happened nationwide.[76]

In providing schooling for girls, the cities were especially protective of them, employing special measures to keep them segregated from boys. Not only did they have separate classrooms, but in one school in Toulouse they entered and left school at different times. Protectiveness can also be seen in the tendency of parents to send more daughters than sons to congregationalist schools. In Toulouse in 1861, 56 percent of the boys, but 83 percent of girls attended religious schools. In Bordeaux in 1874, 15 percent of the school boys, but 76 percent of the girls were enrolled in congregational schools.[77]

CENTRAL GOVERNMENT

Although France's educational system appeared to become increasingly centralized during the nineteenth century, with Paris attempting to impose a common, standardized educational policy on the country, the localities retained considerable autonomy. At mid-century, the prefect of the Gironde admonished the mayor of Bordeaux that his school system was inadequate: three of his schools were overcrowded and dirty. The mayor answered that nothing could be done; the city had insufficient funds, and in time these schools would be replaced by new ones. The prefect, his powers limited to admonishment, accepted this answer as adequate.[78]

National laws regulated such things as minimum classroom space per student, but did not suddenly produce the desired effects. In Marseille, for example, one-third of all girls were enrolled in schools that were too crowded. Inspectors were supposed to enforce these national standards, but even though they recorded shortcomings year after year, the responsibility of bringing change to the schools was in the hands of the municipalities.

Inspectors were few in number and could not visit all classrooms even once a year. In 1903, there was 1 inspector for 250 teachers. And when inspectors did visit a classroom, many were aware that their functions went beyond enforcing regulations. They were also supposed to encourage education, which sometimes meant being sensitive to local interests. On an official visit to a Saint-Etienne school, an inspector found the director completely incompetent, but concluded that since "Mme Jauffret belongs to an excellent family of councilors-general . . . it is impossible to take any [disciplinary] action against her."[79] Local realities set limits to centralization.

While recommendations abounded regarding what might be taught and for how many hours weekly, no national standards were issued until the 1880s. But even then schools' problems were not resolved. Writing in 1887, two inspectors lamented the lack of a truly national education system and the persistence of variety "according to the province, the department, the arrondissement, the canton, the commune. . . ."[80] The Marseille school district, in spite of the national law on mandatory school attendance issued in 1882, had a quarter of the school-age children not attending; in 1891, 20 percent were still not attending. After the turn of the century, when the obligatory school attendance law had been in force for nearly a generation, Lyon and Bordeaux still had hordes of school-age children frequenting the streets.[81]

The municipalities played a determining role in the establishment of a modern educational system. They had taken the initiative in setting the pace of education, experimenting with various models, and in many cases their examples were to inform the national policies which eventually were adopted. And when Paris decreed policies, they were shaped and changed to fit local exigencies and capacities. The national educational system was on paper uniform and centralized, but the variety that flourished at the locale revealed the richness in diversity and the power of local government to shape and influence even a program as ostensibly centralized (by the 1880s) as the French educational system.

6

"The Primary Schools of Enlightened Men":
The Municipal Theaters

*I*n the ancien régime, the monarchy reaped prestige by sponsoring a variety of cultural expressions such as the Académie française and the Comédie française. Local government, before and after the Revolution, also basked in the luster of cultural sponsorships; such activities reaped glory for the municipality, solidified the authority of the local elite and educated and entertained the general public.

Although it became common in the twentieth century to claim that localities were bereft of culture and needed direction from the French central government to flourish, the historic record reveals a very large number of municipalities, particularly in the nineteenth century, to have actively sponsored culture.[1] Each of the cities in this study had an art museum and a theater, but it was the theater that was at the center of municipal cultural concerns, in terms of both the time spent in municipal chambers discussing the offerings of the official stage and the proportion of the budget spent on it. The theater even became a subject of electoral politics—a status not reached by the local museum, or scientific society.[2] While many independent purveyors of amusements, such as jugglers, acrobats, magicians, and singers entertained urbanites, high culture in the form of classical plays and operas was offered mainly in the municipal theaters, (we shall, following French practice, use the term "theater" for both plays and operas).

The value set on this form of culture might be gauged by noting that municipalities spent more on theaters than on subsidies to local churches.

Even during the relatively religious first half of the nineteenth century, Lyon theater subsidies were twice to three times those expended on the churches. In a later, more anticlerical era, the ratio went as high as five to one. In the 1880s, support for the churches disappeared, while theaters continued to receive healthy subsidies. To take a comparison that might strike some as more important, until the mid-nineteenth century, more was spent on the theaters than on schooling. In the 1840s, Marseille's annual expenditure was 90,000 francs on primary education and 100,000 francs for the city theater; in Bordeaux the subsidy was 45,000 francs on the theater and 44,000 on the schools. Lyon's theater expenditure for 1845 came to three-quarters of that expended on education. Not until the second half of the century did the relationship between public schooling and theater expenses change, and the latter began to lag behind. In the late 1860s, Lyon's primary school budget was three times the amount expended on theater; Marseille's was double.[3]

Municipalities and their leaders through the nineteenth and early twentieth centuries viewed the theater as just as worthy of support as basic services. "Just as a city cannot call itself a beautiful city if it does not perfectly light up its avenues, it cannot have the pretension of being a great city if it has no theater," a Marseille city councilor declared. The mayor of Toulouse insisted that a city needed a theater as much as "a railroad, a telegraph, primary schools, academies, water, and gas. . . ."[4] Actually, provision of a theater preceded many services that might be considered more important today. Cities subsidized theater productions before they had established a municipal school system, a corps of firemen, garbage collection, or a regular police service.

BUILDINGS

The importance of the municipal theater was signaled by its building, which in most cases was intended to be one of the most sumptuous edifices in the city. Lyon's first municipal theater, built in 1756, was designed by the architect Jacques Soufflot. A half-ellipse, it had excellent acoustics and made architectural history; contemporaries considered it the most beautiful theater building in Europe.[5] In the 1820s, the city council decided to tear it down and replace it with a large neoclassical building seating 1,800 people. The city spent 4 million francs on the new theater, making it Lyon's single largest building project up to that time. It was intended, as a prefect a generation later put it, to "provide the second city of France with a monument which in every way would by its splendor and importance be worthy of it."[6] It was built long before Lyon thought it could afford to build its own schools (they were rented until the 1870s) or water system (first established in the 1840s).

Bordeaux built its theater in 1780, designed by the famous architect Victor Louis and inspired by Soufflot's theater in Lyon; Bordeaux in turn became the most splendid theater building of its time. A neoclassical design dominating the square on which it sat, it won wide renown. A travel book in the 1840s said that "no theater in France can be compared with ours."[7] It inspired Charles Garnier's plans for the Paris Opera 80 years later, and it still remains Bordeaux's most stately building, symbolizing the city's aristocratic pretensions.

In Marseille, a private stock company built a theater in 1787, modeled after the one in Bordeaux. For years, the Mediterranean port was the only major French city that did not own its municipal theater building; finally, in 1882, it purchased the building. The interior was refurbished, making it, as a local official exulted, "one of the most beautiful theaters of France."[8]

Saint-Etienne, a working-class city, could afford no such luxuries. Its first permanent structure in which plays were performed was a shanty, acquired in 1764. In 1787, a barber received permission to transform his shop into a theater. But it too was substandard and a fire hazard; it was closed down in 1792. Five years later, the municipality converted a chapel that had belonged to the Minimes friars into the city's first structurally solid theater building. Then, for reasons unknown, it moved to a narrow rented room "in which the audience is stuffed."[9] In the 1820s, the city began to consider building a theater, but did nothing about it. Finally, in 1853, after the city became the departmental capital, it spent 250,000 francs to construct what was intended to be a provisional building. It housed the municipal theater for 75 years. Ugly and unimpressive in most every way, the building became blackened by city soot and weakened by shifting subsoil; but it appears to have had great acoustics. The building burned down in 1928 and was finally replaced 40 years later by the more substantial Maison du peuple.[10] For all its shortcomings, the building of 1853 was a high priority item on the city's agenda. The city fathers chose to build it rather than providing more fountains for the working classes to combat water shortages.[11]

The Toulouse theater occupied a wing of the city hall beginning in 1542. As early as 1808, plans were made to build a new, freestanding opera house across from city hall, the Capitole, which was and continues to be the chief symbol of the city. But the anticipated cost, 1 million francs, was prohibitive, and for a quarter of that amount, the existing theater was redone in 1816.[12] During the Second Empire, Toulousains revived the old plans. It was necessary, a petition of the day proclaimed, for "the dignity of a city like Toulouse to have an opera hall . . . which was grandiose and monumental."[13] Several architectural projects resembling Garnier's Opera in Paris were submitted.[14] When the cost of a new Toulouse theater was estimated at 4 million francs, city fathers had second thoughts, and Toulouse still has no freestanding municipal theater building. Instead, the city decided to renovate its theater wing at an estimated cost of 500,000 francs, though the repairs ended up costing 1.4 million francs—due in part, it was suspected, to contractors' overcharges.[15] Combining the theater and the Capitole under one roof added to the luster of the city hall, making clear that the glory of the municipal theater, one of the best provincial operas, was due to the munificence of the city administration.

PURPOSES

The theater was seen as a tool of the monarchy in the ancien régime. During the Revolution, it was seen as no less a weapon in the struggle for the minds of men. The revolutionary leader Bertrand Barère proclaimed theaters "the primary schools of enlightened men." The National Convention authorized municipalities to run theaters "to present the plays most appropriate to educate the public and develop republican enthusiasm (former l'esprit public et développer l'énergie républicaine.")[16] Several decades later, Victor Hugo declared the theater "a branch of popular education, responsible for public morality."[17] Early on during the Restoration, the minister of interior noted that if well directed, the theater offered the educated class "the noblest of relaxation." And if well supervised, it "could spread healthy and useful ideas."[18]

Local officials believed fervently in the utility of the theater. City councilmen—many of whom were educated in the classics—saw in the theater a morally uplifting force that transmitted the true and the beautiful. They subscribed to the philosopher Victor Cousin's assertion that "by the means of sight and sound, art penetrates the soul." Alfred Fabre, the Marseille historian and city council member, stated in an 1844 report to the council that the theater had moral and aesthetic roles to play. A few years later, another city councilor described the theater as a moralizing force, showing the triumph of virtue over vice and inspiring the development of the other sciences and arts. Many of the bourgeois supporters of the theater would have agreed with the Bordeaux historian who described the theater as like all fine arts in "bringing us closer to the infinite by representing ideas by symbols which speak at the same time to the senses, the soul and reason. . . ."[19]

With the introduction of universal male suffrage, some hoped that the theater could educate the common man and help make him into a responsible citizen. It was claimed that the theater educated the masses, preventing them from being misled and offering them valuable models. High culture, its supporters argued, would raise the values of the common man and prevent him from sinking into barbarism. Classical theater and opera would prevent the population from resorting to popular music halls and cafés, "which by their nature are not apt to develop moral instincts," declared the Marseille mayor in 1867.[20]

The edifying cultural spectacles the municipality offered its residents could, it was thought, keep vice away from the masses. One of the foremost representatives of the Marseille bourgeoisie, a city councilman, argued that official culture lifted the intellectual and moral level of the working class. "It is far preferable that the workers take a healthy and elevated pleasure in hearing Carmen or Sigurd rather than waste their Sundays and evenings in a bar swilling alcohol and listening to obscene and stupid songs." Many officials in other cities echoed these sentiments throughout the nineteenth century.[21]

Early on, the theater was seen as a way of distracting urban dwellers and thus ensuring public safety. It was no coincidence that theaters in the country were regulated by the same minister who was responsible for securing public order, the minister of interior. One minister of interior described theaters as providing officials "with the means of occupying during leisure hours an anxious population, which, abandoned to itself, could become dangerous.[22] In the Year XI, the mayor of Toulouse equated a well functioning theater with "public tranquillity," and a generation later the Bordeaux city council declared that the "public and political order" of the city depended on the theater's staying open.[23] Theaters, the Marseille municipal council declared, were the site for the gathering of "this crowd of foreigners, of idle people without family ties . . . who without honest distraction could compromise public tranquillity." In Lyon, the theater was seen as especially important, even necessary for the distraction of the working class, although that did not prevent workers from rising up in revolt in 1831 and 1834. At mid-century, the theaters were still associated with "grave questions of security," according to a Toulouse municipal councilor.[24]

Under the watchful eye of the police commissioners, who were required to be present in the theater, the crowds were presumably more controllable indoors than on the street. Without a theater, one councilor said the action of the police "would be paralyzed." The theater, the prefect of the Haute-Garonne claimed, provided a convenient gathering place, easily observable by the police and especially useful in a city such as Toulouse, with large numbers of young people (it was a university and garrison town). The city council had a similar view, arguing in 1855 that, "In a city with a mobile and varied population of schools, military garrisons and workers," it was advantageous to have a theater where the population could be conveniently supervised. In rebuilding Lyon's second theater, the Célestins, in the 1870s, the municipal commission in charge of the project claimed that the theater was particularly easy to oversee, unlike "the thousands of pleasure spots where evening idleness attracts young people and workers."[25]

To both national and local officials, the theater seemed a relatively safe arena for venting feelings. An observer in 1786 described the audience in the Bordeaux theater conducting a "charivari." Charles Tilly has argued that the charivari, a traditional mode of protest in villages, became in the nineteenth century a means to express political opinions in cities, often in the confines of the theater.[26] In Toulouse in the 1820s, theater audiences (especially working-class patrons in the pit) sometimes applauded passages that seemed to be alluding to the Revolution, "and let out cries of 'Vive la liberté.'" Continued acts, such as "seditious behavior," by Toulouse students led to the theater's being closed. The Marseille theater also was the scene of demonstrations, both royalist and anti-royalist; the occasion was a showing of *The Barber of Seville*.[27] Decades later, in 1872, when a singer, known as a Republican and maybe Communard, was invited to perform in Marseille, he was booed by the Royalists and cheered by the workers in the pit. When the two groups came to blows, soldiers with drawn bayonets had to be called in to separate them. In the heated atmosphere of the Dreyfus Affair, at the end of the century, the Marseille theater became a site for voicing pro-Dreyfusard sentiment, and "Vive Picquart" and "Vive Zola" were often yelled by enthusiastic theatergoers.[28]

The theater, in addition to its other assets, was seen as having economic value by providing a large number of individuals with a livelihood: managers, actors, stagehands, hawkers of various sorts. The Goncourt brothers, Edmond and Jules, estimated in the 1850s that in Paris alone, one thousand actors, actresses, and directors depended for their livelihood upon the stage. An estimate covering all of France was that 10,000 persons made their living directly or indirectly from the stage.[29]

For the five cities in this study, various estimates exist of the number of people who depended for their livelihood on the theater. In the 1830s, the number in Bordeaux was said to be 300 to 400 individuals; the following decade, it was said to be 300 families. In Marseille, a few years later, the estimate was 150 families; in 1878, it was 200 families; and a few years after the turn of the century, the theater supposedly provided a living for 1,500 people. In Toulouse toward the end of the century, it was estimated that the theater employed 200 individuals.[30] These estimates, often flung out in the heat of debate, are less than reliable. In 1877, during a Bordeaux city council debate, it was claimed that 215 families depended on the theater for their livelihood; a day later, the figure had increased to 300.[31]

Whatever the exact numbers, it is certain that many more persons' livings were indirectly affected. Theaters attracted merchants, lawyers, notaries, and others who visited with or without their families from smaller communes in the region. Lyon's theater, for instance, drew audiences not only from neighboring Villefranche but also from cities within a radius of 100 kilometers, cities such as Saint-Etienne, Grenoble, and Chambéry, which had rail links to Lyon.[32] Out-of-town theatergoers stayed in city hotels; rented local apartments; supped in restaurants; had drinks in cafés; and bought jewelry, gloves, clothing, and other luxuries. The "multitudes of families" who swooped down on Toulouse each theater season, it was estimated in the 1890s, spent hundreds of thousands of francs yearly.[33]

The municipal theater also had a role to play in upholding a city's eminence. In its contract with the theatrical director, the Lyon municipality specified in 1873 that the performances should be "appropriate and worthy of the second city of France." Marseille, supporters of its theater said in 1844, was in antiquity "the sister of Athens;" was it not then fitting for it to have a theater worthy of this rank? Toulouse, city councilmen argued, had an ancient reputation for its support of culture that had to be preserved; it was the capital of the Midi and thus had certain responsibilities. While Toulouse may not have been competitive in industry and commerce with other large cities, its genius lay in "its superiority in the arts and sciences"— or so went the mayor's proud boast in 1880. In Bordeaux, a city councilman argued that the Grand Théâtre was "the glory of the city."[34]

Theaters often became objects of inter-urban rivalry. The Marseille theater director was tapping into a well of common concerns when he asked, "Can the great city of Marseille do less than Bordeaux and Lyon, its rivals?" Even cities "of third and fourth rank" in the kingdom had a theater, and therefore Marseille could not forego having one, a supporter argued.[35] City councilors were well aware of municipal theaters in other cities and jealously defended the standing of their own, fearing they would be outranked by theaters in rival cities.[36]

AUDIENCES

During most of the nineteenth century, theater was a form of entertainment for all classes. A municipality that wanted to retain popular support needed to be cognizant of the demand for a steady supply of quality plays and operas.

The theater was a major social gathering place. The working classes occupied the pit, often coming equipped with bread, sausage, and wine for a long evening of amusement. In the loges occupied by the upper classes, all kinds of activities went on; from flirting to conducting business negotiations. In the Marseille theater, businessmen discussed their business affairs, "except when there were ballet performances." They attended several times a week, and Stendhal observed on a visit in 1837 that the port city's theater was "just a more elegant form of a café and a more jovial form of the stock exchange." Another traveler to Marseille confirmed these views, describing the merchants as showing little interest in the spectacle they were attending: "Little do they care if Scribe's comedy or Dumas' drama is being shown; there is no drama or comedy as worthy as trade; no music by Meyerbeer or Rossini equals the pleasant sound of money. . . ." And the ladies felt constrained to spend large sums on their theater dresses and paraded them proudly.[37] The provincial theater, just like the Comédie française in Paris, was, as *Le Temps* put it in 1883, a place where "very chic people come to greet each other."[38]

Unlike Parisians, who, according to a recent study, learned the art of listening by the 1840s, provincials were not awed by musical or theatrical performances.[39] Enough spectators of all classes brought their dogs with them that the practice had to be forbidden by special regulation in Marseille, "regardless of the part of the theater the spectator intends to seat himself in."[40] The public's inattention and noise were great. A Dutch visitor to the Bordeaux opera in 1819 noted that when the famous Talma was not on stage, the pit made so much noise that other actors could not be heard. Stendhal, after visiting the Marseille theater, remarked that "the first difficulty of an actor is to gain the silence of the audience."[41] Often the audience members, especially those in the pit, were so busy chatting, yelling, and playing pranks that they did not heed what was happening on stage. An inhabitant of Saint-Etienne reminisced about the experiences he and his family had of the theater at the turn of the twentieth century: "If we remembered little of the plot of the scene we had just witnessed, at least we had had a good meal in company," he wrote.[42]

Municipalities ignored the public at their peril. In Toulouse, the large student contingent attending one performance in 1817 started yelling during intermission, demanding Talma be brought to the city. When told that the director had been unable to secure the actor's services, the students rioted, wounding two policemen before soldiers dispersed them and the performance was canceled.[43] The following year, the director, perhaps with heightened motivation, brought Talma to the city. Saint-Etienne audiences were accustomed to hiss, *siffler*, so vociferously during the unsatisfactory 1839 theater season that the city came to be known as "Sifflepolis."[44] In Toulouse, when a singer's voice gave out midway through an aria, the public yelled, whistled, and sang; the performance was stopped, and the police emptied the theater. An angry crowd of 200 persons proceeded to the house of the director, threw stones at it, and had to be dispersed by the police. When the theater director in Lyon appeared to scrimp on singers by not hiring the best, a fortnight of disorders broke out in the Grand Théâtre, and the hall had to be forcibly evacuated several nights by armed force.[45] An historian of the Toulouse theater writes that throughout the century audiences came armed with "sticks, hammers, and whistles"; in 1836 they wielded trumpets. To reduce injury, the Lyon and Marseille mayors forbade spectators from bringing in "sabers, weapons, walking sticks, whips, umbrellas, or staffs of any sort."[46]

Municipalities and theater directors who wanted to preserve public order had to see to it that performances were of high quality to satisfy the audiences; otherwise they risked major disorders. Raphaël Félix, brother of the famous actress known as Rachel and director of the Lyon theater, was so notoriously parsimonious in paying actors and providing scenery that he won the hostility of both actors and audiences. Things reached a climax one night when, to escape an angry mob, he fled the theater disguised as a monk. The crowd, out for blood, moved on to his domicile, tore up the pavement, and used the pieces as projectiles. Some members of the mob, which eventually numbered 10,000, broke in and threatened to burn down the house. It took a regiment to disperse them.[47] The director, evidently surmising that he no longer enjoyed public support, resigned.

Audiences often intruded into the performances, saluting actors and actresses with too little or too much respect. When Mademoiselle George, whose great beauty once had attracted Napoleon's favors, appeared in Lyon, her audiences, outraged by her obvious antiquity, greeted her with catcalls of "camel." But when the beloved Talma was ending his engagement in Bordeaux in 1819, the theater public violently sought to force the director to keep him on.[48]

Audiences were extremely demanding and regularly made and broke performers' careers. Toulouse was particularly famous for its tough audiences, which prided themselves on knowing and appreciating music. One of the city's great singers remarked in 1830 that if one's career survived there it could do so anywhere.[49] The Marseille audiences were extremely harsh. When a young singer made her debut in *Mignon*, she was mercilessly booed off the stage; she took to her bed and died 22 days later. Paris newspapers accused the audience of causing her death, but the historian of the Marseille stage defended his fellow Marseillais by suggesting that the singer had an advanced case of tuberculosis when she arrived in the city and was in no condition to sing.[50] When a barrelmaker with a good voice was singing in *Les Huguenots* in Marseille and came to the famous line "My

God what shall I do?" someone in the audience yelled—to its general amusement—"Resign and make barrels!" The singer did. In 1902, when Massenet's *Sappho* was put on in Marseille, the role of the young Provençal woman Iréne was sung by an American soprano, a Miss Parkinson. Instead of employing the appropriate Provençal accent for her performance in Provence's principal city, Miss Parkinson retained the unmistakable accent of her native shore, leading to howls of protest and a riot; the director was forced to resign.[51]

At times, the applause and the protests were premeditated and organized. Claques could be arranged for various purposes. At the Paris Opéra, the most famous claque leader was Auguste Levasseur, known to his contemporaries as simply "Auguste." In the 1830s, he was in the regular employ of the Opéra, and it was his role to create enthusiasm for works and actors unfamiliar to the public.[52]

In the provinces, claques were used similarly. They were available for rent to anyone, not just the director or the actors but also persons with hostile intent, as indicated by the rates for their services in Lyon: from 5 francs for "ordinary salvo of applause," 50 francs for "unlimited curtain calls," an unspecified sum for "sneers, laughter, and other indications of disapproval." In Marseille in 1810, a playwright hired a claque to applaud his work; when this stratagem failed, he had to flee the city. Half a century later, a theater director, according to a city councilman, mounted a claque for an unusual purpose—to get rid of talented and expensive performers by booing and hissing them off the stage while applauding less talented and cheaper actors.[53]

Mayhem in the theater was routine; authorities expected it, and under certain conditions viewed it as legitimate. A prefect who attended the Toulouse theater in 1823 and heard the catcalls and whistling from the audience wrote the mayor: "I recognize that the displeasure of the public is well founded . . . the actors should never have appeared on the Toulouse scene; none have a reputation." Whistling in the theater was considered a legitimate means of expression—only if the whistling degenerated into general disorder was it forbidden. A municipal commission of Lyon noted in 1842 that "if the public is demanding, it has the right to be so, given the sacrifices of the commune." Lyon's contract with a new theater director in 1873 specified that the city would not reimburse him for any destruction to his property that occurred in a riot due to his poor direction.[54]

After mid-century, a variety of systems attempted to formalize the public's intervention. When actors debuted, they often had to win public acclaim in three performances before being given a contract. In some cities, cheering and booing were officially registered by police commissioners, councilmen, or representatives of theater subscribers.[55] Other cities set up a small commission of city councilmen and audience representatives to make the decision after the third performance. In Saint-Etienne, an 1878 regulation allowed the audience to decide an actor's fate by a show of hands during the first two appearances, and by ballot at the third peformance.[56] Such democratic measures never quite succeeded in quelling public outbreaks of enthusiasm or approbation, however, and municipalities continued to contend with popular pressures.

How broadly representative were theater audiences? The contemporary evidence is mixed, and much of the testimony is colored by whether the observation was made by a friend or foe of municipal subventions. Typical of proponents of subsidies was the Marseille councilman who claimed that "the artisans, the people, are the ones who frequent the theater the most." In Lyon at about the same time, a councilman claimed that as a result of an increase in salaries and more of a taste for luxuries, "the workers are increasingly going to the theater," and some were even sitting in the loges. Those on the opposite side argued that the theater audiences were socially circumscribed. In Lyon, Mayor Jean-François Terme described the theater as "the pleasure of a few." In the 1860s, a Bordeaux city councilor stated that the worker who works every day does not go to the theater." A Socialist city councilman in Marseille in 1885 claimed that "workers rarely go to the theater." And even proponents of subsidies claimed that audiences were unrepresentative of the city population; the Marseille historian Fabre noted in the 1840s that 99 percent of the population did not attend the theater.[57]

Yet evidence independent of the debate on the merits of subsidies suggests that audiences were drawn from several social strata. The memoirs of the poet Victor Gelu for the 1820s and 1830s reveal that he went to the theater in Marseille with "clerks, employees, but also artisans, laborers, stevedoers."[58] Proof of lower-class attendance at the theater also comes from contemporaries' complaints. In Toulouse in the 1830s, the theater director lamented that there were only two types of seats—the first occupied by the bourgeois, the second not fit for "the good worker, the honest artisan" to bring his family with him because of "the women of ill repute who occupied them." In the 1860s, a Marseille councilman complained that a working man could not take his family to the cheap third gallery because of the kinds of people who were there, presumably persons below the working class. In Saint-Etienne, however, the subprefect described the theater audience as consisting of "only the middle class and the workers." In the 1850s, a government official, wishing to berate the Lyon worker for wastefulness, wrote that "theater is his favorite pastime."[59]

Audiences in the official provincial theaters seem to have been less homogeneous than the audiences in Paris. In the capital, the classical repertoire performed at the Opéra, the Opéra comique, and the Comédie française seems to have served exclusively the bourgeoisie, while the more popular types of vaudeville, plays, and light musicals were the preserve of artisans and workers.[60] Once non-official, private theaters were allowed after the 1860s, workers favored them, although they never seem to have totally abandoned the official theaters in the provinces.

In Paris, ticket prices made it nearly impossible for workers to attend the official theater. Tickets at the Paris Opéra varied between 16 francs and 2.50 francs in 1860; at the Théâtre français, the most expensive seat was 8 francs, while the cheapest seat was 2 francs. Scalping evidently was common, making tickets even more expensive.[61] In the provinces, tickets were priced more modestly; in 1844, the cost of tickets at the Grand-Théâtre and the Célestins in Lyon ranged from a high of 3 or 4 francs to a low of .60 francs. In later years, while the price of the cheapest tickets remained the same, the most expensive seats increased. At the Grand-Théâtre of Lyon, they had increased to 5 francs by 1855 but had remained unchanged at the Céléstins. At the beginning of the twentieth century, the price of theater tickets (in spite of inflation and increased earnings) was the same in Saint-Etienne as it had been half a century earlier. Prices in Toulouse changed little from mid-century to the end of the century, varying between 3.50 francs to .50 francs, with half price for students. In Marseille, ticket prices were somewhat higher: from 1.50 francs to 4 francs in the 1860s, and 2 francs to 6 francs at the end of the century.[62]

Attending the official theater undoubtedly represented a luxury for workers that could be indulged in only once in a while. The earnings of a worker in Marseille in the 1840s, for instance, was 2.7 francs a day, and in the 1890s, 4 francs a day.[63] Having to pay one-quarter of a day's earnings for a ticket made frequent theater-going difficult, but it was not out of reach for workers. The demand for lower-price tickets was so high—or the number of lower-price tickets was so limited—that in Saint-Etienne in the 1890s, according to one city councilman, they were bought up a year in advance.[64]

While the evidence is not definitive, it seems reasonable to conclude that the middle classes attended the theater in great numbers and with considerable regularity, while a far smaller proportion of workers attended, and with less frequency.

SUBSIDIES

During the ancien régime, municipal theaters were run by private directors who hired their own troupes and were responsible for the programs.

The designation "municipal" meant that the theater was provided with the protection of a monopoly in presenting plays, operas, and classical dance programs, and that it also received municipal subsidies. It was common for French municipalities to provide subsidies; many southern cities did so as early as the sixteenth century, and by the eighteenth century all the cities in this study (except Saint-Etienne, which did not yet have a municipal theater) proffered such assistance.[65]

The Revolution of 1789 brought an end to this practice. The national government provided subsidies to the official theaters in Paris, but it did not provide support to the provincial theaters. Neither did the municipalities. To make ends meet, the Bordeaux theater director rented the hall out as a gambling den during the day and allowed it to serve as a pickup place for prostitutes at night.[66] These were temporary stratagems, eventually banned.

When funding was restored in the nineteenth century, it was done at first on an ad hoc basis. Marseille provided the theater director with a 15,000-franc subsidy to help him pay the rent in 1813; four years later, he received 10,000 francs so he could continue the season. When the director in Bordeaux resigned, his theater indebted by over 100,000 francs, no one would apply for the position. To make it attractive, the city had to provide the theater free rent along with a subvention of 20,000 francs. Marseille's first regular subsidy, planned by the council at the beginning of the theatrical season, was 6,000 francs in 1821; the following year, it doubled the amount. Toulouse also provided a theater subsidy that year, of 12,000 francs. Of course, such sums were modest compared to the Paris Opera, which received subsidies from the national government of 950,000 francs in 1830.[67]

Table 6.1: Theater Subsidies of Five French Municipalities, 1831-1910

	1831	1849	1862	1866	1890	1910
Bordeaux	40,000	96,000	14,400*	234,000	234,000	250,000
Lyon	90,000	19,000	200,000	250,000	250,000	300,000
Marseille	50,000	120,000	200,000*	250,000	150,000	300,000
Toulouse	12,000	51,666	80,000*	87,000	110,000	155,000
Saint-Etienne	—	3,300	20,000	50,000	—	27,000

* In addition, rent on the theater was free.
Source: City budgets.

At first the subsidies were seen as temporary forms of assistance for theaters in difficulty; the sums were listed as "extraordinary expenses." Only gradually did it become clear that these subventions would be necessary on a regular basis, and eventually they fell under the regular budget.

Once started, subsidies grew faster than just about any other budget item (see table 6.1).

When deprived of financial support, theaters usually closed down for a season, but subsidies were no guarantee of success; theater directors followed each other in quick succession, as they either went broke or became discouraged at their prospects. In Marseille, the average term of a director in the 60 years following the opening of the Grand Théâtre was 31 months; in the second half of the nineteenth century, it was 23 months. Toulouse in the first 20 years of the nineteenth century, had eight directors, all of whom became insolvent. Bordeaux in the 25 years between 1822 and 1847 had 17 directors, of whom 15 went into bankruptcy.[68] "Bankruptcy and ruin is the normal end" to a theater director's career, a mid-nineteenth century commentator wrote. And later in the century, the situation apparently remained unchanged. A Marseille author quipped that "bankruptcy is nearly always the last act of the [directors'] play."[69]

The financial difficulties of directors sometimes had dire consequences. One director in Marseille in the 1820s allegedly became so distraught about his 150,000 francs debt that he went mad and had to be interned in the local mad house. In several cities, directors failed to pay their actors, then fled without leaving a forwarding address. In 1914, the Toulouse director, broke after paying all his debts, was reduced to petitioning the city council for a position as a singing teacher in order to make a living.[70] Confirming the financial problems in directing a municipal theater was the low number of candidates seeking to fill a vacant directorship—usually two or three. Luckily for the cities, someone nearly always came along who was confident or foolhardy enough to believe that in spite of the record of his predecessors, he could find the right formula to bring in the audiences and make a profit and pull the theater out of its difficulties.

Costs

Contemporaries had many explanations for the rising cost of the theater, and their analyses seem to coincide with those of drama critics and historians. Low attendance was one main factor. In Lyon in the 1840s, the theater was virtually empty half the week. In Bordeaux, the mayor observed that the theater frequently was three-quarters unoccupied. Low attendance in Marseille also was noted; the journalist Joseph Méry found that in summer his fellow citizens preferred the cool outdoor breezes and that during the winter season only regular subscribers usually attended.[71] In several cities, it was claimed, residents were too busy making money to be interested in the arts. Even in Toulouse, where enthusiasm for the arts was well known, the mayor noted in 1876 that theater attendance was low. In 1910, a Bordeaux newspaper claimed that whereas local audiences once had attended the theater regularly—nearly daily—they now did so only when there was an exceptional performance. That same year, a meeting of municipal officials from major French cities described theaters as decadent, their halls deserted.[72]

Contemporaries cited several reasons for low attendance, among them the lack of variety in the fare.[73] Other forms of entertainment, such as café concerts sprang up to fill the gap and provide competition. Itinerant magicians, rope walkers, and jugglers drew audiences. There were circuses: Lyon had a permanent one, and Marseille had one briefly in 1830. Music halls of various sorts opened in the second half of the century, and by 1914 all of the cities in this study had their own Folie Bergères and Alcazar.[74]

After the 1860s, when private, nonofficial theaters were allowed, they flourished with non-classical repertoires. In Saint-Etienne between 1848 and 1866, a dozen such theaters opened. One show offered living tableaux of such scenes as "Terrestrial paradise," "The massacre of the Innocents," and "The Baptism of Jesus Christ." After the turn of the century, newer forms of entertainment, including film and sports, further undercut the theater.[75] All such offerings provided sharp competition to the official theaters.

Another factor behind rising costs was an increase in actors' salaries. In Paris, their salaries rose between the 1820s and the 1860s by an estimated 70 percent. Major actors and singers commanded substantial salaries. The 1840 contract the Comédie française signed with the actress known as Rachel, specified that she would have a base annual salary of 27,000 francs, with an additional 15,000 francs per performance after her fiftieth. Nourritt, starring at the Paris Opéra, received 30,000 francs in 1830; Naudin was paid 110,000 francs in 1866, while Mme. Geymard received 60,000 frs.[76] The provinces followed the same pattern. A Bordeaux commentator claimed that whereas at the beginning of the nineteenth century a contralto earned 5,000-6,000 francs a year, in 1831 he earned between 12,000 and 18,000 francs. A first ballerina earned, he wrote, 4,000 francs at the beginning of the century, 14,000 francs in 1831.[77] City officials complained; Lyon's mayor noted disapprovingly that "a singer receives a higher salary than a cabinet minister, a dancer than a prefect." In Marseille and Bordeaux, city councilors murmured against "the exaggerated pretensions of the public and the actors." But the public clamored for these stars; a highlight in the history of the Marseille opera was the appearance in 1861 of Adelina Patti, the American singer, who at the time was reputed to be the best paid performer in the world.[78]

Costs also went up as a result of an insistence on lavish stage settings. An emphasis on producing exactitude of scenery and even costumes developed in the 1830s. When Halévy's *La Juive* was produced at the Paris Opéra in 1835, the scenery alone cost 150,000 francs. In Bordeaux, a growing taste for grand opera led audiences to demand "luxury and pomp" in the productions. Once content with hardly any scenery at all, the Bordeaux theater in 1831 produced a season so lavish that expenses for scenery alone often outran the income from ticket sales.[79]

Of less import, but still a factor in the high cost of running theaters, was the combination of regulations and traditions requiring the theater director to provide a large number of free seats for members of the city council, municipal and prefectural administrators, students of the local conservatory, and members of the local and regional press. In Toulouse, approximately 100 seats were free at each show and in Lyon 56. In Bordeaux, the mayor, councilmen, and national officials who were locally posted, along with their families, were guaranteed free seats, and occupied one-quarter of the Grand Théâtre.[80]

Several proposals were made to combat the rising costs. One was to abolish subventions, which, one argument went, only encouraged the actors' high wage demands and the directors' appetite for sumptuous scenery. A city could not implement such a policy in isolation, however, since it feared losing its directors and performing troupes to cities that retained their subsidies. If all cities ended them, however, the problem would be resolved. Marseille in vain petitioned the minister of interior to forbid giving subventions to theaters throughout the realm. In 1877, a Marseille councilman suggested that as a first step toward national abolition, the port city should end its subsidy, but the potential risks prevented adoption of the measure.[81]

Another possible solution was to provide national financing of local theaters. After all, the national government supported theaters in the capital and presumably it could provide similar help to the provinces.[82] But that was a costly proposal to which the national government was distinctly unsympathetic. Not until the twentieth century was it willing to subsidize provincial theaters.

Other initiatives were attempted. At the turn of the century, Mayor Antoine Gailleton of Lyon suggested that the major cities establish a provincial troupe to perform by turns in each sponsoring city. In 1911, under the chairmanship of the Toulouse mayor, large-city mayors met to adopt such a plan but thought it could not be implemented before 1915. By then, of course, more pressing issues dominated the scene. Forty years later, however, such a project succeeded with the founding of the Réunion des théâtres lyriques municipaux.[83] So cities continued to be faced with high bills for their theaters.

CONTROVERSIES

The subvention issue was a subject of intense municipal debate throughout the nineteenth century. Often, dozens of pages of a city council's minutes were devoted to discussions about the city theater. A Marseille councilor complained of the excessive time that he and his colleagues were spending on the question. The topic was so controversial that councilmen during one council session debated whether the measure should be decided by secret ballot or by roll call.[84]

The issue tested liberal city councils, which in gingerly fashion were probing the limits of government intervention. After all, asked a mayor of Lyon, a noted liberal of the July Monarchy, was the theater not a business enterprise like any other which should be exposed to all the risks of success or failure? And 30 years later, a Marseille councilor reminded his colleagues that the rules of political economy indicated that any enterprise that could not support itself did not deserve to survive. But the evidence seemed to be clear: private enterprise could not meet the needs of the arts; hence subsidies were essential.[85]

In spite of the support for liberalism in most city councils until the latter part of the nineteenth century, none found sufficient reason to cancel theater subsidies. If a theater could exist without subsidies, it could do so only by offering a repertoire which, the budget reporter for the Saint-Etienne city council noted, "had a distant relationship with literary works."[86]

The question of theater subsidies helped sharpen the debate over the proper priorities of city councils. A Lyon councilor asked in the revolutionary year 1848, when unemployment was particularly severe and city assistance for the unemployed was insufficient, how the municipality could justify providing a theater subsidy; there were more important things to do with the city's limited funds. But despite the excellence of his argument, the subsidy continued. A left-wing Republican city councilman asked how Marseille could justify spending more on its theater than on schools. Another critic of the subsidy said the money could be better used to lower property taxes affecting the poor or to supply drinking water. Subsidies to the theater were misplaced: "Art is good, but water even better." In the Bordeaux city council, the Republican opposition to the imperial regime pointed out that more was spent in direct and hidden subsidies to the theater than on education. In Lyon, a councilor asked in 1873 whether it was appropriate to provide large theater subsidies "when there are so many poor to relieve."[87]

A clever stratagem introduced as early as the fifteenth century helped assuage some citizens' guilt over the theater subsidies: the theaters paid "poor taxes."[88] A proportion varying between 5 percent and 10 percent of a theater's income went as a subsidy to fund poor houses. With apparent sincerity, supporters of the theaters argued that subsidies allowed them to bring in revenues for the care of the poor. But the income from a theater's poor tax was less than the subsidy that the municipality granted the theater. In Bordeaux and Lyon, though it was surprisingly high, it still represented only two-thirds of the subvention in the 1850s; in Toulouse in the 1890s, it was only 10 percent.[89]

While the theater tax may have given the privileged classes a clearer conscience, the political left attacked the subsidies during most of the nineteenth century. Some left-wing parties upon coming to power experimented with abolishing the subsidy. Lyon's Mayor Gailleton, a Radical with Socialist sympathies, decided to abolish the city subsidy in 1882; but when the season started without opera (the director claimed he could not offer the most expensive part of a regular repertoire without city funds), the opening night performance was interrupted with yells from the audience of "Subvention! Down with Gailleton!" Out in the streets, hostile crowds dispersed only after a cavalry charge, then went on to the mayor's house and yelled insults at him.[90] Soon thereafter Gailleton had to capitulate and restore the subsidy.

A more systematic assault on the theater subsidies came from the Socialists, who by the end of the nineteenth century had gained considerable representation in major cities and in some cases dominated them. In opposition, the Socialists had vigorously attacked the cultural policies of the bourgeois parties that "exclusively benefited the needs of the dominant class" while neglecting those of the working class. The party at a national conference in Lyon committed itself in 1880 to abolishing theater subventions.[91]

Although the Socialists had a clearly spelled-out program toward the theater, few of them abided by it. In Toulouse in the 1890s, the Socialists were in an alliance with the bourgeois Radicals. Some of the more extreme Socialists suggested abolishing the subsidy, but cultural policy was not a sufficiently important issue to break up the political alliance. Appealing to fellow Socialists, Jean Jaurès, a moderate, a lycée professor, and the future leader of the French Socialist party, argued in favor of the subsidy, assuring his comrades that eventually the workers would have access to the theater, so that it was not in the long run a class issue. Furthermore, the theater would improve the taste of the poor, and it was important for all citizens that "the literary glory of the city of Toulouse" be preserved. While a more uncompromising Socialist argued that the city should consider cultural expenditures only after it met its social responsibilities, Jaurès declared, "I do not separate the progress of democracy and socialism from intellectual developments."[92]

In Marseille, the Socialists did not need to compose a policy jointly with bourgeois parties; they controlled the city council for ten years, beginning in 1892. Nevertheless, they had trouble hammering out a consistent subvention policy. Many councilmen made declarations against subventions at a session in 1893. As one declared, "When we cannot fund the schools [or help] the poor, we should not offer a subvention to the theater."[93] But another councilor, concerned about the impression his party might be giving, declared that "we must prove that art and socialism are not incompatible." Eventually the council abolished the subvention, an action that led to mass protests. The municipality reversed its decision within five months. But that was hardly the end of the affair. Four years later, the municipality abolished the subvention a second time. It was prepared for theatergoers' protests and, on the first night after the vote, placed 150 police agents in the theater. They may have averted catastrophe, but could not prevent pandemonium; "an indescribable tumult" broke out in the hall, the historian of the Marseille theater writes. A few days later, the assistant mayor in charge of cultural affairs, who was especially reviled by the public, resigned. Unruly crowds gathered in front of the offices of the prefect, and 2,000 noisy citizens gave vent to their anger under the windows of the mayor's home. The theater had to be closed down; eventually, the council swallowed its pride and restored the subvention.[94]

In Saint-Etienne, the Socialists, who first won control over the municipality in 1888, decided at the turn of the century to put their imprint on the theater. Like their bourgeois predecessors, they thought the theater could be a vehicle to transform the populace. They insisted that the directors give a number of free performances and even specified that there should be "Socialist" plays. But the performances were poorly attended by the very people they were intended for, and the financial difficulties of the directors led them toward the end of each season to hire fewer and fewer accomplished artists and to put on "vulgar" plays. Furthermore, to save money the directors cut out opera, making Saint-Etienne the only major city without a lyrical season. Hoping to improve the quality of the theater and in accordance with their ideological predispositions, the Socialists in 1905 municipalized the theater. The theater now performed Ibsen, a favorite of the Socialists, and the audiences stayed away in droves.

Whereas it had been Saint-Etienne's bourgeois who had spoken of the theater's spiritual values and the Socialists who had opposed subventions in the name of more pressing social concerns, the tables now were reversed. A leading liberal opponent of the Socialist municipality in Saint-Etienne, objecting to municipal support of the theater, declared, "may those who want it pay for it." And another opponent, echoing words that a generation earlier might have been spoken by Socialists, complained, "we do not have the right to expend on such extravagances in the face of the growing needs of welfare, hygiene, the street system, and schools." It was the Socialists who argued in favor of the theater in the name of practicality and culture. A prosperous theater would prevent people from going to nearby Lyon and thus keep spending money within the city limits. Moreover, the workers were in need of "intellectual nourishment. . . . It is anti-democratic and anti-Socialist to be niggardly with subsidies for the theater." The Socialist mayor was willing to envisage a subsidy of 200,000 francs to 300,000 francs a year, which, for Saint-Etienne, was a sizable proportion of the budget.[95] Power thus had prompted Socialists to change their tune; they had come to see cultural activities as a legitimate function of a municipality.

In the face of increasing municipal costs, the proportion of city budgets that the municipal theater absorbed went down during the nineteenth century, and this in part helps explain the reduced tensions that this issue caused. The theater and opera remained visible and proud aspects of the life of a city and its government, and by 1914, when all major parties had had experience in governing, this ceased being an issue of partisan politics and class antagonism. A consensus had developed on the cultural responsibilities of local government.

7

Public Health

*T*he public health of urban dwellers was mainly the responsibility of municipalities. In the ancien régime, some aspects of public health in port cities, especially quarantines, had been administered by royal agents. But after the Revolution, legislation established municipal powers and provided them with authority over public health. During the nineteenth century, city government played an increasingly interventionist role in improving public health.

SANITARY INTERVENTION

In the face of an increasing population and the concomitant growth in the problems of urban sanitation, it became imperative for cities to take a more interventionist role in ensuring public health. Many reformers in the years 1820-40 had seen in the "environment" a cause for the spread of disease. Health studies revealed that mortality rates varied depending on living conditions—people living in wealthy neighborhoods, with broad avenues and plenty of air, sun, water, sewers, and dwellings of sufficient size had longer life spans than the poor, who were deprived of all these amenities.[1]

The cholera epidemic in 1832 underscored the belief that dirt and crowdedness "spontaneously give rise to the most serious illnesses."[2] The outbreak of cholera intensified concerns over public health, but they did not, as many historians agree, mark any radical departure in the field of public health.[3] However, threats of epidemics, which seemed more real after the 1832 cholera outbreak, made public authorities more willing to favor public health needs over the rights of private property. In Lyon, two doctors who had been members of the Public Health Council and were particularly active in promoting public health declared in the 1840s that "in matters of health one must compel men to do that which is useful and avoid that which is harmful. In that regard the inhabitants of a large city have to be treated as minors. . . . if sanitation had not been legislated, it would never have existed."[4] Regulatory bodies were needed to enforce standards of public health. Beginning in 1802, Paris had an advisory standing health council; it served as a model for similar bodies established in the provinces. Lyon and Marseille each founded one in 1822, and Bordeaux in 1831, apparently under the threat of the impending cholera epidemic that had already hit eastern Europe. While the councils were empowered to give advice, the authority of these groups was limited; often, city administrations were not receptive to unsolicited sanitary advice. Frequently the councils favored property owners and were reluctant to impose strict demands on them. The Lyon council in 1824 declared its responsibility to be the conciliation of public health with "respect for the sacred rights of property owners."[5]

In addition to city health commissions, there were departmental ones. But they also had limited authority. The careful and well-considered advice the health committee of the Gironde gave Bordeaux regarding water supply and sewage in the 1830s was blithely ignored by the municipality. In 1849, health commissions were made mandatory for all departments, but they also had limited authority. Like the city councils, they were only advisory organs. Several factors, including their miniscule budgets, circumscribed their activities. While the commissions were required to publish their reports, few of them did so regularly. Typically they did no on-site inspections but made decisions based on examinations of files. No inspectors were available to enforce health rules; in the department of the Gironde, for example, it was 1871 before the first inspector was hired.[6] The councils exercised their responsibilities in the whole department and only occasionally dealt with urban affairs, thus playing but a minor role in securing public health in cities.

In the 1880s, hygienists became a well-organized group, and their concerns about the dangers to public health began to receive a better hearing. Under their pressure, Parliament in 1902 passed a public health law which included the requirement that every city with a population greater than 20,000 have a bureau of hygiene, endowed with increased powers.

Many municipalities did not wait for the 1902 law to establish bureaus of hygiene. Inspired by the example of Turin and Brussels, Le Havre, under the reform-minded Mayor Jules Siegfried, established such a council in 1879. Saint-Etienne in 1884, Toulouse in 1889, Lyon and Bordeaux in 1890, and Marseille in 1893 followed suit. The bureaus were not equally successful: Toulouse's ceased functioning within a few months of its creation, and Bordeaux's folded three years later, and neither was reestablished until the national law of 1902 made them mandatory. When the national law of 1902 required a bureau, the Toulouse city fathers tarried in establishing it, and it was 1907 before one started functioning. Bordeaux's did not operate according to law; its director was supposed to be approved by the national commission of public health, but such approval was not sought until the 1930s.[7]

By midcentury, grabage pickup became a municipal responsibililty. In the 1910s, Bordeaux motorized the service. (Reproduced with the kind permission of Michel Suffran, Bordeaux.)

The section of the 1902 law requiring cities that had higher-than-average mortality rates to take corrective measures was not enforced by the national government. All the cities in this study, except Lyon, suffered death rates higher than the national average for cities with more than 100,000 inhabitants, yet there was no effective intervention to correct the situation.[8]

Cities in compliance with the 1902 law, in having mortality rates below the national average, escaped close scrutiny. If the average for the city met national standards, central authorities could not intervene on behalf of less favored neighborhoods with higher mortality rates.

In the field of public health regulation, municipalities played a modest role. But they ameliorated and expanded services to improve public health, such as the supply of water and the removal of waste. As a result of increased activism, municipalities made their cities cleaner and healthier. While it is hard to calculate the direct impact that sanitary policies had on mortality rates, they contributed to a decline toward the end of the era in our study.

IMPROVING URBAN WATER SUPPLIES

The growing concern after the late eighteenth century about the impact of the environment on public health led to a growing awareness of the need for cleaner cities. A Lyon physician noted that dirty and unsanitary conditions in poor neighborhoods led to greater disease there than in other neighborhoods. Bad odors were identified with "bad air," which was thought to exude "malignant exhalations." Beginning in the 1830s, physicians suggested that cities rid themselves of these dangers by cleaning the streets with plenty of running water and letting fresh air circulate.[9] Although the disease's etiology was unknown, the cholera epidemic in 1832, and a less dramatic but equally lethal outbreak of typhoid fever, had medical experts preaching the value of providing large water supplies. Lack of water, two Lyonnais pamphleteers wrote in the 1830s, led the working class to be dirty and unhealthy. "Abundant water," a city councilor declared, "strongly contributes to the health and adornment of a city."[10]

The problem of water supply was constant throughout the nineteenth century as populations grew, industrial needs developed, and a new attitude toward public and personal hygiene developed. At the beginning of the century, a city's water came from private and public wells and fountains. The amount and the quality of water available were drastically below standards that a later age would consider minimal. Improvement in the quality and quantity of water ameliorated both inhabitants' comfort and health. More water meant cleaner streets, better flushing of sewers, cleaner dwellings, and—toward the end of the century—improved personal hygiene.

In the early part of the nineteenth century, water was brought into the home by people who carried it themselves, or who had their servants carry it from the nearest well or pump. Some residents bought it from water-carriers, who were common sights in cities such as Toulouse in the 1810s; "robust men, with a leather hat on their head, yelling with all their strength "Aïgo! Aïgo!"[11]

Most water was drawn from public sources: city wells and fountains. At the end of the eighteenth century, Lyon's water supply came from 90 public fountains, 200 cisterns, and 2,000 wells. These sources, it was estimated, provided only ten liters of water per inhabitant daily. A decline in the water supply and population growth led to a drop in the per-capita supply; by 1833, Lyon's public fountains were thought to supply only 1.33 liters per inhabitant.[12] In Bordeaux in 1806, the amount of public water available was 3.5 liters per inhabitant—a quantity that had not been improved on by 1841. Such a small amount hardly met personal consumption needs. The city engineer noted that many citizens, short of clean water, had resorted to bathing in nearby swamps and were "dressed in clothing infected with the smell of the marsh." Some bathers, risking the current of the Garonne, drowned.[13]

The supply of water was so low that cities could not successfully withstand drought and other emergencies. Marseille was particularly hard hit in 1834. People dug desperately, hoping in vain to find new water supplies. The few fountains that had not yet run dry and the Huveau stream were besieged by such unruly crowds that the police had to keep them in line. The little water that was drawn was hoarded, every drop "considered as precious as wine."[14]

Saint-Etienne had far too few public fountains: only one at the beginning of the nineteenth century, three as late as 1827. Water was available from private wells and directly from the Furan and Furet rivers. But their regular supply was no more than 40 liters per person, and in the drought of 1834 they provided but 15 liters per person. They were also polluted, though the water was potable. Saint-Etienne actually had the highest quantity per person of the five cities in this study, for it still had a small population.[15] With increased population this advantage disappeared.

The quality of the water in the cities was also frequently poor. Wells often were not protected from contamination from cesspools or foreign objects. Lyonnais in one neighborhood complained of finding in "said well huge dead rats coming from the canal" and latrines washing into the wells "so that a month later it smells of rotten water." An investigation in 1840 showed that a canal in which butchers threw the remains of dead animals leaked directly into Lyon's city wells.[16]

In the first three decades of the century, cities felt little responsibility to provide more and better water. Costs were a major stumbling block. Bordeaux was reluctant to indebt itself. Since 1809, it had considered a plan to bring more water to the city but felt it could not find the quarter-million francs needed.[17] Lyon contemplated improving its water supply in the 1820s but was discouraged by the cost. It considered a plan costing 180,000 francs yearly, but also felt it could not afford the outlay, while at the same time it built a four-million-franc theater.[18]

Toulouse took measures only after a councilman left the city 50,000 francs in his will on the understanding that it would be used to facilitate water distribution or be forfeited. Most of the cities in this study were on major rivers, and it is puzzling why they found it so difficult to tap nearby sources. A possible model for the use of locally available water was developed in Toulouse, partly thanks to the 50,000-franc bequest. Inspired by the example of Paris and cities in Britain, Toulouse built a pump in the 1820s to distribute filtered water from the Garonne River; the total cost was a million francs. An unsuspected advantage of the city's sand filter was to provide water free of bacteria. Downriver, Bordeaux could not repeat the experience, for by the time the Garonne reached the port it had collected so much silt that Toulouse's technique would not work there. Lyon, as a contemporary remarked, should have been able to resolve its water supply problem, since it sat on not one but two major rivers. The Sâone was too muddy, but the Rhône was a good source, and a pumping station, installed on it in 1832, provided water to 37 fountains, though the flow was weak and the water unfiltered. Saint-Etienne built 22 more fountains for a total of 25 in 1827, but that was still a modest number for a population of 40,000.[19]

The July Monarchy

Industrialization made local political elites aware that time was money. Two of the leading Lyonnais public health officials, eager to appeal to them, argued that supplying homes with water would save people interminable hours that could be used for working.[20] Water of course also had direct industrial uses; it operated steam engines in Marseille in the 1830s and was used in various industrial processes.

Industrialization also made water projects more feasible, for changes in manufacture drastically reduced the price of cast iron pipe, making it twice as cheap in 1825 as it had been at the end of the eighteenth century and four times cheaper still by 1850.[21]

Reduced costs made it easier to finance the increased amount of water that public health proponents were demanding. Water was no longer viewed as a luxury. The Marseille Mayor, Max Consolat, told his council in 1837 that an adequate water supply was "a question of life or death . . . whatever it costs . . ." A few years later, the mayor of Bordeaux declared that bringing more water to the city was the most important issue the city faced. In Lyon, it was reported that the citizens were demanding that all neighborhoods be equally supplied with water. No longer was it viewed as an investment of less importance than the city theater. Cities that had seen dramatic growth began to realize that it would continue and that they had to supply water for a burgeoning population. The Parisian water engineer hired by Bordeaux told the city it had not only to take care of its present needs but also plan for future city growth and the development of industry, which would be requiring additional water sources.[22]

The examples of other cities often crowded the minds of municipal officials, who were remarkably well informed about accomplishments in France and abroad. Toulouse had installed its water-pumping system inspired by similar systems in Paris and British cities. When Lyon's mayor, Dr. Jean-François Terme, the first of a long line of medical men who played leading roles in the city, proposed building an ambitious water system, he cited not only the examples of Paris, Toulouse, and various British cities but also Genoa, Philadelphia, and Rome. Bordeaux's mayor pointed to projects in Marseille and Paris, and noted that even third-rate cities—much to Bordeaux's shame—were forging ahead in supplying themselves with water.[23] A recent historian of French public health has argued that Lyon's progress was due to its medical doctors, who also occupied important political posts.[24] While they were important in Lyon's sanitation policies, similar reforms were adopted in other cities without the active participation of medical doctors in local municipal councils.

Estimates of how much water each inhabitant needed were quite low; until the 1840s, 20 liters was considered more than sufficient. Toulouse's new water system provided 80 liters per inhabitant, far more than other cities; Paris in the 1830s only provided 7.5 liters per person. Dijon had the record before mid-century, with 240 liters per inhabitant in 1839, a superabundant amount at the time.[25]

In the 1840s, city residents began to expect much higher water supplies. A prominent member of the Corps des Ponts et chaussées, the state-run engineering corps, argued that large cities such as Lyon should supply 80 liters per person a day to ensure "satisfactory conditions of hygiene." That was double what the city council had suggested a few years earlier. Cities succumbed to what a Brussels newspaper called "a water mania" and the 1840s saw the laying of foundations for ambitious water projects.[26]

In Lyon, the city council, after lengthy debates on extending the water sources and improving water quality, decided on a plan of action in 1846. But these efforts were interrupted by the revolution of 1848, and it was under the authoritarian prefect Claude Vaïse that a new water system was finally installed with a filtering station on the Rhône, upriver from the city.[27] Bordeaux floated a four-million-franc-loan in 1842 to build an aqueduct from the Taillan stream to the city, though complications delayed its construction until the 1850s. Marseille embarked on the most ambitious project; the cost of its aqueduct from the Durance River, originally projected to cost 10 million francs, rose to 26 million francs before it was finished in 1849. The canal was 87 kilometers long, 9.40 meters wide, and 2.40 meters deep—an astounding project for that era. When the Durance waters reached Marseille, the city for the first time gained a reliable water supply. This feat belongs to the municipality that initiated the project and saw it to a successful conclusion.

The Second Empire and Beyond

While a flurry of activity occurred during the Second Empire, many of its water schemes represented the completion of projects that had been proposed or started earlier. That was the case in Lyon, Bordeaux, and Marseille. Saint-Etienne's damming of the Furan River had not been considered earlier, however, and the credit for this four-million-franc project belongs to the Second Empire.

Although the projects of the 1840s through the 1860s led to the provision of more water per inhabitant-Bordeaux in the 1860s enjoyed 100 liters per person a day, Saint-Etienne 139 liters-these projects failed to solve water distribution problems. Population growth around mid-century quickly wiped out the progress that had been made. Toulouse's population doubled after the 1820s and suddenly the 80 liters per inhabitant disappeared; it was half that by 1856. New neighborhoods had sprung up, and they lacked water.[28]

The Second Empire had trouble keeping up with the dramatic population growth, but even when the growth rate slowed, water supplies proved inadequate. In all our cities, there were complaints that there was insufficient water to clean the streets, and in summertime water often was reduced to a trickle. While Marseille still had an ample supply, it was polluted, entering the city in open canals.[29]

While the French seemed averse to bathing, the practice gained adherents in the 1880s. As a result of medical findings showing that cleanliness discouraged the spread of disease, personal cleanliness was understood as no longer a private matter but one of general public concern, and it was advocated by doctors and reformers. As the habit spread, a Bordeaux city commission noted "The public gets quickly habituated to its new comforts, and a measure which in the past it greeted as enormous progress, it now sees as lagging behind its desires. . . ." Whereas around 1860 the amount of water needed per person generally had been thought to be 60 liters a day, after the 1880s it was more like 1,000 liters, and 200 liters was certainly the minimum. In Toulouse, water-supply experts and the city council agreed that a minimum of 300 liters per inhabitant was desirable.[30] In the last two decades of the nineteenth century, a new spurt in water supplies occurred. Bordeaux undertook new water projects to meet the city's added needs. Only now, as an historian has remarked, did Bordeaux have the water supply that its location had denied it.[31] But this project was barely finished when this amount was seen as insufficient. In Lyon, the daily supply went from 117 liters per person in the late 1870s to 188 liters by the turn of the century, so that the city was finally able to supply each resident as much water as the Romans had supplied.[32] By 1912, it was supplying 304 liters per person. Marseille extended its water supplies beginning in the 1890s, and by 1908 the city was providing 2,300 liters per person. Saint-Etienne envisioned an ambitious aqueduct from the Lignon River. One problem after another caused delays, however, and the project was not built until after World War II.[33] Toulouse expanded its water supply to 265 liters per person by 1902.

While municipalities increased the amount of water coming into the city, the amount did not always keep up with population (see Table 7.1).

Table 7.1: Water Supply in selected French cities, 1892–1908
(in Liters per Person per Day)

	1892	1902	1908
Bordeaux	218	175	490
Lyon	116	188	183
Marseille	765	—	2300
Saint-Etienne	210	207	185
Toulouse	100	265	268

Source: A. Debauve and Edouard Imbeaux, *Assainissement des villes, distribution d'eau,* 2 (Paris: H. Dunod & E. Pinat, 1906), 11-12; André Chantemesse & E. Mosny, *Hygiène générale des villes* (Paris: Baillière, 1906).

A study in 1892 showed that the 12 million inhabitants of France's 691 cities with populations over 10,000 enjoyed a per-capita daily supply of 111 liters, an average far below that for the cities in this study (except Toulouse). And international comparisons in the early twentieth century also showed these cities to be competitive: Berlin provided 113 liters per capita, Munich 150, San Francisco 328, and New York 522. Philadelphia, the largest American city with the most water per inhabitant—1,030 liters—supplied half as much per person as Marseille did in 1903.[34]

Until the 1880s, municipalities were mainly concerned with the quantity of water available; only thereafter did quality gain equal importance. By the 1880s, it was generally known that infected water supplies were the cause of the spread of cholera and typhoid, especially the latter.[35] Increased supplies of water allowed cities to be free from urban wells, which often were polluted. When new freshwater supplies were brought to Bordeaux in 1888, the typhoid death rate dropped from seven in 10,000 in 1886-87 to four in 10,000 the following year. After Lyon forbade the use of well water in 1890, it became one of the three cities in France with populations over 100,000 having the lowest typhoid rate.[36]

The Central Government

Jean-Pierre Goubert has argued that France expanded water supplies during authoritarian regimes, while it was lax under more liberal ones. The record for the five cities does not show such a pattern. The July Monarchy, more liberal than the Restoration, certainly was a greater era of water expansion than its predecessor. And while projects were built under the Second Empire, many had been initiated by the earlier regime. Whereas the total supply of water available for each city increased under the Second Empire, judged by criteria such as the amount available per person and in some cases quality, one could argue there was some deterioration under the authoritarian regime. Goubert also suggests that the central government was more enlightened than municipalities on water policy, pushing reluctant local governments to expand their water systems. That may sometimes have been the case, but most of the initiative came from the municipalities themselves. In the first half of the nineteenth century, the most spectacular provincial water project was in Marseille, and that was a local accomplishment. There were even times when the central government blocked a city's efforts to increase its water supply. Toulouse's effort in the 1890s, for example, was delayed by a national administration hostile to the local Radicals.[37]

Indifference on the part of the central government regarding the water question may be surmised by its failure to collect information on supply and quality. No ministry coordinated such information; instead it was scattered among the ministries of finance, interior, agriculture, and commerce. As a commentator noted at the time, countries far better known than France for their decentralized traditions, such as Britain, Germany, and the United States, had centralized information on water supplies.[38]

The large provincial cities recognized their continuing obligations to supply water for citizens, and provided amounts beyond the national or even the urban norm. And they did so without national coercion or intervention; most water projects were locally developed. In cases in which prefects played prominent roles, they were carrying out local initiatives. Where some municipalities lagged was in water quality. In 1902, the national government passed a law requiring every commune to have safe drinking water. Toulouse began to comply only in 1905, and in 1921 it still had done so incompletely.[39] Marseille had a higher typhoid incidence than other large cities, and only after four years of debate and threats from the national government did it install a filter system to purify the water.[40] Luckily it was not revisited by a cholera epidemic, such as the one that had hit it in 1884.

DISTRIBUTION

When nineteenth-century cities thought of their responsibility to supply water, it was usually in terms of feeding a central fountain from which citizens could draw their water. In the 1820s, Toulouse distributed water from the Garonne to 91 fountains across the city; houses in all but two neighborhoods were within 200 meters of a fountain, or about a three-minute walk. In Bordeaux in the 1860s, no house was more than 300 meters from the nearest fountain.[41]

The possibility of piping water directly into homes was considered early on. Toulouse offered homeowners piped water in the 1820s, but few opted for this choice since it cost money and the water at the fountain was free. Lyon started talking about piping water into homes in the 1840s; Bordeaux actually started piping after 1857. In Saint-Etienne, piping water into homes was suggested as early as 1851.[42]

When Lyon went through urban renewal in the 1850s, it piped water into the apartments in new luxury buildings erected on the Rue Impériale. The irony, as two Lyon hygienists pointed out, was that the rich who lived on the street had servants who could bring them all the water they needed, while the poorer people living elsewhere had less immediate access to water; barely 200 out of 10,000 houses had running water.[43]

There was resistance to bringing water into every dwelling. The cost had to be paid by the owner. Installing water in existing houses also meant piercing walls and floors, and many proprietors were reluctant to take on these additional costs.

Running water in homes was exceptional; in 1892, less than half the 691 French cities with populations over 10,000 had water running into residences. And in those that did, houses with running water were always a minority. In Paris, 58 percent of the houses had running water in 1882, whereas in Bordeaux only a third of the buildings (9,716 of 28,363) had running water. In Lyon in the 1880s, of 16,000 houses, two-thirds were not connected to piped water; of 150,000 apartments, only 20,000 were served with water. In Marseille, only a quarter of the households enjoyed piped water by 1895.[44] In nearby Saint-Etienne, a law was passed in 1906 requiring every floor (but not necessarily every apartment) in newly built houses to have running water. Still, that did not affect most of the housing, which antedated the law; by 1914, only half the houses had piped water.[45]

The cities in this study made substantial progress over the nineteenth century in supplying water to most of their inhabitants. A telling development occurred in the provision of water fountains. While city fountains also existed, in the words of the Bordeaux public works director in 1841, "for the ornamentation of public squares," their main role until mid-century was to supply water for neighborhood residents and for street cleaning.[46] By the end of the nineteenth century, fountains no longer served such practical purposes; rather, they were erected for purely aesthetic reasons, the spectacular *Monument to the Girondins* in Bordeaux and Bartholdi's *The Saône and its Tributaries* in Lyon being prime examples. They are testimony to the fact that these French cities and their water-supply systems were no longer submerged in the ancien régime. The quantity had significantly improved, and while there were still problems with the quality, some of the cities had also made important strides in assuring a cleaner and healthier water supply.

Increased water had an impact on waste disposal. As more water became available, more dirt could be washed away, but also more sewers were built to drain increased effluent away from the city.

WASTE DISPOSAL

Before the eighteenth century, human waste had a variety of uses within the city. Human fertilizer was prized by gardeners within the city and by farmers on its outskirts. It also had industrial uses: for curing leather and dyeing cloth, for instance. By the mid-eighteenth century, however, some of the most polluting industries had moved to smaller cities or even to the countryside. Chemicals replaced human and animal waste in dyeing processes.[47] So waste became less useful and cities found fewer reasons to retain it and became, instead, interested in its disposal.

By the early nineteenth century, there was a strong medical consensus as to the unhealthiness of waste in the city. Medical experts and reformers, believing diseases were spread by stagnant water, filth, and bad odors, recommended the building of storm sewers; leveling of streets; digging of cesspools; and removal of industrial, animal, and human debris from the city. A series of studies by medical practitioners and others in the 1830s and 1840s revealed possible connections between dirty and unhealthy neighborhoods and high mortality rates, the best known being Louis René Villermé's *Tableau de l'état physique moral des ouvriers* (1840).[48]

Complaints began to grow regarding the stench of cities; such complaints reflected the changing attitudes toward dirt of all kinds since the eighteenth century. The French were becoming increasingly intolerant of bad smells, seeing them not only as denoting a lack of refinement but also suggesting possible disease. The Mayor of Toulouse and a public health official spoke of "unhealthy smells," seeing them as carriers of disease.[49]

For many, the relationship between dirt, bad odors, and disease was not in doubt. After cholera struck, municipal officials, seeing dirt as a major cause for the epidemic, decided to clean up their cities. Cleanliness, as the Marseille mayor was to note, was "the best protection." In an influential article, published half a century ago, Erwin Ackerknecht argued that those insisting on the environmental causes of cholera—the "anti-contagionists"—were economic liberals, driven by a desire to avoid quarantines and allow free trade to prosper. But if that were true, then Marseille's campaign against cholera would have differed from cities less dependent upon outside trade. But that was not the case. While the argument between contagionists and anti-contagionists raged in all our cities, the balance in Marseille appears as elsewhere to have been in favor of the latter.[50]

The 1832 cholera epidemic, which killed 102,000 French people, was blamed on the prevalence of dirt in streets and dwellings.[51] Among the five cities, Marseille was worst hit by the cholera epidemic. The first attack, in 1832, caused 865 deaths there. A second attack followed in 1834, when people fleeing from nearby Toulon brought it with them. Half the population of Marseille in turn fled, but 2,189 Marseillais died in July and August 1835. Bordeaux lost 344 citizens in 1832, while Lyon reported only four. While deaths in the provincial cities were modest compared with Paris, the epidemic spurred efforts all over Europe to control the disposal of human waste.[52] The increased fear of the possibly unhealthy nature of various forms of urban refuse, combined with changes in its economic utility, made municipalities more eager to manage and evacuate it.

The disposal of waste represented a series of intricate problems for French cities in the nineteenth century. For convenience, one might distinguish three products that had to be removed from the city: garbage, rainwater, and human excrement. Very often, however, these three were not conveniently separate: garbage, muddy water, and human waste were often intermingled on streets. In 1805, the Toulouse mayor described the *boues*, or mud, heaped along house walls and into the streets as consisting of "kitchen scraps," "the waste of the house," and the "excrement that every individual accumulates in his habitat."[53] It was not until the 1840s that people began to differentiate these elements.

Garbage pickup

Garbage contributed significantly to the city waste problems. As from time immemorial, people commonly threw their trash on the street, and in their attempts to regulate cleanliness, cities met with as little success as they had for centuries. In Marseille, the city put up signs prohibiting the dumping of trash on the street, but to no avail; a municipal councilor suggested that the city forego the expense since the signs were neither obeyed nor enforced. As late as the turn of the century, Marseillais continued to heap their garbage at curbs, or against house walls. The less conscientious flung their garbage out the window; "many of our streets until late in the morning and again in the evening are transformed into real garbage dumps and dunghills," an authoritative study remarked.[54]

Cities did not take responsibility for removing garbage; it was left to the private sector. In Lyon, for instance, it was estimated in 1802 that a thousand people made their living picking up the city's waste and selling it for fertilizer or other uses. The most common garbage removers were the ragpickers, who typically rummaged through the refuse for valuables but left the rest behind.[55]

To ensure a more thorough pickup of city waste, monopoly responsibility was given to private companies, which paid fees to the city for the right to haul away all the garbage, thereby cutting out the ragpickers and other gleaners. Under this system, waste materials were perceived as an asset. Rags made paper, for example, and bones made glue. Toulouse had such a system in place as early as 1740; in 1819, it received 10,551 francs for this monopoly. Lyon, with a much larger supply of waste, received thrice that amount. Saint-Etienne, still a small town, provided such an unprofitable source in 1811 that it had trouble finding an entrepreneur willing to pay 20 francs for the monopoly.

Garbage collection eventually became unprofitable almost everywhere. The increasingly variegated nature of the refuse, along with the development of other sources for making fertilizer, paper, and glue, led to a decline in its value. Entrepreneurs, rather than paying for the privilege of picking up waste, now were paid by the city. By mid-century, Bordeaux and Marseille paid entrepreneurs to collect the garbage.[56] Less as a result of a conscious policy decision and more because of changing market conditions, garbage pickup became a municipal responsibility. For years assigned to the private sector, it became around mid-century a public charge.

Cities were slow to adopt trash cans. As late as the 1880s, garbage in Bordeaux, especially in the working-class neighborhoods, was stored along sidewalks and houses to be shoveled up by garbage collectors into horse-drawn carts. In 1859, Saint-Etienne provided a can in which people were expected to deposit their trash, but the rules were not followed and had to be reissued repeatedly. The city legislated a standard-size garbage can with a lid in 1906. In 1856, Lyon passed a law stipulating that residents use trash cans holding 45 liters and made of canvas or wood; in 1878, the requirement became mandatory and stipulated a container of 50 liters. The example of Lyon was widely admired and appears to have influenced the introduction of the standard trash can in Paris by the Prefect of the Seine, Eugène Poubelle, in 1884. In fact, as early as the 1860s, the Lyon administration was offering suggestions and models for trash removal to the capital, an example of a provincial city inspiring Paris. In Toulouse, the first Socialist Mayor, Albert Bedouce, introduced a standard-size metal can in 1906. Like Parisians who had named the trash can Poubelle, so Toulousains affectionately named theirs the Bedoucette. On its regular round, the Toulouse city trash service would pick up the can with its contents, leave a clean one behind, empty and clean out the old one, and then on the next round, return it. Toulouse was the first French city to have such a system.[57]

In Marseille on the eve of the upcoming International Colonial Exposition of 1906, a councilor suggested that the city make trash cans mandatory, but the proposal was buried in committee. Not until 1913 was the garbage can used in Marseille and then experimentally in the fancy Avenue de la République neighborhood.[58]

Street-sweeping was considered the responsibility of city inhabitants until mid-century; property owners were expected to sweep the streets in front of their homes or businesses. The cholera epidemic of 1832 led the Toulouse mayor to issue reminders to do so; but the habit seems to have lasted only as long as the emergency, for in 1854, when another cholera epidemic threatened, the local Conseil de salubrité had to remind the municipality to have the streets regularly swept. In Lyon, a law passed in 1855 allowed residents to pay fees to the city and ignore the street-cleaning obligation. Since only a third paid the fee, cleaning the rest of the city still depended on property owners' sense of cleanliness and responsibility, which never was very high. In the 1870s, the city moved to take on this responsibility itself; it hired a private street-cleaning company.[59] In Saint-Etienne, the chronology of events was quite similar. In Marseille in 1872, the city council was still debating whether to reinstitute the law requiring property owners to sweep in front of their houses; the proposal was defeated by the mayor's tie-breaking vote. In Toulouse, the law requiring property owners to sweep appears to have fallen into disuse sometime in the 1870s; after the turn of the century, the mayor decided that "this responsibility belongs to the municipal service."[60]

Cities began barring animals at various times over the century. After the 1830s, slaughterhouses were moved to the peripheries. Saint-Etienne lagged behind; in the 1840s, it still commonly had homes right next to butcheries and slaughterhouses, and residents had to endure rotting heaps of entrails and carcasses that were kept around "far too long."[61] In 1833, Marseille forbade the moving of goats through the city; in 1868, it barred the moving of chickens, ducks, geese, or other animals that might dirty the streets. In 1853, it forbade the keeping of animals altogether.[62] But these prohibitions clearly were not enforced, for in 1884, when yet another cholera epidemic hit the Mediterranean port, its council forbade raising rabbits, pigs, goats, pigeons, and all kinds of poultry. In Bordeaux in 1884, 1,000 houses contained chickens and pigeons. In Saint-Etienne as late as 1900 the departmental health commission allowed a pork farmer to establish his sties in the center of the city as long as he maintained no more than 28 pigs. In 1906, farm animals were still allowed in city limits as long as they were kept in stables, as city regulations required.[63]

If the number of farm animals dropped in most cities, the number of horses remained large; they not only were used for private transportation but they also powered the growing public transport system. Horses in the streets of major cities numbered in the tens of thousands; Paris had 80,000 horses in 1880, Marseille 15,000 horses in 1896.[64] These animals contributed their share to the filth that accumulated on city streets.

While trash removal was by no means perfected by the end of our period, there was less of it strewn along the streets. More was collected, and it was better sealed in trash cans. Such changes probably reduced the amount of flies, a common carrier of the typhoid and the cholera germs, which could live for prolonged periods in refuse.

RAINWATER

Most urban dwellers lived in mud much of the year. The wet surfaces were thought to be unhealthy, exuding "miasmas," or unhealthy vapors. The draining of cities was considered important to public health. Storm sewers—intended for runoff of rainwater and other effluents but not primarily human waste—were rare in French cities; only exclusive neighborhoods usually had them. The first French city to have a complete sewer system was Saint-Etienne, built in 1806. It was a small town with a large river, the Furan, into which the sewer could conveniently run. As it grew from a village to a city, it was able to keep up its sewer building. The other cities in this study had grown quite large before the value of sewers were recognized, and for them providing adequate sewers was a much larger task than for Saint-Etienne.[65] Most rain water simply ran down or off the streets until it found the lowest point, typically the rivers in four cities in this study, and the sea in the case of Marseille.

The cholera epidemic of 1832 appears to have stimulated municipalities to increase their storm sewers. By the end of the 1830s, Toulouse had built sewers for its main thoroughfares, but they barely helped. Streets were in terrible condition, and sidewalks unknown. After a rain, it was common for streets to be inundated; one student's memoirs of Toulouse in the 1830s claims "it happened often that the surprised pedestrian was swimming rather than walking in the middle of certain streets which had been turned into real torrents." Enterprising individuals put down planks and required fee payments for their use; others charged to carry people across puddles piggy-back. That people actually paid for such services suggests that the situations a rainfall could create were indeed dire.[66]

In Bordeaux as in Toulouse after the cholera epidemic of 1832, a few sewers were built, but they were not very effective; during high tide some would back up and inundate the city. Not until the 1860s did the cities try to build a sewer system connecting the existing sewers, adding new ones, and facilitating their smooth operation. The supply of storm sewers remained limited. Although during the Second Empire large sums were expended on storm sewers, as late as 1885 barely a quarter of the streets were equipped with storm sewers; in Lyon and Marseille it was about a third.[67]

HUMAN WASTE

The growing concern about the health risks that dirt and bad smells supposedly posed led municipalities to become involved in the disposal of human waste. For a long time, cities had a laissez-faire attitude and only gradually imposed effective controls. It was common for house dwellers to toss the contents of their nightpots onto the streets. While Bordeaux had forbidden this practice as early as 1585, the law was not enforced. Marseille was notorious for its inhabitants' practice of throwing their waste out the window. The city fathers forbade the practice in 1830; yet in 1844, when a Parisian chambermaid in Paris was arrested for emptying a pot onto the street, she defended her action with the explanation that that was how it was done in her native city of Marseille. And, in fact, as late as 1853, the Mediterranean port still found it necessary to forbid such practices.[68]

Human waste frequently piled up in the streets. In Toulouse, an 1832 report triggered by the cholera epidemic described one neighborhood, the tenth *arrondissement,* whose narrow streets were "veritable latrines." Houses either lacked latrines, requiring people to resort to the street, or contained ones in such terrible condition that they overflowed into the street. Saint-Cyprien, another poor neighborhood, had a "nearly total lack of latrines," which forced the inhabitants to "convert the streets into latrines." A sanitation committee report complained of cesspools that had not been emptied for 18 years. The same year in Bordeaux, a similar health inspection, also triggered by fear of cholera, revealed that "the number of houses without latrines is considerable." Even in many that were equipped, the miserly landlords, not wishing to pay to have them emptied, forbade tenants to use them.[69]

While cities gradually were able to reduce the use of the streets as privies, occasional polluters were harder to control. Marseille evidently was notorious for this practice, for when in the 1860s a delicate city councilman in Saint-Etienne wished to mention it he called it "the same spectacle as was the case in Marseille." At the turn of the century, certain streets in Marseille were still known as places where people went to relieve themselves at night. But obviously there had been changes in popular behavior; half a century earlier, Marseillais would not have required the cover of darkness to fulfill pressing needs.[70]

A Lyon newspaper felt it necessary to suggest that a law be passed against the custom and to urge that public latrines be built over the river. In the 1860s, the city, in an official decree, complained of "the inconvenience to public health and decency" posed by "the great number of people who urinate in the streets and the alleys of houses, against monuments, public buildings, houses. . . ."[71]

Legal ordinances forbidding people from relieving themselves in public were disregarded. In the 1840s in Bordeaux, 200 persons a day were given warnings for relieving themselves in the Jardin public. Angered, some countered that they had been in the habit of so doing for the last 30 years. In Toulouse, an ordinance of 1827, repeated again in 1830, forbade that practice along with the throwing of objects from windows. But the practice was still not totally unknown toward the end of the century, when the local paper described a street as having been converted into a latrine by workers in a nearby factory, soldiers from the local barracks, and "pedestrians in a hurry." The street that was cited was the city's major thoroughfare, the Rue Alsace-Lorraine.[72]

Whether dumped out of windows and doors onto public space or finding its way there more directly, human waste became part of the general urban mud. In a sharply hilly city such as Marseille, waste from the high ground, for instance the Cours Julien area, would flow down into the port where it would join the waste from the ships anchored there, making the harbor "a true chamber pot of the city." It killed the fish, which floated dead on the water's surface. The smells evidently were horrific; a contemporary wrote that while the Marseillais could get used to the smell, strangers "found a stay in our city unbearable." Indeed, after Charles Dickens visited Marseille in 1851, he described the "great harbor full of stagnant water and befouled . . . which in hot weather is dreadful in the last degree." Hippolyte Taine, arriving in Marseille a decade later, remarked that the water in the port was "of an extraordinary colour; it is a reservoir of diluted filth."[73]

Cesspits and Tubs

The municipally approved method of human waste disposal was the cesspit that was emptied from time to time. A team of men would be lowered with ropes into the pit and would, with pails and spades, dig out the matter, then load it up onto a cart and haul it out of the city. It was a job so fraught with danger that the Lyon municipality required a medical doctor and policeman to be present during the process; it forbade men to perform the job when drunk and stipulated that workers had to be provided with ample rope, which had to be well anchored.[74] The process of emptying the pits created such a stench, a Marseille physician wrote, that it affected persons living in the highest apartments even with windows closed; people of "exquisite sensitivity were known to have fainted." Permitted only at night, the job of emptying a pit could take four or five nights—a dramatic event in the life of any neighborhood.[75]

In Paris beginning in the 1820s, pumps were used in cleaning out cesspits; they reduced accident risk and allowed the pit to remain closed during the process. But it was the 1870s before such technology was common in provincial cities. Lyon decreed in 1872 that only the pump method was to be used, but with no entrepreneur willing to take on the task, the rule was a dead letter. Toulouse mostly depended upon cesspools, which after the 1880s were regularly pumped out by a steam-operated pump. While pumps sped up the process, it was still very unpleasant.[76]

Human excrement usually was moved out of a city by a private company, which paid the city for this monopoly. Individual carriers, *gadouarts*, in Toulouse complained about this practice, however, and in 1829 they were given back the right to contract individually with owners of outhouses. Marseille strictly enforced the monopoly; an inhabitant could cart off the contents of his own outhouse only if he was using it to fertilize his own farmland outside the city. The income to Marseille was modest, 263 francs in 1838, but at least the city treasury did not have to pay for the service. In 1841, Bordeaux hired an "inspector of clandestine night soil men" to prevent thefts and enforce the monopoly. Continued thefts led Bordeaux to hire two additional municipal guards in 1847.[77]

A growing alternative to cesspits was tubs. Typically these tubs, having a volume of 250 liters, were removed from outhouses and emptied weekly. Introduced in Paris in 1819, they were later adopted in the provinces. By the 1860s, two-thirds of the 23,000 buildings in Marseille had these *fosses mobiles*. The owner brought the tub to the front of the house, where it was picked up by a yellow cart. These carts, in the words of a local poet, struck "terror" in those sighting them because of their smell.[78]

Most of our cities, however, continued to depend on cesspits. Because of the expense and inconvenience, many property owners found ways to circumvent the need to empty the pits. The cheapest way was to let their contents leak into the subsoil or to connect them to the storm sewers. In the 1860s, laws in Bordeaux, Marseille, and Toulouse forbade such procedures and required impermeable pits. But citizens brazenly ignored the regulations. In Marseille, one third of the buildings had latrines illicitly connected to the storm sewers or flowing directly into the streets, transforming the soil into what a contemporary called "fecal terrain."[79] The Marseille city engineer estimated that his fellow citizens produced 300 cubic meters of human waste each day, while only 90 cubic meters was removed; the difference, he surmised, was disposed of illegally. In Bordeaux, a number of cesspits were leakproof, one medical doctor wrote in 1875, "but too many are not." The situation was no different in Toulouse or Lyon; in the latter the city violated its own rules by connecting the public urinals, when they were established, to the storm sewers.[80] As water use increased, making it necessary to empty cesspits far more often, a new device came to the rescue: the divider. This system became common in Paris and among the cities in this study was first tried in Lyon. The *tinettes filtrés* or *système diviseur,* it was claimed, retained solid waste and let out only liquids, but a study conducted in 1882 in the national hygiene journal, the *Annales d'hygiène publique et de médecine légale,* denounced the device as a fraud. While it slowed down the evacuation of solid wastes, they still ended up in the storm sewers. An investigation of the holding tanks showed them to contain "but papers, remains of all sorts: vegetable matter, broken bottle ends, linen, bones, hair. . . ."[81]

Effluent into the storm sewer thus retained the contents of the cesspools. The sewers, forced to carry foreign matter, were often stopped up and had to be cleaned out. Sewer cleaning was dangerous work. In 1898 in Toulouse, for instance, six workers were nearly asphyxiated and had to be pulled out of the sewer; one died.[82]

As water supplies increased, more water in all cities was used to cleanse the toilets and for personal hygiene. A Bordeaux daily estimated in 1904 that cesspools were filling up "at least ten times faster than before," necessitating monthly emptying.[83] The costs of each emptying also went up because, being far more watery, the contents were worth less to the night soil company. Another reason for the drop in value of human waste was the increasing use of chemical fertilizers. The stratagem of escaping payment for emptying the cesspool by perforating the holding tanks or cesspools and linking them up with the storm sewer or nearby streams continued and probably became more frequent as the cost and frequency of emptying pits went up. A Bordeaux public health physician noted that many houses were able to go without having their pits emptied sometimes for five and more years. A survey of 1885 even mentioned a 20-year period. "A very large number of cesspools are never emptied," a city commission concluded. Of the 28,000 houses in Bordeaux in 1885, 8,000 had impermeable or close to impermeable cesspools, but the rest leaked into the storm sewer system.[84] With time, the proportion of houses following regulations increased; in Bordeaux in 1895, 37.5 percent of the cesspools were regularly emptied as compared to 29 percent in 1885, but there were now still the same number of houses violating the rules (20,000). "If the Bordelais have the reputation of making good wine," a physician remarked, "they don't have one for practicing good hygiene."[85]

In all five cities, the subsoil remained saturated with sewage. As population and water usage increased, the situation worsened; the wells became dangerous sources of infection. An outbreak of typhoid in Lyon was blamed on polluted well water in 1908. A greater sensitivity to the resulting bad smells had also developed. As a Bordeaux newspaper put it, "Our forefathers withstood without complaining these fetid smells. . . . More refined, perhaps equipped with a more delicate smell, we are beginning to revolt against this stink."[86] Something had to be done, and cities were thinking about solutions.

Unitary Sewers

A proper sewage system required plenty of water and large sewer pipes large enough to accommodate both rainwater and human waste. Such a system had been introduced for the first time in modern Europe in London in 1848 (the Romans, of course, had this system centuries earlier). It was termed the unitary system, *tout à l'égout*. The London system served through the rest of the nineteenth century as a model for other European cities. By 1865, 40 British cities had this amenity. Cities in other countries followed: by the 1870s, Berlin, Danzig, and Brussels. French public officials, medical doctors, and public health reformers made constant reference to the experiences of foreign cities when considering sewage disposal. After mid-century, Lyonnais medical authorities considered the London example but dismissed it as unsanitary and as hurtful to agricultural interests that depended upon fertilizer from the city. In January 1873, Lyon sent its city engineer to London to study the city's sewer system, but he learned little after finding to his dismay that none of the officials he contacted spoke French.[87]

The first of the cities in this study to attempt a unitary system of sorts was Saint-Etienne in 1854; it sent human waste into the storm sewers, both closed and open, that emptied into the Furan River. But the ditches and existing sewers were too narrow and inadequate in terms of water flow, and the pipe stopped up. When the water level was low, as was often the case, the waste material lay at the bottom and rotted; in one neighborhood, "nearly all year it was impossible to open any windows that looked onto this sewer." The system appeared to have a negative impact on health conditions; while French citizens had a life expectancy of 36 years, Saint-Etienne's citizens had but 26 at mid-century. Correcting the sewage situation would, it was believed, significantly improve these statistics.

The Saint-Etienne system was unitary, of course, only in the sense that waste and water flowed in the same pipes. It lacked the wide, covered sewers and generous amounts of water that were the hallmark of a truly unitary system. In the late 1860s, Saint-Etienne became the first of the five cities in this study to have a truly unitary system. The measure was made practical by use of the Furan River; the waterway, in the words of a medical doctor, "could be considered as Saint-Etienne's major sewer." This important reform, which brought lengthy battles with agricultural interests in other cities, was accomplished rapidly in Saint-Etienne, which had few farm interests to consider. Yet even in this compact city not all housing was connected to the unitary system. Some sewage still flowed in the open air, and not all the channels were covered; at the end of the century, a third of Saint-Etienne's population was still thought to depend on cesspits.[88]

By 1889, 250 European cities had adopted the unitary system. In France by the early 1880s, Grenoble, Saint-Etienne, and Reims were the only municipalities with citywide systems. Paris did not start building its system until 1894; it cost 117.5 million francs. Foreign example, rather than a Parisian one, was the point of reference of provincial cities wishing to adopt a unitary system.[89]

MARSEILLE

The most spectacular adoption of the unitary system in France was Marseille's. The motivation was provided by the outbreak of cholera in 1884-85, which killed 3,000 persons. The city had always had a high death rate from transmissible diseases, which accounted for about a third of all deaths through the 1880s. Marseille's overall death rate also was dramatic in the 1880s—around 32 per thousand—compared with 22 per thousand for France as a whole. While the death rate was going down in most cities, that was not the case in Marseille; it had been 29.4 per thousand in 1866. Compared with other major French cities, Marseille's record was poor; the average death rate for France's 50 largest cities was 25.6 per thousand. For other cities in this study, it was Bordeaux, 25.4 per thousand; Lyon, 22.2 per thousand; Saint-Etienne, 21.1 per thousand; and Toulouse, 26.3 per thousand.[90]

The Marseille cholera outbreak triggered a national debate. For the contemporary observers there was no doubt about the source of the epidemic. Comparative figures within the city appeared to confirm the linkage between sewage and mortality. Dr. Henri Mireur, assistant mayor and member of the sanitation commission, found that the most exposed neighborhoods, such as the one around city hall by the port with a mortality rate of 47.4 per thousand, lacked sewage facilities—the inhabitants dumped their waste into open streams—while the neighborhood with the lowest mortality, the Port-les-Iles, had its houses linked to a unitary sewer system. While Dr. Mireur recognized there were many other possible causes for differences in mortality, such as crowding, availability of water, and width of streets, the sewage system seemed the crucial factor. He called for the establishment of the unitary system.[91]

In 1883, the German Robert Koch discovered that the *cholera vibrio,* living in the small intestine, was communicated through contact with an infected person's feces, which often spread via drinking water, food or clothing. The purity of drinking water was especially important. Marseille authorities, however, seem not to have been particularly impressed by the need to improve their water quality as a means of fighting the cholera epidemic. Instead the emphasis was on improving sewage disposal; the latter would, of course, indirectly have had an impact on water quality, for leading sewage away from the city reduced the infection of the water supply.

The cholera epidemic was an economic disaster for the port city. 100,000 Marseillais fled the city and fewer people visited it. In 1884, a third fewer passengers arrived by sea, and a sixth fewer left; 3,233 fewer ships, with 1.3 million less tons of cargo, served the port in July-November 1884 than in the same period in 1883.[92] The local chamber of commerce was alarmed at the economic impact and appealed to the government to provide help to clean up the city. The drop in the port's trade hurt not only the city but also the nation, for all ships in and out of Marseille were embargoed.

Given the extensive rail traffic between the port city and the rest of France, the disease also posed a danger to the nation. That was the conclusion of health authorities and the minister of commerce, who visited the city almost immediately after cholera broke out. Prime Minister Charles Freycinet was probably sympathetic to the cause of public health; as a young man he had gone on a tour of Europe studying public health questions. Yet the national government was slow to act; proposals tarried in various ministry offices for nearly two years. And then all the government promised was to pay half the expenses of a sanitation project if it cost less than 600,000 francs—barely a drop in the pipe. For all the denunciation of Marseille's lack of interest in public health and efficiency, the city proved to be far more active than the national government in trying to find a solution.[93]

The economic elite of the city, shocked by the economic repercussions of the cholera epidemic, became concerned; the chamber of commerce weighed in heavily in favor of the unitary system. The city's deputy and assistant mayor Jules Charles-Roux, head of one of the largest shipping companies, tried to enlist the help of the French Parliament to bring in such a system.[94]

But the city engineer, who even before the cholera epidemic had considered putting in new sewers, was opposed to the unitary sewer system. He believed, as did many Parisian experts at the time, that such a system would spread rather than hinder disease by creating "a subterranean sea of filth and excrement." He also saw that it would mean the loss of rich fertilizer and the 410,000 francs it brought into the city each year. Instead, he recommended the Berliet system, which pulled waste through sewers with multiple pumps but without using water.[95] This system had been first tried in Lyon and had been greeted by *Le Temps* as a preferable alternative. But it was not well tested, and in trying to convince the Marseille city council to adopt it, one of its promoters made such exaggerated claims and bribed so many city councilmen that when the shenanigans were revealed, the plan was dead. Several other alternate plans were also considered.[96]

It was not until 1890 that the city council voted to build a unitary system. The vote was heavily in favor, 29 to 3. The city hired the engineer Louis Genis, who had built the Brussels system and was in the process of building the one in Paris. The projected cost was 33.5 million francs, to be paid by a surcharge in taxes imposed upon householders for 50 years. But the revenue collected was far from covering the expenses and in the end the regular city budget was also heavily laden with the financial obligations occasioned by the project. In addition, vast local economic interests were mobilized to invest in a public works company to build the system.[97]

The unitary system became the subject of intense political controversy. Mayor Félix Baret, a moderate Republican who had favored the new system, was faced by vigorous opposition in the 1892 municipal elections from the Socialists. Their candidate Dr. Siméon Flaissières, was running on a platform opposed to the sewer system. The doctor attacked the project not only because of its expense but also because of its threat to public health; it would spread bacteria and disease through the sewers to the whole city.[98] The Socialists won, but they continued the sewer-building program, mainly because the funds had already been voted and they saw it as a way to provide work and extensive patronage—at its height the project employed 3,200 people.[99]

As construction progressed, charges of graft, corruption, collusion, and misappropriations of various sorts were continuous. In 1894-95, a newspaper started up that was solely devoted to publishing a barrage of such charges; in an allusion to the contemporaneous national scandal, it was named *Le Panama Marseillais*.

When building was completed in 1903, the city required all houses to be connected to the new system. But enforcement was a problem, and in 1913 nearly one third of the city, or 10,000 houses, was still not connected.[100] Nonetheless, the general health benefits predicted for unitary systems were reaped in Marseille. Whereas the mortality rate had been 30 per thousand in the 1880s, by 1905 it had fallen to 21.46.

Marseille provided an example to cities, concerned about public health. But it also served as a warning to municipalities interested in adopting a unitary system. The financial outlay had been even larger than anticipated, costing in the end 43 million francs. The expenses had added to the city's debts, making the city very difficult to govern. City councils were so torn apart over how to finance the debt that they often found it difficult to consider other pressing projects.[101]

The other cities in this study also considered adopting the unitary system, but were intimidated by the costs involved. Bordeaux, Lyon, and Toulouse continued with their outdated sewer systems until well after World War II. Not until the 1960s did Toulouse have a unitary system; as late as 1954, only 5 percent of its dwellings had sewer connections, the rest still relied on cesspits. Lyon did not require connection to a unitary sewer until 1961.[102]

If French medical doctors, reformers, and local politicians knew and understood the value of waste evacuation, cities were singularly uninterested in paying for it. The engineer who built the Marseille system explained the limited political advantage accruing to a municipality building a sewer system. Public works above ground could be seen and appreciated, Louis Genis said, but underground and for something as vague as public health, they were perceived as "money buried in the ground and of no direct benefit."[103]

171

But there was a rational calculation involved in resisting the unitary system. Public health officials had vigorously connected the unitary system with declining death rates. But after the turn of the century that did not necessarily hold true. Better water distribution systems, urban renewal projects, and raised standards of living improved mortality statistics for many cities—even those without unitary sewer systems. Belonging to the latter category, Bordeaux and Lyon had mortality rates that were reasonably low—in 1903, 19.12 per thousand and 19.41 per thousand, respectively—and better than the rate in Marseille, which was already partly enjoying the unitary system but yet had a 25.04 per thousand mortality rate; or Saint-Etienne, which did have a unitary system and yet had a 20.72 mortality rate. Toulouse, without having installed the unitary system, cut its mortality rate from 26.17 in 1886 to 22.8 in 1903. Cholera did not return to haunt France after 1884. Typhoid fever, which was seen as particularly prone to spread in cities with poor sanitation, had become less lethal even for cities that had not installed a unitary system (see table 7.2).

Table 7.2: Typhoid Mortality Rates per 100,000 in Selected French Cities, 1886–1903

	1886	1903
Paris	452	193
Lyon*	295	211
Saint-Etienne	287	239
Marseille	1040	407
Toulouse*	802	248
Bordeaux*	620	174

*Cities with no unitary system in 1903.
Source: A. Debeauve & Edouard Imbeaux, *Assainissement des villes-distribution d'eau*, 2 (Paris: H. Dunod & E. Pinat, 1906), 461.

Except for the unpleasant smells issuing from storm sewers, there seemed no pressing reason to change a system that was reasonably acceptable, eschewing the high death rates which had marked earlier decades. These statistics seemed to confirm the conclusion of one of France's leading experts on water and sewers, "the unitary system represents an enormous expense, out of proportion sometimes with the advantages it represents." A generation later, another expert echoed the same view when he described the unitary system as "a luxury [that] can only be applied in rich cities."[104] And that seemed to be an opinion most French city councils subscribed to.

HOUSING

To the public health movement, housing was both a social and a health issue. Many reformers in the years 1820–40 had seen housing conditions as a cause for the spread of disease. Many physicians and reformers suspected that slums were the breeding grounds of various diseases. Dirt not only in streets but also in dwellings was seen as creating miasmas and infecting the inhabitants. Fears of infested slums, reinforced by the trauma of the 1832 cholera epidemic, convinced those interested in public health that housing had to be improved. Bettering the housing of the poor would improve their lives, while also maintaining a city's public health. It was even seen by some as a governmental obligation to ensure that it happened.[105] City governments attempted to regulate housing quality, increasingly intruding in an arena that had been considered a private preserve.

Controlling Housing

The need to control housing quality was very real, given the prevalence of slums, which worsened as cities faced an increasing influx of population. Housing, especially of the poor, was usually wretched. It was commonly dirty and crowded. Dwellings often were bereft of light and without windows; many were dank. The medical reformer Louis Villermé described Lyon's housing in the 1830s as "repulsively dirty." To render the city healthy, half of its housing would have to be destroyed, the official departmental hygiene council concluded at midcentury.[106] In Bordeaux, an inspection in 1884 revealed that 4,000 of the city's 28,000 houses were "unsanitary."[107]

France had a very high tuberculosis rate throughout the century.[108] In 1882, Robert Koch discovered the tuberculosis bacillus. Its breeding ground was recognized to be dark, dank areas, such as those common in slums, and crowding ensured the easy spread of the disease from individual to individual. Koch's findings gave a scientific underpinning to reformers' and physicians' long-standing belief that slums were a source of disease.

As with other contagious diseases, social reformers were able to point to the fact that tuberculosis did not strike only the poor; it could and did also threaten the more fortunate. As one important public health official, Paul Brouardel, Dean of the Paris Medical Faculty, put it, if the tuberculosis bacillus were allowed to "attack our neighbors, we or our family will in our turn be attacked." Or as a study on workers' housing put it, between poor and rich neighborhoods "the distance is quickly crossed." Hence, slums were a matter of concern for the whole community.[109]

In times of emergency, municipalities were sympathetic to medical advice to regulate housing, but otherwise their intervention was limited and episodic. The Bordeaux Academy of Medecine, in an 1817 prize competition, crowned the writer of an essay who forcefully argued for regulation of housing: "The rights of the individual end where those of society start. A civilized society has the right to insist that all its members live in healthy housing and to forbid those projects inspired by monetary interests at the cost of the interests of the majority of the population."[110]

In emergencies, such as the cholera outbreak, the health councils inspected houses and issued recommendations, but they did not impose radical measures. In Lyon, for instance, the public health commission, appointed to combat cholera in 1832, was no longer functioning three years later, when the city had to contend with a return of the epidemic.

The Law of 1850

By the 1840s, a national sense seems to have formed behind the notion that some stronger intervention was necessary. Cities were acknowledged to be centers of disease that led to high death rates. Fears of French degeneration arose; the elite imagined a lower class "degenerated" and reduced to a "bastard race," unable to defend the fatherland in case of war. The trauma of revolution in 1848 inspired the desire for reforms that would ensure social stability—among them the control of housing quality.[111]

Under the influence of these concerns, the National Assembly in 1850 passed a law authorizing municipalities to establish official bodies called *commissions des logements insalubres* (commissions on unhealthy dwellings) to regulate housing quality. In operation, however, the law was disappointing. The commissions could regulate rental, but not owner-occupied, housing. Thus a large proportion of housing was not subject to control. In 1894, for instance, one-fifth of the housing in cities with populations over 100,000 were owner occupied. Another severe restriction was that the commissions could inspect only housing on which it received complaints; it could not initiate inspections. And penalties were light: a commission could fine owners between 16 and 100 francs for a violation, and only a year later, if the improvements stipulated had not been carried out, could it levy a fine equivalent to the cost of the improvements and double the original fine. The law provided careful safeguards for the property owner, including several levels of appeal against commission decisions—all the way, if necessary, to the Conseil d'état. As a Lyonnais reformer complained, "matters could drag on . . . while the tenant was suffering."[112] Furthermore, these commissions were not mandatory; cities could decide not to establish them.

None of the housing commissions of the five cities in this study functioned continuously and regularly in the half-century after 1850. Most of these cities were reluctant to institute a commission. Saint-Etienne refused to establish one, claiming that the city was healthy; the real reason for its resistance was opposition to what it saw as unwarranted government intervention. If a commission on housing quality were established, the municipal council asked, what was to prevent the formation of commissions to ensure that people had "healthy and abundant food, supplies of linen, furniture, fuel, clothes?" Under prefectural pressure, the city finally did establish a housing commission in 1859, but soon thereafter, it went defunct. Toulouse, 30 years after the law's passage, still did not have a commission. Marseille, subsequent to another cholera outbreak, established a housing commission in 1854, but as soon as the danger of disease appeared to be ended, the commission ceased to function. It was reinstituted as a result of prefectural pressure in 1878, only soon to expire again; in 1890, a social reformer described it as "existing only on paper." The Bordeaux commission was not established until 1854, and it too came as a result of prefectural pressure.[113]

When they functioned, these commissions did not take an activist role. In Lyon, the commission members examined few lodgings because of their respect for "the inviolability of the home." Four years after its establishment, the Bordeaux commission had visited only 54 buildings, and it appeared to hesitate to condemn the *hôtels des miracles,* crowded hotels for the poor, because of a supposedly double rationale: concern for the interests of the property owners and over where the displaced poor would find alternative housing.[114]

When weighing the interests of public health versus private property, a critic wrote at the end of the century, the commissions tended to come out on the side of the latter. The Marseille commission, according to a contemporary, only once to his knowledge imposed a fine on a landlord. Throughout most of the nineteenth century, a French legal historian writes, property took priority over dirt ("La propreté a été longtemps victime de la propriété").[115]

Housing commissions had little power to enforce even the limited provisions of the law; after finding a property owner in violation of the code, they also usually often found him reluctant to accept their dictates. Commissions often had to consider and reconsider cases with no tangible results. Property owners sidestepped the law with impunity. "Many property owners promised to make improvements and declared they had, when that was not so," the Bordeaux commission reported. In other cases, the Bordeaux commission limited the number of renters allowed in the *garnis,* the cheap lodging houses, only to have a far larger number accommodated. And there was little that could be done, given the shortage of personnel available for inspection. When violators were caught, the fines were too low to deter lawbreaking. Almost nothing could move a landlord to make improvements. Even under the impact of the cholera epidemic in Marseille in 1884, landlords refused to repair houses which the commission had cited as needing attention.[116]

Members of the housing commissions were volunteers who carried out inspections in their free time and so could not be as active as was necessary. In 1889, one Bordeaux commission member was a hundred files behind in his inspections; many members had not processed complaints that were four or five years old. Even so, the commission apparently became more active in the 1880s than it had been previously. In 1876-82, for example, the commission examined 120 cases a year, whereas between 1884 and 88, the number of cases examined rose to a thousand.[117]

The laws of 1884 and 1902

The law passed in 1884 which spelled out municipal authority including the provision that mayors were in charge of public health, might have been construed to allow them to impose additional standards in housing. But the interpretation of the law restricted mayoral power. After a mayor ordered a landlord to install water in a crowded apartment house, the Conseil d'état struck down the provision in 1885, arguing that supplying water was not a matter of public health but rather a convenience. The Conseil d'état some years later further limited municipal powers by ruling that while a city might indicate that each house ought to have privies, it could not indicate how many, and that while a city could demand that houses have water, it could not state what kind; the method by which a city standard was to be reached was left to the owner.[118]

Localities were usually also in favor of weakening regulations. While public health officials strenuously argued for greater intervention, the general public would have been aghast, a noted hygienist wrote, if a mayor had imposed water or sewage disposal rules on a property owner. Yet, he argued, such measures were necessary: "all civilized countries feel the necessity to protect public health." France, he added, was notoriously lagging in this domain.[119]

The 1902 public health law gave municipalities more extensive powers, and even imposed mandatory standards on them. These powers were particularly useful in controlling housing. No longer was owner-occupied housing immune from inspection; all housing was subject to city control.

Housing deemed dangerous to its inhabitants could be pulled down as under the 1850 law, but now so could housing that represented a health hazard to neighboring dwellings. If housing improvements were ordered and the owner failed to comply, the city could charge the expenses to the owner. A national norm was established: if a commune had a death rate higher than the national average three years in a row, an investigation was mandatory—and so were any housing improvements that might be ordered.

The law had shortcomings, too. Some of the rules hampered the bureaus' effectiveness. For example, the value of slums needing to be expropriated was determined by a commission chosen from among city voters—often property owners who were sympathetic to the slum owners and as a consequence inflated the value of the property. These inflated costs discouraged expropriation and slum clearance. And, rather than being headed by a sanitary expert, the bureaus were chaired by the mayor, who potentially could be swayed by electoral considerations rather than purely sanitary ones. "The municipalities are too afraid of their voters," a legal treatise noted. The limited scope of the national law and the weak way it was enforced both at the national and the local level led Georges Clemenceau to say that "Everyone is attempting to paralyze it."[120]

It was too much to expect that the 1902 law could deal effectively with the accumulated problems of the past. Even in a city such as Lyon, with a municipality headed by Herriot that favored housing inspection, the task was too big. In 1902-1903, only 200 of Lyon's 20,000 houses were inspected; in 1911 complaints regarding 2,000 dwellings were investigated. But the city had only one housing inspector, and it was estimated it would take him ten years to inspect all the housing. Hiring more inspectors was considered financially prohibitive; but maybe that was just a cover for the lack of zeal of which the national director of hygiene had in 1909 complained.[121]

Municipal authorities were well aware of the problems that strict adherence to the housing regulations would bring on; if all substandard housing were suddenly condemned, many residents would find themselves shelterless. In Saint-Etienne, one third to a quarter of the population, it was estimated, would be thrown into the street.[122] Obviously, the law could not be followed blindly. And limited zeal went into enforcing it.

Richard J. Evans, in his monumental *Death in Hamburg,* insists that the public health policy of the German city was not dictated by narrow sanitary interests, but rather reflected general political and ideological currents.[123] Thus the failure of the Hamburg city fathers to take appropriate preventive measures against cholera is seen as reflective of their narrow oligarchical interests and their devotion to liberal ideology. Only after Hamburg was devastated by the cholera epidemic of 1892, which killed 8,600 inhabitants, did the city senate take the appropriate sanitary action and adopt a central filtered water system.

Among our cities, Marseille was the hardest hit by cholera in 1884. While the city fathers had done little to avert the epidemic, once it struck, its business and political elite championed government intervention even though it violated their liberal convictions. Ironically, in the Mediterranean port city, it was the Socialists who were reluctant to support the building of a unitary sewer and the liberals who favored it. So the neat correlation between liberalism and opposition to public health schemes does not quite fit the French case.

If some cities appear as interventionist in certain areas of public health, they were not in others. Toulouse was an early pioneer in its water policy, but not in waste management and housing control. Lyon's water policy was advanced, and while it led in the disposal of garbage, it did not in the management of human waste. Saint-Etienne received a unitary sewer and a water system from a liberal ruling elite; the water system was to become inadequate later in the century under the Socialists.

Given the resources at their disposal, city fathers on the whole were, regardless of their ideological commitments, conservative. They tried to limit their activities to that which was strictly necessary, trying to avoid—until it became unavoidable—large expenses and ambitious projects. And with rare exception in our French cities, councilmen, if representing the business elite or the workers, did not aggressively advance public sanitation.

Reformers and historians have seen the central government as a force favoring public health being resisted by the stubborn forces of localism.[124] But it would be hard to maintain such a general thesis. Water supplies were expanded in the decades between 1820 and 1840, sewers and waste disposal were somewhat later established—also before the central government intervened. Many cities founded bureaus of hygiene before they became mandatory. In regards to controlling housing quality, the central government was ahead of local initiative—especially reluctant to intervene in this form of private property. The 1902 law on public health made localities accountable to the central government, marking a decline in local autonomy and greater intrusiveness by the national government (although cities, as long as they had mortality rates below the national average, still retained considerable freedom in public health policy). And when all was said and done, the central government had limited authority; the director of public health in the ministry of interior, Léon Mirman, said in 1912 that his ministry could recommend, even threaten "but it cannot constrain" municipalities.[125]

Modest as their accomplishments were, cities had throughout the century become more interventionist and provided greater sanitary comforts.

The record of the provincial cities seems to show improved public health to be the result of a gradual, incremental policy. The decades spanning 1820 and 1840 reveal the development of a public health ethos. Cities then began to take measures they hoped would prevent epidemics and disease. Thereafter, such measures steadily expanded. If three of our five cities had no unitary sewers, all had tried to provide a water supply that would keep up, or in some cases surpass, previous per capita supplies. There was some improvement in street cleaning and garbage disposal. Lower typhoid rates and the disappearance of the threat of cholera after the end of the century seem to be testimony to an improved health environment.

In French terms, there had been progress. But compared to their foreign neighbors, French cities lagged behind. Much of French sanitation seemed archaic, its cities were bereft of unitary sewers, housing was dirty and far less regulated than in Britain or Germany. While cholera had disappeared, and typhoid and tuberculosis was lower than it had been earlier, it was estimated that the French rate in these frequent killer diseases at the turn of the twentieth century was double that of Britain and Germany. If Republicanism, which had taken root in our cities in the 1860s and in the nation the following decade, expressed great faith in progress and technology, few Republicans, however, showed zeal in applying these values to resolve public health problems in the city.

8

Municipal Welfare

B y the second half of the eighteenth century, an apparent increase
in the number of poor persons in France and a growing concern
for their well being, together with a decline in charitable bequests to religious foundations, led to advocacy of state intervention on their behalf.
Difficulties in carrying out such measures prompted the national government in the later phase of the Revolution and during Napoleon's Empire
to vest city councils with responsibility for care of the poor and destitute.[1]
If municipalities took on these tasks reluctantly at first, they gradually expanded services on their own initiative, going far beyond nationally mandated programs.

Poverty and physical misery existed all over France, but it was particularly
concentrated and visible in cities. Local governments in the nineteenth century employed various strategies: they tried to repress vagabondage and begging; and provided hospices for the aged, children, and the physically
disabled; while departments administered local poor houses, the *dépôts de
mendicité*. Municipalities provided for the poor or those temporarily faced by
hard luck with outdoor relief and various other services.

Local welfare measures established the principle of government responsibility for providing social services long before major national involvement occurred toward the end of the nineteenth century, an
involvement that formed the basis for the modern welfare state in France.[2]

What is striking about local welfare services through at least the middle of the nineteenth century and in many cases beyond is how little innovation occurred. Attitudes and institutions that existed or at least had been proposed during the ancien régime or the Revolution endured. As in the ancien régime, the ruling urban elites employed various forms of repression against the poor, whom they viewed as a menace and as repulsive in their public show of misery. Old and new institutions were employed to care for the poor. The Hôpital, charged in the ancien regime with care for the sick, the poor and various deviants, evolved into several specialized institutions in the nineteenth century. The *dépôts de mendicité* continued in fits and starts. The local welfare board, the *bureau de bienfaisance,* established during the Revolution, provided the largest amount of care with its outdoor relief programs. During economic emergencies, cities improvised public works programs and soup kitchens. Municipalities established pawnshops to help the poor tide themselves over hard times.

A generation ago, two American social scientists, Francis Fox Piven and Richard A. Cloward, proposed to use labor supply as the explanatory variable for shifts in welfare programs in the United States. A recent essay has employed the paradigm for a French city, seeing its welfare program responding to shifting labor supplies. According to this interpretation, the city fathers provided welfare to ensure a steady reserve army of labor and, when that was unnecessary, reduced aid to the poor and unemployed. A single explanation for a city's welfare system provides a procrustean bed, incapable of explaining the complex of motives for local assistance programs. Comparing urban programs for the poor, I find that the weight of local traditions, the fear of urban unrest, and ideological and political concerns were more important in shaping welfare policies.[3]

THE PROBLEM OF THE POOR

Liberal ideology, developed in the eighteenth century and dominating much of the nineteenth century in France, insisted that the poor had no right to charity. Any assistance given should be limited; the poor should be discouraged from depending on aid and should be encouraged by every means possible to become self-sufficient.[4] The free market had to be allowed to regulate itself. Faced with an economic downturn, the Saint-Etienne mayor in 1832 declared the need to abstain from any interference. "We must gain time; later by the force of things, the regulating law of the universe will re-establish the balance that was upset."[5]

Poverty was viewed as being, to a large degree, the result of vice. In Lyon, the large number of abandoned children in the post-Napoleonic years was seen as being a result of "the lack of self-control by the parents . . . and the absence of religion."[6]

Providing aid for the poor, most elite members of society feared, would make the recipient lazy and dependent, sapping "a society, the foundations of which are order, work, and family." In 1826, the prefect of the Rhône opposed a special tax to help alleviate the conditions of the needy, since it would "infallibly" make the population less likely to seek employment. The Toulouse city council in 1843 deliberately paid low wages to unemployed persons working on public projects "to avoid providing a reward for laziness." The fear was that charity, if made a right, would destroy personal initiative and render pauperism chronic; the only individuals who had a right to charity were children and the insane. Even in regard to the aged, local authorities in Lyon suggested that providing for them would lead "to lack of foresight and dissipation."[7]

The poor who were housed in hospices were described as "wicked poor," who had been reduced to their circumstances by vice. In 1808, a Bordeaux philanthropic group stated that "most of the misfortune" of the poor was "caused by lack of foresight, immorality, incapacity, laziness and all the vices that normally lead to poverty." The mayor of Marseille in 1850 provided a long list of the causes of poverty in his city, the main ones being "the immorality, debauchery, and bad habits of the poor; of ten who are sick, four or five are so because of poor conduct and vice." The cure, he suggested, was religion and hard work.[8]

In 1835, Alexis de Tocqueville suggested a strange paradox: the richer the country, the more people on welfare. One of his contemporaries, Viscount Villeneuve-Bargemont, the prefect of the Nord, who also wrote on pauperism, thought 5 percent of the country's population was poor. In the industrial north, however, probably 10 percent was poor. In manufacturing cities, he observed, the number of poor had doubled in recent years and he posited an axiom that he found paradoxical: "the more a country has rich industrial entrepreneurs, the more it has poor workers." Such circumstances could be read in two ways. On one hand, rich societies may have marginalized more individuals and reduced them to pauperism—a common view in those years when industrialization indeed harshly affected large numbers of people. Joseph De Gérando observed that the same cause that "produced wealth in modern societies"—the freedom to work—had also created a growth in the able-bodied indigent, while the Lyon welfare board observed in 1841 that "misery grows with the progress of industry." On the other hand, the availability of wealth could also be seen as providing opportunities for people so inclined to live on charity, a complaint already frequent in the eighteenth century.[9]

The fear that charity would wean the poor from work and discipline had grown up in the sixteenth century, when Europeans ceased thinking of the poor as objects of salvation. No longer were the poor thought of as the representatives of Christ to whom charity would be deemed an act of piety that opened the gates of heaven to the benefactors. Rather, they were seen as a social and administrative problem, and city and national administrators began worrying how to separate the "deserving" poor from the lazy and slothful.[10]

The ancien régime and the Revolution wrestled with the task of differentiating the "deserving" from the "undeserving" poor; this quandary continued into the nineteenth century. The Lyon Academy of Science in 1818 provided a prize for the best essay on "Which persons have the right to call on the benefits of public sympathy? And by what means can one make charity profitable to those who give and those who receive?" No one entered the essay that year; the following year, Baron Joseph De Gérando, a Lyonnais who would become internationally renowned for his writings on the problems of the poor, submitted a winning essay, introduced by the quote "The least worthy form of charity is that which gives but gold."[11] Vice must not be rewarded. Such attitudes continued through the nineteenth century, reinforced by the ethic of work and labor espoused by the leaders and beneficiaries of a growing industrial economy.

While Catholics in the 1820s and 1830s often expressed a concern for the poor that blamed the capitalist system, rather than the poor, this trend is hardly reflected in municipal policies. If in cities such as Lyon many of the municipal councilors were ardent Catholics and personally gave to the poor, when they functioned as city magistrates they mostly worried about the drain the poor represented on the city's budget.[12]

Assistance at the local level had to be provided in a way that would not play to what were seen as the already existing vices of the poor. In 1836, the president of the Lyon Hospice général, a banker and one of the city's preeminent citizens, affirmed the principle that "our first responsibility is to carefully avoid allowing our . . . assistance to encourage poverty and reward dissipation and lack of foresight." Lyon's *ordre moral* municipality in the 1870s claimed that assistance did not necessarily go to the most needy, but rather to "the cleverest," and thus was "an encouragement to laziness and to the neglect of filial piety." The Bordeaux officials in charge of the assistance program insisted that "aid must be withheld from the lazy and immoral poor." And even Socialists, usually sympathetic to the plight of the poor, were at times troubled by the thought that there might be "unworthy" poor; Marseille's popular Socialist mayor Flaissères asked in 1892, "Is it really the unfortunates who receive [assistance]? It goes to those who need it least, but have the least pride, the least dignity."[13]

Whatever the reasons, by the 1840s a large army of the poor, labeled *les classes dangereuses* had developed.[14] While the elites might rage against the poor, they also recognized that it was in their interest to alleviate the worst miseries. Tanneguy Duchâtel, who advised Charles X on the poor, described charity—both private and public—as creating "social harmony." Baron de Gérando explained at the beginning of his work that the poor posed a threat "to peace, order, health, property." Poverty led to vice of all sorts; hence, if society wanted to protect itself, it had to provide some forms of assistance. Much later in the century, Jules Siegfried, social reformer and mayor of Le Havre, declared that charity was necessary to reduce riots and revolutions, "which are of use to no one."[15]

Such attitudes also were expressed by local elites in the five cities of this study. Both the Bordeaux and the Saint-Etienne city councils in the aftermath of the July Revolution voted special funds to employ the poor on public works projects to ensure "public tranquillity" and "the peace of citizens." In Saint-Etienne, the prefect warned that since "workers are unemployed, public tranquillity is threatened." When, during the economic crisis that culminated in the 1848 Revolution, the city decided to hire a hundred unemployed workers, the police commissioner, entrusted with public safety, pleaded for the hiring of five or six hundred. That presumably would facilitate his peace-keeping responsibilities. Marseille mayor Max Consolat argued in 1840 that the new water aqueduct, in addition to its obvious benefits in bringing water to the city, would ensure "constant work to numerous workers, preventing frightful disorders. . . ." In Toulouse, a Republican leader and future mayor, Roquelaine, in 1848 proposed, in light of massive unemployment, a program of "vast public works in the interest of both humanity and order."[16]

Sometimes the suggestion that welfare could preserve public order came from the poor themselves. In 1847, the hungry people of Bordeaux carried signs threatening that if bread prices were not lowered, "the people will rise and the four corners of the city will be set ablaze." The city council promptly issued bread coupons. Although collective violence was more common and its danger was more overtly recognized in the first half of the nineteenth century, toward the end of the century welfare services were still in some cases thought of as a form of insurance against disorder. The mayor of Toulouse in the 1890s justified his public works program by declaring that it was "the duty of a truly republican municipality, which also was concerned with public tranquillity, to alleviate the conditions of the unfortunate."[17] So the care of the poor as a mechanism of social control, as a way of ensuring social peace, was a strong motivation for local charitable activities.

REPRESSION

Municipalities tried various stratagems to control the symptom of poverty most troubling to urban elites—vagabondage and begging. After the Napoleonic wars, France suffered from a severe economic downturn that drove the poor into the city, increasing the number of urban beggars and others with no clear means of employment.

The influx of the poor alarmed contemporaries. In 1816, Madame Remusat, wife of the Toulouse prefect, noted that "Toulouse is inundated with beggars." Marseille heard repeated complaints that the city was overrun. A report of 1824 spoke of an increase in the number of beggars importuning passersby in the Mediterranean port with "plaintive cries"; others, "to rouse compassion, drag themselves along the pavement or show themselves half-nude to expose disgusting wounds or mutilated limbs." Children so young they "could barely utter a few words," were trained to beg. The poor of northern Italy arrived in Marseille in rags with neither resources nor employment; living crowded in stables and cellars, the Savoyards were a health hazard, the mayor wrote in 1832, the year that cholera hit France.[18]

Begging was viewed as a crime. The Marseille historian and councilman, Augustin Fabre, stated in the 1840s that it was important to remove beggars from society, for "there must not be habits of laziness. The honest worker, earning his daily bread by the sweat of his brow, must not be confronted by the sight of the degraded being who has but to put out his hand to make his daily living." The mayor of the second *arrondissement* of Lyon (under the second empire each *arrondissement* in Lyon was provided with an appointed mayor) denounced begging as "at once a menace, a disgrace, and an affront. A menace because beggars could form the unruly crowds which challenged authority," a disgrace because beggary "dishonors a society." Begging was theft, a reward for laziness, an affront to charity. At the end of the century, a Toulouse newspaper declared begging to be an act "against safety and public morality." So begging needed to be discouraged and even proscribed. Such strictures existed regardless of the economic cycle; it was there in the mid-century when the silk merchants of Lyon wanted to retain labor in Lyon, and after the 1870s when the industry was in crisis and a steady supply of labor was no longer desired.[19]

Cities in the provinces attempted various experiments to repress begging. In Toulouse and Marseille—continuing a custom from the ancien régime—beggars who were outsiders (not born in the city) were forbidden to solicit, for as Toulouse authorities declared in an ordinance of 1831, "their presence is alarming to the citizens." Non-native beggars often were expelled by force. Toulouse in 1807 assigned four of its twenty-three policemen to "repress begging and vagabondage." This marked a return to the eighteenth century, when the city had used *archers des pauvres* to police beggars. In addition to the stick, Toulouse also proffered a carrot to outsiders: 15 centimes per league to leave for a nearby commune. But this was not very effective, most non-native beggars soon reappeared.[20]

While Marseille and Toulouse barred outsiders from begging, they allowed local ones. A residency requirement was necessary, Toulouse authorities explained, because every municipality owed a duty toward "its own poor to protect them from foreign beggars whose competition diminishes their resources. . . ." Locals who were considered "worthy" poor—invalids, the aged, and children—could register as beggars in both Toulouse and Marseille. Toulouse even provided tokens for registered beggars to wear. The number registering varied widely, usually reflecting not economic conditions but levels of enforcement and advantages of registration. Marseille registered 138 beggars in 1808, but only 87 in 1827. Toulouse registered 337 in 1842. Only a small proportion of beggars registered.[21]

An easier policy to regulate was to forbid all forms of begging. Toulouse, in a curious show of faith in the literacy of the poor, hung a sign on the outskirts of the city in 1848 proclaiming, "Begging in the Commune of Toulouse is forbidden." It advised its citizens against giving alms, and prosecuted those who sought alms. In the 1840s, one-tenth of persons arrested in Saint-Etienne and over one-third of all those arrested in Marseille and Toulouse were charged with begging or vagabondage. Even the infirm were arrested; in Saint-Etienne, 83 percent of beggars arrested in 1858 suffered some physical disability.[22]

Begging persisted throughout the century. Although it was forbidden in the whole department of the Gironde, Bordeaux in the 1870s was supposedly infested by beggars. A municipal councilor called begging, "this plague of our times." Even able-bodied persons, he contended, had joined the ranks of beggars. In Toulouse, a city councilman complained that "begging spreads daily in our streets." In Lyon in 1881, the prefect felt it necessary to put up signs at the city's entrance forbidding begging. Toward the end of the century, complaints were still rife about the prevalence of begging—a Toulouse newspaper complained that the city was "invaded by a swarm of beggars."[23]

If contemporary accounts are to be believed, the problems of beggary had not been satisfactorily resolved by the municipalities. On the other hand, it is likely that in the early part of the nineteenth century, the elites were quite hardened to the frequent view of poverty and misery while toward the end of our period of study, people were probably more sensitive, more easily shocked by begging and vagabondage. Nationally, prosecution for begging increased by 120 percent and for vagabondage by 139 percent in the years 1886-90.[24] While municipal councilors expressed outrage at the prevalence of begging both in the early and later part of the century, its frequency may have declined.

Dépôts de Mendicité

To get the poorest out of public sight and at the same time render them economically useful the ancien régime confined large numbers of vagrants and beggars in *hôpitaux généraux*. In 1767, a law provided for their confinement in separate institutions, the *dépôts de mendicité*.[25] The *dépôts* soon fell into disuse but were revived by a Napoleonic law in 1808, providing every department with a *dépôt de mendicité* located in the departmental capital. All the cities in this study, except Saint-Etienne, which until 1855 was not a departmental capital, had a *dépôt* and served many of the cities' poor.

Napoleon's purpose was to reduce beggary by making the *dépôts* so unpleasant as to discourage the exercise of that profession. Thus the *dépôts* were set up to punish the "unworthy poor."[26] Nonetheless, as a result of lack of space in other types of institutions and administrative confusion, the *dépôts* also housed many "worthy" poor. In the Bouches-du-Rhône, a prefectural decree of 1811 ordered the *dépôt* to accept the infirm, the aged and "abandoned children, orphans, lazy beggars and vagabonds." The Marseille *dépôt* thus contained a mixture of categories: 56 inmates were aged, 131 handicapped either physically or mentally (this number included "maniacs and insane"), 6 had venereal disease, 24 were prostitutes, 3 were infants, 14 were juvenile delinquents, 77 abandoned children, and 25 (probably beggars) were physically apt. In the Toulouse *dépôt*, nearly half of the male beggars in 1810-16 were over age 60. Many of the adult inmates were in poor health. Of the 200 persons incarcerated in 1818, only 60 were physically capable of working.[27]

Continuing traditions established in the eighteenth century, the *dépôts* were workhouses. Charity was to bring no escape from labor; as the chairman of the Revolutionary Assembly's Comité de mendicité, Rochefoucauld-Liancourt proclaimed, "If the poor have the right to demand of society, 'Give me the means to live,' it has the right to answer, 'Give me your labor.'" The labor requirement would ensure that no one embraced public charity to avoid hard work and would also help defray the cost of assistance. In Marseille, more than half of the *dépôt*'s inmates, or 196, worked in a shop, mainly producing textiles; another one- sixth of them helped in the daily tasks of running the *dépôt*, such as preparing meals. At the end of the century, the *dépôt* in Lyon still required its wards to work seven to eight hours daily. Bordeaux drafted the strongest members of the *dépôt* to sweep the streets; the elderly manufactured rope. Toulouse marketed the products of its inmates' labor, but that brought in such a low income that the departmental *dépôt* was discontinued in 1815. The *dépôts* in Bordeaux and Toulouse (a municipal one had been created after the departmental one was closed) brought in around 3,000 francs a year by mid-century, while Marseille's produced 22,000 francs. But whatever income they generated, as Louis Moreau-Christophe, a mid-century authority on pauperism, noted, the *dépôts* were more expensive to operate than anticipated and certainly did not pay for themselves.[28]

The *dépôts* were made as disagreeable as possible, since, in the words of a government inspector, they were meant to subjugate the poor "to more or less arduous labor, and be sufficiently unremunerative so that occupations which can be found in the free industry are always preferred. . . ." The Marseille *dépôt*, its director declared, was to be "a correctional establishment, rather than a shelter . . . a menace to the beggar and not a charitable asylum." The purpose of the *dépôt*, the prefect of the Gironde explained, was to inspire the poor to avoid it "by all the means of their position and their industry." The Toulouse *dépôt* fed its inmates only bread and water; their treatment was so harsh that its hapless inmates tried to flee the institution.[29]

The *dépôts*, although established by the central government, did not have uniform fates; local needs and authorities shaped them. At midcentury, Marseille's *dépôt* incarcerated 200 persons a year, four-fifths of whom came from outside the department, many being foreign born. In the 1860s, there were about 330 inmates, over 90 percent of whom were not Marseillais. Although the *dépôt* was intended for the "unworthy" poor, half its wards were sickly or aged. The institution was closed in 1902 by the Socialist mayor, but his Conservative successor reopened it in 1905 as a measure "against the invasion of the city by beggars from all countries."[30]

When, after the departmental *dépôt* in Toulouse was closed in 1815, the city established its own *dépôt*. It was a rather modest operation. In 1840 it had 49 inmates and five years later but 35; the following year there were 60. Many were more than 80 years old. One woman was a 100. Most of the inmates were needy, physically unfit, and unable to earn their living. Thus the *dépôt* actually served the "worthy poor," the aged and incapacitated; nonetheless, it continued to be punitive. Its inmates, for example, were forced to wear prison uniforms. The *dépôt* survived until 1890.[31]

The departmental *dépôt* of Bordeaux seems to have closed its doors soon after opening. But in 1827 a private charitable organization enjoying a 40,000-franc city subsidy revived it, and it lodged about 350 people. Beggars were given a choice of being institutionalized there or leaving the department. It was still in operation in the 1890s, housing 211 wards, of whom 18 were beggars, the rest presumably the infirm.[32]

Lyon revived its *dépôt* in 1829, since "society wishes to be spared the hideous view of beggary and the serious abuses which it causes." It appears to have housed 100 beggars. In 1859, it housed 321 inmates, of whom 264 were voluntary admissions and 67 were involuntary. At the end of the century, the *dépôt* housed a *maison de retraite*—a retirement home—for those voluntarily entering.[33]

Relatively little archival material exists to tell us about the conditions reigning in the *dépôts*, but what is found confirms the pathetic conditions, even for the "deserving" poor. The Toulouse *dépôt* was run so frugally that it spent but two-thirds of its allocated daily funds, 39 centimes per inmate. The one in Bordeaux was a little more generous, spending the allocated 56 centimes per inmate per day. The Marseille *dépôt* in the 1880s was reported to be in physical ruins, about to fall at any time, "a permanent danger for people's security both inside and outside the establishment. . . ." The building housing the *dépôt* in Lyon was described in the 1880's as "not unlike a prison." If the residents wanted to leave in order to see a friend or relative they had to ask for permission 15 days in advance.[34]

The efficacy of the *dépôts* in combating public beggary was debated by contemporaries. Moreau-Christophe complained that the *dépôts* had not proved to be effective deterrents to begging. In Bordeaux, the prefect and a city councilman prematurely declared that the *dépôt* had frightened off all the beggars, freeing the city from more than a thousand who had once wandered the streets. But shortly thereafter, a Protestant minister wrote that no sooner had Bordeaux set up a *dépôt* than it was filled, unable to accommodate all those who should have been institutionalized, and public begging continued. The immediate effect of establishing the *dépôt* in Lyon, according to the same minister, was that it diminished the number of poor; yet three or four years after its founding, "we were molested by beggars along the whole road."[35]

The *dépôt* had not been very effective at repressing beggary. In time, it changed from being an instrument of repression and dissuasion to becoming more clearly a charitable institution—more akin to the hospice.

THE HOSPICES

In the Middle Ages, the *hôpital*, run by clerics, was a place that received poor aged persons, abandoned children, sick and infirm patients, the mentally ill, pilgrims, and other travelers. By order of the police, the *hôpital* also took in beggars, vagabonds, and individuals deemed morally corrupt, such as prostitutes. In a long, slow process, the institution split in the nineteenth century into two separate establishments: the hospital, where the poor who were sick received medical attention; and the hospice, the asylum for abandoned children and the aged. By mid-century, a distinction developed between the needy and the sick (who also were, however, needy).[36] This division was, however, never airtight. Even in the twentieth century, French hospitals continued to house large numbers of people who were socially, rather than medically, needy. In 1971, the French medical inspectorate estimated that 26 percent of those hospitalized were there for social, rather than medical, reasons.[37]

Administering both the hospital and the hospice throughout the nineteenth and early twentieth centuries was the local Commission d'hospices, whose members came from the cities' political, philanthropic, and medical elites. The commission received its income from charitable private donations and municipal subsidies. But the latter were the major source of income for all the commissions, except the one in Lyon, which had better-endowed foundations and larger properties than the commissions in other cities in this study. Lyon had a tradition of pious giving to the poor, unrivaled by any of the other cities. The Lyon Commission d'hospices owned large amounts of real estate, especially properties in the Brotteaux and Guillotière neighborhoods on the right bank of the Rhône that had been acquired over several centuries. Between 1820 and 1914, the income from these investments totaled 367 million francs.[38] In 1888, when the Lyon hospice foundation had an income of 4.2 million francs, income endowment for Marseille was 666,000 francs and for Bordeaux 505,000 francs. Lyon's hospice and hospital system was so generously endowed that it did without municipal subsidies.

During the ancien régime, General Hospitals, also known as hospices, provided institutional care for the "deserving" poor, the lame, the blind, the aged, orphans, and poor, usually single, expectant mothers. The first institution devoted to such purposes, was the Charité of Lyon, founded in 1622, which became a model in the seventeenth century for enclosing the poor.[39] The hospices survived the Revolution and throughout the nineteenth century sheltered various categories of the indigent.

The criteria for institutionalizing people in hospices were confused and varied by period and locale. Both in Lyon and Marseille, the poor, the infirm, and orphans were commingled during much of the nineteenth century. Lyon had no segregation by sexes; a single ward in Lyon contained 164 men and 220 women. An inspector, writing of the Lyon hospice in the mid-nineteenth century, described it as "a spectacle that nothing can prepare one for. . . ." Mixing of sexes and age groups continued in Lyon into the twentieth century. Some cities, however, did segregate various groups. Bordeaux by the 1840s had established separate pavilions for the "incurable," the aged, the insane, and foundlings. In 1906, a circular from the minister of interior demanded separation of children and the aged.[40]

Early on, Bordeaux established a separate service for abandoned children. A new building, erected in 1886, housed 250 children.

Many of the wards presented appalling conditions. In Marseille, it was remarked in the late 1830s that the hospice was located in a crowded neighborhood with "foul air." It was far too small for the 1,100 persons housed in it. While by the 1870s it had reduced its population to 800, it was still severely overcrowded. Only in 1890 was it replaced by a new building. The courtyard of the Lyon hospice in the 1830s was filled with latrines; sheds of various sorts; and cages in which chickens, rabbits, and pigs were raised—it provided a mixture of ripe odors. Because of the shortage of space, authorities had an extra floor installed in the large tall wards; the result was that the upper floor was not tall enough to accommodate patients and staff standing erect. An inspection report in 1883 described the Charité, built in the seventeenth century, as an anachronism, lacking "modern hospital hygiene." It was always overcrowded; in 1910, a ward intended for 60 people housed a 100. The building survived until it was torn down in the 1930s to make way for the city's central post office.[41]

Bordeaux's pavilions were all in deplorable condition. Because the one that housed the aged failed to shelter its occupants adequately, during the hard winter of 1829-30 a quarter of them died. In 1855, Bordeaux had projected a single new hospice to house all those needing institutionalization, but in the end only a home for the aged was built. It opened in 1877. Spacious and airy, it had innumerable stairs, which proved difficult for the aged to climb. The other buildings remained inferior. In 1855, the hospice for foundlings had been described as unhygienic, its wards humid, poorly aired and poorly lit, its walls ready to fall down in places. Thirty years and several plans later the foundlings finally were provided with a new building. The maternity ward was poorly heated, and the women staying there caught "serious diseases."[42]

Many of the hospices were overwhelmed after the mid-century by the arrival in the cities of a large migrant population that was less likely than the native-born to have relatives nearby on whom it could depend in case of ill health or unemployment. As part of the urban economy, the newcomers could not readily be refused services. In the Bordeaux hospices between 1869 and 1878, 4,500 of 7,500 patients were migrant indigents whose commune of residence could not be billed. Hence the cost of their institutionalization had to be financed by the Bordeaux hospital system. Faced with increased costs, Toulouse, wishing to balance its welfare budget, closed the gates of its hospice "to a multitude of unfortunates whose sufferings are certain and position excessively deplorable." In Bordeaux, a report of 1871 noted the long waiting lists for entry into the home for the aged. It usually took 15 to 18 months after one was first registered before one was admitted. The new hospice, Pellegrin, built in 1877 to accommodate the increasing demand, was soon overwhelmed. In 1888, of 478 persons who signed a waiting list to enter the Hospice de vieillards et incurables, only one was admitted, and he had waited for over five-and-a-half years. That is an extreme example, but even the normal waiting period was three to four years. Toulouse, given its slow growth, had a surprisingly large hospice, with 1,000 beds at mid-century. Its ability to accommodate needs varied. In 1846, it had a waiting list of 100 persons; in 1872, 109 beds were vacant. Admission was not based on pure need; a student of welfare in Lyon has shown that throughout the nineteenth century admission was based on clientage and in some cases on the ability of the applicants or their supporters to pay the hospices (2,000 francs guaranteed lifetime care).[43]

By the end of the nineteenth century, Saint-Etienne, while building a new hospital to take into account the dramatic growth in the city's population, had made no plans for its hospice. The aged and crippled had to wait for years before they could gain admission "if they did not die before." The buildings were recognized in 1900 as run down, insufficient in size and quality for their residents. Only in May 1914 was the decision made to erect a new building, with 768 beds. The war intervened, and it was not built until 1932.[44]

The poor, many authorities feared, would grow too comfortable in the hospices. In Marseille in the 1880s, hospice inmates were restricted to two meals a day, receiving no food between 6:00 P.M. and 11 A.M. In Bordeaux, the hospice for foundlings was operated with severe discipline, requiring children to work in industries established within its walls. In Lyon at mid-century, a medieval custom still persisted of having the aged from the Charité accompany funeral processions. It tired the aged to climb the steep incline to the cemetery to such a degree that "several among them fell sick; others fainted on the way and were brought back to the hospital, dying." A reform exempted the aged from having to climb the steep incline, yet they still had to continue to provide escorts for funerals. Stern discipline continued. When in 1884 several pensioners left the grounds of the hospice to celebrate July 14th, they were disciplined.[45]

Since institutional care had been developed by local authorities, the cities in this study had varying capacities to provide hospice care. In 1824, Bordeaux had 640 beds, while Toulouse had 885 and Marseille 1,075. In 1860, Lyon had 1,620 beds, while Saint-Etienne had 584.[46] In proportion to populations, hospice capacities varied among cities, although they with time represented a lower proportion of people and budgets (see table 8.1).

The variations in the supply of hospice beds were not necessarily a reflection of need, or even of municipal funding. Marseille was the most poorly supplied in relation to its population, but its city council was not ungenerous with its support. In 1885, it provided a 750,000-franc subsidy, while Bordeaux provided 509,000 francs, Saint-Etienne 85,000 francs, and Lyon none. Yet Lyon had the largest number of beds in its hospices (although the number was not particularly high in proportion to its population).[47]

Toulouse had the most hospice beds per population because its stock of beds was built up early, when the city was rich and growing. It had been able to draw on centuries of local philanthropy. Relative to the other cities, Toulouse grew slowly, and hence in relation to its population during the nineteenth century it had an abundance of hospice space. During the century, while Toulouse added 100,000 inhabitants, Lyon and Marseille increased their populations by 340,000 and 390,000 respectively, so the latter were overwhelmed.

Table 8.1: Hospice Services in Selected French Cities, 1825-1894

	Number of Beds per 1,000 Population			City Budget (percent expended)	
	1825	*1869*	*1894*	*1825*	*1894*
Lyon	9.0	5.0	3.9	20	0.0
Bordeaux	5.9	4.8	3.2	14.3	5.6
Marseille	5.5	3.6	1.7	29.0	6.3
Toulouse	9.7	10.9	5.4	20.0	6.3
Saint-Etienne	6.3	3.8	4.9	13.7	1.7

Source: Ministère de l'intérieure, *Rapport au Roi sur les hôpitaux, les hospices et les services de bienfaisance* (Paris; Imprimerie royale, 1837), 18-19; France. Ministère de l'intérieure. *Situation administrative et financière des hôpitaux et hospices de l'empire*, 1 (Paris: Imprimerie nationale, 1869); Napias, "Budgets municipaux," 272-73; idem., "Etudes d'assistance publique. Budgets municipaux et budgets hospitaliers," *Revue générale d'administration* (1896), 6-13; J.P. Pointe, *Histoire topographique et médicale du Grand Hotel-Dieu de Lyon* (Lyon: Ch. Savy, 1842), 196.

Representing a large part of the city budget in the early nineteenth century, hospice expenditures late in the century embodied a far smaller proportion. In part, this change was due to the increase in a growing type of assistance, outdoor relief. In the early part of the century, hospice care was considered an important means of aiding the poor. But with time this strategy changed. In general, our cities institutionalized fewer people in hospices, and in proportion to the population there was a marked decline in the number of hospice beds available. Lyon and Marseille reduced the number of hospices beds available from 1,620 (in 1860) to 1,544 (in 1894), and from 1,075 (in 1835) to 679 (in 1894), respectively. While the other cities increased their hospice capacity, it was a modest increase.

The hospice had provided institutional care for the poor; gradually in the latter part of the nineteenth century it concentrated on the sick in certain categories. In Lyon, the old Charité became the hospital for women and children. It increasingly became a medical institution rather than a caregiver for the destitute. The hospices declined in importance as a smaller proportion of the population was being confined. As Michel Foucault noted, the era of the "grand confinement," begun in the seventeenth century, had come to an end in the early nineteenth century as new means of social control were established.[48]

OUTDOOR RELIEF: THE BUREAU DE BIENFAISANCE

The decline in confinement was accompanied by the growth in outdoor relief, an alternative favored by most officials dealing with welfare. This form of aid, administered in every commune by a *bureau of bienfaisance* (welfare bureau), was established by the Revolution. The bureau was run by a five-member committee appointed by the municipality and approved by the prefect. The mayor was a member. The bureau could receive funds from private donors, as well as allocations from the city budget; most funds came from the latter. Whereas the ancien régime had emphasized the hospice as the institution providing aid for the poor, the Revolution emphasized outdoor relief provided by the welfare bureau.[49] It was, of course, cheaper to let poor persons live at home or wherever they could outside the institution and be provided with the aid they might need from time to time.

The role of the *bureaux de bienfaisance* grew throughout the nineteenth century as authorities placed more and more emphasis on de-institutionalizing the poor. The minister of interior in 1837 noted that outdoor relief was not only cheaper than institutional care but also less disruptive of family ties. By not putting the poor and crippled in hospices but rather providing them with outdoor relief, the city, a noted Lyon physician proclaimed, would leave them to be more responsible for their own well being without taking them away from their relatives' "affection and devotion."[50]

The *bureau de bienfaisance* in each city, according to shifting criteria and considerations, drew up lists of people who qualified for allocations in cash, food, kindling wood, or clothes. The bureaus' mode of operation and rationale were well articulated in 1884 by the Bordeaux assistant mayor of public assistance:

> The goal of the Bureau de bienfaisance is not to provide those who want to do nothing with abundance, it has no other mission than to come to the aid of those who are in abject poverty. It attenuates to a limited degree their condition, but it does not provide for the total needs of its charges. To some it gives soup, to others clothing or a wool blanket, to others who are sick medication. . . . [51]

A sizable segment of the population was usually on the city rolls. Paris routinely supported one-twelfth of its population, and during economic crises it could support almost a third, or the bulk of the working class. As a result of the miseries created by the Napoleonic wars, Marseille in 1811 had 40,000 persons, or nearly half the population, on its rolls. Paris at the time had more than 100,000 persons, or 15 percent, on the dole. In Bordeaux, 17 percent of the population was receiving city aid in the 1820s, and

20 percent in the 1830s. Thereafter, the proportion steadily declined, reaching 8 percent in 1891. Lyon had 6 percent of its population receiving welfare in the 1820s, 7 percent in the 1830s, and 10 percent in the 1840s.[52]

Cities were far more likely than rural areas to provide assistance for the poor; in the hungry 1840s, when the cities in this study provided aid to between 10 percent and 20 percent of their inhabitants, it was but 5 percent nationally.[53] Most rural communes did not have *bureaux of bienfaisance;* only a fourth of all French communes had them, and only 5 percent had funding that made their operation anything more than nominal. Toward the end of the nineteenth century, slightly more than half of all French communes had bureaus, and many of the rural ones still provided purely nominal services.[54]

Differences in the proportion of the population admitted to the welfare rolls in various cities are shown by looking at the figures for 1847, a year that was uniformly harsh. That year, the proportion of the population receiving assistance in Paris was 8.5 percent, Lyon 10 percent, Marseille and Bordeaux 16 percent, and Toulouse 20 percent. Later, in the early 1870s, 8.1 percent of the Bordeaux inhabitants were on the city dole, 10.9 percent in Lyon, 9.7 percent in Marseille, 8.1 percent in Saint-Etienne, and 13.2 percent in Toulouse. The smaller contrast in the size of the welfare rolls of the various cities in the 1870s may be due to the greater homogenization of society as rails and roads penetrated the country, creating a more uniform economy that was less affected by vagaries of the local economy.

Most aid was in kind, reflecting the continuing suspicion that the poor were wasteful and would not properly employ what they were given. Welfare legislation in the year V offered material rather than pecuniary assistance; charitable institutions could buy in bulk and hence get goods at a lower price and—probably more important—the *bureaux de bienfaisance* could have the certainty that "the aid provided will not be misdirected and foolishly spent." Emphasis on aid in kind continued throughout the century; in 1871, three-fourths of expenditures of the largest bureaus were in kind. While food often was the principal item disbursed, that was not always the case. In the 1840s, the Bordeaux bureau spent 56 percent of its funds on food assistance, Toulouse 44 percent, and Saint-Etienne 34 percent; but Marseille spent only 15 percent. In Bordeaux in 1869-79, the single largest outlay after food was for clothes, followed by heating fuel. After 1879, these two switched and more was spent on heat than clothing. In Lyon, the largest amount (41 percent) was for food—followed by medicine (17 percent), and fuel (14 percent). Bureaus rarely gave out cash. In the 1840s, cash constituted 1.5 percent of outlays in Bordeaux and 2 percent in Toulouse. Marseille was exceptional, with 21 percent of its dole in cash. In 1869, cash constituted less than 1 percent of outlays in Bordeaux; in 1890, it was 3 percent. In 1911, Saint-Etienne provided 7.5 percent of its aid in cash. This comparatively high proportion reflected grants mandated for the indigent aged.[55]

The average amount of aid to indigents varied according to municipality. In the 1840s, it was nationally 11 francs; for Bordeaux, 12.9 francs; Lyon, 15.5 francs; Marseille, 6 francs. In 1871, the amount per assisted person was in Bordeaux 14.7 francs; Lyon, 25.5 francs; Marseille, 13.3 francs; Saint-Etienne, 5.4 francs; and Toulouse, 13 francs. All these amounts except Lyon's were below the national average of 14.9 francs and the Parisian average of 28.6 francs. By the 1890s, most cities in this study improved their per-capita contribution—Marseille disbursed 24.8 francs, for example, and Bordeaux 21.4 francs—while the national average had risen only to 19.3 francs.[56]

The general trend in the later part of the nineteenth century was to provide more aid to a smaller proportion of population. From 1872 to 1911, the number aided by welfare bureaus in four of the most urbanized departments declined by 20 percent, even though the population had grown by 31 percent in the same period, while the average expenditure in these four departments rose from 16.9 francs to 42.2 francs. Not all the cities in this study followed this trend. Lyon, after providing aid to 27,000 paupers in 1891, reduced the number to 11,500 in 1893, and, as a result, the amount per person went up dramatically, from 16.41 francs per person to 46.4 francs per person. The smaller number of people provided with assistance after the 1870s in Lyon has been cited as evidence of an increased indifference towards the poor. This new callousness, it is argued, was due to the decline of the silk industry and the emergence of heavy industry. As a result, there was less need to maintain a large reserve army of unemployed in economic downturns—and aid was cut.[57] But instead the opposite happened: more aid was provided for the truly needy, replacing the previous policy of providing paltry sums to a very large number.

And if the number aided (without regard to the amount provided per needy person) is supposed to be the test of a municipality's response to a labor supply that has become redundant, the experience of other cities ought to provide similar results. But that was not the case. Lyon's neighbor Saint-Etienne, which also saw a decline in the silk industry by the 1880s, did not witness an accompanying decline in the number of poor provided with assistance. Saint-Etienne's population grew by 7 percent in the years 1891-1906, but the number on its welfare list increased by 78 percent (the amount provided per person, however, fell from 50 francs per person in 1891, to 33 in 1907). And while Marseille, until the 1880s, diminished the proportion of people aided, it then started increasing it; the city became more industrial towards the end of the century, yet the number of persons on the rolls rose faster than the city population. In 1886, 16,000 people, representing 4.2 percent of the population, rose by 1903 to 33,000, representing 7.9 percent of the population. The amount given per recipient fell for the same period from 26 to 17 francs. Toulouse, while an artisanal city throughout this period, was more industrial towards the end than previously, yet the number on the dole grew: in 1885, it provided for 7,300 indigents (4.9 percent of the population); and in 1894, 13,000 (8.7 percent). While the population of Toulouse grew by 9 percent in the years 1886-1912, the number of people provided with assistance grew 74 percent.[58]

Variations in numbers on the dole and average amounts of the grants cannot be easily explained. A mechanical explanation, based on an abstract paradigm, proves unsatisfactory. Although the variations reflect no recognizable changes in the political makeup of city councils, one is tempted to attribute the increasing number of welfare recipients at times to politicians' desire to increase their electoral support. In Saint-Etienne, for instance, the city raised its contribution to the bureau before the elections of 1897.

The manner in which special funds, which the *bureaux d'assistance* did not distribute, were disbursed suggests that authorities could be swayed by political considerations in making welfare allocations. In Marseille, Saint-Etienne, and Toulouse, political clientage appears to have been particularly important. Some assistance was handed out directly by city councilmen. The Toulouse city council, approving emergency funding during the winter of 1868, provided that the funds be distributed by city councilmen to those they deemed needy. In some cities, mayors had discretionary powers to distribute funds to the poor. The single largest amount under the heading of "miscellaneous" in the Bordeaux budget in 1885 was spent by the mayor as discretionary aid, and Lyon's mayor also expended a large amount. Toulouse's mayor, upon the recommendation of city councilmen, distributed aid out of his special funds to the needy. But evidently not all councilmen had the mayor's ear. One councilor, a member of the political opposition, complained that his constituents were never given access to these funds. In 1894, Toulouse councilmen and the mayor handed out bread coupons worth 20,000 francs, which they distributed with no accounting. It was, in the words of an historian of Toulouse welfare, "the means to be popular for certain councilmen." The city also used its unique *dizeniers,* block leaders, who served as electoral agents, to distribute aid funds. They undoubtedly allowed political considerations to play a role in providing assistance. In the latter part of the century, Marseille councilmen attending council meetings were provided with 150 food coupons which could be disbursed at will. They were not always distributed to the most impoverished; supposedly people with incomes as high as five francs a day were receiving food coupons. A scandal occurred in the 1890s when a councilman gave the coupons to his mother, who apparently was not needy.

The use of welfare rolls for political purposes was common enough that in a discussion of poverty at the national level, it was recognized as one of the major problems besetting assistance programs. The former head of the welfare division in the ministry of interior, the well-known Henri Monod, lamented in 1909 "the tendency of certain elected bodies to register on the [assistance] list political allies who could do well without any aid."[59]

The emphasis on providing welfare support—although of limited amounts—to a large number of persons appears to have been more frequent in cities experiencing tight political races, such as Marseille, Saint-Etienne, and Toulouse. In Lyon and Bordeaux, the political situation was usually predictable—in the former, the Left, and in the latter, the Center was well organized and usually had no need to resort to padding the welfare rolls to win elections or stay in power.

Programmatically, the Left was committed to welfare, while the Right was skeptical, but such contrasts did not necessarily transcend the rhetorical realm. When the Socialists came to power in Saint-Etienne in 1888, they increased the subsidy to the *bureau de bienfaisance* by 50 percent from 36,000 francs per year to 54,000. It reached 209,000 francs in 1903—nearly a fourfold increase in the municipal subsidy over 15 years. Once these large subsidies became common, even Conservatives who temporarily gained control over city hall maintained them, cutting them only 8 percent in 1907. But the example of Saint-Etienne does not allow for generalizations. In Marseille, the Socialists won city hall in 1892, but did not increase the subsidy until 1897—and then by 20 percent, followed in the ensuing year by another increase of 30 percent. Then the Socialists, faced with a tight budget, cut back the subsidy to the 1897 level. A Conservative victory in 1902 left the subsidy intact. Bordeaux, even without a change in the political makeup of its city administration, increased its subsidy by 30 percent between 1879 and 1885. The amount spent per person by bureaus in the cities in this study was lowest in Saint-Etienne, even though it was a Socialist city beginning in 1888. The percentage of the city budget going as a subvention to the bureau was lowest in Socialist Marseille, at .5 percent; while Socialist Saint-Etienne expended 2 percent; and Lyon, where the Socialists participated in a coalition, expended 2.5 percent. In some cases, Socialist victories at the municipal level meant increased welfare expenditures, but not invariably.[60]

Table 8.2: Municipal Welfare Expenditures in Selected French Cities, 1878-1910 (Percent of Budget)

	1878	1898	1910
Bordeaux	15.0	13.0	14.0
Lyon	12.4	12.4	11.5
Marseille	13.0	12.5	12.0
Saint-Etienne	9.0	14.0	6.9
Toulouse	14.8	12.0	6.8

Source: François Cavaignac, "La Politique budgétaire de la municipalité de Toulouse de 1888 à 1900" (Unpublished Maîtrise thesis, 1973), 130; City budgets.

Looking at poor relief across France in the mid-nineteenth century, the English historian Roger Price characterized it as haphazard, inadequate, and disorganized. It continued to be so throughout the century. A law professor writing in the 1880s described the confused ways in which the bureaus dealt with the poor: "Aid is distributed without thought or plan to the poor who complain the most, not necessarily to those who are most unfortunate." Twenty years later, an editorial in the respected regional newspaper *Dépêche de Toulouse* saw these and other problems still besetting the granting of aid through the bureaus.

> Everything is insufficient, the resources as well as the methods used. Budgets are small and are allocated into far too small amounts of aid. The aid is distributed with insufficient care or intelligence. The cure has to fit the patient. The indigent totally unable to work should be provided with aid; the needy who are unemployed should be given work. Instead the bureaus distribute in a uniform and mechanical fashion.[61]

Some communes gave more support to hospices than to outdoor relief programs. Adding the major expenses together, however, one finds roughly equivalent proportions of the municipal budgets of the cities in this study spent on "assistance," or welfare—all higher than the national average which fluctuated for the years indicated between 5 and 6.3 percent.[62]

PRIVATE CHARITY

In addition to the aid provided municipalities, there was considerable private charitable activity. No one knows how much money was spent. In 1876, the archivist of Marseille estimated that private charities provided two million francs a year for 30,000 to 40,000 needy persons; toward the end of the century, the figure was five million francs. A student of the assistance programs in Marseille enumerated more than 150 active private philanthropic groups, from societies offering assistance to expectant mothers, orphans and sailors, to a trade school for Jewish children. In Saint-Etienne, an estimated half of the four million francs a year spent on care for the poor and the sick came from private charities. Lyon, endowed with somewhere between 245 and 300 private charitable organizations, provided around 13 million francs annually in 1906, while city services expended 8 million francs. A common assumption was that private charity equaled all state and local assistance combined, but it often exceeded it. Even more than official welfare services, the private ones were disorganized, arbitrarily distributed, and not necessarily directed toward the most needy-as contemporaries and later historians have remarked.[63]

OTHER MEASURES

Emergency Assistance

On an ad hoc basis, the municipalities made special forms of aid available for the poor. In the first half of the century, when the poor were often vulnerable to poor harvests and skyrocketing food prices, municipalities initiated various measures to provide help. While such measures were frequent in the first half of the century, they did not entirely cease thereafter. In 1810, in the face of big increases in food prices, the mayor of Toulouse provided aid. In 1812, the misery was so widespread that the city administration handed out 4,000 bowls of soup a day (in a city with 65,000 inhabitants). In Lyon, in the face of crop failure in 1817, the city council voted a "poor tax," bringing in an extra 55,000 francs for what a contemporary described as "relief of the poor. . . . Our streets are filled day and night with a considerable multitude of beggars of every sex and age." A particularly bad winter in 1844 led the Toulouse city council to vote 10,000 francs for bread coupons for the needy. In 1847, a difficult year in most of France, Bordeaux provided bread for 21,700 persons, Toulouse for 20,000. In 1848, Saint-Etienne opened soup kitchens. The Toulouse municipality did the same thing in 1853 to assuage the effects of severe unemployment. In the winter of 1867, Toulouse approved a combination of special funds to provide bread coupons and public works.[64]

While the problems of food supplies had been generally resolved by mid-century, municipalities still sometimes intervened to help the workers through particularly grim seasons of unemployment. In Saint-Etienne, heavy unemployment among the ribbon workers led the city to establish food distribution centers, *fourneaux économiques,* which handed out meals at 5 centimes each. In 22 weeks in 1857, they distributed 11,128 meals. In 1867-68, they prepared 148,559 meals. During the Commune in 1871 and the high unemployment years in 1884 and 1906, Saint-Etienne's soup kitchens reopened. In 1884, a particularly difficult year in Saint-Etienne, the city voted an extra 300,000 francs for relief and public works; 50,000 francs was distributed in 10 to 15 franc amounts to 3,600 workers.[65]

Lyon, in the face of a crisis in the silk industry in the 1870s, started an international fund drive to aid the silk workers; the municipality provided 200,000 francs of the 700,000 francs raised, including Paris's 50,000 francs, Marseille's 10,000 francs, and Bordeaux's and Toulouse's 5,000 francs each. Contributions came from as far away as Egypt, Morocco, and Uruguay. In 1884, when the silk workers again faced hardships, the city again came to their rescue.[66]

Many urban improvement projects provided employment. When in 1816 the public works commission in Bordeaux recommended a program of street widening for health and beautification reasons, it added that the project would give employment to "a large number of workers." Welfare rolls could swell when public works ceased; the Bordeaux municipality explained in 1820 that the 1,100 person increase in its welfare rolls was due to the completion the year before of the demolition of the Chateau Trompette.

In Lyon, workers organized into *ateliers de charité,* but unlike those of the ancien régime, which were factories run with the labor of the poor, these were brigades building public works. They were created to prevent "the consequences which need and idleness of a large number of individuals easy to mislead" could cause. The downturn of the economy subsequent to the July Revolution in 1830 led the Saint-Etienne city council to provide 75,000 francs for a series of public works. At the same time, Bordeaux voted 130,000 francs to provide "work to those without." Employing people in public works provided salaries instead of handouts, which, the city council observed, would have humiliated the unemployed. The measure would not only provide city improvements but also ensure "public tranquillity." In 1831-32, 513 workers were employed daily in Bordeaux removing and planting trees and clearing ditches.[67]

During a recession in 1836, Saint-Etienne voted 25,000 francs to put 500 unemployed to work at a franc per day. In 1843, Toulouse provided work for able-bodied beggars organized into an *atelier de charité,* but the pay was low: .70 francs per day for a man, .40 francs for a woman, and .30 for a child.[68]

In 1848, many cities provided work for the unemployed. In Bordeaux, beginning in April, eight work sites performing various kinds of public works employed 1,800 laborers at a total cost of 8,000-9,000 francs a week.

Both Toulouse and Lyon established similar projects. Lyon's city architect argued for public works projects solely to alleviate unemployment. Marseille provided considerable work to the unemployed as it sought to finish the aqueduct connecting the city to the Durance River. Within the city walls there was also work leveling major streets and terracing the Prado. Marseille may have put as many as half its unemployed to work. As in Paris, Marseille had its national workshops; the port city spent 200,000 francs a week to keep these workshops going in the spring of 1848. Much of the work was just make-work; an historian has estimated that 870,000 francs were spent per month between March and May 1848, mainly to keep the poor employed. In 1848, Lyon spent over a million francs on the national workshops, providing work for 30,000 men, though a republican opponent described the public works as "movements of earth from one place to another." Saint-Etienne also established public works to feed the unemployed and thus, the city fathers hoped, preserve public order.[69]

In the second half of the century, public works continued as a means to aid the unemployed. Beginning in the 1880s, Saint-Etienne created public works almost yearly to help alleviate unemployment. The Toulouse city council voted a public works budget in 1895 "to assure employment for workers during the winter." The Radical party, the mayor of Toulouse proclaimed, was traditionally committed to public works, not only because they embellished the city but also because they gave "workers, artisans, and industrialists as much work as possible." Often the rationale for urban renewal projects was their ability to generate employment for the jobless (see chapter 9).

Some employment was more temporary, although probably of some use to the cities. Brigades of street sweepers were hired during hard times. In 1879, Bordeaux had indigents sweep the streets at night, for in the daytime, a city official explained, they did not want to make known their misery. Given the poor street lighting, one can imagine that street-cleaning at night was at best perfunctory. Reviewing in 1910 why street-cleaning was a municipal service in Toulouse and most other cities, a local official explained,

> In all French cities, street cleaning is the last resort for the unemployed, the poor, the failed. In employing all these unfortunates in cleaning the streets, municipalities have found the practical means of replacing charity with work . . .[70]

Municipal Pawnshops

The persistence of the pawnshop in our era suggests the continuity of old forms of assistance, first started in the middle ages. The lack of adequate credit institutions for the rich and especially for the poor ensured the survival of municipal pawnshops.

While there were private pawnshops, beginning in the Middle Ages, charitable organizations operated such institutions, charging little or no interest to help see the poor through temporary hard times. To fight usurious private pawnshops, an Italian monk established a charitable one in Peruggia in 1462. By the end of the fifteenth century, there were over 80 in the Italian peninsula. The Dutch Republic emulated Italy, and in the beginning of the seventeenth century in France, a number of reformers—most prominent among them Théophraste Renaudot—suggested the establishment of government-run pawnshops. While these projects aborted, royal edicts toward the end of the century allowed municipal-run pawn shops that charged minimal fees to operate on a non-profit basis. Montpellier opened the first municipal pawnshop in 1684. Of the cities in this study, the first to have one was Marseille, in 1696. A royal edict in 1777 established a municipal pawnshop in Paris, inspiring the establishment of more such institutions in provincial cities. Bordeaux opened one the following year, but it soon failed. The Revolution abolished public pawnshops, but they started up again at the beginning of the nineteenth century.[71]

The usefulness of pawnshops was recognized under Napoleon. His minister of interior asked the prefects to establish them, since pawnshops were "necessary to the relief of the poor." Bordeaux started a municipal pawnshop in 1801, Marseille in 1807, and Lyon in 1810. But the Toulouse city council unanimously refused to establish a pawnshop in 1817. Influenced by royalism and traditional Catholicism, the council rejected pawnshops as "a monster of usury. The city of Toulouse is not in a situation where it has to sacrifice religious and political principles to the interests of money." Pawnshops, the council argued, encouraged bad morals, tempting people to live above their means and giving them assistance when they fell into financial difficulties as a result of having been careless or irresponsible. For ten years, the council repeatedly turned down requests for such an institution. Finally, in 1827, it created a pawnshop, but one that charged no interest. That meant it was financed by a subvention and the sale of non-reclaimed objects, usually those of value. As for Saint-Etienne, in the early part of the nineteenth century it was too small and too poor to consider opening a pawnshop, but even later, after the city grew, it still did not found a pawnshop.

Municipal pawnshops were regarded as a welfare measure. De Watteville, a national welfare inspector, described these pawnshops in 1846 as useful to the poor; they put limits to usury, reduce begging in providing working men with the means to take care of emergencies such as sickness, unemployment, or some other accident; and contributes to the honor of the poor citizen in saving him from resorting to unworthy means to provide himself with money.[72]

The Toulouse city council declared pawnshops "indispensable in the large cities, where there is great poverty; they serve as complements to the welfare institutions. . . ." Most of the pawnshops were underwritten by the Commission d'hospices, a sign that they were fulfilling a charitable mission.[73]

The pawnshops, particularly in the early years, charged high interest rates. When Bordeaux opened its pawnshop in 1802, the interest rate was 24 percent; it was lowered to 18 percent in 1806, 15 percent in 1830, 10 percent in 1840, 9 percent in 1843, 8 percent in 1879, and 6 percent in 1886. Marseille's opened with an interest rate of 18 percent, which national and local commentators observed "was not an act of charity." It too went steadily down, to 10 percent in 1815, 6 percent in 1834, and 5.75 percent in 1890. The Toulouse pawnshop at first charged no interest rates but eventually charged rates no different from other cities.[74] The highest interest rates typically were charged on items of lowest value. Thus the Lyon pawnshop in the 1840s charged 12 percent on goods valued under 1,000 francs and 8 percent for items worth more than 2,000 francs. As De Watteville noted, "This way of proceeding is as illogical as it is uncharitable." Honoré de Balzac, who had occasion to use the Parisian pawnshop, called it "the king of usury."[75]

The average worth of pawned goods varied considerably between cities. Around 1850, the average value per item pawned ranged from 51.9 francs in Bordeaux to 15 francs in Lyon. In 1900, it ranged from 26.9 francs in Toulouse to 16.5 francs in Lyon. Toulouse's average value at mid-century, 41.45 francs, reflected the shop's lack of funding and hence its inability to accept pawns from the poorest part of the population. More accommodating to the poor was Bordeaux, where a minimum pawn of 3 francs was accepted.[76]

The poor often had to pawn items they needed in times of emergency. During the hard year of 1848, the government provided grants to pawnshops to release such items to their owners. During harsh winters, the Bordeaux and Toulouse municipalities provided funds so the pawnshops could return blankets and mattresses, the most commonly pawned items, to their owners.[77]

The well-off and even the wealthy at times used the pawnshops to alleviate temporary cash-flow problems or to safely store valuable items while away on business or vacation. But most of the customers continued to be the poor. In Marseille, half the items pawned in 1885 were valued under 10 francs. In Toulouse in 1901, two-thirds of the pawned items were worth less than ten francs. While workers were the most frequent users of the pawnshop, others employed it too. In 1893, 34 percent of the Marseille pawnshop clients were workers, 33 percent were employees, 11 percent small tradesmen, 9 percent rentiers, 6 percent in liberal professions, 4 percent merchants, and 3 percent agriculturists.[78]

Saint-Etienne's lack of a municipal pawnshop is striking. France overall had at least 50, and many of them were in towns far smaller than Saint-Etienne. Beginning in the early 1840s, various plans for a pawnshop surfaced, but none was implemented. One reason may be that Lyon's pawnshop was not far away and operated a branch in Saint-Etienne. The public demanded a pawnshop in Saint-Etienne, and the Socialists promised one in their platform during the municipal elections of 1896. That same year, a petition signed by 40 housewives, miners, hairdressers, mattress makers, and traveling salesmen asked the council to establish a pawnshop, since "the only pawnshop which now exists is in Lyon and it does not accept clothes; it demands jewels. We . . . have no jewels; we gave up our wedding bands long ago. We have only our clothes to spare, and at present they are refused for pawning." Nonetheless, the poor people of Saint-Etienne had to wait until 1914 for a municipal pawnshop to open.[79]

In Paris, the municipal pawnshop by the end of the nineteenth century played a less crucial role in the life of the poor. Workers' mutual aid societies developed beginning in the 1860s; state intervention assured workers' compensation, retirement benefits, and medical care for the indigent. These new forms of assistance appears to have saved many from the pawnshop.[80] In the provinces, however, such a trend was still not apparent before the war. Typically, pawnshops accepted an increasing number of objects and lent larger sums. Even towards the end of our period, pawnshop were still playing an important role in helping the poor.

TOWARD THE WELFARE STATE

At the national level, reformers and legislators were deeply concerned with France's demographic crisis, which was a result of a falling birth rate, and they seemed in large part to have supported social legislation out of patriotic, pronatalist concerns. While such concerns were mentioned by private charitable groups in some cities, for instance Lyon, they were not championed in the city halls or local welfare bureaus included in this study.[81] The absence of such a debate in city halls was probably due to the fact that many of the institutions assigned by the national government to deal with children and women were departmental, rather than municipal. Yet municipalities continued to provide local welfare for many, which included poor women, single mothers, and families with children. Such issues could have given occasion to address welfare in the language of gender and populationism. And yet that was not done. Municipalities' lack of interest in natalism suggest that appeals to the population problem may not have been as deeply and broadly felt as some historians have believed. Rather, the national appeal to natalism may reflect a discourse crafted to win support from groups and regions within the nation who otherwise might not have supported measures improving the lot of children and mothers.

Municipalities created welfare programs to provide for needs they could see in front of their own eyes—poor people without enough to eat and lacking satisfactory shelter, children who were abandoned, sick people who had no care, infants who were malnourished, workers temporarily out of work. Local elites understood the need for social programs that would alleviate the worst misery, reduce the offending sight of public begging and other forms of human misery, and ensure social peace within the city. Under the influence of new forms of production and political ideologies, class divisions threatened the common identity of urban dwellers. Limited as municipal welfare was, it was throughout the nineteenth century the only source of public assistance reinforcing class cohesion.

While there were some changes over time in the disbursal of welfare, the most striking fact is the persistence of older traditions of dealing with the poor, attitudes and methods going back to the ancien régime. Also, local elites appeared to respond to the poor with little regard for changing economic needs of their services—rather, it was an empirical expansion of services to meet growing needs.

The municipalities initiated many programs before the national government did so. Most welfare was provided by local government; in 1885, only 3 percent of the funds spent on assistance to the poor came from the national government. By the end of the nineteenth century, the national government began to mandate welfare responsibilities to local governments. A law of 1893 made it obligatory for departments and communes to provide free medical assistance to the indigent, a law of 1905 provided assistance to the aged who were infirm or incurably ill, and finally two laws of 1913 provided assistance to unmarried mothers and to large families. While these laws show a national interest in the lot of the poor, the burden was to be carried by departments and especially municipalities.[82]

Some of our cities had initiated programs prior to their being mandated by Paris. All of our cities provided medical care and general care for the indigent throughout the nineteenth century prior to the respective laws of 1893 and of 1905 that made these services mandatory. The difference was that the national laws made this aid obligatory to *all* the people who were needy and set minimum amounts that were to be received. Lyon resisted the law for ten years, not because it did not provide aid, but rather because it saw the legislation as an intrusion of the central government. The mandatory laws increased the cost of welfare in some cases. The 1905 law, for example, stipulated 60 francs a year for the aged indigent, Saint-Etienne provided less, and its budget felt the effect of the new law. Marseille, on the other hand, already provided 80 francs per person a year to the aged indigent. The Toulouse welfare budget rose by 200,000 francs between 1910 and 1914—mainly because of the new mandates. Budgets were in some cases hard hit, and the mandates explain some steep rises in welfare expenses. The fact that the modest national laws raised welfare costs for the cities suggests that their previous contributions were low, but those contributions still represented the only type of public assistance then available.

As a result of the new national laws and the municipalities' own increased commitments, total outlays on welfare increased significantly. French communes disbursed on welfare 550 percent more in 1909 than in 1890. Our cities increased their outlays, although they were not quite as dramatic as they were for the many small towns and villages. Lyon's expenditures went from 1.1 million francs to 2 million francs, Marseille from 1.2 million francs to 2.3 million francs, Toulouse from 431,000 to 1.4 million francs.

During this period, the role of the state in providing for welfare increased considerably. In 1890, the national government provided 4 million out of 42.6 million francs, or 9 percent of the national expenditure on welfare; by 1909, it provided 39 percent of the national expenditures. While the national government was increasingly taking on responsibilities for welfare, even at the end of our period most of the expenditures in this field still came from local government units, especially large cities.

The total aid provided by both national and local units were admittedly modest by comparison with some of France's neighbors. While in 1912 the French spent 34.9 francs per pauper, the British spent the equivalent of 180 francs, more than five times as much as the French. In relation to its own legacy, however, France had made important strides forward.[83]

Assistance at the local level preceded a national sense of government responsibility for the poor and disinherited. And it might be argued that the notion of the welfare society, "l'état providence," developed in a rudimentary fashion within the walls of the city, where it was pioneered before it became national policy in the twentieth century.

9

Reorganizing Urban Space

*I*n the face of economic and demographic growth, French cities in the nineteenth century needed to rebuild. Many launched ambitious programs around mid-century to reorganize urban space: they broadened and straightened out major traffic arteries, built new city squares and enlarged old ones, and created major city parks. The best-known and most spectacular transformation occurred in Paris, and it provided a model by which all urban renewal was measured. But provincial municipalities also launched ambitious attempts to establish control over their urban environments, and these efforts represented the largest single financial outlay by all major municipalities in the nineteenth century. What happened in mid-century was foreshadowed by several earlier experiments in city planning.

ANTECEDENTS

Urban planning antedated the nineteenth century. In the Renaissance, cities had instituted various programs intended to facilitate the movement of troops and goods. Large and wide streets gained aesthetic value, and renewal programs often were called programs of beautification, *embellissement*.

French cities adopted particularly important attempts at urban planning in the eighteenth century, as city administrators, medical doctors, and purveyors of the new discipline of statistics posited a relationship between commerce, industry, population, wealth, quality of housing, and mortality and morbidity in cities. Urbanists, borrowing from biology, described the city as having lungs, arteries, and, a heart, and as experiencing circulation or asphyxia, depending on how successfully a city was managed. That century saw an attempt at planning intended to ensure easier circulation of people and goods and less crowding, with more air and sunlight and thus better health. Cities developed numerous proposals, although most of them remained unrealized.[1]

The five cities in this study were at this time active in drawing up schemes for urban renewal. Throughout the eighteenth century, the city administrators attempted to widen and straighten streets, build large squares to ensure circulation and health, and erect bridges and quays that helped trade. The most dramatic urban transformation in the five cities during the eighteenth century occurred in Bordeaux. The provincial intendant, Louis Tourny, tore down much of the old city fabric; constructed wide avenues and the grand Place Royale; and imposed stately, standard classical facades on the new, sumptuous residences that were built. The grandeur of these transformations put its mark on the whole city, making it the "classical city." In fact, this style still gives the city its imprint.

The historian Jean-Pierre Poussou ascribes Bordeaux's changes to the determined actions of the intendant Tourny, who struggled against an obdurate local council. That may be an accurate description of Bordeaux, but in other cities local elites appear to have played major roles in eighteenth-century urban transformation.[2] Particularly strong examples are found in Lyon, Marseille, and Toulouse, where the elites built new squares, major *allées*, and quays.[3]

The Revolution on the whole was not a propitious time for urban transformation. Cities were short of funds and embroiled in numerous political disputes. In Lyon, however, the Revolution opened up new possibilities. Under the ancien régime, the Church owned extensive property in the center of Lyon and had successfully resisted attempts by the city to acquire church land or to impose regulations on its holdings. But as a result of the Revolution, the sale of clerical property in October 1794 made some of this real estate available to the city, and it could impose long overdue changes. The city took sides against the National Convention, and in reprisal Paris ordered the razing of the city. The fanciest area, around the Place Bellecour, was partly razed, but the city fathers were able to channel the destruction to more useful purposes; some old houses along the Sâone, very much in need of removal, were also torn down.[4]

Napoleon started a national effort in 1807 to encourage urban renewal when a law was passed requiring municipalities to adopt citywide plans. It also required mapping the city (many cities did not have complete city maps) and devising plans to straighten and widen principal urban arteries. Marseille had already established a partial plan in 1801, and a few other cities had already embarked on a number of urban schemes.[5] All the cities in this study were slow, however, to respond to the Napoleonic order to establish a citywide plan. By 1810, the Bordeaux city engineer still had not finished his plan. Lyon voted in 1808 to spend 100,000 francs a year "to acquire and destroy houses or parts of houses that obstruct the public street." This was a piecemeal approach and did not constitute the carrying out of a general plan. In Marseille and Toulouse, the plans were delayed several times and were not finished until 1825. In Saint-Etienne, the city council discussed the law of 1807 but failed to adopt the required plan.[6] Municipalities fell short of the overall comprehensive city planning that the Napoleonic decree of 1807 had mandated.[7] Yet, even during the years of Napoleonic rule and of the Restoration, significant projects were launched that changed urban space.

While many cities failed to adopt the more daring proposals for change, they were far from inactive. The Bordeaux city council enlarged 200 streets, and built the Place Quinconces, where the Château Trompette, torn down in 1818, had stood. And a very important contribution to public health and the reduction of stench was the transfer of the slaughterhouses from the city center to a peripheral area. A long-sought bridge, crossing the Garonne and joining Bordeaux to the suburb of La Bastide, was built; the hospital Saint-André was erected.

On what had been the outskirts of Toulouse, the city built an imposing square with a uniform facade and five radiating avenues, the Place Angoulême (later the Place Lafayette, and still later the Place Wilson). First planned in the 1780s, then delayed because of political instability and financial and technical problems, the square was finished in its present oval form in 1834 with an impressive, uniform, classical three-story facade of buildings enclosing it. It was connected to the canal (then the main means of transportation for the city) by a 60-meter-wide-mall that had tree-bordered walks on each side (later known as the Allées Jean Jaurès). The Place Angoulême/Lafayette stood out in contrast to the rest of the city, which Stendhal described as "ugly," "not having three houses in a row the facade of which forms a straight line."

Saint-Etienne had an energetic mayor, Hippolyte Royet, who during his rule (1819-30) attempted to meet many of the city's needs. He erected the Bourse and City Hall buildings, covered that part of the Furan River flowing through the city, and enlarged streets, notably the major artery, the Route de Roanne. New churches, a monumental fountain, and a new slaughterhouse were erected. The suburbs were annexed, nearly doubling the surface of the city. Royet remained true to his personal motto, adopted from Napoleon: "Impossible is not French."[8]

Compared with transformations that were to occur later, the early-nineteenth-century urbanist programs were modest, but it seems unfair to dismiss them as nonexistent and to say, as Roger Chartier has, that no provincial city was to see any urban planning or projects under Napoleon and the Restoration.[9]

THE JULY MONARCHY

The July Monarchy, in the provinces as in Paris, brought with it programs of city rebuilding and planning, and laid the basis for the dramatic transformations that were to occur in the following regime. The need for urban renewal became far greater in the 1840s as urban population growth really took off. Whereas, with the exception of Saint-Etienne, all the cities in this study had been demographically stagnant in the 40 years after the Revolution, these cities now experienced significant growth.

The crowding and the growing industry and trade created increasing hustle and bustle on city streets, revealing them to be far too narrow. New railroad connections made the cities even more crowded, as passengers and goods boarded and disembarked. While the cholera epidemic of the 1830s did not hit all cities, every municipality recognized itself to be vulnerable. While the causes of cholera were unknown, it was recognized that cholera hit areas that were crowded, dark, and damp; to avoid disease, open areas and wide streets, allowing the flow of fresh air and sunshine, were recognized as important. Traffic needs, as well as health and aesthetic considerations, led to the movement to reorganize urban space.

Under the influence of the mass uprisings of 1831 and 1834, the Lyon city fathers felt the need to transform the city. As one of them stated, "It is a powerful and noble means of moralizing people to prove to them by highly useful acts that they are the objects of the solicitude of their magistrates." Also, Lyon's rank as the second largest city in the kingdom seemed to call for special policies. "It is important that our city maintain the position of second city of the kingdom," a councilman declared; "it cannot remain immobile in the face of improvements and the progress of most of the large cities of France. . . . The love of progress is spreading everywhere."[10]

Lyon was far more crowded than other cities in this study, with houses of four or five floors, sometimes even seven, tightly wedged against each other. A contemporary author described Lyon's houses as "black, tall, ugly . . . which crush you, hide the sky and light; the mud on the streets never dry." Jules Michelet denounced Lyon as "a decidedly second-rate city . . . a city almost everywhere black and shadowy. . . ."[11]

While necessity dictated that the old Lyon slums be torn down, there were also good opportunities for urban renewal, especially the newly available ecclesiastical land, providing sites for city squares, public buildings, and major arteries.[12] Lyon's mayor from 1830 to 1848 was the distinguished medical doctor, Jean-François Terme, who shared with the council his conviction that urban renewal would improve public health.

In the 1830s and 1840s, other major urban transformations were implemented in Lyon. Seven new bridges were built across the city rivers; the slaughterhouses were moved away from the center of the city; new quays were built to control the flooding rivers; several streets were widened and lengthened, and many were provided with sidewalks. The transformations occurring in Lyon in the late 1840s were seen by a local observer as bringing in a truly revolutionary age. "Never on Greek or Roman soil, even at the time of the Florentines or the Luccans, was there a comparable movement of workers and building," he declared triumphantly.[13]

Other cities also embarked on programs of urban transformation. In 1837, a Toulouse city commission announced a dynamic rationale for changing the city: ease of communications "shortens distance; brings closer to the consumer the objects that nature or habits make desirable, and develop the three things that society needs: industry, commerce and agriculture." Canals, railroads, and national roads contributed, but so did the widening of city streets—which also enhanced public cleanliness and health. If in the past streets had been built narrowly to shelter people from sunlight and winds, now the increase in traffic made it necessary to build broad avenues. Aesthetic considerations, common in the eighteenth century, persisted as an argument for urban renewal. Cities, the Toulouse city council declared, have to concern themselves with their beautification, *embellissements*. "It is by their monuments, the layout of their streets, their squares, that cities reveal their wealth, the capacities and taste, the genius of their inhabitants." Toulouse in the 1830s and 1840s built boulevards on the sites of its former walls. Its cemetery and slaughterhouses were moved to the outskirts of the city, and two new bridges across the Garonne were erected to ease traffic flow.[14]

Commercial concerns led Marseille to build not only a new set of quays on the port but also a new port, the Joliette. Concerned about the increasing crowdedness of the city and the difficulty of circulation, the city council enlarged and extended streets, such as the Rue Paradis and Rue Saint-Barbe, making them into major arteries.

Saint-Etienne, too, underwent important changes. Contemporaries visiting the industrial city for the first time during this period were sometimes aghast; Stendhal dismissed it as "simply an English city . . . where the streets are wide and dark as in England." A Lyon journalist described its old city as "but a heap of poor houses . . ." But for those who had known the city before, progress was clear. A guide to the region in 1849 noted how surprised a visitor would be who had not been in the city for 30 years. He would not recognize it: "The broad streets of that epoch are now but alleys in comparison with the broad avenues that are open everywhere." New large squares and public buildings stood out. The city purchased a terrain in 1839, developed it in 1848-49, and opened it as the Jardin des Plantes in 1856.[15]

Municipalities did not take on the full burden of city renewal; much still depended on the private sector. Cities saw it as quite natural for private individuals to play roles in providing urban amenities. When the monies granted by Napoleon to build the Bordeaux bridge over the Garonne ran out, a local wine and cloth merchant, Balguerie-Stuttenberg, finished the bridge in 1822 and then collected tolls. In Saint-Etienne, the city council voted to enlarge and extend a major avenue after the property owners agreed to share the cost.[16] Some of the most spectacular examples of urban renewal in Marseille, including the development of the Avenue Prado and four other large avenues in the 1830s, were the result of private initiative and financing, although admittedly with a good subsidy from the city.

One reason why French cities were so timid in launching projects was their failure to anticipate population growth. To contemporaries, it was far from obvious that the growth of the 1830s and 1840s would continue. Saint-Etienne, when trying to become a departmental capital in the 1790s, had claimed it would have a population "soon to exceed 100,000," but that was but a vain boast to impress the revolutionary assembly. One could take more seriously Mayor Royet's prediction in 1819 that the population of Saint-Etienne, then 24,000, would soon reach a maximum of 40,000. He based his estimates on the example of "various cities in France and abroad with which we can compare ourselves in terms of industrial resources." But few authorities in the city took steps in anticipation of future growth. The experience Saint-Etienne had with its cemetery reveals the extent to which it failed to prepare for growth. It acquired burial grounds in 1819, but this land was filled by 1825. It had to annex more land in 1836 and still more in 1840.[17]

Other cities failed to plan for demographic growth and one of its byproducts—increased deaths. In Lyon the Loyasse cemetery, started in

1807, had to be expanded repeatedly thereafter: in 1831, 1834, and again in 1853. In Marseille the Saint-Charles cemetery, opened in 1821, was built with no anticipation of the need for additional space. Established in an area surrounded by streets and avenues, it offered no possibility of expansion, and within a couple of decades it no longer could meet the city's needs.[18]

When enlarging the port or building an auxiliary one became a pressing issue in Marseille in the 1840s, an essayist warned: "The essential is to stay away from any extravaganza and not do anything too ambitious. . . . If, in a few centuries, Marseille has a population of half a million and its port is insufficient, then it can be taken care of." Who would have thought Marseille would reach that goal within half a century? One concerned Toulousain, after suggesting in a one-volume work a series of urban improvements for his city, added, "I am not saying that all my ideas have to be executed in ten years, or in twenty . . . we should fulfill only some, our children some others, the rest will be done after them. . . ." In Bordeaux, the city commission considered street improvements, but concluded there was no hurry: "The existence of cities is not measured by generations; for them centuries are like years in the life of a man."[19]

Some historians have been severe with the shortcomings of municipalities in the 1830s and 1840s, pointing out their failure to modernize the urban environment.[20] But it must be noted that this era laid the groundwork for the dynamic years that followed. Cities not only physically changed their urban space in the 1830s and 1840s, they also created important blueprints for the future. In Marseille, many buildings, though not built, were nevertheless planned, laying the basis for their construction during the Second Empire. They include the Hôpital de la Conception, the new Cathedral, the Palace of the Bourse, the Museum of Longchamp, and the Faculté des sciences. If funds were insufficient for building large avenues, nevertheless Marseille's council specified that as soon as it had the monies it would begin building. In Toulouse, this period also saw the laying of ambitious foundations. Urbain Vitry, the city architect in the 1840s, drew up a new city plan, based on the 1807 designs by his uncle (also city architect), Jacques Pascal Virebent. As revised by Vitry, the plan was the basis for Toulouse's urban renewal projects from the Second Empire until the 1970s.[21]

The 1830s and 1840s were important years in bringing about and imagining urban change. Like the prefect Rambuteau in Paris, whose widening of streets; tearing down of slums; and vision of a new, restructured Paris was to lay the basis for Haussmann, so in the provinces the activities of the municipalities during the July monarchy to an important extent set the stage for the transformation that was to come.[22]

FINANCING CITY IMPROVEMENTS

A powerful impediment to introducing more ambitious urban projects until mid-century was the difficulty cities had in imagining how they would pay for the astronomical costs that even the more modest urban programs would necessitate. Cities, it was thought, should spend on urban improvement projects only what they could afford, preferably out of current income.

Toulouse's mayor declared in 1805 that the first obligation of the city budget was to meet basic needs: administration, police, lighting, and hospices. All funds needed for reparation, "even the most urgent ones, as well as beautification, must be taken out of the remaining funds." The mayor realized that there might be unforeseen expenses that could not be delayed, "for instance the collapse of an aqueduct or the breach in a city wall." Such expenses should be paid out of a reserve fund the mayor suggested the city establish. But even for emergencies, the thought of taking out a loan did not occur. To borrow money was clearly anathema; noting that the Lyon budget included debts, the mayor urged the council to see to it that they were paid off immediately, for "the credit of a city is like that of the head of a household or a merchant. . . ."[23]

When Lyon's mayor issued an ambitious list of improvements for the city, his suggestion on how to finance them was to "create the funds in advance." In other words, he wanted to save money from the regular operating budget, then use the funds to carry out a project. When he stepped down in 1826, still guarding a budget with income higher than expenditures, he proudly told his successor, "Your inheritance, I have preserved it intact."[24]

Loans, if taken, were infrequent. The one major loan floated in Marseille in the 1820s was for the popular (but inutile) triumphal arch celebrating the expedition to Spain. Even then, the official cautious attitude toward loans can be seen in the division of the 350,000-franc loan into several sections. As one section of borrowed money was used up, another would be borrowed. "Borrowing the totality of the sum would be premature," the city explained on a poster, "and would needlessly undermine the city's finances making it pay interest on a sum it was not using while it would be lying uselessly in its treasury."[25]

When loans were taken, it was with great circumspection. Bordeaux issued its first bonds in 1817 to raze the Château Trompette area, but only reluctantly. Bordeaux thereafter refrained from borrowing money for public works; after the Revolution of 1830 it did take a 1.5-million-franc loan, but that was to cover a deficit in the regular operating budget. In spite of obvious and declared needs for urban improvements, Bordeaux officials proudly announced their opposition to loans and their dedication to "having our expenses square with those of our income."[26]

Lyon borrowed ten million francs between 1827 and 1847 to allow it to carry on major projects and meet emergencies such as the flood of 1840. But the Lyon council, faced in 1830 with the financial difficulties of the Revolution, regretted the loans it had been taking shortly before, calling them "harmful." While some important projects were built in Lyon in the 1840s, most that were discussed during the July Monarchy ended up being tabled for fear of the expenses involved.[27]

In Toulouse, the mayor claimed that funds remaining after the required operating costs were met were sufficient to deal with the needed capital investments. He warned against taking out any loans, for they would cause "disorder in our finances," lead to higher taxes, and "anger the citizens." When city income went up and projects long desired might have been realized, the mayor continued to preach fiscal prudence.[28]

The national government also discouraged municipal indebtedness. The minister of interior in a circular warned municipalities against contracting loans for frivolous purposes and urged limiting them to "actual, pressing needs that are clearly proven." Loans were to be taken for a short period; this stipulation meant that yearly payments would be large and daunting.[29]

When Marseille desperately needed more water, a special commission of the municipal council in 1834 recommended against financing the project with a loan. To do so would throw "too great a complication into the administration [of the city], which ought to be as simple as that of a family." Also, by taking a loan and saddling future generations with its payments, the municipality would be guilty of an "egoism unworthy of the council of a great city." In the end, when the funding of the canal had to be decided, a loan was floated. But it created such a heavy debt that no other project was considered. Mayor Consolat had taken the brave step to build the canal, but this visionary act did not extend to other projects.[30] Thus, a strong ideological underpinning had developed against carrying out public works by floating loans. Such credits were essential, if anything important and large were to be accomplished. Otherwise, projects would have to be done piecemeal—as in fact they were.

But while this conservatism was often expressed and practiced, it is also important to note that this is the same period during which developed a more dynamic attitude toward public spending. A minority formed a theory that was to become dominant in the next generation, making it possible for municipalities to finance the ambitious projects of the Second Empire. The prefect in the Lyon region in the 1820s insisted that the city could extend its resources by the credit it enjoyed from being rich, well run, and faithful in paying back past debts. To fulfill various plans of improvement in Lyon, the mayor suggested in 1826 a "temporary" loan. A pamphleteer in Bordeaux in the same decade suggested a program of urban renewal that could be financed with a four-million-franc loan. The improvements would lead to an increase in population, trade, and investments, which in turn would lead to a higher income for the city and thus would more than recoup the original outlay.[31]

The Marseille city council was, as stated, originally opposed to financing the canal with loans. But while other cities might forego ambitious projects rather than float loans, Marseille could not do so. It had to have water. And the rationale for the loan was one useful to all those thinking of large public improvement projects. The finance committee of the Marseille city council put it this way: "The canal is a project of the future; it is then only just that part of the expense be carried by the next generation that will be enjoying its benefits." The conclusion, therefore, was to make overall plans and implement them by large-scale loans. While these dynamic ideas did not dominate thinking on municipal credit during the July Monarchy, they helped prepare for dynamic growth later. If the city fathers during the July Monarchy had not accomplished as much as their successors, they had suggested and laid the foundation for some of the directions the latter were to take.

THE SECOND EMPIRE

Urban renewal that had been in the planning stages was brought to reality in many cities during the 1850s. Financially, the cities in this study were better off, benefiting from the general growth in the economy. Having made considerable economic progress and anticipating even more, municipalities found it easier to envision borrowing money and paying off loans with future income. They also began to realize that if they were crowded and congested now, they would only become more so in the future.

The discourse that had started in the eighteenth century on the need to make cities not only more beautiful but also healthier continued through the first part of the nineteenth century, and the growing urban population seemed to lend urgency to these concerns. Medical doctors and social reformers insisted on the need to transform the city so that it would no longer be the devourer of populations. Cholera swept several cities after 1832. Epidemics occurred in 1846 and 1849; between 1833 and 1866, Marseille was swept six times by the dreaded disease. Even in cities not afflicted by cholera, the disease represented a warning of what might happen. Other illnesses, such as tuberculosis, also flourished in such environs and contributed to high death rates.

Suffrage during the July Monarchy was limited to men of property, and thus city councilors came from that milieu. Even with the introduction of universal male suffrage in 1848, the makeup of councils changed little. Councils during the Second Empire were still nearly exclusively drawn from the propertied class. Still, even though the very wealthy lived in exclusive neighborhoods—such as the Bellecour in Lyon, the Chartron in Bordeaux, the suburbs in Toulouse, and on large lots along the Prado in Marseille—they were not immune from developments among what were commonly called "the dangerous and working classes." Self-preservation played a role in the concern shown by city elites; slums were threats not only to their denizens but also to the rest of the community.

EXPECTATIONS OF GROWTH

During the two decades spanning the Second Empire, populations of the cities in this study grew to an unprecedented degree: Bordeaux grew by 50 percent, Lyon by 70 percent, Marseille by 60 percent, Saint-Etienne by 100 percent, and Toulouse by 38 percent. (These increases include annexation of suburbs, acts that had an especially important impact on Lyon and Saint-Etienne.) This growth led city leaders to believe the process would continue. If Marseille had 300,000 people in 1857, "[the number] is probably very much lower than the future has in store for us," a city councilman declared. One journalist estimated that within a generation Marseille's population would be half a million; another, writing in 1862, predicted quite accurately that a century later the city would have 800,000 people. Bordeaux officials in 1878 predicted that by the end of the century the city would have a population of 300,000. In Saint-Etienne, expansion was seen as the norm, the city population had tripled in the first three decades of the nineteenth century. "Everything leads one to believe," a city councilman announced, "that this growth is far from ended." In Marseille, a commission of the city council declared that there was "urgency for the municipal administration to provide at the same time for the needs of the present as well as the future."[32]

The expectation of continued growth was reflected in the cities' acquisition of cemeteries. While in the first half of the nineteenth century, municipalities repeatedly had to acquire more space for burial ground as their projections of need were exceeded, in the second half, cities more successfully anticipated future needs. Marseille acquired additional properties for the Saint Pierre cemetery, making it large enough, the municipality hoped, for a city twice Marseille's size. Actually, the city's needs outgrew these land needs, and Marseille had to acquire more cemetery land in 1874. But at least the interval between acquisitions had lengthened. In Lyon, the city engineer's ambition was to annex the old Sara military camp next to the Loyasse cemetery and thus fulfill the "very distant" needs of the city "for about a century." Toulouse's population grew far more slowly; its new cemetery, the Terre Cabade, built in the suburbs in 1840 to resemble the Père Lachaise cemetery in Paris, fulfilled the city's space needs better than had earlier cemeteries located in the center of the city.[33]

CREDIT

Population growth provided a larger tax base, and hence cities anticipated increased income. Municipalities quickly changed their attitude toward credit. In the career of Bordeaux mayor Antoine Gautier, one can observe the change within just a few years. In 1852, he warned the city council of the dangers of indebtedness, and the need to keep reserve funds available for unforeseeable eventualities. Five years later, he was an ardent supporter of floating loans. Cities were not like households, the Bordeaux mayor declared, for unlike families, a city was enriched by growth in numbers and did not have limits to its duration in time. Urban development, he argued, would lead to greater city income, which in turn could finance yet further improvements. A local booster of Bordeaux improvements insisted that "a great city is not administered like a household, its business is no longer handled as in the past. Spend in order to earn, that is the first principle of political economy, borrow in order to increase hundredfold one's capital, that is the rule of empires and cities."[34] Large public works did not have to be financed immediately. The "life of communes is counted in centuries," Saint-Etienne's mayor pointed out in 1851. Through loans, officials argued in both Saint-Etienne and Lyon, future generations would assume the burden of the benefits that were going to accrue to them.[35]

The successful implementation of ambitious projects with loans encouraged further borrowing. Whereas Mayor Gautier had borrowed 5 million francs, his successor took out loans totaling 17 million francs. Times had changed, as a former Lyon city councilor remarked; while his city had hesitated to take out loans in the 1820s, now there were no such inhibitions. "Other times, other mores; other persons, other principles. Other needs, other obligations. Who would today seriously question the utility for Lyon of a moderate debt?" The standard of what constituted a "moderate" debt had changed: cities were not reluctant to take out loans that in earlier times would have been thought astronomical.

The state made these loans possible in 1852 by establishing the Crédit foncier, which was empowered to lend to communes at a very reasonable rate. Thus, when Lyon borrowed for its urban projects, it received 8.2 million francs at 4.45 percent interest, a lower rate than if the city had directly floated loans. Beginning in 1860, the state also allowed cities to borrow funds for 50-year periods rather than only 20.[36] That meant lower yearly payments, and thus cities could more calmly envisage taking on larger debt.

PARIS AND OTHER MODELS

It is customary to see the dramatic urban programs that started in the provinces in the 1850s as modeled after, and directed by, Paris. In actuality, the relationship was complex and tangled. Certainly, the central government helped. A new decree in 1852 allowed the expropriation of all surfaces necessary for the erection of new arteries, and enlarged the right to remaining buildings that were unsanitary as well as to remaining areas that if built on would be unsanitary.[37] This decree was a powerful tool, and the central government deserves credit for it; yet acknowledging that is not the same as ascribing to Paris full responsibility for all the changes that occurred in the provincial cities.

The set of transformations that began in Paris are named after the authoritarian prefect of the Seine, Baron Georges Haussmann, who ran roughshod over Paris to realize his and Emperor Napoleon III's plans. It has often been assumed that the transformations in the provincial cities also occurred by fiat from the capital, but many localities showed remarkable enterprise, carrying on their urban renewal with little regard to the Parisian example. Much of the urban renewal in the provinces during the Second Empire was a realization or continuation of plans developed long before Haussmann came to the scene—in some cases going back to the eighteenth century.

Many cities served as models. Paris without doubt served as a useful reference; the accomplishments of the capital were often referred to as an archetype of what should be done in provincial cities.[38] Many of the provincial cities referred to the experience of fellow provincial cities.[39] Foreign cities were also compelling models. Mayors and city councilors spoke of various accomplishments of foreign cities, which they asked for information; among these were Belfast, Berlin, Brussels, Florence, Frankfurt, Liverpool, London, Munich, Newcastle, Philadelphia, Stettin, Stockholm, Venice, and Vilna. In Marseille, city officials alluded to London, Liverpool, and New York as models of how a city could and should respond to urban growth.[40]

LOCAL INITIATIVES

Bordeaux

In many cases, municipalities played the major role in rebuilding their cities. In the case of Bordeaux, the locale dictated both its priorities and the rate at which change occurred. The city's increased wealth and self-confidence inspired the municipality to engage in new, ambitious projects under the leadership of Mayor Gautier. The mayor believed Bordeaux was at the dawn of an unprecedented era. As a result of the introduction of railroads and steamships, Bordeaux seemed destined for spectacular growth, more so than any other city in France except Paris. Anticipating the building of the Suez and Panama canals, he declared Bordeaux to be the natural point connecting both.

In the 1850s, Bordeaux lengthened and widened several important streets. The old market and its surroundings burned down in a fire in 1855, providing the opportunity to rebuild the area with "healthier" houses, replacing fifteenth- and sixteenth-century structures, "these rat and cholera nests," as Mayor Gautier called them. He even bemoaned the fire's failure to destroy more.[41]

In 1855, the city enlarged, restored, and landscaped the *jardin public,* which it had neglected after the Revolution, letting it become a dumping ground for garbage and a place of uneasy coexistence between promenaders and soldiers carrying out target practice. The park was transformed into an English garden by plans drawn up by Adolphe Alphand before he joined Haussmann's team in Paris.[42] With an artificial lake in its middle, the park had a lot of charm and was frequently used by the citizens. A much larger park, the Parc Bordelais, was established by a private group of philanthropists on the outskirts of the city in 1863, but it hardly served the common people and was beset by financial difficulties that allowed the city to acquire it in 1878.

During the Second Empire, the city spent more than 25 million francs on its urban projects, "a colossal effort," say the historians of nineteenth-century Bordeaux.[43] Yet, considering the city's needs and resources, its accomplishments were modest. The center of the city was left essentially untouched; there were none of the major piercings—in the sense of surgically cutting through existing streets and blocks—that, for instance, marked Lyon and Marseille. Bordeaux already had excellent eighteenth-century peripheral boulevards that allowed for ease of travel. To get from one end of the city to another, one did not necessarily have to carve new arteries through the middle of the city. But that meant that unhealthy slums continued to fester in the very center of town.

Lyon

In Lyon, the need for transformation of the urban fabric seemed particularly important. A dirty, crowded city (far more crowded than Paris or any other French city at the time), it was also prone to political contention. It had risen up in revolt in 1831, 1834, and 1848, and had given far less support to Louis Napoleon's presidential candidacy in 1848 or his coup d'état in 1851 than the department of the Rhône as a whole. As a result, the central government of Louis Napoleon took a direct hand in rebuilding the city. The historian of the urbanization of Lyon in the Second Empire lists four reasons why Louis Napoleon favored such a program: to provide for the dissatisfied and unemployed, to provide the bourgeoisie with investment opportunities and increase business activities, to boost his popularity with the citizens, and to provide large avenues through which troops could be easily moved.[44]

In terms of population, Lyon was the second largest city in France, and it must have seemed natural to Louis Napoleon to model the governance of Lyon on that of the capital. He appointed the prefect of the Rhône, Claude Marius Vaïsse, to the additional posts of police prefect and mayor of Lyon. He also stripped the city of an elected city council. The projects accomplished in Lyon thus were done under the impetus of the authoritarian prefect, though local initiative was by no means impossible. Several of the prefect's plans echoed earlier city council schemes, and when he wanted to carry them out, he found that he had to modify them in the face of local opposition.

The focus of Vaïsse's projects was the very center of the city, between the Place Terreaux and Place Bellecour. Vaïsse built a large avenue, the Rue Impériale, connecting the two. It was specifically intended to ensure internal security; the military governor had urged its building to "move soldiers easily to the center of the city." The prefect subscribed to this argument and saw an additional security advantage: getting rid of the narrow streets would deprive rioters of their favorite battlefields.[45]

The Rue Impériale and, paralleling it, the Rue Impératrice, also linked the city center to the rail station. Given the important role that the railroad was to have for Lyon, making it a major crossroad, the city had to be prepared to receive "a considerable excess of population." The rail presented a major impetus for street widening. The transformed city would in turn help facilitate the development of the national economy. The minister of interior, Victor Persigny, remarked that "cities are part of the national network; they are instruments of wealth." In Lyon, it was crucial to prepare for the impact of the rail, since the city was to be the single largest hub outside the capital. In 1863, nearly 3 million passengers and 1.2 million tons of goods arrived or embarked at the Lyon rail stations.[46] One can clearly see the increased ambitions of the Second Empire. While in the 1830s the widest street built was the Rue Centrale at 12 meters across, the Rue Impériale measured 25 meters.(The project tore down 500 houses, dislodging 12,000 people.)

The prefect annexed some of the suburbs, thus giving the city more space to grow and incidentally establishing control over what had been seen as the particularly unruly workers living there. Annexation had been a long-term desire of the municipality, but it had been frustrated by the resistance of people in the concerned areas. The prefect was able to ignore previous protests and by fiat annex the outlying communes.

Prefect Vaïsse also built the Tête d'or park, declaring that the park would become "the green space [la campagne] of those who don't have it."[47] The largest provincial city park in France (at 200 hectares), it provided nearly as much green space as all the Parisian parks combined (263 hectares). The Tête d'or park was, however, on the outskirts of the city, too far away for most people of limited means to reach. And no other green spaces existed in the city.

Vaïsse's many ambitious projects led to an outlay of 120 million francs in the 11 years following 1853. City indebtedness, which had been 11 million francs in 1852, increased more than eightfold, reaching 93 million francs in 1871. The major investments, however, came from local private sources, estimated to have been two to three times the governmental expenditures.[48] If the prefect, appointed by Paris, had been able much of the time to ignore the local government with impunity, his success was still due in part to the willingness of local capital to invest and build the new boulevards with their luxury buildings.

Marseille

The central government also played a crucial role in city renewal in Marseille. As France's major port, Marseille was to be built up to maintain the nation's predominance as a Mediterranean power. In light of the dramatic population increase, authorities recognized the need to transform the city: to create wider streets, connect parts of the city to the outskirts, acquire and develop land while it was still available, and provide the city with amenities. The crowding, particularly intense in the poorest neighborhoods huddled around the port, needed to be alleviated. The economic need to enlarge the port facilities conveniently merged with the human needs. The new port, built in the 1840s, had to be expanded, and a thoroughfare connecting it to the old port had to be established. Creating such an artery would also have the advantage of clearing some of the port's worst slums. The large avenue, to be called the Rue Impériale (later Rue République), was to cut right through the urban fabric. The cost of the project was immense, over 100 million francs.

Napoleon III sent a powerful prefect, Emile de Maupas, to Marseille to oversee the urban projects. Whereas in Lyon the municipal government had been abolished, and hence there was no official local institutional resistance to the prefect, in Marseille the city council was maintained, and it was able to amend Maupas's determined efforts. The city council's fears of excessive financial outlays, its desire to preserve as much as possible of the old city, and many technical considerations reduced Maupas's projects and delayed them until 1862. The prefect got his way only after he replaced the elected municipal council with an appointed one. And eventually, when an elected council returned, its opposition drove the prefect out of office.[49]

By far the most ambitious project, the one that came to symbolize the whole effort, was the new Rue Impériale, 25 meters wide. The undertaking involved not only removal of a whole hill but also the destruction of 935 houses, and the complete removal of 38 streets and partial removal of 23 others. In the process, 16,000 inhabitants had to move. It represented the single largest debris-removal project in France up to that time, totaling 1.5 million cubic meters.[50]

Large land speculators became involved in Marseille's urban renewal. The city sold land bordering the new avenue to private groups, which were to develop it and build luxury housing with an imposing uniform facade along the new avenue. While in the 1840s the private groups involved in urban projects were composed of Marseillais, the scale of this undertaking attracted outside groups. But the Rue Impériale turned out to be a dismal commercial failure. Jules Mirès, who initiated the project, went broke in 1860, even before construction started. He was replaced by the Pereire brothers, who also went broke when profits failed to materialize. The expected influx of population to the Rue Impériale did not occur. The supply of housing outpaced demand; for decades, a large number of apartments remained unsold and unrented. The wealthy, accustomed to living in the hilly area away from the port, stubbornly stayed there in what remained the prestigious neighborhood, while the port area continued to be associated with crime and vice. The Rue Impériale, intended as a site for fancy stores and rich tenants, had to settle for artisans. Of 8,000 apartments erected in the Rue Impériale scheme, 1,200 were still empty in 1900. Only in 1910, as a result of housing shortage, were these apartments finally occupied.[51]

The Rue Lit de Cavaux in Marseille. One of the narrow, dark, and unhealthy alleys torn down to build the imposing new artery, the Rue Impériale, later Rue de la République.

Although the Rue Impériale was the only instance in Marseille of "Haussmannian piercing," some major arteries, such as the Rue d'Aix and Rue de Noailles, were widened from six to thirty meters, while some others were widened and lengthened. A number of important public buildings were erected: a new prefecture, the Majore Cathedral (replacing a twelfth-century cathedral that was unceremoniously torn down), the Palais Longchamp Museum, a new Bourse, and the imperial Palais du Pharo. And like so many cities in this period, Marseille received its park, the Borély. The architect of the Bois de Boulogne, Alphand, served as a consultant on the building of the French garden. Located on the city heights, it was an agreeable site, open to breezes from the sea. But it was still at the margins of the city.

Contemporary observers applauded the overall transformation of the Mediterranean city. "It was the kind of progress," said one, "which only the United States of America seemed to be able to achieve." Another, the philosopher Hippolyte Taine, was overwhelmed by the extent of the urban programs in Marseille. "Nothing like it has been seen on the Mediterranean shores since the most famous days of Alexandria, Rome, or Carthage."[52]

Toulouse

In Toulouse, the transformation effort was far less ambitious, yet the city did see change. As in so many cities, the new rail line meant that Toulouse was faced with an influx of population and goods. The city had grown impressively, doubling from a population of 52,000 in the 1820s to over 100,000 in 1855, the date of its rail opening. A commission of the city council noted in 1856 that plans adopted in the 1830s for the gradual alignment of streets were insufficient for the flow of goods and people, "the consequence of the railed roads." The city would need to carve several major arteries to connect the city center to the railroad station and the periphery. It was imperative, the mayor told his council, to widen and straighten streets, build new squares and covered markets, and finish rebuilding of the Capitole, the city hall.[53]

If traffic control was the main goal, street enlargement also had public health as a goal in Toulouse as elsewhere. The mayor told the council that narrow streets endangered public health; "The first responsibility of an intelligent administration must be to give the inhabitants of a large city air, water and light," the mayor declared.[54]

The single largest project, adopted in the late 1850s, was the building of two large boulevards that would cross each other, as in Paris. There was to be a longitudinal avenue (later called Alsace-Lorraine) and a transversal one (later called Metz). The former would link the railroad to the center, then extend beyond that to serve as a north-south artery. The latter would provide east-west communications. While the large arteries of Paris, Lyon, and Marseille were 25 meters wide, those in Toulouse, the municipality decided, would be less ambitious, only 16 meters (4 of which would be sidewalks).

City authorities, hoping the national government would finance the venture, argued that the artery was part of the national highway system. But Paris, although eager to see the project carried out, was not so eager to pay for it. It insisted that local resources be used. The two thoroughfares were not completed until a decade or two into the Third Republic.

Nonetheless, something was accomplished. As in Lyon and to some degree in Marseille, the central government played a pivotal role in Toulouse and was able in the end to overcome the deadlock that developed in the city council. Yet it would be wrong to analyze the situation as having been shaped entirely by the central government.[55] It was, after all the mayor, Count Jean-Marie Campaigno, who, through his personal contacts (he was a childhood friend of Empress Eugenie), first brought the attention of the central government to the project. It was the effective opposition of local political and economic forces that diminished the final plan adopted by the central government.[56]

Saint-Etienne

The mid-century urban projects in Saint-Etienne were the least impressive of the five cities. One reason was that the condition of the city itself was more modest. Saint-Etienne was bereft even of basic services, and these had to be established before any grandiose plans could be implemented. Like the other cities, Saint-Etienne built a large avenue, the Rue des Jardins (now Rue Michel Rondet), connecting the rail station to the city center. Mayor Faure-Belon, one of the richest men in the city, did much to improve the city during his decade as mayor, during 1855-65. He helped erect the largest artery in the city, the Cours Fauriel, the 40-meter-wide promenade connecting the two railroad stations. He also established a water-supply system and erected a new prefecture, a city hall, a park, and school buildings.[57]

Some observers ascribe the city's modest urban renewal programs to the social make-up of the city council. During the half century between 1815 and 1870, it has been argued, councilors belonged to "a hard-working and frugal petite bourgeoisie." But actually the municipality had more of an elite membership.[58] During the July Monarchy and even the Second Empire, the councils numbered among their members the very richest men in the city.[59] So the timidity probably reflected the values of the dominant bourgeoisie. Even the rich in this poor city lived unostentatiously, plowing most of their profits back into their businesses and factories. Given its resources, the city assumed large loans to finance its urban projects. While the per-person city debt had been 38.54 francs in 1854, less than ten years later it had nearly doubled, to 74.04 francs per head.[60] Compared with earlier eras, during the Second Empire the city engaged in significant disbursements on capital improvements: 7.8 percent of the total urban renewal expenditures for the years 1815-70 were spent during the Restoration, 16.13 percent during the July Monarchy, and 71.73 percent during the Second Empire.[61] The semi-official historian Louis Gras, archivist of the local chamber of commerce, while criticizing the city fathers for their modest urban programs, remarked that "if Saint-Etienne did not become a beautiful city, it improved considerably over what it had been previously."[62]

THE REPUBLICAN ERA

Urban projects, planned and realized under Napoleon III, were received critically by the Second Empire's Republican opposition in the cities in this study. Many motives stirred the opposition. Of course, nearly anything done by the Empire received criticism from an opposition that questioned the legitimacy of Napoleon III's rule. There was fundamental suspicion of the authoritarian methods that accompanied the realization of the programs. Corruption had been involved in giving hugely profitable contracts to developers. Municipalities had spent large sums of money and instituted higher taxes, providing the Republicans with useful ammunition. Attitudes born in opposition shaped later attitudes toward urban projects when Republicans came to power after the late 1860s, and explain in part their conservative outlook on city rebuilding.

Republican Opponents

While the projects in Toulouse during the Second Empire were relatively modest, one Republican opponent of the Empire, Jules Ferry, denounced them as "Babylonian and pathological."[63] Ferry had also been a leader of the opposition in Paris to Haussmanization. Too much was being done too fast for critics of the regime. An opposition newspaper complained that there appeared to be the desire "to achieve in a few years the gradual needs of future generations."[64] When public sentiment could express itself in Toulouse as a result of free elections in 1869, the Republican council denounced its predecessors in strong language. The imperially appointed Toulouse commission members, who had floated the large public debts, were attacked by the Republican mayor Ebelot as "these men who for three years did not hesitate to exhaust the finances of the city and ruin its present and future resources in useless works."[65]

In Marseille in the 1864 municipal election campaign, the Republicans argued against the arbitrariness and authoritarianism of the urban schemes of the prefect. They favored, they claimed, better water, sewer, and lighting services, thus supporting progress, and opposing only "Babylonian projects."[66]

During the Empire, there had been great fears of the added debt cities were incurring. While the imperially appointed mayor of Bordeaux was willing to go ahead with the necessary loans, the city's major newspapers opposed them and the popularly elected city councilors were far more cautious, for they "fear unpopularity," the prefect reported. Loans and large expenditures were in bad odor.[67] Correctly, the Lyon deputy in the Corps législatif criticized the projects in his city for having indebted it into the next century. If the Marseille municipality was now saddled with a 100-million-francs debt, it was the fault of the central government, a Republican opponent complained.[68]

The enlargement of streets, razing of blocks, and building of new housing had gone hand-in-hand with speculation and corruption. In many cases, the speculations turned out to be not so profitable, as in Marseille and Toulouse, and notorious scandals accompanied some of these ventures, as in Toulouse. There, special favors had been granted the Caune company, to which city property had been sold at considerably below market value, and contractors building the public works projects appear to have been allowed to overcharge for their services. After the fall of the Empire, the Republican financial commission in Marseille denounced the previous regime for local policies that led to "mad expenses, waste, and dissipation."[69] The prefect in Marseille, for instance, had built his official palace at a cost of eight million francs.

Property owners, feeling threatened by the modernization schemes, had extolled local rule. And to some degree, all these cities, strongly Republican, had identified the urbanization schemes with the hated authoritarianism of the personal regime of the Second Empire. Critics stressed the arbitrariness and illegality of the expropriations. The Republican deputy from Lyon, while admitting that some urbanization schemes in his city had been necessary, felt others were not, but the main thrust of his criticism was that they had been arbitrarily imposed.[70]

Republicans, who had been such ardent critics of imperial excess, intended when they came to power to be frugal as an outward symbol of their seriousness. As the Republican leader who later became Marseille's mayor, Félix Baret, put it, "The Republican system intends to be frugal so it cannot be said of it what was said of the others." A generation later, Republicans in Bordeaux proclaimed that a positive balance in the budget was the hallmark of a Republican regime, "while the regime of deficits is . . . the other [regime.]"[71] The attacks on the urban policies of the Second Empire shaped a Republican aversion to ambitious plans for city rebuilding, and in part explain the modest policies of the subsequent decades.

The Third Republic

When the Republic was founded in 1870, there was no overriding enthusiasm for ambitious urban projects. Much of the hesitation was shaped by opposition to Napoleon III's urban policies. But it was also due to the large debts incurred by these schemes. The urban policies of the Second Empire mortgaged the future, making it difficult to consider new ambitious projects. In the 1870s, the debts of the five cities were as follows: Toulouse, 6.9 million francs; Saint-Etienne, 9.6 million; Bordeaux, 29.4 million; Lyon, 70.6 million; and Marseille, 107.7 million. That represented roughly twice Toulouse's yearly budgetary income, thrice Saint-Etienne's, four times Bordeaux's, six times Lyon's, and nine times Marseille's.[72] Paris's indebtedness—which had created such alarm among contemporaries—was by contrast only 4.5 times greater than its yearly budget. Lyon's and Marseille's yearly debt payments were intimidatingly high; in 1875, Lyon allocated nearly half, and Marseille more than half, of its regular city income to pay off debt and interest.[73]

Such large debts made it difficult for municipalities after 1870 to envisage engaging in new projects. Compared with the Second Empire, there was a slowdown during the following four years in the rate of urban transformation. Yet urban transformation occurred then, too. A survey of the city rebuilding programs of the five municipalities in this study reveals rational responses based on local needs and finances.

Toulouse

Of the five cities, Toulouse accomplished the least in urban renewal during the Second Empire, and came through it least indebted. The city was aware of the projects it needed to complete and could—relative to the other four cities—envisage increased indebtedness with some equanimity. And so it was the city in which the greatest amount of urban renewal occurred in the years after 1870.

After the fall of the Empire, the Republicans in Toulouse tried to scuttle the plan for large avenues, and only the appointment by the central government of a non-elected commission to replace the contentious municipality allowed the project to move forward. When a democratically elected municipality returned to power, it appeared to be too late: the ground for the projects had been acquired, the plans adopted, and some rebuilding started.[74] Of the two major cross streets, finished under the names Rue Alsace-Lorraine and Rue de Metz, the first was intended to connect the center of the city in a straight line to the railroad station. When finished in 1874, it did not, however, follow a straight trajectory—that would have required more funds and political muscle than the municipality was willing to expend. The Rue de Metz was finally finished in 1884.

The accomplishments by the municipality in this period reveal that local initiative was able to engage in ambitious projects. Toulouse Republicans overcame their initial opposition, completed the unfinished schemes of their predecessors, and even went beyond them. Mayor Ebelot, critic of the Second Empire, helped carry out its original plans. The Opportunist mayor was followed in the late 1880s by the Radicals who, though critical of Ebelot, nevertheless continued extensive urban programs.

The Radicals' support for urban projects in Toulouse was based essentially on the employment they offered; Radicals rarely mentioned public health and traffic concerns. The competitive political situation in the city seemed to ensure victory to the party that could promise full employment. In a town of workers and artisans, with little industry, public works was a good source of employment. As Mayor Ournac put it, "we must give work to the workers who need it, spend money and let others earn it." The extent to which the main intention of the public works was employment may be gauged in the rules the city council adopted to hire only local workers and use locally produced materials.[75]

The program of urban improvements was, of course, appreciated for its own sake; city inhabitants appreciated wider, safer, cleaner streets and a good water delivery system. Radicals presented themselves as the party of urban reform. Mayor Serres and the Radical newspaper urged voters to reward the party for its accomplishments in urban improvement. In running for office in 1892, the Radicals promised water accessible to everyone; that had essentially been assured the following year. This accomplishment alone, the *Dépêche de Toulouse* argued, made the Radicals worthy of reelection.[76]

Sometimes the twin goals of providing both urban improvements and employment failed to coincide. The Toulouse sidewalks had always been notoriously poor. Stendhal had complained about them in the 1830s; the few that existed contained small sharp stones that were uncomfortable to walk on. In the 1850s, when new sidewalks were built of flat, tile-like material known as *pavé à l'alsacienne*, the beneficiaries of the work were contractors from out of town, for no manufacturer in Toulouse produced the pavement. The program petered out. In the 1890s, two-thirds of the city streets still needed sidewalks. When new ones were built, neither *pavé* nor asphalt was employed, but rather the traditional pointy stones—because that system provided employment for local artisans.[77] Providing employment was more important than the comfort of pedestrians.

The most ambitious urban renewal project in Toulouse was the building of the Rue Alsace-Lorraine. Started in the late 1850s, it was only completed 15 years later and was neither as broad nor straight as initially intended.

The Toulouse municipality oversaw a number of projects, but considering the city's needs, the urban transformations were modest. Still, compared with other major cities, it appeared to lag behind. The city had not drawn up a general plan since Vitry's in 1841. Toulouse, the doyen of the city's historians writes, remained throughout the nineteenth century but a "grand village." Until 1914, he added, it was "a city of the Middle Ages, living by the rhythm of a rural economy, surrounded by prestigious monuments."[78]

Bordeaux

The Republican era saw little urban change in Bordeaux before World War I. Growth slowed down; the city grew by 50 percent during the Second Empire, by 30 percent in the next two decades, and by only 5 percent from 1890 until the outbreak of the war. The city became less ambitious in its urbanization schemes. The city council seemed to agree with the member who told his colleagues in 1880 that he recognized the need for broader avenues, larger squares, and more and larger parks, but given the costs involved, the need could not be filled. "To try and remedy this situation would, I know, be demanding the impossible, hence I am not demanding it." Throughout the decade, the fear of incurring new expenses kept the municipality from carrying out any major projects. The dominant municipal party, the Opportunists, in running for reelection, boasted of "the remarkable financial balance of our city, of the city's "spirit of economy."[79]

Some streets were built and squares created, fulfilling plans drawn up during the Second Empire. Two major arteries went in: the Rue Duffour-Dubergier and the Cours Pasteur. Toward the end of the century, several projects helped to rebuild the old city center and remove what a member of the local public health commission, Dr. Charles Levieux, had called "a veritable cloaque." The hope was also that the projects would stem the movement of people out of the city to the suburbs by providing a healthier and more elegant downtown.[80]

To accomplish these goals, the council considered between 1882 and 1904 several ambitious projects that would tie the center of the city to the railroad station, the Gare du Midi. Considerable dispute arose over where to locate the Grande voie, alternatively suggested to be between 22 and 30 meters wide. Ten different plans were considered, costing between 25.8 and 33.6 million francs. A non-official source presented the daunting estimate of 50 million francs.[81]

The Grande voie became the object of political debate, an issue dividing the Right from the Left, in 1896.[82] In 1900, the Left ran on a platform that promised to build the Grande voie, but after winning the election, Mayor Louis Lande decided for budgetary reasons to bury the plan, explaining that "we must not let ourselves be carried away by the seductiveness of these great projects."[83]

In the midst of these debates, Bordeaux was prey to dramatic changes in the political makeup of its councils, swinging from Opportunist to Radical and even Monarchist (in an unholy alliance with the Socialists), and thus plans considered by one council were completely revised by succeeding ones.[84] None instituted an overall city plan. The city should have been able to embark on more ambitious schemes. Its conservatism was revealed in its finances in 1912: with a population 50 percent larger than that of Saint-Etienne or Toulouse, it had a comparable debt.[85] No major transformations of Bordeaux occurred in the prewar period. And the worst slums, which had festered throughout the nineteenth century, had to await destruction by bombing during World War II before being replaced.

Lyon

In Lyon, urban clearance in the first four decades of the Third Republic was modest compared with that during the Second Empire. One important project instituted in the 1880s was the rebuilding of the Groleé neighborhood, a slum in the middle of the city that had been left untouched during the Second Empire. Renewing the Grolée was the pet project of Mayor Antoine Gailleton, head surgeon of the Antiquaille Hospital. A very popular mayor, he ran the city for nearly 20 years (1881-1900), and in spite of opposition was able to get the proposal adopted.[86]

Lyon badly needed a new slaughterhouse, and the city planned to erect a new one in 1880. It was a quarter-century before the local architect Tony Garnier was hired to build it; then several other delays followed, so that it was not completed until 1928—nearly half a century after it was first approved.[87] Such slowness on projects suggests Lyonnais had reservations about urban renewal, quite a different state of affairs from the days of Prefect Vaïsse's decisive actions during the Second Empire.

Except for Mayor Gailleton, the only city magistrate who attempted to bring urban change to Lyon was Mayor Herriot. He tried to launch some ambitious street building, extending the Rue République (formerly Impériale) and adding a large boulevard that would provide a much-needed peripheral route. But the boulevard was not built. Herriot also appointed a commission of experts in 1912 to provide a comprehensive plan for the city.[88] Moreover, Herriot hoped to provide national and international leadership in urban planning by sponsoring an international urban exposition in Lyon in May-November 1914. But all of his projects were cast aside by the outbreak of war in August. Little had been accomplished. An historian after the war described Lyon as "an uncompleted city; it lacks elegance in many regards."[89]

Marseille

In Marseille, the population growth slowed somewhat but not significantly—increasing by 50 percent during the Second Empire and by 40 percent in the next two decades. As in Lyon, but far more seriously, the Second Empire's projects had left major portions of Marseille's slums untouched. In spite of the transformations, slums around the old port and stock exchange remained, and traffic continued to get tied up in narrow streets.

Around the turn of the century, the municipality cast caution aside and finally approved a major renewal project around the old port as well as other ambitious public works, including a new city hall, some new peripheral boulevards, and an extension of the Rue Colbert. The old port project was to cost 37 million francs, of which a third was to come from private speculators. In 1905, the area behind the Bourse was expropriated and razed. But no buildings were erected. The area remained a series of empty lots, and next to it the slum surrounding the city hall survived until Hitler ordered its destruction in 1943 in reprisal for the ambush of German soldiers in this red-light district. Not until the 1960s were these areas rebuilt.[90]

Failure to finish the Bourse project or to even envision clearing the slum around the city hall was due to lack of interest by local investors. Financial resources had not been available locally even for the projects of the Second Empire; these resources, it will be remembered, came from Paris financiers. And they had gone bankrupt. Better terms of return were available in industry, colonial trade, and other ventures.[91]

In spite of the strong Socialist control of the city council and the Socialist Party's concerns for the poor and underprivileged—which were, for instance, translated into better welfare provisions and ambitious schemes of municipalization—the council could not see its way to implement a program of slum clearance. The municipality was unable and unwilling to shoulder the burden for modernizing the city. It had spent a fortune on the sewer system in the 1890s and considered itself far too indebted to carry any greater debts. Compared with the other cities in this study, Marseille indeed was strapped. In 1910, its total debts amounted to 92 million francs, which was less than Lyon's 98 million francs, but with far higher annual debt payments: 8.8 million francs compared to 4.9 million francs for Lyon. The difference was due to the longer repayment period that Lyon had been able to secure-60 years compared to 33 for Marseille.[92] Even on the eve of World War II, as one historian of the city put it, the city retained "a complex imprint of archaism and modernity."[93]

Saint-Etienne

Saint-Etienne remained intensely practical, introducing minimal changes in the years 1870-1914. The city increased its water supply; widened streets; built a new marketplace; erected a new slaughterhouse and hospital; and covered the Furan River, which served the city as a sewer.[94]

The city was unbelievably dirty; in its midst were large factories belching smoke and soot. Residential areas were not separated from the manufacturing districts; disorder was apparent throughout the city. It consisted, an observer at the turn of the century noted, of just a "heap of houses." And what was available was terribly overcrowded; in fact, in 1911, Saint-Etienne had the highest number of inhabitants per apartment in France, and was commonly known as "slum city."[95]

Lacking any monuments of distinction; polluted, ugly, and overcrowded, Saint-Etienne needed—its visitors recognized this—a radical rebuilding. As a 1908 guide to the city put it, "Nothing to see, coal miners' city. . . ." But the city fathers seemed remarkably satisfied with things as they were. In the nine-teenth century, the bourgeoisie that dominated the city councils may at times have cast jealous eyes on nearby Lyon, but the Socialists who gained control in the 1890s took an even narrower view. The novelist Marc Leguet has a fictional city councilman saying, "Saint-Etienne is a beautiful city . . . Saint-Etienne is excellent, it is much better than Saint-Chamond," a small in-significant mining town nearby.[96] In reality, a Socialist mayor at the turn of the century, when attacked for not running a clean city, is supposed to have retorted, "But Rive de Giers or Firminy are still dirtier."[97]

A poor city with a modest income, Saint-Etienne could not consider ambitious projects. And, as already noted, the city was governed by people from modest backgrounds with limited ambitions. Even though urban re-building projects would have helped working people, improving their con-dition of living and providing them with employment, Socialists were not at the forefront of urban renewal in any of our cities they came to control. In part, that was the legacy of the suspicions that had developed toward the speculations associated with urban renewal during the Second Empire. Ac-cusations from conservative opponents who called them spendthrifts and advocates of increased government control may also have intimidated the Socialists, rendering them less eager to transform the urban environment. Nonetheless, for a city its size and resources, Saint-Etienne had probably strained its resources fairly far; in 1910, it had a total debt of 40 million francs, while Toulouse, with a population the same size, had a debt of 32 million francs.[98]

On the eve of the war, many understood the shortcomings of major French cities. There was a desire to bring more order to them. City plan-ners at the turn of the century formed a professional group, calling them-selves protagonists of "public art," or "civic art." An urban reform group, the Musée social, in 1907 established a "section of social hygiene," presided over by the deputy and social reformer, Jules Siegfried. Among them, a group mainly consisting of architects founded, in 1911, the Société française des urbanistes, which saw itself as endowed with a professional mission to order and transform the city.[99]

One of the leading members of this emerging profession, Georges Risler, suggested that France adopt planning as England had. Engineers were particularly impressed by the wide avenues and city planning evident in American cities.[100] Others admired German and Austrian accomplish-ments. In comparison to all these countries, France clearly lagged in urban planning.[101]

In the face of the cities' growth and their seeming inability to adapt, Par-liament considered making urban planning mandatory in 1908. The legislature, largely representing rural interests, was unwilling to address the issue and did so only in 1919. The law was weakly enforced and it was first as a result of a Vichy decree in 1943 that city planning became effective.[102]

The historian Jean-Paul Brunet argued that various practices of the central government and its failure to provide financial assistance limited the capacity of cities in the nineteenth century to plan and carry out programs of urban renewal.[103] But at a time when less than 40 percent of the population was urban, cities were rarely regarded as a national charge. In the era of our study, both successes and failures to transform the urban environ belonged principally to the municipalities.

10

Municipalization

*T*he growing commitment of nineteenth-century French cities to bettering the lives of their inhabitants involved them in more functions, including the takeover of some services previously performed by private enterprise. The growing ambition of cities to own and control street cleaning, water, gas, electricity, and transportation services suggest a desire to further extend the reach of municipal government.

In the late nineteenth century, municipal socialism developed as both a doctrine and practice. The doctrine emphasized that municipalization could serve as a school on the local level for the goal of socialism—the public appropriation of the means of production. The practice, developed in many European nations and several states in the United States, was not always connected to Socialism; it was usually inspired by the desire of municipalities to ensure high-quality, low-cost services for their citizens, which the market did not always provide. If not necessarily inspired by Socialist doctrines or aspirations, the practice in the late nineteenth century was commonly designated as "municipal socialism."

MUNICIPILIZATION WITHOUT IDEOLOGY

While municipalization was more widely considered towards the end of the nineteenth century than in earlier decades, it was connected to earlier practices and did not represent as radical an innovation as both its supporters and opponents at times suggested. Although France was the nation in which a rich and varied form of Socialism flourished throughout the nineteenth century, the transfer of ownership and direction of city services to the municipality were, through much of the century, free of ideological considerations.

In the early nineteenth century, many French cities established municipal control of various services previously in private hands. For purposes of public health and order, national legislation provided that marketplaces (in 1790), weighing services (in 1790), and slaughterhouses (in 1811) be put under the control of municipalities.[1] City administrations erected the buildings to house these services and staffed them with market inspectors and veterinarians, respectively. Retailers and wholesalers paid the cities for the services provided.

One early city initiative to municipalize a private service was the collection of city tolls, the *octroi*. During the ancien régime, the *octroi* were in the hands of tax farmers, who collected the tolls while paying a fixed amount to the city. It was said that they were particularly rapacious, and when the *octrois* were restored in 1799, municipalities took over what had been a private service. While the service shifted several times between private and municipal control, it ended up a city service—in Lyon in 1807, Toulouse in 1808, and Bordeaux in 1842.

Municipalities considered taking over private services in a variety of situations. Emergencies might trigger such proposals; in Marseille, the quality of service from the private street-cleaning company in the face of the cholera threat in 1832 was particularly appalling, and the city therefore decided to municipalize the enterprise, although only briefly. In other cases, cities took over private services when they ceased to function. Street-cleaning services, run by private contractors and paid by cities, were sometimes taken over on an interim basis by the municipalities when the contracts ran out or the companies went bankrupt and no new entrepreneurs could be found.[2] In some cases, once a service had been municipalized in the face of what was thought to be a temporary emergency, it remained a city service; that was the case with the street-cleaning in Bordeaux.

REASONS FOR MUNICIPALIZING

Although until the 1880s economic liberals ruled all the councils of the cities in this study, pragmatism rather than ideology dominated city decisions to municipalize. In 1841, the Marseille city council debated whether it should dig the canal that was to provide its water supply or hire a private company to do so. The two points of view reflected quite closely the poles of opinion on city activism heard throughout much of the century. Against the city's taking on the task was Councilor Tarague, who appeared to fear that the lack of competing agencies would lead to abuse of power: "to concentrate in the same person the power to command, direct, oversee, execute, and receive the works is a flagrant violation of all rules. . . ." On the opposite side, Councilor Dumas argued that any private company given the job would make profits that could better accrue to the city, and that letting a private company build the canal was not the most efficient method, for the process undoubtedly would lead to disputes between the city and the entrepreneur, and considerably slow down the project. Dumas won the argument. In Bordeaux, the mayor argued that the city should run the waterworks, thus benefiting from the profits and ensuring that the service would be properly performed; and in fact, the city in 1852 became one of the first in France to municipalize waterworks.[3]

Efficiency and city control, rather than ideology, informed the argument in favor of municipalization. In Lyon in the 1840s one city councilman, a wealthy rail magnate, explained that the city should build the new waterworks instead of entrusting the work to a concession company, for thus the city could save the profits the company would be pocketing. The expectation of financial advantage for the city also lay behind the decision of the Lyon mayor, a staunch liberal, to have the city build and run a cattle market, since it would be cheaper than having a private company do so.[4]

Even though the first three-quarters of the century was the heyday of liberalism and city governments were usually well stocked with representatives of the business class, they were remarkably open minded in regard to whether the city's business should be conducted by its own employees or by a private entrepreneur on behalf of the city. If the business elite that served on the councils believed in free trade and the advantages of entrepreneurship, they nevertheless often advocated that the municipality conduct a project or run a service, believing it would save the city money and be more efficient.

Often the impetus for municipalization came from frustration over the quality of a private service. Street-cleaning, water, gas, and transportation companies often fell short of fulfilling their contractual obligations, and this led to continuing friction with city officials, many of whom saw in municipalization a resolution to these frustrations. In Saint-Etienne, the street-cleaning service was municipalized in 1837 to improve it. Bordeaux and Marseille, off and on through the century, took over the street-cleaning services, Bordeaux permanently in 1889 and Marseille in 1903. The advantage, it was argued in Bordeaux, was that private entrepreneurs, in an attempt to keep costs down, would barely fulfill their minimum obligations, while a city service would "tend to improve, extend its action where it was necessary." Municipalization of the street-cleaning service in Toulouse in 1905 was explained as necessary, given the poor performance of the previous private service. The Toulouse director of public works (who undoubtedly had a vested interest in protecting his bureaucracy) insisted that the city retain control over its street-cleaning force, for thus it could determine the quality of the service; if it were returned to a private entrepreneur, there would be endless discussions about the quality of the effort.[5]

Many other city services operated by private companies were deemed as unsatisfactory. From the establishment of gas lighting in Bordeaux, there were persistent complaints about the poor quality of the gas and the haphazard service rendered by the company. One evening in the midst of debating the poor service, the city council found itself in darkness because the gas quality was too poor to keep the lamps lit in the city hall chambers. Within a year, the city felt constrained to seek legal redress, filing seven different suits against the company.[6]

Many utility companies resisted demands to extend and improve their service if they saw no gain to be had. Companies preferred building infrastructure in neighborhoods with high use, while neglecting those, mostly poor, which could be expected to have low consumption. In Lyon, the new electricity company in 1895 did not provide current for the Croix-Rousse, St Georges, or Fourvière areas.[7]

In public transport it was the same story. The Lyon transportation company was stingy with the number of lines and trams it ran, and with their comfort. As one councilor put it, "When the company sees an interest in establishing a new line it does so, but when it has no interest in doing so, it leaves whole neighborhoods with no service." When the tram company added wagons, they were old ones from the Ouest-Parisien line. And with electrification the company insisted on installing ugly wires in the center of the city, instead of the more aesthetically pleasing underground connectors. In Bordeaux, the city administration conducted a lengthy and finally successful campaign to prevent the electrical trams from installing overhead wires in the city center. No sooner had that been accomplished, however, when conflicts in interpretation about the contract forced the city to threaten a law suit. In Saint-Etienne, the tram company provided old wagons that were not replaced until World War II, making the city one of the cities with the oldest trams in the nation. In Toulouse, the Pons tram company resisted electrification and only under the threat of municipalization did it finally give in, making Toulouse the last of all large French cities to adopt this new source of power for trams.[8]

Some of the concessionary companies were dishonest and took advantage of the cities and their inhabitants. In Marseille, a local entrepreneur, Jules Mirès, signed an agreement with the city to run the local gas works; taking advantage of a contractual oversight to specify the price for private users, he charged them double the public rate. When the contract ran out, the gas company during the next four years—until a new contract was signed—doubled its bill to the city. In the 1870s, after the city entered into a profit-sharing arrangement with the gas company, an audit revealed the company's deliberate underreporting of its profits in order to evade paying its fair share.[9]

Private concessionary companies resisted technical innovations, finding it commercially advantageous to maintain traditional services for which they often had long-term contracts. For instance, municipalities had given gas companies decades-long monopolies to provide lighting for both private consumers and public buildings and streets. Cities wanting to install electricity found that the gas companies insisted on their monopoly rights, and only if these companies were allowed to generate electricity was the adoption of electricity free of strife. Elsewhere, municipalities had to provide compensation or wait until the gas company's monopoly expired. As a result of these legal impediments, small towns, which often had no contracts with gas companies, were more likely to have electrical lighting than big cities.

When the Edison Company in Saint-Etienne started a modest effort to light major thoroughfares, the gas company sued for infringement of contract, and the city had to pay it 750,000 francs.[10] In Bordeaux, the gas company allowed the city to provide electrical lighting in three squares, but sued when the city fathers wanted to extend the area served. The Conseil d'état favored the gas company, which claimed damages of 9.2 million francs. Toulouse was enjoined by the Conseil d'état from using electricity until 1910 unless it compensated the gas company.[11]

Legal obstacles were removed in 1912, when the Conseil d'état declared that if a city wished to have electrical power, it first had to offer the gas company (if it had a monopoly over lighting) the opportunity to produce electricity; if the company refused, the city could then enter into a contract with an electrical company. But until this decision was reached, cities experienced considerable frustration.

Relations between municipalities and the concessionary companies were often antagonistic; municipalities found the companies uncooperative and even confrontational. Complaints did not emanate only from Socialists, who were opponents of private enterprise; they also came from municipalities that had a strong representation of liberal businessmen. In the 1840s, the mayor of Lyon complained about the unreliability and rapaciousness of the gas company; in the 1880s, the Bordeaux city fathers, also political moderates, denounced their gas company for negotiating in bad faith and for foot-dragging. "Not for an instance," they complained, "has it avoided trying to evade its contractual obligations."[12] Municipalities did not have the authority to levy fines on companies that openly broke their contracts; the only power a municipality had, noted the assistant mayor of Bordeaux in charge of transportation, was "insister encore et insister toujours."[13]

Utility companies had large numbers of workers, and around the turn of the century these workers' conditions of employment became a matter of concern in several city halls. In Marseille the gas company apparently misused its political clout with regard to its workers. According to police reports, it promised bonuses to its employees if the Conservative candidate was elected mayor, while threatening to fire them if he was defeated. The poor treatment of workers led councilors in Bordeaux and Toulouse to suggest municipalization as the solution.[14]

An implicit advantage that municipalization provided was to offer a convenient form of patronage. In the case of the street- cleaning service, patronage meant jobs for a large number of unskilled laborers. Marseille, upon municipalizing the street- cleaning service in 1832, provided 96 men with city employment. Bordeaux in 1883 put 180 street-sweepers on its rolls (from the 80 who had been under private auspices). City employees were a useful electoral force for a municipality. It was no accident that in 1905 at the Bordeaux street-cleaners' banquet, the municipality was fulsomely praised by its employees.[15]

Given the high cost of utilities provided by private companies, cities believed they could lower expenses and make the comforts available to more of their inhabitants. Utility costs were far higher in France than in Britain or Germany. In 1892, a cubic meter of gas in France ranged in cost from .28 to .35 francs, while in London it was .10. A decade later, a cubic meter for individual private use ranged from .17 in Marseille to .23 in Toulouse.[16]

Municipalization could lower costs for consumers, but also contribute to public health. The Lyon private water company charged higher rates than service providers in any of our other cities. Municipalization in 1898 led to a drop in the price of water by two-thirds, and, as a result, both consumption and the number of consumers increased. Whereas in 1898, 7 percent of the population subscribed to the water service, six years after municipalization 12 percent did. And the amount of water consumed had risen by 11 percent. It was clearly a socially progressive move, with public health and hygiene benefiting from municipalization.[17]

Perhaps the most important argument in favor of municipalization was that it would bring in extra income to a city's coffers. The profitability of municipalization was so well known that legal treatises argued city governments used the device to cover their deficits.[18] Information from abroad seemed to confirm this view. An 1871 Bordeaux mission to Germany and England returned with reports of the profitability of municipalized utility companies in both countries. A study at the end of the century on municipalization in England also revealed the financial advantages of such measures. Of 18 cities that had taken over gas works, only one had lost money as a result.[19]

France itself could point to convincing examples of profits that municipalities could gain by taking over utility services. Municipalizing the waterworks in Bordeaux had proved to be profitable. In 1870, for instance, the city had an income of 400,000 francs from selling water while expending only 66,000 francs; by 1900, the city had become less greedy but was still making good profits on its water works of 500,000 francs on a gross revenue of 1.1 millions francs. Lyon was late in municipalizing its water. But when it did, in 1900, the financial benefits immediately became clear. Even though it paid large yearly compensation payments to the private company from which it had purchased the water system, it was making a 100,000-franc profit in 1902. By 1913, profits had increased tenfold, reaching a million francs. Lyon also made profits on its municipalized slaughterhouses and markets. It was the anticipated unprofitability of municipalizing the theater that made Mayor Augagneur initially reluctant to municipalize it. The step, he believed, would bring in only "a few thousands of francs." But municipalization of other services would "help the city meet its needs."[20]

In Saint-Etienne, the Socialists projected an annual income of 170,000 francs if they municipalized the gas works. In Bordeaux, it was argued that municipalizing the gas service would provide the city exchequer with additional income. In both Lyon and Saint-Etienne, municipalizing the gas works found support as a means of reducing taxes or offsetting increasing city costs. Even opponents of municipalization claimed that while it was economically inefficient, it helped balance city budgets.[21]

Muncipalization, it appears, could also help finance ambitious social measures. In Toulouse, a Socialist suggested municipalizing the gas works to help expand social services, while the Lyon city council thought a similar move could pay for workers' housing.[22]

The example of other countries inspired many French city governments to consider municipalization. Some foreign cities had municipalized public utilities quite early. Leipzig in 1838, Kolmar in 1851, and Copenhagen in 1858 had municipalized their gas works, while Edinburgh had municipalized its water system in 1847.[23]

The monthly journal, *Annales de la régie directe,* regularly reported on the worldwide trend toward municipalization, providing examples from Germany, Italy, England, the United States, and even Japan. The English example was frequently cited in the contemporary literature on municipalization; in 1904, 1,945 English cities had municipalized their waterworks, 152 their gas works, and 118 their tram systems.[24]

Individual French municipalities sent missions abroad to learn about municipalization. The Bordeaux city council in 1871 sent a two-man team to England and Germany. Given the recent war with Prussia, the mission to Germany was perhaps surprising. But the French, as Alan Mitchell has shown, were eager to learn from their recent enemies.[25] The mission enthusiastically reported on the advantages of municipalizing the lighting system—it would provide Bordeaux with added income and a more modern system. Nonetheless, the city council did not act, perhaps dissuaded by the seven million francs in compensation it would have had to pay the gas company.[26]

At the turn of the century, Lyon and Saint Etienne sent delegations to Britain to visit, among other cities, Manchester, Glasgow, and Edinburgh. They came back with glowing reports of efficient and profit-making public services. Proponents of municipalization, accused of being socialists, found in the British experience useful evidence that one could favor such measures without being a "collectivist"; across the Channel, even conservatives municipalized.[27] Foreign example served as both a model and a political alibi for municipalization.

SOCIALISTS AND RADICALS

Socialists provided a current of thought favorable to municipalization. The term "municipal Socialism" was first used by the Allemanist strand of French socialists, who suggested that socialism first establish a base in the commune before conquering the nation.[28]

French socialists, who were divided on so many issues, also disagreed about the wisdom of municipalism. The Marxist Jules Guesde was at first opposed, declaring, "Revolution—that is, expropriation—first, then public services." Guesde at first dismissed as fraudulent, based on deliberately falsified data, reports that municipalization was bringing in profits to city governments.[29] But by 1891, the Guesdist party included a plank on municipalization. Guesde came to see electoral advantage in the ameliorative programs that might go along with municipalization, predicting that the hundred or so communes that had passed into Socialist hands in 1892 would in future elections increase to 10,000 to 15,000 communes. The municipality could become a school for socialism and be a step on the road to rendering all of France socialist; they could be "springboards for our subsequent struggles." Yet for Guesdists, municipal socialism continued to be a tactical device; at a congress in Ivry in 1900, the Guesdists affirmed, "There is not and cannot be a communal socialism."[30]

More moderate socialists were wedded to the principle. Independents, such as Benoît Mâlon, and Possibilists, such as Paul Brousse, had faith in the notion of building socialism from the ground up, starting with the commune. Municipal socialism, Mâlon declared, was "the linchpin of the future."[31] The international Socialist Congress, meeting in Paris in 1900, affirmed this principle as well, seeing municipalization as "an excellent laboratory of decentralized economic life and at the same time a political fortress for localized majorities of Socialists against the bourgeois majority of the central government." At its national congress in 1911, the recently united Socialist party, the Section française internationale ouvrière (SFIO), voted in favor of municipalization, seeing it as serving the needs of the working class.[32]

Beginning in the late 1880s, the Socialist party began to make inroads in major French cities. Saint-Etienne in 1888 was the first large city to have a Socialist mayor; and in the municipal elections of 1892, Socialists captured the city halls of Roubaix, Marseille, Narbonne, Montluçon, and Toulon. In the 1896 elections, Socialists gained 1.4 million votes on the first ballot, captured control over 150 municipalities, and won a sizable minority representation in Bordeaux, Lyon, Saint-Etienne, and Toulouse. Upon being elected mayor, Dr. Flaissières of Marseille promised to carry out the program of the Lyon Socialist Congress, which, among other points, had declared itself in favor of municipalization. Socialists in the Marseille city council proclaimed municipalization to be a hopeful step in spreading socialism to the region and from there to all of France.[33]

To many Socialists, it was an article of faith that municipalization would occur. In Saint-Etienne, the Socialists had run on a platform that promised the abolition of all "monopolies," a platform essentially aimed at private utility companies. In addition to socializing such means of production, Saint-Etienne Socialists had also specific social goals in mind; they intended to build a hydroelectric plant on the Lignon River to make it possible for craftsmen, equipped with small electric motors, to compete with larger plants and survive the wave of industrialization. None of these plans were realized; the Socialists municipalized neither the theater, the gas and electricity works, the trams, nor the garbage service. The Lignon plan fell victim to opposition from the central government, then to regional interests, and finally to a lack of municipal resolve. Of his Socialist principles, Mayor Ledin was to say cynically that they were "like beautiful girls, to be violated."[34]

Socialist city administrations experimented with municipalizing the local theater. In Marseille, Socialists argued that culture was too important to be left to the profit motive, to be treated "like merchandise that one buys and sells." Opera "should be distributed to all like air and light; everyone, the humble and the mighty, should in a well-organized society receive their share. There ought to be a law that obligates communes to complete the education of their citizens . . . by providing absolutely free the master works of our national genius and even that of foreigners." By controlling the stage, the municipality imagined it could educate the populace. It could "strike the imagination, sight, and reason with the resources of art."

The experiment started auspiciously enough with the hiring of an experienced director, the former director of both the Grand Théâtre of Lyon and the Opéra comique of Paris. Municipalization was accompanied by a dramatic effort toward democratization. Admission to the third and fourth balconies were reduced to 75 and 30 centimes, respectively, in anticipation of the time when tickets would presumably be free. The low prices attracted people in search of shelter but not necessarily privacy. "Unabashed" young lovers, the historian of the Marseille theater tells us, "gave demonstrations" of their passion. To put an end to this development, ticket prices were raised somewhat, and utopia was indefinitely delayed; free theater was never implemented. Even worse, the theater failed to win audience approval. The public disapproved of the fare it was offered and often became unruly; then the director resigned. Unperturbed, the Socialists continued their experiment, but they lost the elections in 1902, and the new council returned the theater to private hands with a subvention of 250,000 francs.[35]

Lyon, which at the turn of the century had a very progressive municipality run by Radicals and Socialists, municipalized its theater in 1902, arguing that this measure would improve quality. Given the sums the city was expending in subsidies, the argument went, it might as well directly run the stage. The municipalized theater was not carefully administered, however, and by the time the experiment ended in 1906, the city had expended 1.4 million francs. The Socialists were disillusioned by the experience. In spite of lower ticket prices, the theater had failed to change its clientele, and there were after all worthier causes to support. Mayor Herriot returned the theater into private hands in 1905.[36]

In Saint-Etienne, the Socialist municipality, hoping to improve the quality of its stage presentations and live out its ideological predispositions, municipalized the theater in 1905. When the theater performed Ibsen, a favorite of the Socialists, the audiences, as has been mentioned in chapter 6, stayed home. Two years after municipalizing the theater, the Socialists lost the elections of 1908, and the theater was returned to private hands.

THE RADICALS AND MUNICIPALIZATION

On the principle of municipalization, the Socialists often had backing from the Radicals. At the national level, the Radical party, with a strong peasant and petit bourgeois base, could not afford to alienate its constituents, and it therefore eschewed state intervention in the economy.[37] But at the municipal level, where their support was less heterogeneous, Radicals, depending on the local situation, sometimes favored an active policy of intervention in the economy. Some Radical cities municipalized, or at least desired to: Lyon under Herriot, for instance. In that city, a municipalization program cemented the local Radical alliance with the Socialists. But in Toulouse, also under Radical control, municipalization was far less advanced. There Radicals and Socialists were in competition with each other, and municipalization was an issue that divided them. The Radicals, in search of middle-class support, fearing financial difficulties, and hesitant to embark on a policy obstructed by the national government, opposed municipalization. But when animated by anticlericalism, they were able to sidestep their principles. In 1905, the city council decreed municipalization of funeral services, which were previously in the hands of the Church. In Lyon, principle and ideological commitments could combine; the anticlerical municipality of Radicals and Socialists built a city-run crematorium. This was not just, as the city commission report stated, a contribution to "public health and hygiene," but also a mark of one's "emancipation from all dogma and superstition" (the Catholic Church opposed cremation).[38]

MUNICIPALIZATION AND ITS ENEMIES

A strong strain of liberal thought opposed municipalization; one notable opponent was the influential liberal economist, Paul Leroy-Beaulieu. While he noted that municipalization was broadly practiced in Britain and the United States, he claimed that it led to corruption, favoritism, and abrupt policy-switching as a result of electoral changes. He suggested that cities be prohibited from all forms of municipalization. The advantages of private enterprise, he argued, were that it could be flexible, adapting to new situations, and because it was motivated by profits, would be more dynamic and efficient than a city-run service.[39]

To private entrepreneurs, municipalization signified unwanted competition. It seemed unfair to liberals, who argued that tax-paying entrepreneurs were being harmed with tax monies and their freedom to trade was being undermined. Furthermore, it was economically inefficient and led to "state socialism, which ends in collectivism."[40]

Other critics pointed to ever-increasing expenditures to show that municipalization was leading cities to the brink of bankruptcy. The example of Elbeuf was often cited. That city's mayor, a local lycée professor under the influence of "municipalization mania" (*municipalisatiomanie*), had municipalized the garbage, water, electricity, gas, and funeral services. In 1911, after discovering that his city had a deficit of 180,000 francs in a budget of 800,000 francs, he committed suicide in the cellar of Elbeuf's city hall. Opponents of municipalization pointed to this tragedy as a warning to other municipalities that might be similarly tempted.[41]

Vested interests fought municipalization of various sorts, one of the most successful efforts coming from public transport companies. They appear to have convinced the public that the cities did not have the competence to run such a complex service as public transportation.[42] The possible inefficiency of a municipalized service might be seen in the street-cleaning service in Toulouse, which in 1905, after it had been municipalized, cost 450,000 francs a year, while allegedly a private entrepreneur could have performed the same service for 250,000 francs.[43]

Legal Constraints

When cities attempted to municipalize city services, they often found themselves stymied by legal constraints. The Conseil d'état, hostile to most forms of municipalization, ruled that if a private company could adequately perform a service, there was no reason for a city to take on such functions. Its interpretations, however, were inconsistent. For instance, after the mid-nineteenth century, it allowed city municipalization of waterworks because it determined that such an act served the public good. Bordeaux in 1852 and Grenoble in 1855 were among the first large cities to municipalize their water systems. By 1892, 438 communes had done so, of which 284 had populations over 5,000. But in spite of the favorable ruling regarding municipalization of water, the Conseil d'état was hostile toward the municipalization of gas. It struck down the attempt by Tourcoing in 1875, and nearby Roubaix two years later. The administrative court ruled that owning and running gas works might risk city finances, while the desire for profits might lead a city to provide poor services. After 1905, the conseil permitted the municipalization of gas works, but only on a case-by-case basis. Thus, Marseille was able to municipalize its gas works in 1907. Until World War I, the decisions of the conseil appeared muddled and confused and were so portrayed by contemporary legal scholars.[44]

The Conseil blocked many attempts at municipalization, arguing that cities should not usurp the functions of private enterprise. In 1887, the court declared that since the running of buses and trams was an entrepreneurial activity it could not legitimately be performed by a city. When Roubaix, under Socialist control, established a municipal pharmacy in 1892, the court declared it illegal, as it did when Lille decided in 1900 to municipalize the night soil-pickup service. The latter, the court declared, could be carried out by a municipality only if private services were unavailable. As a result of the active discouragement of the Conseil, by 1910 only eight communes, of which only three were large (Tourcoing, Valence, and Grenoble) had municipalized their electrical plants.[45]

The Conseil d'état showed greater flexibility after about 1905. Two young Socialists appointed to the court, Paul Grunebaum-Ballin and Léon Blum, the future Socialist statesman, are believed to have played a role in issuing decisions rendering the conseil more open-minded regarding municipalization, but still no strong general endorsement of such a practice came down before 1914.

Writers on French municipalization remark that France lagged behind many other countries in the rate of municipalization; usually they have pointed to the central government as the main impediment.[46] And Socialists themselves often pointed to central government control and bureaucratic red tape as undermining their schemes to municipalize various services.[47] Certainly the *Conseil d'état* and prefects at times nullified attempts to municipalize various services, but municipalities never fully took advantage of the possibilities they had. For instance, it was legal for cities to municipalize water services after mid-century, yet many cities waited decades before doing so. Saint-Etienne Socialists had not even municipalized services that many bourgeois city governments had successfully taken over. None of our five cities exploited all the legal possibilities that existed. Although cities were permitted in 1912 to provide municipal housing, none rushed in to meet this widely recognized need. So while the central government sometimes exercised its authority to stymie municipalization, city governments also bear the responsibility for not having been bolder.

There was little uniformity across cities in the municipalization of services. Bordeaux municipalized its trash service in 1889, but neither Lyon nor Saint-Etienne had done so before the start of World War I. Nor was there any apparent logic in the sequence by which particular enterprises were municipalized; although Lyon and Saint-Etienne had not taken over the trash service, for example, they had municipalized their theaters. Political labels do not provide particularly helpful guideposts for municipal action; if Socialist Marseille was active in municipalizing, Socialist Saint-Etienne was not. Radicals in Toulouse opposed municipalization; those in Lyon supported it. Liberal Bordeaux municipalized its water service in

1852, nearly half a century before Radical-and Socialist-dominated Lyon did so. The Opportunist municipality in Bordeaux municipalized its street-cleaning service in 1889; Socialist Marseille waited until 1903.

If municipalization was the subject of a national debate and became the program of the Socialist party, at the local level, it was at most applied sporadically and unevenly-revealing again the individual character of each municipality, colored by the local constellation of political forces and the varying commitments of local leaders.

Uneven and incomplete though it was, municipalization of urban services reflected cities' growing concern for their citizens' well being and the expanded powers of city governments. Their spheres of influence had grown considerably during the nineteenth century.

Except for the nationalization of some rail lines, the State had not appropriated any of the manufacturing or service industries. Only in 1936-37, during the Popular Front, and more extensively immediately after the Liberation in 1944-45, did the state nationalize major firms in the private sector.[48] Long before then, however, government municipalities had pioneered—as they had in a number of other arenas—in the social appropriation of some major utilities.

Afterword

*I*n the summer of 1889, Paris was the site of a world exposition. Held on the occasion of the centenary of the Revolution, the exposition was also noteworthy for providing the engineer Gustave Eiffel the opportunity to build entirely out of steel what was then the tallest building in the world. In celebrating itself, the Republic chose especially to honor the mayors of France. In them, it saw a reflection of itself, of its successful institutionalization. All 37,000 mayors were invited, and 11,182 accepted the invitation. They came from all over France, joining in the procession that started at the recently rebuilt Paris Hotel de Ville and ending at the exposition center on the Trocadéro (across the Seine from the Eiffel tower). It was led by Camille Chautemps, president of the Paris city council (the capital did not have a mayor until 1975). Representing a city of two million people at the head of this august procession, Chautemps was flanked by the mayors of the smallest communes of France, Mayor Robert of Bressancourt (Marne, with a population of 20 people) and Mayor Nolle of Vaudberland (Seine-et-Oise, with 48 inhabitants).

There was a festive and folkloric air about the slowly moving procession. Many people were dressed in their local costumes. Especially noticeable were those from Brittany, with their large black felt hats and jackets covered with metallic buttons, or those from the Basque country, with their berets. The head of the cortege reached the hall at 5 P.M. It was two hours later before the end of the procession had finally reached the hall and was seated to an unaccustomed early dinner. For the banquet, 80,000 plates were used, which if stacked, would have been six times higher than the nearby Eiffel Tower. They were served a nine-course meal, to the copious accompaniment of 30,000 bottles of wine.[1]

That the Republic would honor its mayors in this spectacular fashion made sense. Local government had in the nineteenth century served as a kind of nursery for democracy. Communal inhabitants (both appointed and elected) had become accustomed to deliberating and resolving their issues on their own. In many large cities by mid-century, opposition to Napoleon III's dictatorship was pronounced, producing Republican municipal councils, which were wedded to the installation of a democratic Republic. They provided some of the important bases of support for the Third Republic. The new regime depended upon the support of local Republican leaders, who helped bring in the vote during regional and national elections, and who ensured that local schools, monuments, and street signs celebrated the values associated with the Republic.[2] And since one could occupy office at both the local and national level, many mayors and city councilmen were distinguished members of Parliament, the Senate, and even the ministerial cabinets. Serving the Republic, they also advanced the interests of their communes.

Local interests were well defended. The historian Hippolyte Taine noted with regret in 1875 in his *Origins of Contemporary France* that the centralizing ambition of the French State to bring communes under firm central control had failed, leaving France "since 1789 with 44,000 small, nearly sovereign states. . . ."[3]

Through the nineteenth century, municipalities developed a strong presence. To be sure, cities were not insular; their inhabitants increasingly were swept up into national economic networks. Nationally based political ideologies and movements often mobilized urban-dwellers. Yet cities were able to maintain a surprising sense of identity in the nineteenth century. It is true that outside forces often challenged both the economic and the political authority of local elites. Within cities, notes of disharmony could be heard; interests of class and neighborhood clashed. Democratization gave voice to different political groupings. Yet municipal elites were able to preserve their position by forging and maintaining a strong identity for a city. They did so by a sharp increase in activism, and by lending the city significance through an increasingly imposing physical presence: through the erection of prestigious public buildings, statues, and impressive large avenues. The well-being of the inhabitants was increasingly taken in charge by the municipality; social cohesion and public safety was assured by welfare services, schools, police, and fire services. Cities often spent prodigious sums on opera and theater. Municipalities, especially of large cities, provided an ever-increasing number of services to meet the needs of their citizens.

Had individuals who had lived in a French city at the beginning of the nineteenth century visited it a hundred years later, they would not have recognized it. Cities had, of course, grown in population, but what might have been even more striking was the multitude of activities that urban governments had taken on. In 1800, they were not necessarily concerned with education; by the 1880s—before the central government took over much of the responsibility for public instruction—municipalities played the major role in providing primary schooling. By trial and error, they had developed fire and police departments and a municipal civil service to meet the needs of communities that had grown dramatically in both area and population. Cities rearranged urban space, tearing down old slums and replacing them in many cases with broad, tree-lined avenues or attractive squares. Cities built waterlines, storm sewers, and gas lines; they provided street lighting and supervised the development of omnibus and tram systems; in some cases, they even municipalized some of these services.

If, broadly speaking, the nineteenth century is the era in which the state increasingly intervened in the lives of its citizens, municipal governments had by far the greatest impact on the daily lives of urban dwellers. The services provided by the central government were few compared to those that municipalities dispensed in the nineteenth century. Through the nineteenth century, local government expenditures grew faster than national expenditures; in 1836, communal budgets represented 16 percent of the French national budget, compared to 30.2 percent in 1912 (a level, incidentally, it was never again to approach). After World War I, the role of the central government expanded dramatically. If one excludes the high debt payments of the central government, local government budgets during the years before the war were higher than those of the central government.[4]

The lack of centralization and the importance of local decisionmaking can be understood by looking at the varying dates at which municipalities initiated various programs. Cities had different timelines for providing universal schooling, instituting extensive police and fire protection, and providing welfare services. The timelines for adopting new technologies were also diverse. If Saint-Etienne adopted the unitary sewer system in the 1850s, and Marseille in the 1890s, none of the other cities in this study did so until after World War II. Municipalization of city services also occurred at different times.

The capital, in adopting urban innovations, was by no means always the leader of the pack; at times, it lagged behind some provincial cities, for instance in public transportation and garbage collection. In the latter field, it looked to Bordeaux, Lyon, and Marseille for models to emulate.[5] Nor did provincial cities always look to Paris as a model for their actions. Often, they were more curious about urban experiences abroad, collecting information on the water-supply system of Philadelphia, the sewer system of

London, and housing control in German cities, and maintaining correspondence with such cities. The provincial cities, which are the subject of this study, were open to the outside world—comparing themselves to and learning from other French and foreign cities.

All over Europe, cities were learning from each other. They corresponded with each other, inquiring about each other's policies. In France, they not only corresponded with towns of similar and larger size, but also with significantly smaller towns in the hope of learning from them. Usually, however, the larger cities served as models for smaller towns. Bourges corresponded with larger cities to learn how they carried out certain policies, for instance floating municipal loans; its correspondents included Bordeaux, Dijon, Nantes, and Rouen. Many small-town administrations wrote the Lyon city government for information on its municipal services, among them in the years 1909-16 were Bourges, Chalon-sur-Saône, Roanne, and Valenciennes.[6] Thus, many of the changes that occurred in the large cities had an impact beyond their limits, shaping the general urban scene in nineteenth-century France.

Much changed in the era following World War I. Used to playing a large role during the conflict, the central government became increasingly intrusive. In some cases, the State had taken over previous municipal functions even before the war, notably in the 1880s with regard to primary education. But the war accelerated this process. City planning, by a law in 1919, became a national responsibility. Public housing, previously left to municipalities and local philanthropic organizations, became a national charge with the passing of the Loucheur law of 1928.

The war accelerated urbanization. By 1931, more than 50 percent of France's population was urban. Increasingly, it made sense for the national government to carry out policies of importance to city dwellers. World War II brought the Vichy government into power. Its authoritarian predilections and necessities dictated by war and occupation led to further centralized control. Cities' major tax revenues, the *octrois*, were suppressed and replaced by a state-collected sales tax. Local welfare agencies, the hospitals and hospices, were nationalized in 1942. And after World War II, the full-blown welfare state was introduced, eclipsing local welfare efforts. The destruction during the war of many cities necessitated a national effort of urban rebuilding. Both the financing and decision making changed foci; rather than municipalities, the State played the major role in removing slums; building new avenues and squares; and installing the infrastructure to provide for public health, transportation, and many other amenities.

The mayors' banquet of 1889 may have been the high noon of municipalism. Local power was within a generation to diminish. Yet studies conducted a century later still showed that French local government through various stratagems—many of an informal nature—was able to elude central control and maintain remarkable room to maneuver.[7] On the whole, municipalities' powers to transform the urban physical, social, and cultural environment was reduced from what it had been in the nineteenth century. The achievements of that century, however, still mark to a considerable degree the urban landscape we know today.

Abbreviations to Notes

City council minutes are entered as follows: city, date of meeting. Thus, for instance, the entry: Toulouse. 13 January 1878, refers to the city and date of council meeting.

A.D.G. Departmental archives of the Gironde.
A.D.R. Departmental Archives of the Rhône.
A.M.B. Municipal archives of Bordeaux.
A.M.L. Municipal archives of Lyon.
A.M.M. Municipal archives of Marseille.
A.M.S.E. Municipal Archives of Saint-Etienne.
A.M.T. Municipal Archives of Toulouse.
A.N. National Archives.

Notes

PREFACE

1. Aristide Guilbert, *Histoire des villes françaises* 1 (Paris: Bureau des publications illustres, 1844), xii.

2. For the development of urban studies in France in the fields of geography, statistics, and sociology, see Gilles Montigny, *De la ville à l'urbanisation* (Paris: Harmattan, 1992). François Bédarida, "The Growth of Urban History in France: Some Methodological Trends," in H.J. Dyos, ed., *The Study of Urban History* (New York: St. Martin's Press, 1968), 48.

3. Georges Dupeux, "Immigration urbaine et secteurs économiques," *Annales du midi*, 85 (1973), 209; Andrew Lees and Lynn Lees, eds., *The Urbanization of European Society in the Nineteenth Century* (1976), 233; Serge Chassagne, "L'histoire des villes: une opération de renovation historiographique," in F. Bayer, et al., *Villes et campagnes, XV-XXe siècles* (Lyon: Presses universitaires de Lyon, 1977), 18.

4. Georges Duby, ed. *Histoire urbaine de la France.* 5 vols. (Paris: Seuil, 1981-1985). While the Privat publishing house in Toulouse has been issuing one-volume histories of French cities for years, it has produced a particularly large number of fine quality in the last couple of decades. Class mobility has been studied by Sewell in Marseille, and by Pinol in Lyon: William H. Sewell, Jr. *Structure and Mobility: The Men and Women of Marseille, 1820-1870* (New York: Cambridge University Press, 1985); Jean-Luc Pinol, *Les mobilités de la grande ville* (Paris: Presses de la Fondation nationale des sciences politiques, 1991). Demography has been studied by Guillaume in Bordeaux: Pierre Guillaume, *La population de Bordeaux au xix siècle* (Paris: Armand Colin, 1972). Merriman has looked at the phenomenon of the dangerous marginal classes, camped on the outskirts of many French cities: John M. Merriman, *The Margins of City Life—Explorations on the French Urban Frontier, 1815-1851* (New York: Oxford University Press, 1991). Aminzade has examined the social dimensions of political radicalism both within the confines of a single city and comparatively among several: Ronald Aminzade, *Class, Politics, and Early Industrial Capitalism: A Study of Mid-Nineteenth Century Toulouse, France* (Albany: State University of New York Press, 1981), and *Ballots and Barricades—Class Formation and Republic Politics in France, 1830-1871* (Princeton: Princeton University Press, 1993).

5. S.G. Checkland, "Toward a Definition of Urban History ," in H.J. Dyos, ed., *The Study of Urban History*, 353.

6. Jean-Paul Brunet, *Un demi siècle d'action municipale à Saint Denis la Rouge, 1890-1939* (Paris: Cujas, 1981), 1; also see Philip B. Uninsky and Charles A. Tamason, "French Cities in the 18th and 19th Centuries," *Trends in History*, II, 1 (Fall 1981), 37.

7. These works include the history of Belleville by Gérard Jacquemet, *Belleville au xix siècle, du faubourg à la ville* (Paris: Ecole des hautes études en sciences sociales, 1984); of Toulouse by Jean Nevers, "Système politico-administrative communal et pouvoir local en milieu urbain-étude d'un cas: la municipalité radicale-socialiste de Toulouse (1888-1906)," Unpublished thesis, 3ème cycle, Sociology, University of Toulouse, 1975; of Saint-Denis by Brunet, *Un demi siècle*;

and of Saint-Etienne for diffferent eras, A. Martourey, "Formation et gestion d'une agglomération industrielle au XIXème siècle, Saint-Etienne de 1815 à 1870," (Unpublished Doctorat d'état, University of Lyon, II, 1984), 4 vols; Jean Lorcin, "Economie et comportements sociaux et politiques—La région de Saint-Etienne de la grande dépression à la seconde guerre mondiale." (Unpublished Thesis, Dr. d'état, University of Paris, 1987). 9 vols; Maurice Agulhon, *Histoire de Toulon* (Toulouse: Privat, 1976), 9; others have also called for such efforts, Bernard Lepetit and Jean-Luc Pinol, "France," *European Urban History—Prospect and Retrospect*, ed. Richard Rodger (London: Leicester University Press, 1993); A. Lees, *Cities Perceived: Urban Society in European and American Thought, 1820-1940* (New York: Columbia University Press, 1985), 88.

8.   John M. Merriman, "Introduction," in Merriman, ed., *French Cities in the Nineteenth Century* (New York: Holmes and Meier, 1981), 12; Jean-Luc Pinol, "L'histoire urbaine contemporaine en France," Jean-Louis Biget and Jean-Claude Hervé, eds., *Panoramas urbains—situation de l'histoire des villes* (Fontenay/ Saint Cloud: E.N.S. editions, 1995), 214-15.

9.   Contrary to Anthony Sutcliffe, who observed that French city autonomy had ended by the mid-nineteenth century, I would argue that considerable autonomy continued thereafter. Anthony Sutcliffe, "In Search of the Urban Variable," Derek Fraser and A. Sutcliffe, eds., *The Pursuit of Urban History* (London: Edward Arnold, 1983), 263.

10.   Lepetit and Pinol, "France," 88.

11.   R. Martineau, *Les secrétaires de mairie* (Paris: Bonvalot-Jouve, 1906), 9.

12.   Edouard Herriot, in Alain Charre, "L'organisation esthétique des villes et les projets d'urbanisme à Lyon, 1905-1914," (Unpublished Thèse, Histoire de l'art, Lyon, University of Lyon, II, 1983).

13.   Alfred Picard, *Le bilan d'un siècle (1801-1900)* 2 (Paris: Imprimerie nationale, 1906), 269.

14.   Guilbert, *Histoire des villes françaises* 1:xii

15.   Peter McPhee, *A Social History of France, 1780-1880* (New York: Routledge, 1992), 200.

INTRODUCTION

1.   Georges Dupeux, "Croissance urbaine,: *Revue d'histoire économique et sociale,* 52 (1974), 18; Jean-Pierre Poussou, "Migrations et peuplement," in Jacques Dupaquier, et al., *Histoire de la population francaise,* 3 (Paris: Presses universitaires de France, 1988), 199.

2.   The French census bureau defined as urban a community with more than 2,000 people.

Introduction: A Tale of Five Cities

3. Marie-André Prost, *La hiérachie des villes* (Paris: Gauthier-Villars, 1965), 20.

4. Adna Ferrin Weber, *The Growth of Cities in the Nineteenth Century—A Study in Statistics* (New York: Columbia University Press, 1899), 16.

5. Paul Meuriot, "Du progrès général des grandes villes en Europe de 1800 à nos jours," *Congrès international et exposition comparative des villes* ser. II (Brussels, 1913), 62.

6. Paul Meuriot, *Des agglomérations urbaines dans l'Europe contemporaine* (Paris: Belin, 1898), 64.

7. Rousseau, q. in Emmanuel Leroy Ladurie, "Baroque et Lumières," Georges Duby, ed., *Histoire de la France urbaine*, 3 (Paris: Seuil, 1981), 290.

8. André Armengaud, "Industrialisation et démographie dans la France du xixe siècle," in Pierre Léon, François Crouzet & Richard Fascon, eds. *L'industrialisation en Europe au xixe siècle* (Paris: CNRS, 1972) 189; Bernard Lepetit, "Armature urbaine et organisation de l'espace dans la France préindustrielle" (Paris: University of Paris, Dr. d'état, 1987), 795.

9. Georges Dupeux, "Immigration urbaine et secteurs économiques," *Annales du midi*, 85 (1973), 209-15.

10. Pierre Léon, *Histoire économique et sociale de la France*, 2 (Paris: Presses universitaires de France, 1976), 619-22.

11. Maurice Agulhon, *Histoire de la France rurale, 1789-1914. Apogée et crise de la civilisation paysanne*, 3 (Paris: Seuil, 1976), 60-2, 388, 395-401, 456-57, 222-23; Jean Bouvier et al., *Histoire économique et sociale de la France*, 4 (Paris: Presses universitaires de France, 1979), 364-69, 101-103; Ted W. Margadant, *Urban Rivalries in the French Revolution* (Princeton: Princeton University Press, 1992), ch. 11; Jacques Dupaquier, *Histoire de la population française*, 3 (Paris: Presses universitaires de France, 1988), 179-92.

12. Edmond About, q. in Jean Guillou, *L'émigration des campagnes vers les villes et ses conséquences économiques et sociales* (Paris: Rousseau, 1905), 108-109.

13. About, q. in Guillou, *L'émigration*, 108-109.

14. Weber, *The Growth of Cities*, 77.

15. Gilbert Chinard, "Notes sur le voyage de H. W. Longfellow," *Revue philomatique* (1916), 61; Gautier, quoted in *Pétite Gironde*, 25 May 1903; Victor Cambon, *La France au travail*, II (Paris: Pierre Roger, 1913), 17.

16. A. Charles, "La modernisation du port de Bordeaux sous le second empire—les grands travaux et le nouvel equipement," *Revue historique de Bordeaux et du département de la Gironde* (1962), 25-49; Joan Droege Casey, *Bordeaux. Colonial Port of Nineteenth Century France* (New York: Arno Press, 1981), 161.

17. *Le Temps*, 7 August 1882; Emile Camau, *Marseille au xxème siecle. Tableau historique et statistique* (Paris: Guillaumin, 1905), 800; Bouvier, *Histoire économique et sociale*, 4, 207.

18. Louis Desgraves and Georges Dupeux, *Bordeaux au xix siècle* (Bordeaux: Fédération historique du Sud-ouest, 1969), 193.

19. Pierre Guillaume, "Essai sur la composition et la répartition de la fortune bordelaise au milieu du xix e siècle," *Revue d'histoire économique et sociale*, 43 (1965), 350-51; Louis Papy, "Réflexions géographiques sur l'histoire de Bordeaux," *Mélanges offerts au Professeur A. Meynier—La pensée géographique française contemporaine* (Saint-Brieux: Université de Haute-Bretagne Presses, 1972), 530-34.

20. Charles Higounet, *Histoire de Bordeaux* (Toulouse: Privat, 1980), 317.

21. Jeanne Labarthe, "Les salaires à Bordeaux entre 1850 et 1870," (Unpublished D.E.S., Bordeaux, n.d.), 20.

22. Guillaume, "Essai sur la composition," 321.

23. Pierre Guillaume, "Bordeaux, chef lieu de la Gironde," *Bordeaux, 2000 ans d'histoire* (Bordeaux: Musée d'Aquitaine, 1973), 453; Henry James, *A Little Tour in France* (New York: Houghton Mifflin, 1897), 127.

24. "Rapport sur la situation de l'instruction primaire dans le département de la Gironde au 31 décembre 1855," F^{17}9326, A.N.

25. J. Dumas, "Le rôle de l'industrie dans la croissance métropole de Bordeaux," *CESURB* (1983), 44; Théophile Malvezin, *Histoire du commerce de Bordeaux*, 4 (Bordeaux: A Bellier, 1892), 251.

26. Anon. *Bordeaux. Aperçu historique, sol, population, industrie, commerce, administration*, 1 (Bordeaux: Feret & fils, 1892), 326.

27. Desgraves, *Bordeaux au 19e siècle*, 239; A. Charles, "Mouvement démographique de la Gironde," *Annales du midi*, 69 (1957), 135-57.

28. C. Higounet, *Histoire de Bordeaux*, 290-91; Pierre Guillaume, *La population de Bordeaux au xixè siècle* (Paris: Armand Colin, 1972), ch 4.

29. Georges Dupeux, "Bordeaux et les désert Aquitaine, une métropole provinciale et sa région au xixe siècle," P. Butel and L.M. Cullen, eds. *Cities and Merchants—French and Irish Perspectives on Urban Development, 1500-1900* (Dublin: Trinity University, 1986), 33-34.

30. Maurice Garden, *Lyon et les Lyonnais au XVIIIe siècle* (Paris: Belles Lettres, 1970); Pierre Dockès, *Historique de la société d'économie politique et d'économie sociale de Lyon, 1866-1966* (Lyon: Bonnavint, 1967?), 15; Henriette Pommmier et al., *Soierie lyonnaise, 1850-1940* (Lyon: CNRS, 1980), 44.

31. Alexis Bailleux de Marisy, *Transformation des grandes villes de France* (Paris: Hachette, 1867), 112.

32. Pierre Cayez, "Industries anciennes et industries nouvelles à Lyon au début du xxè siècle," *Histoire, économie et société*, 13, 2 (1994), 321-42.

33. Auguste Von Kotzebue, "Souvenirs de Paris, 1805," extract in *Revue du Lyonnais*, 3 (1836); Jules Michelet, *Tableau de la France*, ed. Lucien Refort (Paris: Société des Belles Lettres, 1934), 64; Paul Sauzet, "Traits distinctifs du caractère Lyonnais," *Mé-*

moires de l'académie impériale des sciences, belles lettres et arts de Lyon, 14 (1868-1869), 217; Taine, q. in Louis Trénard, "Lyon et ses visages aux temps modernes," *Mélanges offerts à André Latreille* (Lyon: Centre d'histoire du catholicisme, 1972), 473.

34. E. Rolland and D. Clouzet, *Dictionnaire illustrée des communes du département du Rhône,* 2 (Lyon: C. Dizain, 1903); *Documents rélatifs au projet de budget de 1889* (Lyon, 1889), 70.

35. A. Chatelain, *Les migrants temporaires en France de 1800 à 1914,* II (Lille, 1976), 591; idem., "L'attraction des trois plus grandes agglomérations françaises: Paris-Lyon-Marseille en 1891," *Annales de démographie historique* (1971), 30-31; Gilbert Garrier, *Paysans du beaujolais et du lyonnais, 1800-1970* (Grenoble: Presses universitaires de Grenoble, 1973), 113-14, 479-86.

36. Emile Camau, *Marseille au xxème siècle. Tableau historique et statistique* (Paris: Guillaumin, 1905), 11; William H. Sewell, Jr., *Structure and Mobility—The Men and Women of Marseille, 1820-1870* (New York: Cambridge University Press, 1985), 23-30; Marcel Roncayolo, "Croissance et division sociale de l'espace urbain. Essai sur la genèse des tructures urbaines de Marseille," (Unpublished Dr. d'état, University of Paris, 1981), 200.

37. Marcel Roncayolo, "Les grandes villes françaises—Marseille," *Notes et études documentaires,* no. 3013 (July 29, 1963), 48; Sewell, *Structure and Mobility,* 146-52.

38. Edouard Baratier, *Histoire de Marseille* (Toulouse: Privat, 1973), 385-86.

39. Abbé Louis Dorna, *Histoire de Saint-Etienne* (Saint-Etienne: Dumas, 1970), 12, 159; Maxime Perrin, *La région industrielle de Saint-Etienne* (Tours: Arrault, 1937), 222.

40. Perrin, *Saint-Etienne,* 222; L. Babu, "L'industrie metallurgique dans la région de Saint-Etienne," *Annales des mines,* 9th ser., XV (1899), 357-462.

41. The engineer Piebard, q. in M. Descreux, *Notices biographiques stéphanoises* (Saint-Etienne: Constantine, 1868), 271.

42. Victor Janneson, *Monographie et histoire de la ville de Saint-Etienne* (Saint-Etienne: Le Hénaff, 1892), 195.

43. Rapport sur la situation des industries de Lyon et de Saint-Etienne fait au nom de la commission d'enquête sur la situation des ouvriers de l'industrie et de l'agriculture en France par M. de Lanessan, député, annexe no. 3446, séance 26 December 1884. *Documents parlementaires,* 2290-95.

44. Louis Gache, "Le commerce à Saint-Etienne," in Gilbert Gardes, *Grande encyclopédie du Forez et des communes de la Loire—La ville de Saint-Etienne* (Le Coteau: Horvath, 1984), 250-310.

45. Perrin, *Saint-Etienne,* 224, 226.

46. Jacques Schnetzler, *Les industries et les hommes dans la région stéphanoise* (Saint-Etienne: Feuillet blanc, 1975), 276-277.

47. Jean Merley, "Elements pour l'étude de la formation de la population stéphanoise à l'aube de la révolution industrielle," *Démographie urbaine* (Lyon: Centre d'histoire économique et sociale de la région lyonnaise, 1977), 265; Jacqueline Quintin and Michèle Tomas, "L'origine de la population de Saint-Etienne," *Les villes du massif central* [*Actes du colloque de Saint-Etienne, 27-28 Novembre 1970*] (Saint-Etienne: Centre d'études foréziennes, 1971), 52, 56.

48. The 149,000 figure was probably an undercount to avoid paying the extra subsidies to education that cities with populations over 150,000 were required to pay.

49. Q. in Jean Lorcin, "Economie et comportements sociaux et politiques—La région de Saint-Etienne de la grande dépression à la seconde guerre mondiale," (Unpublished Dr. d'état, University of Paris, 1987), 204.

50. Aristide Guilbert, *Histoire des villes de France*, 1 (Paris: Bureau des publications illustres, 1844), 433.

51. Guilbert, *Histoire*, I:433; Armand Audiganne, *Les populations ouvrières et les industries de la France dans le mouvement social du xixe siècle*, 2 (Paris: Capelle, 1900), 85; F. Bertaux, *Les grandes villes de France* (Paris: 1900), 178.

52. Audiganne, *Les populations* 2:80; Guilbert, *Histoire*, I:433; newspaper, quoted in Lorcin, "Economie et comportements," 1517, 1529.

53. Jean Coppolani, *Toulouse, étude de géographie urbaine* (Toulouse: Privat, 1954), ix-xiv, 82; idem, *Toulouse au xxe siècle* (Toulouse: Privat, 1963), 11-18.

54. Henri Lerner, *La Dépêche de Toulouse, journal de la démocratie*, 2 vols. (Toulouse: Université de Toulouse, 1978); *Petite Gironde*, 26 September 1905.

55. Edmond de Planet, "Statistique industrielle du département de la Haute-Garonne," *Mémoires de l'académie impériale des sciences de Toulouse*, 6th ser. vol III (1867), 227; Charles & Decomble, "Voie de communication," Association française pour l'avancement des sciences, *Toulouse*, I (Toulouse: Privat, 1887), 160; Jacques Boisgontier, *Toulouse* (Toulouse: Christine Bonneton, 1990), 93; Philippe Wolff, *Histoire de Toulouse* (Toulouse: Privat, 1988), 458.

56. Quoted in Jean Fourcassié, *Une ville à l'époque romantique: Toulouse* (Paris: Plon, 1953) 86; Toulouse. 26 July 1876; similar observations in July 1872, q. in Marie-France Brive, "La politique économique de la ville de Toulouse de 1870 à 1880" (Unpublished D.E.S., University of Toulouse, 1967), 81; Henry James, *A Little Tour in France* (New York: Houghton Mifflin, 1897), 173.

57. Raymond Abellio, *Une dernière mémoire-un faubourg de Toulouse, 1907-1927* (Paris: Gallimard, 1971), 43; Calixte Couffin, "L'influence de la ville de Toulouse sur l'agriculture des terrasses garonaises de la Rive gauche," *Revue géographique des pyrenées et du sud-ouest*, 28 (1957), 363; Marie Thérèse Plégat, "L'évolution démographique d'une ville française au xixè siècle, l'exemple de Toulouse," *Annales du midi*, 64 (1952), 237.

58. Boisgontier et al., *Toulouse*, 92; Plégat,"L'évolution," 237.

59. Coppolani, *Toulouse au xxe siècle*, 39, 46; Plégat, "L'évolution," 241.

60. Coppolani, *Etudes géographiques*, 130-47; Plégat, "L'évolution," 237; for the social transformations of Toulouse, see Ronald Aminzade, *Class, Politics, and Early Industrial Capitalism—A Study of Mid-Nineteenth Century Toulouse, France* (Albany: State University of New York Press, 1981), 15-45.

61. The ideologies shaping a strong sense of localism are brilliantly studied in the case of Lyon, Pierre-Yves Saunier, *L'esprit lyonnais, xixe-xxe siècle* (Paris: CNRS, 1995); Jean Bouvier, *Histoire économique et sociale de la France*, 4 (Paris: Seuil, 1979), 399.

62. Margadant, *Urban Rivalries*; idem. "La culture urbaine et la mobilisation politique autour de la division du royaume en départements et districts," Bruno Benoit, ed. *Ville et révolution française* (Lyon: Institut d'études politiques, 1994), 29-37.

63. Quoted in Paul Masson, ed., *Les Bouches-du-Rhône, encyclopédie départementale*, 5 (Marseille: Archives départementales des Bouches-du-Rhône, 1929), 66-67; Reichhardt in 1792, q. in Rolland and Clouzet, *Dictionnaire*, 2: 9; Joseph Bard, *Itinéraire de Dijon à Lyon* (Lyon: Librairie générale, 1851), 213; J Morin, *Histoire de Lyon* (Paris: Ladrange, 1846), xx; Antoine Baton, *La patrie lyonnaise* (Lyon: Legendre, 1914).

64. Christian Barbier, *Les Communes de la Loire: l'application du droit municipal dans un département* (Saint-Etienne: Université de Saint-Etienne, 1976), 15.

65. Marseille. 14 December 1844; Bard, *Itinéraire de Dijon*, 197; idem., *Le département du Rhône—histoire, statistique, géographie* (Paris: A. Brun, 1858), 41; Lyon. 13 April 1908; Adolphe Thiers, *Les Pyrenées et le Midi de la France* (Paris: Ponthieu, 1822), 429-30; Méry, quoted in Félix Tavernier, "L'avènement de la Canebière," *Marseille*, 3rd. ser, no. 5 (April-June 1965), 10.

66. Lyon. 24 June 1873; Quoted in Madeleine Lasserre, "La création du cimetière de Terre-Cabade à Toulouse au xixe siècle," *Annales du midi*, 106 (Jan.-March 1994), 86; Letter, 25 February 1817, 77R4, A.M.M., also q. in Isabelle Bonnot, ed. *Divines divas et vivat l'opéra!* (Marseille: Archives de la ville, December 1987), 16.

67. A. Hodieu, *Essais de nomenclatures lyonnaises municipales et autres de 1800 à 1865* (Lyon: Thibaudier and Boin, 1866), 113-14; Jean Bienfait, "Le recensement de 1936 à Lyon," *Grandes villes et petites villes, colloque national de démographie, Lyon, 1968* (Paris: CNRS, 1970).

68. Bordeaux. 17 December 1878; *Petite Gironde*, 18 April 1906.

CHAPTER 1

1. Alan Forrest, *Society and Politics in Revolutionary Bordeaux* (New York: Oxford University Press, 1975); W.D. Edmonds, *Jacobinism and the Revolt of Lyon, 1789-1793* (New York: Clarendon Press, 1990).

2. V. L. Bourrilly, *La vie et les institutions municipales de Marseille des origines au xixe siècle* (Marseille: Sémaphore, 1935), 83; Mairie de Marseille, "Observations sur le projet

de suppression de la mairie unique et du conseil municipal," (Paris: Serrière, 1859), 3; F. Baud," Caractères géneraux du parti libéral à Lyon sous la restauration," *Revue d'histoire de Lyon*, 12 (1913), 223; Prefect of Rhône to Minister of interior, 1 February 1820, 4M1, A.D.R.; Prefect to Minister of interior, 3 March 1828, 4M1, A.D.R.; Cathérine Pélissier, "Les sociabilités patriciennes à Lyon du milieu du dix neuvième siècle à 1914," (Doctorat de l'université, Lyon II, 1993), 13.

3. Henri Blaquière, Yves Castan and Pierre Gérard, *Documents Toulousains sur l'histoire de France*, 4 (Toulouse: Conseil général de la Haute-Garonne, 1962), 37; Vincent Wright, "Comment les préfets se voyaient," in Jacques Aubert, et al., Les préfets en France (1800-1940) (Geneva: Droz, 1978), 149-50; Camille Jullian, *Histoire de Bordeaux depuis les origines jusqu'en 1895* (Bordeaux: Ferret et fils, 1895), 632.

4. Louis M. Greenberg, *Sisters of Liberty* (Cambridge, MA: Harvard University Press, 1971); Jeanne Gaillard, *Communes de Province, Commune de Paris* (Paris: Flammarion, 1971). For the merger of the social and local in the communes, see Ronald Aminzade, *Ballots and Barricades—Class Formation and Republican Politics in France, 1830-1871* (Princeton: Princeton University Press, 1993), 209-51.

5. Marseille. 20 October 1865; Pierre-Honoré Thomas, *Lyon en 1860* (Lyon: Aimé Vingtrinier, 1860); Edouard Baratier, *Histoire de Marseille* (Toulouse: Privat, 1987), 250; Jacky Meaudre, "La poussée urbaine à Saint-Etienne (1815-1872)," (Unpublished Diplôme d'études supérieures, University of Lyon, 1967).

6. Albert Babeau, *La ville sous l'ancien regime*, 2 vols. (Paris: Didier, 1884).

7. Mirabeau, q. in François Burdeau, *Histoire de l'administration française du 18e au 20e siècle* (Paris: Montchrestien, 1989), 21; and Ibid, 49.

8. Pierre Deyon, *Paris et ses provinces* (Paris: Armand Colin, 1992), 48-51, 88-93; Steven D. Kale, *Legitimism and the Reconstruction of French Society, 1852-1883* (Baton Rouge, LA: Louisiana State University Press, 1992), 89-110, ascribes the decentralizing attitudes of legitimism less to calculation and more to earnest conviction.

9. Suffrage was less limited, however, in local elections than in national elections; there were three million local voters—ten times as many voters as in national elections. This ratio varied a lot, though, according to cities; in Marseille, for instance, in the 1840s, 3,000 men could vote in national elections—4,600 in municipal contests. Félix Tavernier, *Vie quotidienne à Marseille de Louis XIV à Louis-Philippe* (Paris: Hachette, 1973), 216.

10. Jean-François Gilon, "Les élections à Bordeaux sous la seconde république," *Revue historique de Bordeaux*, n.s. (1990-1992), 113; Aminzade, *Class, Politics, and Early Industrial Capitalism*, 158.

11. Quoted in *Le Temps*, 22 January 1864.

12. Toulouse. 17 November 1869.

13. Anon. "La municipalité Emile Fourcand (aout 1870-février 1874)" (University of Bordeaux (Unpublished T.E.R., 1971), 19; "Mémoire à M. le Ministre de l'intérieur—protestation contre les arrêtés de suspension du conseil municipal de

Bordeaux," (Bordeaux: G. Gounoilhou, 1874); Marseille. 9 May 1877; Lyon. 30 May 1872.

14. *Le Temps*, 17 February 1882.

15. A convenient summary of the changing status of Parisian local government can be found in Pierre Debofle et al., *L'administration de Paris* (Paris: Centre de recherches d'histoire et de philologie, 1979).

16. *Le Temps*, 28 March 1873.

17. Eleazar Lavoie, "La révocation des maires (1830-1875), ordre moral ou mise en interdit?" *Etat et pouvoir*, 8 (1992), 37-65; slightly lower figures in John M. Merriman, *The Agony of the Republic—The Repression of the Left in Revolutionary France, 1848-1851* (New Haven, CT: Yale University Press, 1978), 111.

18. Lucien Aune, "Le parti républicain à Marseille, 1869-1879," (Unpublished D.E.S. Aix, 1963), 194; Bordeaux. 18 June 1874.

19. Marseille. 28 March 1887.

20. *Le Temps*, 25 September 1894, *Dépêche de Toulouse*, 10 November 1896; Jean Nevers "Système politico-administrative communal et pouvoir local en milieu urbain— étude d'un cas: la municipalité radicale-socialiste de Toulouse [1888-1906]," (Unpublished thesis, 3ème cycle, Sociology, University of Toulouse, 1975) 9-10.

21. Aune, "Le part républicain," 221, 232; *Le Temps*, 26 January 1895.

22. *Pétite Gironde*, 27 May 1905.

23. Marseille. 23 June 1901.

24. Vivian A. Schmidt, *Democratizing France—The Political and Administrative History of Decentralization* (New York: Cambridge University Press, 1990), ix, 181, 207.

25. Marie-Claude Zanzi, "Les maires de Marseille de 1789 à 1940," Unpublished Mémoire, Diplôme d'études approfondies (henceforth abbreviated as DEA) Droit et administration, Aix-en-Provence, n.d., 19; Laurent Coste, *Le maire et l'empereur-Bordeaux sous le premier empire* (Bordeaux: Société archéologique et historique de Lignan et du canton de Créon, 1993), 67, 87.

26. Bernard Gallinato, "L'entrée en vigueur en Gironde de la loi du 30 juin 1838 sur les aliénés: Incidence budgétaires et difficultés d'application," *Colloque sur l'histoire de la sécurité sociale* [Actes du 110e congrès des sociétés savantes, Montpellier, 1985] (Paris: Association pour l'étude de l'histoire de la sécurité sociale, 1986) 177.

27. Paul Masson, ed, *Les Bouches-du-Rhône, encyclopédie départementale*, 11 (Marseille: Archives départementales des Bouches-du-Rhône, 1913), 263.

28. Marseille. 2 January 1860.

29. "Liste des candidats indiqués pour les places de maires," January 1, 1808, F[lb] I, 242, A.N.; André Latreille, *Histoire de Lyon et du Lyonnais* (Toulouse: Privat, 1975), 307-308; Paul Ronin, *Saint-Etienne à ciel ouvert* (Saint-Etienne: Paul Ronin, 1959), 73.

30. A. Martourey, "Formation et gestion d'une agglomération industrielle au XIXème siècle, Saint-Etienne de 1815 à 1870," (Unpublished Doctorat d'état, Université of Lyon, II, 1984), 860.

31. A.J. Tudesq, "De la monarchie à la République: le maire petit ou grand notable," *Pouvoirs*, 24 (1983), 15.

32. A. Kleinclausz, *Histoire de Lyon*, 3 (Lyon: Pierre Masson, 1952), 254.

33. Antoine Olivesi, "J.B. Brochier (1829-1886)," *Revue de Marseille*, no. 125 (1981), 8.

34. *Le Temps*, 9 February 1882.

35. Quoted in Frédérick Ogé, "Armand Duportal: un préfet extrémiste," *Etat et pouvoir-Actes du colloque de Toulouse (22-23 Octobre 1982)* (Marseille: Presses Universitaires d'Aix-Marseille, 1984), 119.

36. *Le Temps*, 10 August 1863.

37. *Le Temps*, 30 November 1873.

38. The Toulouse example, *Dépêche de Toulouse*, 13 March 1895, 1 September 1895, 30 June 1904; Victor Cambon, *La France au travail*, 2 (Paris: Pierre Roger, 1913), 51.

39. I am using this term to translate the French term *député-maire*. I am avoiding the term "deputy mayor," for fear that it will be seen as the English equivalent of *maire adjoint*, which I have chosen to translate as "assistant mayor."

40. Bernadette Lynch, *Le Comte J. B. Lynch—maire de Bordeaux, 1809-1815* (Bordeaux: Mialhe, 1970), 45.

41. Martourey, "Formation et gestion," 935.

42. Terme, q. in Pierre Bertrand and Louis Jasseron. "Les médecins qui furent maires de Lyon," *Revue lyonnaise de médecine* (December 1958), 196; *Dépêche de Toulouse*, 6 May 1904.

43. Howard C. Payne, *The Police State of Louis Napoleon Bonaparte, 1851-1860* (Seattle: University of Washington Press, 1966), 168-69.

44. Q. in François Burdeau, *Histoire*, 231.

45. J. Lagroye, *Société et politique. J. Chaban-Delmas à Bordeaux* (Paris: Pedone, 1973).

46. Philip Nord, *The Republican Moment—Struggles for Democracy in Nineteenth-Century France* (Cambridge, MA: Harvard University Press, 1995).

47. Martourey, "Formation et gestion," 862-81.

48. Jullian, *Histoire de Bordeaux*, 119; Jean Cavignac, "Les négociants maires de Bordeaux sous la monarchie de Juillet," *Congrès national des sociétés savantes, 108e congrès, Grenoble 1983* (Paris: Comité des travaux historiques et scientifiques, 1984), 293-304.

49. Albert Charles, *La révolution de 1848 et la seconde république à Bordeaux et dans le département de la Gironde* (Bordeaux: Delmas, 1945), 108; Louis Desgraves and

Chapter 1: From City Republic to Republican Cities

Georges Dupeux, *Bordeaux au xix siècle* (Bordeaux: Fédération historique du Sud-ouest, 1969), 164.

50. Roland Caty and Eliane Richard, "Notables au xix siècle," *Marseille*, no. 159 (May 1991), 22-30.

51. *Le Temps*, 14 August 1866; Brémond, *Histoire de l'election municipal . . . Toulouse* (Toulouse, 1865).

52. Norbert Rouland, *Le conseil municipal marseillais et sa politique de la IIe à la IIIe république (1848-1875)* (Aix-en- Provence: Edisud, 1974), 63-64.

53. Martourey, "Formation," 836; David M. Gordon, "Merchants and Capitalists: Industrialization and Provincial Politics at Reims and Saint-Etienne Under the Second Republic and Second Empire," (Ph.D. Dissertation, Brown University, 1978), 324.

54. Q. in Daniel Halévy, *The End of the Notables* (Middletown, CT: Wesleyan University Press, 1974), 94.

55. Marseille. 14 November 1871, 20 February 1877.

56. 10K2, A.M.S.; Jean Lorcin, "Economie et comportements sociaux et politiques— La région de Saint-Etienne de la grande dépression à la seconde guerre mondiale" (Unpublished Thesis, Dr. d'état, University of Paris, 1987), 1333.

57. *Le Temps*, 5 July 1882.

58. Desgraves and Dupeux, *Bordeaux*, 340-343; Commissariat spécial de police, "Rapport," 17 May 1888, 3M683, A.D.G.

59. Olivesi, "Brochier," 8.

60. C. Goyet, R. Martin, G. Soulier "Les conseillers municipaux de Lyon, 1884-1953" *Etude de politique et d'économie régionales*, series 2, *Annales de l'Université de Lyon* (1959), 132-134; Pierre Callet, "En un mois, en un an, Lyon en 1900," *Albums du crocodile* (1958), 11.

61. Nevers, "Système politico-administrative," 36-37; Jacques Cremadeills, "La politique financière, économique et sociale de la municipalité Toulousaine de 1910 à 1920," (Unpublished D.E.S., University of Toulouse, 1967), 251-54.

62. G. Ducaunnes-Duval, "Le Traitement des officiers municipaux pendant la révolution," *Revue historique de Bordeaux*, 16 (1923): 207.

63. Lyon. Thermidor, An XII, Repr. in *Bulletin officiel municipal de Lyon* [henceforth abbreviated as *BOML*] (1 January 1911), 8.

64. Bordeaux. 17 June 1831, 20 July 1831; Lyon.16 November 1846; 14 July 1871.

65. Rouland, *Le conseil municipal*, 169.

66. Marseille. 29 December 1876; Jacqueline Herpin, "Les Milieux dirigeants à Bordeaux sous la troisième république," (Unpublished Diplôme d'études supérieures, University of Bordeaux, 1966), 28.

67. Marseille. 24 January 1842.

68. Marseille. 20 September 1870; Lyon. 6 September 1870; Marseille. 18 November 1878, 15 February 1881, 20 January 1893, 1 February 1897.

69. *Le Temps*, 17 May 1882; *Petite Gironde*, 29 April 1904.

70. *Dépêche de Toulouse*, 8 October 1892; *Le Temps*, 25 January 1889; Marseille. 9 March 1902; J. Delaitre, *La municipalité parisienne et les projets de réforme* (Paris: A. Larose, 1902), 64; Alfred des Cilleuls, *L'administration parisienne sous la 3ème république* (Paris: Picard, 1910), 16-17, 327; *Le Temps*, 9 October 1902.

71. *Dépêche de Toulouse*, 31 July 1903; *Revue municipale*, 21 December 1901; "Commission d'enquête, "Rapport," 8 April 1910, A.M.T.; Marseille. Séance, 21 October 1913.

72. Léon Morgand, *La loi municipale*, 10th edition, 1 (Paris: Berger-Levrault, 1923) 555; *Le Temps*, 9 May 1877; *Le Combat*, 6 December 1903.

73. Alexandre Vivien, *Etudes administratives* 3rd ed., II (Paris: Guillaumin, 1859), 48-49; Bordeaux. 9 October 1865; *Le Temps*, 21 September 1865.

74. Pierre Rosanvallon, *L'état en France de 1789 à nos jours* (Paris: Plon, 1990), 35.

75. Hodieu, *Essai de nomenclature*, (25); Toulouse. 14 March 1850.

76. Toulouse. 8 September, 8 November 1865; Burdeau, *Liberté*, 175.

77. Toulouse. 17 November 1869, 5 September 1870, 22 November 1870, 31 October 1871; Marseille. 13 December 1870; Anon. "La municipalité Emile Fourcand," 19; Lyon. 16 June 1871; Bordeaux. 14 May 1878; Marseille. 11 November 1880, 8 February 1881, 29 September 1881.

CHAPTER 2

1. Montesquieu, *De l'esprit des lois, Oeuvres complètes*, 1 (Paris: Nagel, 1950), 290.

2. Gaston Bertrand, *Des taxes communales d'octroi et de leur établissement et de leur suppression* (Paris: Arthur Rousseau, 1896), 26.

3. Armand Rousselot, *De l'octroi et spécialement de l'octroi de Bordeaux* (Bordeaux: Y. Cadoret, 1907), 67-69; "Mémoire," 30 August 1790, 4000 L2, A.M.B.

4. Frédéric Galtier, *La suppression de l'octroi* (Paris: Arthur Rousseau, 1904), 15; André Cottez, *La régie interessée de l'octroi de Lyon (5 fructidor an VIII-21 mars 1807)* (Paris: Domat-Montchrestien, 1937), 21-22.

5. Anon. "Observations de la municipalité de Bordeaux sur la necessité de supprimer les octrois actuels" (Bordeaux: 1791); Rousselot, *De l'octroi*, 67-69. Robert Laurent is mistaken in claiming that Paris was the first municipality to demand the restoration of the tax, Robert Laurent, *L'octroi de Dijon au xixe siècle* (Paris: SEVPEN, 1960), 1.

6. Galtier, *L'octroi*, 28.

Chapter 2: City Financing

7. Jean Gay, "L'octroi Parisien au xixe siècle," *L'administration locale en Ile-de-France [Mémoires des sociétés historiques et archéologiques de Paris et de l'Ile-de-France]*, 38 (1987), 188; 20 floréal, an XI, reprinted in *Bulletin officiel municipal de Lyon*, (20 March 1910), 260.

8. Frédéric Galtier, *La suppression de l'octroi* (Paris: Arthur Rousseau, 1904), 27.

9. Maxime Du Camp, *Paris, ses organes, ses fonctions et sa vie*, 3rd ed., 6 (Paris: Hachette, 1875), 4.

10. P. Deloynes, *Les octrois et les budgets municipaux* (Paris: Guillaumin, 1871), 32-37.

11. A. Gabriel Desbats, *Le budget municipal* (Paris: Berger-Levrault, 1895), 72, fn.1.

12. M.E. Bonnal, *Traité des octrois* (Paris: Guillaumin, 1873), 154-55.

13. *Liberté du sudouest*, 13 June 1909; *Petite Gironde*, 6 February 1902.

14. Armand Cosson, "Finances locales et consommation urbaine: l'octroi à Nîmes au xixe siècle, " *La ville en pays Languedocian* [*Societe Languedocienne de géographie, Bulletin*, ser. 3, vol. 16 (July-December 1982)], 48; Report of 3-4 May 1815 riot in 4001 L58, A.M.B.; 1814 riot in Marseille is described in Marseille City Council, 28 November 1828; Mayor to Préfet, 25 February 1814, F⁶II Gironde 19, A.N.

15. H.A. Frégier, *Des classes dangereuses de la population dans les grandes villes*, 1 (Paris: J.B. Baillière, 1840), 201-202.

16. Letter from Prefect to Mayor, 24 March 1809, 4001 L58, A.M.B.

17. Bordeaux. 8 June 1825; Préposé en chef de l'octroi to Mayor, 16 August 1831, 4001 L108, A.M.B.

18. Claude Chatelard, *Crime et criminalité dans l'arrondissement de Saint-Etienne au xixe siècle* (Saint-Etienne: Centre d'études foréziennes, 1981), 203; Alfred de Cilleuls, *Histoire de l'administration Parisienne au xix siècle*, 2 (Paris: Champion, 1900), 69; "Rapport sur la situation financière de la ville de Marseille, présenté au conseil municipal le 9 juillet 1840," (Marseille: Hoirs Freissat ainé et Demonchy, 1840) 8.

19. Olibo, "L'octroi de Lyon," 278.

20. Ibid., 279.

21. "Rapport des membres du conseil municipal faisant parti de la commission d'enquête, octrois de Lyon," (Lyon: S. Gallet, 1879); Toulouse. 14 March 1881; *Dépêche de Toulouse*, 9 July 1890, 8 February 1893; 12 November 1888.

22. *Nouvelliste*, 2 September 1911; Lyon, *Documents relatifs au projet de budget de 1885*, 138; Lyon. *Documents rélatifs au projet de budget de 1887* (1886), 226; Cited in Toulouse, 7 November 1888.

23. Richard von Kaufmann, *Die Kommunalfinanzen (Grossbritannien, Frankreich, Preussen)*, 2 (Leipzig: C.L. Hirschfeld, 1906) 257.

24. Desbats, *Le budget municipal*, 97; Auguste Foulon, *Etude sur les octrois* (Nantes: Vve. Mellinet, 1870), 71; Gaston Besnard, *De la suppression des taxes communales d'octroi* (Poitiers: Blois et Roy, 1910), 161-17; François Cavaignac, "La politique bugétaire

273

de la municipalité de Toulouse de 1888 à 1900" (Unpublished Maitrise, University of Toulouse, 1973), 132; Emile Camau, *Marseille au xxème siécle. Tableau historique et statistique* (Paris: Guillaumin, 1905), 121.

25. Louis Villermé, *Etat physique et moral des ouvriers employés dans les manufactures de coton, de laine et de soie,* 1 (Paris: J. Renouard, 1850), 389.

26. Mayor Gailleton, q. in Ville de Bordeaux, *Un siècle d'administration (finances et octrois), 1820-1900,* 2 (Bordeaux: G. Delmas, 1903-1904), 374.

27. John M. Merriman, *The Margins of City Life—Explorations on the French Urban Frontier* (New York: Oxford University Press, 1991).

28. Jean Bouvier, "Le système fiscal français au XIXe siècle- étude critique d'un immobilisme," in Jean Bouvier, ed. *Deux siècles de fiscalité française* (Paris: Mouton, 1973), 226-27.

29. Q. in Robert Schnerb, "Les vicissitudes de l'impôt indirect de la constituante à Napoléon," Jean Bouvier, et al., *Deux siècles,* 68.

30. Gaston Bertrand, *Des taxes communales d'octroi et de leur établissement et de leur suppression* (Paris: Arthur Rousseau, 1896), 38-39; Adolphe Thiers, *De la propriété* (Brussels: C.W. Froment, 1848), ch. iv; *Journal des économistes,* 1866, q. in Foulon, *Etude sur les octrois,* 72-81.

31. Bordeaux. 18 July, 1831; Marseille. 19 November 1830, 16 July 1831.

32. Barillon, "Suppression des octrois," *Revue du Lyonnais,* 14 (1841), 135, 123; also cited in François Dutacq, *Histoire politique de Lyon pendant la révolution de 1848* (Paris: Edouard Cornély, 1910), 61.

33. Bordeaux. 9 May 1845; Max Consolat, "Rapport sur la situation financière de la ville de Marseille, presenté au conseil municipal le 9 juillet 1840," (Marseille: Hoirs Freissat ainé et Demonchy, 1840), 8.

34. Bordeaux. 9 May 1845.

35. Minister of interior Faucher's remark of 1847 cited in A. Chérot, "Etude sur l'abolition et le remplacement des octrois," *Journal des économistes* (April-June 1870), 57.

36. Marseille. 4 January 1849.

37. Bordeaux, 14 May 1866.

38. Letter of Mayor of Brussels to Mayor of Bordeaux, 21 July 1869, 4048L2, AMB.

39. M. Migneret, "Question des octrois, Rapport. Compte rendu des séances des 10-13 decembre 1869," (Paris: Imprimerie nationale, 1870).

40. J. Burot, *Les octrois-étude* (Senlis: Vve Duriez, 1872), 391.

41. Lyon. 6 May 1870.

42. On the riot, Report of June 9, 1869, 4003L2, A.M.B.; Rousselot, *De l'octroi,* 110; "Questionnaire sur la situation de l'octroi," March 1870, 4010L1, A.M.B.; Bordeaux. 2 May 1870, 3 June 1870.

Chapter 2: City Financing

43. Saint-Etienne. 13 July 1870.

44. Marseille. 18 May 1870; Toulouse. 12 July 1870; J. Martel, "Octrois," Léon Say, *Dictionnaire des finances*, 2 (Paris: Berger-Levrault, 1894), 683. Martel claimed that the Commune fire in the Ministry of Finance destroyed the answers to the questionnaires. But as the discussion shows, the answers survived in local archives.

45. Lyon. 30 June, 1871; *Temps*, 6 July 1871; Marseille. 21, 23 December 1870; 30 January 1871; Toulouse. 22 November 1870.

46. Jean Nevers, "Système politico-administratif communal et pouvoir local en milieu urbain-étude d'un cas: la municipalité radicale-socialiste de Toulouse (1888-1906)," (Unpublished thesis, 3ème cycle, Sociology, University of Toulouse, 1975), 253-54; *Dépêche de Toulouse*, 2 December 1894; Armand Charpentier, *Le parti radical et radical-socialiste à travers ses congrès (1901-1911)* (Paris: Griaud, 1913), 310.

47. "Elections municipales lyonnaises. La victoire de la bourgeoisie—ses causes" (Lyon: Beau jeune, 1881); E. Stehelin, *Essais de socialisme municipal* (Paris: Larose, 1901), 13; Commissaire de police to préfet, Bordeaux, 24 January 1892, 3M684, A.D.G; *Question sociale*, 6 February 1892; *Le Temps*, 4 November 1897; Michael McQuillen, "The Development of Municipal Socialism in France, 1880-1914," (Unpublished Ph.D. Thesis, University of Viriginia, 1973), 114-16; Galtier, *Octrois*, 147; Laurent, *L'octroi de Dijon*, 4-5.

48. Ville de Bordeaux, *Bordeaux-Apercu historique*, 2 (Paris; Hachette, 1892), 312, 347, 359, 374; Comité central républicain de Bordeaux, "Programme électoral," n.d. [March 1892?], 3M 684, A.D.G.; *La France*, 29 April 1896; *Petite Gironde*, 29 April 1896.

49. Toulouse. 20 May 1889.

50. Besnard, *De la suppression*, 84.

51. "Rapport presenté à la commission sénatoriale pour la suppression des octrois par l'administration municipale de la ville de Lyon (15 March 1894)," (Lyon: Association typographique, 1894), 6; Gailleton, "Rapport général sur les travaux du conseil municipal de Lyon, 1892-1896," (Lyon: Association typographique, 1896), 28-29; Georges Périé," Rapport presenté au conseil municipal, suppression de l'octroi," (Bordeaux: G. Delmas, 1898), 40, 60-61, 68.

52. C. Blancart, *La suppression des droits d'octroi et les taxes de remplacement* (Paris: Arthur Rousseau, 1910), 50.

53. Lyon. 17 July 1911.

54. Victor Augagneur, "Rapport sur le remplacement de l'octroi par des taxes directes (Lyon: Association typographique, 1896), 4-5; "Rapport sur la suppression de l'octroi," (Lyon: 1898), 7; André George, *Essai sur la suppression de l'octroi de Lyon* (Lyon: Roux, 1904), 9.

55. Q. in George, *Essai*, 21-22.

56. Cited in Lyon. 21 May 1911.

57. Victor Augagneur, "Rapport sur les résultats de la suppression de l'octroi à Lyon." (Lyon: Nouvelle Lyonnaise, 1904); Lyon. 10 July 1911.

58. Nevers, "Système politico-administratif," 257-258; *Dépêche de Toulouse*, 4 January 1893, 4 November 1897, 29 December 1900, 10 July 1901, 29 December 1903; R. Delperie, "Toulouse et sa municipalité, 1900-1910, politique financière, économique et sociale," (Unpublished, D.E.S, University of Toulouse, 1967), 57-58, 72.; Toulouse. 21 May 1908, 29 December 1909.

59. J.B. Brochier, "Rapport sur la suppression partielle ou totale de l'octroi présenté au conseil municipal, 16 November 1880," (Marseille: Méridionale, 1880); Marseille. 4 February 1881, 13 December 1884, 13 April 1886, 4 September 1898, 17 February 1901, 16 June 1901, 25 March 1906, 11 July 1909.

60. *Cri du peuple*, 8 January 1911; Bordeaux. 1 December 1913.

61. Saint Etienne. 17 November, 1888; Letter from prefect to Mayor, 28 January 1889, 2 L192, A.M.S.E.; *Mémorial de la Loire et de la Haute Loire*, 25 November 1888.

62. Saint-Etienne. 9 November 1900, 8 August 1903, 17 March 1905. It is curious that while Limoges was known as the Red City from midcentury on, and the Socialists took power in 1895, they don't seem to have mounted a campaign to abolish the *octrois*, a singular oversight for a party preaching social justice. John Merriman, *The Red City—Limoges and the French Nineteenth Century* (New York: Oxford University Press, 1985).

63. Jean Lorcin, "Le socialisme municipal à Saint-Etienne," *Mélanges offerts à André Latreille* (Lyon: Centre d'histoire du catholicisme, 1972), 577.

64. Emmanuel Couturier, *La question des octrois après la loi du 29 décembre 1897* (Paris: A. Michalon, 1907), 60; in fairness, it should be noted that in spite of this catchy phrasing, the councilman was opposed to the *octrois*. Similar phrasing in H. Barthélemy, "La suppression des octrois et l'expérience de Lyon," *Revue politique et parlementaire*, 4 (May 1895), 275-87.

CHAPTER 3

1. Alfred Neymarck, *Finances contemporaines*, 2 (Paris: Guillaumin, 1904) 467.

2. Max Weber *Economy and Society*, Guenther Roth and Claus Wittich, ed. (New York: Bedminster Press, 1968) 2:220-221, 3: 957, 963, 966-67.

3. Anne-Marie Patault, "Les origines révolutionnaires de la fonction publique: de l'employé au fonctionnaire," *Revue historique de droit français et étranger*, 64 (Janvier-Mars 1986), 391-92.

4. "Observations au compte administratif de 1837," F^6II Gironde 30, A.N.

5. Henry Buisson, *La police, son histoire* (Vichy: Wallon, 1949), 245.

6. Prefect to Minister of interior, 16 June 1806, F⁶II Gironde 13, A.N.; Minister of Finance to Minister of interior, 2 March 1826, F⁶II Gironde 24; Bordeaux. 15 May 1820.

7. 1841 Budget Report, F⁶II Rhône 28, A.N.

8. "Personnel, exercice 1819," 2090 K 1, A.M.B.

9. Théâtre, Directions, 1840-1860, R 2., A.M.L.

10. B. Dumons and G. Pollet, "Pouvoir municipal et fonction administrative: les secrétaires généraux de mairie dans les grandes villes de la région Rhône-Alpes," Conference on "La ville en occident du moyen âge à nos jours," Bourges, 5-7 October 1995; "Rapport fait par M. Monplanet, inspecteur des finances" (1874), 4046 L1, A.M.B.

11. Yves Janvier, "L'industrie des bâtiments à Marseille de 1815 à 1851," (Diplôme d'études supérieures, Aix-en-Provence, 1964), 193.

12. "Etude sur l'octroi de Bordeaux, 19 October 1866, 4000 L6; "Rapport du préposé en chef de l'octroi, 31 May 1872, 4000 L6; 2215 K2, A.M.B.

13. Bruno Dumons and Gilles Pollet, "'Fonctionnaires' municipaux et employés de la ville de Lyon (1870-1914): Légitimité d'un modèle administratif décentralisé," *Revue historique*, 581 (January-March 1992), 117.

14. Letter from Pupire to City Council, n.d. [1790s], 6K3, A.M.M.

15. Marseille, Arrêté, 24 October 1831; Marseille. 11 January 1886.

16. J.F., 2 K33; J.D., also J- M D. 2K33; 14 April 1915, 2K13; M.G., 2K35, A.M.T. [The initials refer to the names of the city employees; their dossiers are alphabetically arranged in the numbered files].

17. *La France*, 24 April 1908.

18. Marseille. Arrêté 11 frimaire, Year III, Arrêté 31 March 1817, 7 September 1830.

19. Arrêté, 29 January 1820, in Pionin, *Code de police municipale de la ville de Lyon* (Lyon: Dumoulin, Ronet and Sibouet, 1840), 285.

20. Marseille. 29 October 1885.

21. Prefect to Minister of interior, 12 November 1825, F⁶. II Gironde 24, A.N.; Prefect to Minister of interior, 4 March 1828, F⁶II Rhône 23, A.N.; Prefect to Mayor, 9 February 1866, q. in Marseille. 16 February 1866.

22. Mayor, quoted in *Le Sémaphore*, 23 November 1849; Marseille. October 1885; Marseille. 24 January 1897. These remarks were not the criticisms of one of the mayor's opponents, but rather of a supporter, and therefore can probably be given credence.

23. Arrêté, 1 April 1873; Toulouse. 29 December 1890; q. in Jean Nevers, "Système politico-administratif communal et pouvoir local en milieu urbain—étude d'un cas: la municipalité radicale-socialiste de Toulouse (1888-1906)," (Unpublished

thesis, 3ème cycle, Sociology, University of Toulouse, 1975) 167; 1 September 1901, K2. 177, A.M.S.E.

24. "Prépose en chef de l'octroi to Mayor, 24 May 1855, 6K 1, A.M.M.; "Etude sur l'octroi de Bordeaux, 19 October 1866, 4000 L6, A.M.B.; Saint-Etienne. Arrêté. 1 September 1901, K2, 177. A.M.S.E.; Lyon. 12 November 1906; Circular of Toulouse Mayor Bedouce, 1906, Copy in Ingénieur 306, A.M.T. ("Ingénieur" is a temporary name for this series while it awaits a new classification); Pierre Yves-Saunier, "La ville et la ville: les hommes et les organismes municipaux de l'aménagement urbain au 19e et 20 e siècles," Recherches contemporaines, no. 3 (1995-1996), 123, 130.

25. An undated report [1830?], 6K3, A.M.M.

26. 6D 214, A.M.T.

27. Préposé en chef to Mayor, 20 April 1865, 2215 K2, A.M.B.

28. "Personnel, exercice 1819," 2090 K 1, A.M.B.; J.B. Dupuch, Quelques observations sur l'administration des finances municipales de Bordeaux (Bordeaux: Lanefranque, 1828), 47-48.

29. Marseille. 10 November 1832; "Etude sur l'octroi de Bordeaux, 19 October 1866, 4000 L6, A.M.B.

30. Préposé en chef to Mayor, 17 October 1866, 2215 K 2, A.M.B.; "Rapport fait par M. Blondel, inspecteur des finances," 24 June 1870, 4046 L 1, A.M.B.

31. Préposé en chef to Myor, 12 August 1865, 2215 K 2, A.M.B.; "Rapport fait par M. Monplanet, inspecteur des finances, 1874," 4046 L 1, A.M.B.; Nevers," Système politico-administratif," 150.

32. "Etat du bureau de correspondence et d'exécution," 25 vendemiaire, Year III, 6K3, A.M.M; Bordeaux. 26 September 1836.

33. A. Martourey, "Formation et gestion d'une agglomération industrielle au xixème siècle, Saint-Etienne de 1815 à 1870," (Unpublished Doctorat d'état, University of Lyon, II, 1984), 1044.

34. Eugene N. Anderson & Pauline R. Anderson, Political Institutions and Social Change in Continental Europe in the Nineteenth Century (Berkeley: University of California Press, 1967), 217.

35. Lyon. Arrêté, 30 May 1881; Saint-Etienne. 1 April 1903.

36. Lyon. "Rapport de la Commission spéciale budgétaire de 1881," (Lyon, 1881), 84; Toulouse. 29 December 1912; Revue municipale, 1-14 February 1907.

37. Toulouse. 1 June 1872; "Etat nominatif des employés du bureau militaire, 25 January 1884," 6 K 1, A.M.M.; Marseille. 19 January 1882; Mayor of Saint-Etienne to Mayor of Lyon, 8 January 1895, K2S, A.M.L.; Toulouse. 16 December 1910.

38. Nevers, "Système politico-administratif," 150-51.

39. Marseille. 6 November 1884, 13-20 November 1910; E. Herriot, "La condition du personnel de la ville de Lyon," Annales de la régie directe 1 (May-June 1909), 129-73,

and *In those Days* (New York: Old and New World Publishers, 1950), 181; Saint-Etienne. 27 December 1907.

40. Lyon Arrêté 4 July 1818; Préposé en chef de l'octroi to Mayor, 24 March 1855, 6 K1, A.M.M.; "Etude sur l'octroi de Bordeaux, 19 October 1866, 4000 L6, A.M.B.; "Rapport du préposé en chef de l'octroi, 31 May 1872, 4000 L6; 2215 K2 , A.M.B.; Nevers, "Système politico-administratif," 150-151.

41. Saint-Etienne. 27 December 1907; Ville de Saint-Etienne, "Service de l'octroi," 30 April 1909.

42. Each of the five city archivists was asked for personnel files of nineteenth-century employees; employee files were not listed in the available archival catalogues. In all but Toulouse, it was claimed that they did not exist; there they were made available on the condition that the names of the individuals not be used. That is why they are identified by initials and by the call numbers of the boxes in which the files are located. I wish to thank the Mayor of Toulouse for granting me permission to use the files, and the assistant archivist, Mme. Maillard, for facilitating the process of consulting them. It turned out that the files for the period before 1914 were meager in information and the secrecy surrounding them unwarranted.

43. E.& J. A., 2K10; J.D.2K29, A.M.T.

44. A.B.; J.C., 2K29, A.M.T.

45. M.C., J.D., 2 K27, A.M.T.

46. M. E., 2 K32, A.M.T.

47. A., J.B., A.C., A.D., B.D., 2 K31, A.M.T.

48. Préposé en chef to Mayor, 20 April 1865, 2215 K2, A.M.B.

49. Marseille. 20 December 1867; 2 January 1880; Georges Bonneau, *Manuel pratique des maires et des conseillers municipaux* (Paris: Marcel Riviere, 1909), 153.

50. Paul Gerbod, et al, *Les épurations administratives, xixe et xxe siècles* (Geneva: Droz, 1977).

51. Arrêté 10 November 1815; Prefet to Mayor, 5 September 1815, 2220 K1, A.M.B.

52. His career conformed to the pattern of opportunities offered by the 1830 Revolution to former Napoleonic officials in the national administration, as described by David Pinkney. Fired for Bonapartism under the Restoration, he was reappointed in August 1830. 6D 244, A.M.T.; David Pinkney, *The Revolution of 1830* (Princeton: Princeton University Press, 1972).

53. Marseille. 24 September 1830; Préposé en chef to Mayor, 22 September 1870, 2215 K3, A.M.B.

54. Marseille. 10 November 1870; Marseille. 5 March 1877; *Le Temps,* January 1, 1877; Frédérick Ogé, "Armand Duportal: un préfet extrémiste," *Etat et pouvoir-Actes du colloque de Toulouse (22-23 October 1982)* (Marseille: Presses Universitaires d'Aix-Marseille, 1984), 123.

55. A. Hodieu, *Essais de nomenclatures lyonnaises municipales et autres de 1800 à 1865* (Lyon: Thibaudier and Boin, 1866), 41-42.

56. Jacques Boisgontier et al., *Toulouse*, (Paris: Bonneton, 1990), 145.

57. Marseille. 5 January 1872, 26 December 1877; The Central Committee q. in *Le Temps*, 25 February 1881.

58. Dumons and Pollet, "Fonctionnaires," 118.

59. Nevers, "Système politico-administratif," 182; *Dépêche de Toulouse*, 20 October 1896, 4 November 1896; *Le Télégramme*, 13 April 1900. Continuous purges at the national level are described in Dominique Chagnollaud, "La naissance du haut fonctionnaire moderne," in Paul Isoart and Christian Bidegarry, eds. *Des républiques francaises* (Paris: Economica, 1988), 348-62.

60. Jean Lorcin, "Economie et comportements sociaux et politiques—La région de Saint-Etienne de la grande dépression à la seconde guerre mondiale." (Unpublished Thesis, Dr. d'état, University of Paris, 1987), 1345, 1379.

61. Nevers, "Système politico-administratif," 161. Nevers cites a different proportion, but he appears to have miscalculated the figures; the examples of professions of the dismissed is in G.G. file, 2 K37, A.M.T.

62. *Le Temps*, 18, 24 December 1878; Commissaire de police to Mayor, 5 March 1892, 3M 684, A.D.G.

63. A.in 1905, J.A.in 1909; 2K37, A.M.T.

64. Marseille. 5 February, 18 December 1878, 22 January 1905; 1882 notes in Bureau de bienfaisance. Affaires diverses, 1889-1933, A.M.L; Marseille. 8 October 1911.

65. Etienne Bellot, *Les hommes du jour à Marseille* (Marseille: Rédaction et administration, 1891), 12-13.

66. Nevers, "Système politico-administratif," 182.

67. Toulouse. 19 December 1879; Jacqueline Félician-Le Corre, "Action sociale de la municipalité de Marseille, 1892-1939," 1 (Unpublished Thesis, 3ème cycle, University Aix-Marseille, I, 1987), 133.

68. Marseille. 13 December 1878, 9 January 1898; "Note de service," 15 July 1910, 8 July 1912, Ingénieur 306, A.M.T. *Petite Gironde*, 28 December 1901.

69. 2215 K5, A.M.B.; Marseille. 3 February 1901.

70. Letter, 26 March 1902. R 18, A.M.L.; Letter from Eugenie Joannet to Mayor, 26 November 1900, R 42, A.M.L.

71. *Dépêche de Toulouse*, 12 November 1903; Marseille. 25 August 1901.

72. Marseille. 14 November 1894, 25 September 1898.

73. Marseille. 14 August 1867; 13 November 1868, 17 May 1878. The charges were made by a city councilman described as disgruntled because his candidates were

not appointed to the public works office. But there was, interestingly enough, no denial of these charges.

74. L. Bruce Fulton, "L'épreuve du Boulangisme à Toulouse: comment les républicains manipulèrent les élections en 1889," *Annales du midi*, 88 (1976), 341; *Temps*, 25 September 1894, 26 January 1895, 9 March 1895.

75. Masson, ed. *Bouches-du-Rhône*, 14: 315-16; "Rapport sur le personnel municipal de 1828 à 1833," n.d. [1833?]; 2090 K1, A.M.B; Prefect to Minister of interior 12 November 1825, F6 II Gironde 24, A.N.; Prefect to Minister of interior, 4 March 1828, F6 II Rhône 23, A.N.; "Rapport fait au nom de la commission des finances sur le projet de budget de l'année 1841," F6 II Rhône 28, A.N.

76. Martourey, "Formation et gestion," 1032.

77. Dumons and Pollet, "Fonctionnaires," 112.

78. Nevers, "Système politico-administratif," 140-41.

79. William H. Sewell, Jr., *Structure and Mobility-The Men and Women of Marseille, 1820-1870* (New York: Cambridge University Press, 1985), 62; Toulouse. 15 January 1907. For clientage in the early part of the century, see Ronald Aminzade, *Class, Politics, and Early Industrial Capitalism—A Study of Mid-Nineteenth Century Toulouse, France* (Albany: State University of New York Press, 1981), 50-54.

80. Jacques Cremadeills, "La politique financière, économique et sociale de la municipalité Toulousaine de 1910 à 1920," (Unpublished D.E.S., University of Toulouse, 1967).

81. Flavie Leniaud-Dallard, "L'assistance sous le consulat et l'empire, (an VIII à 1815)," *Colloque sur l'histoire de la sécurité sociale—Actes du 107e congrès national des sociétés savantes [Brest, 1982]* (Paris: Association pour l'étude de l'histoire de la sécurité sociale, 1983), 111-12; Guy Thuillier, "Pour une histoire des pensions de retraite des fonctionnaires au xixe siècle," *Études et documents-histoire économique et financière de la France*, 4 (1992), 125-78; idem., *Les pensions de retraite des fonctionnaires au xixe siècle* (Paris: Comité d'histoire de la securité sociale, 1994).

82. Cadoux, *Les finances de la ville de Paris*, 16-17.

83. Lyon. 26 November 1819; Toulouse. 20 September 1838; Daniel Sherman, *Worthy Monuments. Art Museums and the Politics of Culture in Nineteenth Century France* (Cambridge, MA: Harvard University Press, 1989), 138.

84. Marie Dinclaux, "La protection contre le risque vieillesse des employés de la ville de Bordeaux au xixe siècle," *Colloque sur l'histoire de la sécurité sociale—Actes du 106e congrès des sociétés savantes* (Paris: Association pour l'étude de l'histoire de la sécurité sociale, 1982), 23, 28; Ville de Bordeaux, *Bordeaux-Aperçu historique*, 2 (Paris: Hachette, 1892), 96-97.

85. Toulouse. 29 December 1896, also q. in *Dépêche de Toulouse*, 30 December 1896; Toulouse. 28, 29 December 1911.

86. Toulouse. 24 May 1876.

87. Conseil municipal de Lyon, "Rapport de Commission spéciale," 1880.

88. *Arrêté du maire de la ville de Bordeaux portant règlement sur le mode d'admission des employés* (Bordeaux: A. Bellier, 1876). Thoenig overemphasizes the extent to which Bordeaux had implemented a *concours* system: Jean-Claude Thoenig, "La politique de l'état à l'égard des personnels des communes (1884-1939)," *Revue francaise d'administration publique*, no. 23 (July-September 1982), 61.

89. Lyon. Arrêté 30 May 1881; *Dépêche de Toulouse*, 23 March 1897; Toulouse. 29 December 1896, 22 July 1914.

90. E. Herriot, "La condition du personnel de la ville de Lyon," *Annales de la régie directe* 1 (May-June 1909), 129-73; idem., *In those Days*, 181.

91. Allegations made in Marseille. 8 October 1911.

92. Marseille. 13, 20 November 1910.

93. Toulouse. 16 December 1910.

94. Toulouse. 11 November 1913, 22 July 1914.

95. R. Martineau, *Les Secrétaires de mairie* (Paris: Bonvalot-Jouve, 1906), 153-62; Thoenig, "La politique," 63.

96. Weber, *Economy and Society*, 2:223, 3:987.

CHAPTER 4

1. Howard C. Payne, *The Police State of Louis Napoleon Bonaparte* (Seattle: University of Washington Press, 1966), 254-56, 258.

2. Prefect to Commissioner of Police, 22 September 1813; Mayor to Prefect, 9 May 1815; Minister of interior to Prefect, 27 June 1816; Prefect of Rhône to Minister of interior, 1 February 1820; 3 March 1828 4M1, A.D.R.; on conflict in Lyon from 1870s to 1914, see A. Kleinclausz, *Histoire de Lyon*, 3 (Lyon: Pierre Masson, 1952), 262-65.

3. *Le message lyonnais*, q. in F. Euvrard, *Historique de l'institution des commissaires de police* (Montpellier: Firmin, Montane & Sicardi, 1910), 117.

4. Ronald Aminzade, *Class, Politics, and Early Industrial Capitalism—A Study of Mid-Nineteenth Century Toulouse, France* (Albany: State University of New York Press, 1981), 115-16, 219.

5. Payne, *The Police State of Louis Napoleon*, 284-85. The 1885 report, q. in Marie-Thérése Vogel, "La police des villes entre local et national, l'administration des polices urbaines sous la troisième république," (Unpublished Doctorat [Nouveau régime], University of Grenoble, II, 1994), 273-80; Hennion report of 1911, reprinted in Vogel, 707-8.

Chapter 4: Police and Fire Services

6. Ville de Lyon, "Revendications de la municipalité au sujet de la police municipal, rapport du maire," (Lyon: Association typographique, 1893); Albert Englinger, *L'organisation de la police administrative-les villes à police d'état* (Paris: Sirey, 1939), 13.

7. Jean-François Tanguy, "Autorité de l'état et libertés locales: le commissaire central de Rennes face au maire et au préfet (1870-1914)," Philippe Vigier et al., *Maintien de l'ordre et polices en France et en Europe au xix siècle* (Paris: Créaphis, 1987), 170. In his study, Benjamin Martin is too much influenced by the formal structure of power, which still left considerable powers in the hands of the prefect, and so Martin overstates the degree of centralization. He also sees the law of 1867 as a centralizing law, rather than one representing a return to the municipalities of previous powers; Benjamin F. Martin, *Crime and Criminal Justice under the Third Republic* (Baton Rouge, LA.: Louisiana State University Press, 1990), 47.

8. Jean Bastier, "Une introduction à l'historiographie des institutions policières françaises," *Annales de l'université des sciences sociales de Toulouse*, 36 (1988), 61-62.

9. Hennion report, repr. in Vogel, "La police des villes," 709.

10. Léopold Pelatant, *De l'organisation de la police* (Dijon: J. Berthoud, 1899), 254, 271, 276; *Bulletin de la société général des prisons* [henceforth abbreviated as *BSGP*] (June 1905), 845; J. Drioux, "Projets de réorganisation de la police en province," *BSGP*, 30 (1908), 342-92.

11. Vogel, "La police des villes," 711.

12. Thomas J. Duesterberg, "Criminology and the Social Order in Nineteenth Century France," (Unpublished Ph.D. Dissertation, Indiana University, 1979), 35, 195; A. Lacassagne, "De la criminalité comparée des villes et des campagnes," *Comptes rendu de la société d'économie politique et d'économie sociale de Lyon* (1882), 238-67; Michelle Perrot, "Délinquence et système pénitentiaire en France au xixe siècle," *Annales, économies, sociétés, civilisations*, 30 (1975), 79.

13. Howard Zehr, *Crime and the Development of Modern Society* (Totowa, NJ: Rowman and Littlefield, 1976), 57, 60-63; David Cohen and Eric A. Johnson, "French Criminality: Urban-Rural Differences in the Nineteenth Century, *Journal of Interdisciplinary History* (Winter 1982), 485-86 which revises on this point the findings of Abdul Qaiyum Lodhi and Charles Tilly, "Urbanization, Crime, and Collective Violence in 19th Century France," *American Journal of Sociology*, 79, 2 (1973), 296-318. The latter article was based on an earlier period, the 1840s, and records of the higher courts, the *cours d'assises*.

14. Cohen and Johnson, "French Criminality," 486; Zehr, *Crime*, 68-69; William H. Sewell, Jr., *Structure and Mobility—The Men and Women of Marseille* (New York: Cambridge University Press, 1985), 221, 231.

15. Louis Chevalier, *Laboring Classes and Dangerous Classes in Paris During the First Half of the Nineteenth Century* (Princeton: Princeton University Press, 1973); Susanna Barrows, *Distorting Mirrors: Visions of the Crowd in Late Nineteenth Century France* (New Haven, CT: Yale University Press, 1981); Robert A. Nye, *Crime, Madness, and Politics in Modern France: The Medical Concept of National Decline* (Princeton: Princeton University Press, 1984).

16. Lyon. 5 May 1832; Marseille. 30 May 1882. The Marseille observation seems borne out by Sewell, *Structure and Mobility*, 221, 231.

17. Bordeaux. 27 July 1906; Thierry Joliveau, *Association d'habitants et urbanisation, l'exemple lyonnais (1880-1983)* (Paris: Conseil national de recherches scientifiques, 1987), 40.

18. Bastier, "Une introduction," 65; Etienne-Félix Guyon, *L'organisation de la police en France* (Paris: Vie universitaire, 1923), 222; Zehr, *Crime*, 68, 118.

19. Marseille. 24 August 1857, 8 August 1862, 30 May 1882, 21 December 1885; Vogel, "La police des villes," 412-14.

20. *BSGP*, (July-October 1907), 1116-17; *BSGP*, (November-December 1908), 1360; Guyon, *L'organisation* , 233.

21. *BSGP* (March 1908).

22. Vogel, "La police des villes," 290-91, 303-305, 309.

23. Ibid., 305-306.

24. Georges Carrot, "L'étatisation des polices urbaines," *Revue de la police nationale*, no. 121 (1984), 40-48.

25. Joseph Rivet, *Les oeuvres de charité et les établissements d'enseignement libre des 1789 à 1945* (Lyon: Missions africaines, 1945), 21.

26. Edmond Lamouzèle, *Essai sur l'organisation de la compagnie du guet et de la garde bourgeoise de Toulouse au XVIIe et XVIIIe siècle* (Paris: H. Champion, 1906), 4-5, 43-44, 46, 66, 108, 113.

27. Toulouse. 18 brumaire, Year IX; Petition signed, 16 April 1817, Lk 17, A.M.T.; *Dépêche de Toulouse*, 16 October 1896; Jean-Luc Laffont, "Les cadres traditionnels de l'institution des dizeniers à Toulouse à l'epoque moderne," Conference on "La ville en occident du moyen âge à nos jours," Bourges, 5-7 October 1995.

28. "Observations du maire de Toulouse, 1806, F⁶II Haute Garonne, 13 A.N.; Toulouse. pluviose, Year XII, L 17, A.M.T.

29. Bordeaux, *Aperçu historique, sol. population, industrie, commerce, administration*, 2 (Paris: Hachette, 1892) 395, 401-402.

30. Bordeaux, *Aperçu*, 2: 407, 409-410.

31. Lyon. 7 nivose, Year IX; Lyon. 8 August 1823; Letter Mayor to Prefect, 2 July, 1823; 6 December 1831, 2M10, A.M.L.; Charles Pionin, *Code de police municipale de la ville de Lyon* (Lyon: Dumoulin, Ronet and Sibuet, 1840), v.

32. Report of Commissaire de police, 20 September 1817, I, 4, A.M.S.E.; Martourey, "Formation et gestion," 621; Paul Ronin, *Saint-Etienne à ciel ouvert* (Saint-Etienne: Paul Ronin, 1959), 85.

33. Consolat, "Rapport . . . 1840.," 12; Georges Carrot, *Histoire de la police française* (Paris: Tallandier, 1992), 155.

34. For instance, Prefect to Mayor, 8 November 1873, 3L22, A.M.T.

35. Toulouse. 18 January 1830.

36. Marseille. 9 July 1840.

37. Marseille. 1 June 1877; *Revue municipale*, 6 April 1901.

38. Saint-Etienne. September 1892.

39. Guyon, *L'organisation*, 222; Marseille. 18 October 1903.

40. Payne, *The Police State of Napoleon III*, 207.

41. Undated memo from the 1830s; prefectural note, 24 January 1855, 4M2, A.D.G.

42. Circulaire of Minister of interior, 13 November 1848, copy in 4M3, A.D.G.

43. "Etat nominatif des dix commissaires de police de Bordeaux," 15 July 1822, 4M14, A.D.G.

44. Minister of interior to Prefect, 10 February 1860, 4M14, A.D.G.

45. F. Euvrard, *Historique*, 115, 203.

46. C.P. Dayre, *Grand manuel de police administratif et judiciaire à l'usage des commissaires de police* (Paris: Marescq, 1877), 134.

47. Minister of interior circular, 13 December 1881, copy in 4M4, A.D.G.

48. J. Drioux, "Projets de réorganisation de la police en province," *Revue pénitentiaire*, 31 (1908), 351; Minister of interior, arrêté 20 November 1908.

49. Decree of 17 May 1809, from Schonbrunn for Bordeaux, 235^I 3, A.M.B.; Arrêté 13 May 1818; Prefectoral arrêté, 27 October 1858.

50. Préfecture du Rhône. *Recueil des arrêtés et règlements de police de la ville de Lyon, année 1874*, (Lyon, 1874), 117-20; Georges Carrot, *Le maintien de l'ordre* 2 (Toulouse: Presses d'institut d'études politiques de Toulouse, 1984), 650.

51. Michel Balmont, "Le carnet d'un policier municipal de la belle époque," *Bulletin du vieux Saint-Etienne*, no. 151, 3rd. sem. (1988), 63-66; Patricia Ann O'Brien, "Urban Growth and Public Order: The Development of a Modern Police Force in Paris, 1829-1854," (Columbia University Unpublished Dissertation, 1973), 311.

52. Toulouse. 27 June 1871; similar opposition in Marseille, Marseille. 16 January 1871.

53. Marseille. 21 December 1885.

54. Léopold Pelatant, *De l'organisation de la police* (Dijon: J. Berthoud, 1899), 254; Henri Chardon, *L'organisation de la police* (Paris: Bossard, 1917), 69.

55. Jean-Jacques Gatein, "Misère et violence à Toulouse au début du xxè siècle (1900-1914)" (Unpublished Maîtrise, University of Toulouse, 1983), 149-53.

56. Note for prefect, undated, [1830s?], 4M3, A.D.R.; Toulouse. 14 February 1843; Bordeaux, *Aperçu*, 2: 411.

57. Lyon. 28 December 1849.

58. "Gardiens de la paix de la ville de Lyon—augmentation de l'effectif," n.d. [1899?]. 4M6 A.D.R.

59. *Bulletin mensuel de la fédération des sociétés amicales des agents de police*, 3 (February 1908), 6-7.

60. Toulouse. 29 December 1906, 24 November 1911.

61. Pelatant, *De l'organsation*, 280.

62. Prefect to Mayor, 4 December 1876, I^I, A.M.S.E.; Commissaire to Mayor, 16 November 1867, 3 June 1873, 3L22, A.M.T.

63. Mayor to Prefect, 21 February 1810, 2475K 1, A.M.B.; for Bordeaux police under Napoleon see also Laurent Coste, *Le maire et l'empereur* (Bordeaux: Société archéologique et historique de Lignan et du canton de Créon, 1993), 236-37; Mayoral notes on commisssaires, 5 November 1823, 4M2, A.D.G.; Prefectoral note, 24 January 1855, 4M2, A.D.G.

64. Q. in Gilles Bollenot, "Police politique et police sécrète à Lyon (1831-1835) (Unpublished Thesis, Institut d'études politiques, Toulouse, 1986) 154, fn. 177.

65. Euvrard, *Historique*, 110; Minister to Prefect, 29 May 1895, 4M25 A.D.G.

66. Euvrard, *Historique*, 203; Drioux, "Projets," 351; Minister of interior, arrêté 20 November 1908.

67. Carrot, *Le maintien de l'ordre* I: 382.

68. "Observations sur la police de Lyon et des communes suburbaines," 1 January 1836, 4M3, A.D.R.; Gilles Bollenot,"Le modèle français de police secrète au début de xixe siècle," Claude Journès, ed. *Police et politique* (Lyon: Presses universitaires de Lyon, 1988), 60.

69. Secretary general circular, 3 June 1854, I ^{1} 4,, A.M.L.; Dainville, Vincent, and Moissonier [no first names provided], *Manuel de police à l'usage des gardiens de la paix de la ville de Lyon* (Lyon: R. Schneider, 1904), 236.

70. Toulouse. 18 January 1830, 24 November 1911.

71. F^6 II Loire 18. A.N.; Prefect to Mayor, 4 December 1876, I^I, A.M.S.E.

72. Adjoint mayor to Mayor, 21 February 1833, 2475, K2, A.M.B.; "Instruction sur le service journalier du corps des sergents de la ville de Bordeaux," 14 August 1851, 7 I^1, A.M.B.; "Rapport confidentiel sur le compte de chaque sergent de ville pendant le mois de décembre 1854," 2475 K2, A.M.B.; "Note confidentielle pour M. le préfet, Du recrutement des divers corps de la police de Bordeaux," n.d. [1880s], 4M15, A.D.G.

73. I^1 1, O, A.M.M; Marseille. 7 February 1897.

74. Georges Hogier-Grison, *La police* (Paris: Ernest Kolb, 1880), 315.

Chapter 4: Police and Fire Services

75. "Observations sur la police de Lyon et des communes suburbaines," 1 January 1836, 4M3, A.D.R.; Marseille. Arrêté, 23 July 1895; Jean-Marc Berlière, "La professionalisation: revendication des policiers au début du xxe siècle, *Revue d'histoire moderne et contemporaine*, 37 (1990), 419; Léopold Pelatant, *De l'organisation de la police* (Dijon: J. Berthoud, 1899), 293; Paul Pichon, *Histoire et organisation des services de police en France* (Issoudun: Laboureur, 1949), 113.

76. Q. in Henry Buisson, *La police, son histoire* (Vichy: Wallon, 1949), 244.

77. *Dépêche de Toulouse*, 29 December 1903, 20 February 1904; Toulouse. 28 December 1903; Marseille. 26 March 1905; "Police de Bordeaux, 1907," 4M16, A.D.G.

78. Robert Pandraud, *Histoire de la police* (Paris: Larrieu-Bonnel, 1977), 150-51.

79. Jean-Marc Berlière, "The Professionalisation of the Police under The Third Republic in France, 1875-1914," Clive Emsley and Barbara Weinberger, eds. *Policing Western Europe—Politics, Professionalism, and Public Order, 1850-1940* (New York: Greenwood Press, 1991), 48-49.

80. Toulouse. Arrêté 15 September 1870; Toulouse. 7, 10, 22 November 1870; 22 January 1871; 17 May 1871; 20 June 1871; 27 June 1871; Marseille. 12 September 1870; Marseille. 25 February 1873; Toulouse. 27 June 1871; 4 December 1873.

81. Saint-Etienne. 24 August 1886; Marseille. 24 March 1893.

82. Carrot, *Le maintien*, 2:327.

83. Report of 1 March 1815, 2H100, A.M.M.; 2H100, A.M.M.

84. Carrot, *Le maintien*, 2:417, 424-25.

85. Félix Tavernier, "Les débuts de la garde nationale," *Marseille*, 3rd. ser, 48 (April-June 1962), 3-14; 49 (July-September 1962), 41-54; Ronald Aminzade, *Class, Politics, and Early Industrial Capitalism—A Study of Mid-Nineteenth Century Toulouse, France* (Albany: State University of New York Press, 1981), 111, 117-19.

86. Marseille. 4 September 1848, 2 October 1848, 4, 25 January 1849, 8 February 1849, 5 March 1849, 11 September 1849, 3 December 1849; 28 October 1850, 29 December 1851.

87. Marseille. 4 September, 24 November 1870.

88. Jean-Louis Loubet del Bayle and Lucien Mandeville, "Le Maintien de l'ordre en France," Jean-Louis Loubet del Bayle, ed. *Police et société* (Toulouse: Centre d'études et de recherches sur la police, 1988), 238.

89. Pierre Miquel, *Les gendarmes* (Paris: Olivier Orban, 1990), 121, 357.

90. Bousquet, 12, Bordeaux, *Aperçu*, I: 326; A. Lacassagne, *Hygiène de Lyon. Compte rendu des travaux du conseil d'hygiène publique et de salubrité du département du Rhône du 1er janvier 1860 au 31 décembre 1885* (Lyon: A. Stock, 1887), 108.

91. Jean Nevers, "Système politico-administratif communal et pouvoir local en milieu urbain—étude d'un cas: la municipalité radicale-socialiste de Toulouse (1888-1906)," (Unpublished thesis, 3ème cycle, Sociology, University of Toulouse, 1975), 152.

92. Miquel, *Les gendarmes*, 268, 295, 301, 341.

93. Bordeaux. *Aperçu*, 2: 427.

94. Marseille. Arrêté, 2 October 1806.

95. Bordeaux. Arrêté, 25 March 1806, 10 June 1808.

96. "Rapport sur le budget de l'an 14," F^6 II Loire 15, A.N.; Rapport 1808," F^6 II Loire 15, A.N.

97. Toulouse. Ordonnance 7 February 1807; Avis 20 January 1810.

98. Francois Bournand, *Le régiment de sapeurs-pompiers de Paris* (Paris: Jules Moutonnet, 1887), 3.

99. Eugène Bottet, "Le corps des pompiers de Lyon," *Rive gauche*, no. 55 (December 1975), 15-20, Bordeaux, *Aperçu*, 2: 427-30.

100. Letter of 31 July, 1833. 3D107, A.M.T.

101. Toulouse. 14 February 1843.

102. Bordeaux. Arrêté 23 november 1837; Toulouse. Arrêté 27 July 1844; Marius Degabriel, *Notes sur la création et l'organisation d'un corps de pompiers* (Lyon: Aimé Vingtrinier, 1871), 4.

103. Marseille. 4 August 1849.

104. Letter from adjoint maire to commandant of garde municipal, 16 April 1823, 236I^1, A.M.B.; 11 October 1831; 22 January 1840, 16 November 1842, 236 I^1, A.M.B.

105. Saint-Etienne. 7 February 1868; List for 1886 in 4H1, A.M.S.E.; Evaluations written 29 January 1889, 30 May 1894, 12 April 1894, 4H1, A.M.S.E.

106. Bousquet, *Suite* (1841), 1.

107. Bordeaux. 1 October 1830; Degabriel, *Notes*, 4; Letter from Conseil de discipline to Mayor, 4 September 1820, 4H 1, A.M.S.E.; Report of fire chief to Mayor, 8 February 1828, 4K36, A.M.S.E.

108. Marseille. 4 August 1849.

109. Toulouse. 13 May 1843.

110. "Règlement général d'ordre intérieur et de service du corps des sapeurs-pompiers" (Marseille: 1876).

111. Martourey, "Formation et gestion," 620-22.

112. Lyon. 9 November 1871; Ville de Lyon, "Projet de réorganisation et de règlement des sapeurs-pompiers de la ville de Lyon-Rapport de la commission spéciale," (Lyon: J. Gallet, 1878), 5; Antoine Baton, *Le théâtre des Celestins* (Lyon: Joseph Buscoz, 1936), 31; Edouard Thiers, *Réorganisation des sapeurs-pompiers de Lyon. Rapport présenté à la commission municipale spéciale* (Lyon: Association typographique, 1881), 40; Lyon. *Documents rélatifs . . . 1909* (1908), 327; *Documents rélatifs . . . 1915* (1914), 201.

113. Ernest Laroche, *Le livre d'or des sapeurs-pompiers de Bordeaux (1809-1889)* (Bordeaux: Gounouillhou, 1889), 9.

114. Thiers, "Réorganisation," 9; Lyon. *Documents divers . . . 1892* (1891), 334.

115. J. Bouissou, *Le Régime des sapeurs pompiers* (Toulouse: G. Mollat, 1911), 32, 50, 135.

CHAPTER 5

1. Robert Gildea, *Education in Provincial France, 1800-1914—a Study of Three Departments* (New York: Oxford University Press, 1983).

2. Marseille. Arrêté, 11 Germinal, Year II, 18 prairial, Year II; Lyon. 15 Thermidor, Year X, reprinted in *BOML*, 12 December 1908, 543; Rapport sur le budget de 1811 par le maire," F^6 II Loire 16, A.N.

3. Marseille city council, q. in J.C. Haron, "Les dernières années de l'empire à Marseille (1810-1814)," (Unpublished Diplôme d'études supérieures, University of Aix-en-Provence, 1959), 34-35; Prefect of Haute-Garonne to Minister of interior, 22 March 1806, F^6 II Haute Garonne, 13, A.N.

4. Bordeaux. 27 May 1831, 4 September 1833, 27 May 1831.

5. Marseille. 23 December 1847.

6. Speech of 31 August 1839, 4R6; 28 August 1840, 4R 7, AMM; Comité d'instruction primaire, 28 November 1839, 4 R 6, AMM; Bordeaux. 4 September 1833.

7. Toulouse. 6 October 1848.

8. Sandra Horvath-Peterson, *Victor Duruy—Liberal Reform in the Second Empire* (Baton Rouge: Louisiana State University Press, 1984), 72-116.

9. Marseille. 18 May 1866.

10. Marseille. 7 May 1872; Toulouse. 17 May 1871; Bordeaux. 3 September 1872; Letter 22 October 1871, Johnston to Mayor, 102R8, A.M.B.

11. Marseille. 7 May 1877.

12. Carnot, quoted in Louis Ariste and Louis Braud, *Histoire populaire de Toulouse depuis les origines jusqu'a ce jour* (Toulouse: Midi républicain, 1898) 804; E. Pariset, "La Fabrique Lyonnaise," *Mémoires de l'académie des sciences de Lyon*, 3rd ser, 6 (1901), 327; q. Geneviève Cavaye, "La Question scolaire à Toulouse à la fin du 19ème siècle," (Unpublished maitrise, University of Toulouse, 1983), 8; Mayor Paul Lande, quoted in *Petite Gironde*, 2 January 1902.

13. Musée pédagogique, *Mémoires et documents scolaires—Documents statistiques sur la situation budgétaire de l'enseignement primaire public* (Paris: Imprimerie nationale, 1888), 9-18; Patrice Grevet, *Besoins populaires et financement public* (Paris: Editions sociales, 1976), 348.

14. Marseille. 1 December 1860.

15. For France as a whole, the trend was of course the same; see Raymond Grew, Patrick J. Harrigan, with James Whitney, "The Availability of Schooling in Nineteenth Century France," *Journal of Interdisciplinary History*, 14 (Summer 1983), 30, 39; idem., "The Catholic Contribution to Universal Schooling, 1850-1906," *Journal of Modern History*, 57 (June 1985), 211-47; idem, "La scolarisation en France, 1829-1906," *Annales, économies, sociétés, civilisations*, 39 (January-February 1984), 116-53; idem, *School, State, and Society—The Growth of Elementary Schooling in Nineteenth-Century France—A Quantitative Analysis* (Ann Arbor: University of Michigan Press, 1992), 31-53.

16. Brunot Théret, Les dépenses d'enseignement et d'assistance en France au xixe siècle: une reévaluation de la rupture républicaine," *Annales, économies, sociétés, civilisations*, no. 6 (November-December 1991), 1345.

17. Irène Servettaz, "L'opposition politique et sociale de la haute bourgeoisie, Lyon sous la monarchie de juillet," (Unpublished Diplôme d'études supérieures, University of Lyon, 1967), 85; Saint-Etienne. 10 August 1836.

18. Maurice Gontard, "Les Ecoles primaires de la France bourgeoise (1833-1875)," (Toulouse: Institut pédagogique national, n.d.), 64-85; R.D. Anderson, *Education in France, 1848-1870* (New York: Oxford University Press, 1975), 41; Katherine Auspitz, *The Radical Bourgeoisie—The Ligue de l'enseignement and the Origins of the Third Republic,1866-1885* (New York: Cambridge University Press, 1982), 15.

19. "Rapport sur la situation de l'instruction primaire dans l'arrondissement de Toulouse, année 1855," F[17]9325, AN; "Rapport sur la situation de l'instruction primaire dans le département de la Gironde au 31 décembre 1855," F[17]9326,A.N.; Anderson, *Education in France*, 162; "Rapport de la commission d'instruction primaire, académie de Lyon," June 1855, F[17]9332, A.N.; Alfred de Cilleuls, *Histoire de l'administration Parisienne au xix siècle*, 2 (Paris: Champion, 1900), 351-2.

20. Anderson, *Education in France*, 131; Gontard, "Les Ecoles," 166; Horvath-Peterson, *Victor Duruy*, 74-81; Patrice Grevet, *Besoins populaires*, 231.

21. Marseille. 11 January 1870, 7 May 1872; M. de Cours, *Rapport sur la situation de l'enseignement primaire* (Toulouse: E. Privat, 1874), 48-49, 57-64; Toulouse. 27 November 1877.

22. Toulouse. 22 November 1870; Marseille. 7 May 1872; Auspitz, *The Radical Bourgeoisie*, 148-49.

23. Paul Masson, *Les Bouches-du-Rhône. Encyclopédie départementale*, 6 (Marseille: Archives départementales, 1914), 3; Meaudre Lapouyade, "Voyage d'un allemand à Bordeaux en 1801," *Revue historique de Bordeaux*, 5 (1912), 235.

24. Q. in Maurice Gontard, *L'enseignement primaire en France de la révolution à la loi Guizot (1789-1833)* (Paris: Belles lettres, 1960), 252; France, Ministère de l'instruction publique et des cultes, *Circulaires et instructions officielles rélatives à l'instruction publique*, 1 (Paris: J. Delalain, 1865), 48.

25. Q. in Gontard, *L'enseignement primaire*, 225.

Chapter 5: Public Schools

26. Budget, 1811. F^6 II, Gironde 16, A.N.

27. Memorandum of city council to National government, undated [1810/2] 1R9, AMT; Toulouse. 26 frimaire, Year 14.

28. Gontard, *L'enseigement primaire*, 317; Circular of 15 March 1816, France, Ministère de l'instruction publique et des cultes, *Circulaires et instructions officielle*, 1: 258.

29. Gontard, q. in Pierre Albertini, *L'école en France, xixe-xxe siècle* (Paris: Hachette, 1992), 37.

30. Sarah Curtis, "Educating the Faithful: Catholic Primary Schooling and the Teaching Congregations in the Diocese of Lyon, 1830-1905," (Unpublished Ph.D. Dissertation, Indiana University, 1994), 241.

31. Délégation cantonale de l'instruction, 16 April 1874," 1R1. A.M.S.E.; Haute-Garonne, "Enseignement primaire (1877)," F^1^{7}9261, A.N.; Marseille. 30 March 1877, 7 December 1880.

32. Lyon. 10 October 1872; Marseille. 7 May 1882, 21 June 1903. Teachers' salaries at the lowest ranks were the same, but teachers beginning at the third rank enjoyed differences in salaries: third rank, 1,500 francs for men, 1,400 francs for women; second rank, 1,800 francs for men, 1,500 francs for women; first rank: 2,000 francs for men, 1,600 francs for women. Frederic Ernest Farrington, *The Public Primary School System in France* (New York: Teacher's College at Columbia University, 1906), 66.

33. Comité communal d'instruction primaire, 2 July 1840, 4R 7, A.M.M.

34. Inspection Report for Marseille, 1833, F^{17*} 89. A.N.; Q. in Marie-Françoise Hautbois, "L'enseignement primaire dans l'arrondissement de Bordeaux de 1830 à 1835," (Unpublished T.E.R., Université de Bordeaux, III, n.d. [1970s]), 103; Etat de situation des écoles primaires, décembre 1834," 6 R 1, AMM; similar complaint in Marseille. 17 June 1831; National inspection report, 1833, F^{17*}89, A.N.; Lucien Gaillard, "L'enseignement primaire à Marseille de la Restauration au second empire," *Marseille*, 3rd ser., no. 99 (October-December 1974), 30.

35. Grew and Harrigan, *School*, 155-163, 174.fn.38; see Curtis, "Educating the Faithful," *passim* for the continuing concern religious orders had to improve their teaching staffs.

36. Circular of 31 January 1829, France, Ministère de l'instruction publique et des cultes, *Circulaires et instructions* 1: 615.

37. Etat de situation des écoles primaires, décembre 1834," 6 R 1, A.M.M.; Comité d'instruction primaire, Etat de situation , 1844," 6R2, A.M.M.; Q. in Maurice Durousset, "La vie ouvrière dans la région stéphanoise," (Unpublished D.E.S., University of Lyon, 1960), 73.

38. Raymond Grew, Patrick J. Harrigan, with James Whitney, "The Availability of Schooling," 40; Grew and Harrigan, *School*, 35.

39. "Rapport de la commission d'instruction primaire, académie de Lyon," June 1855, F^1^{7}9332, A.N.

40. "Etat de situation des écoles publiques et libres, 1875, arrondissement Toulouse," F^{17} 10523, A.N.

41. Pierre Giolitto, *Histoire de l'enseignement primaire au xixe siècle* (Paris: Nathan, 1983), passim.

42. Curtis, "Educating the Faithful," 54; Sylvie Daumas, "L'enseignement primaire à Bordeaux de 1816 à 1833," (Unpublished T.E.R., Université de Bordeaux III, 1986), 113; H. Devun, "La politique scolaire de la ville de Saint-Etienne du premier empire à la IIIe République," (Unpublished, D.E.S., Université de Lyon, n.d.), 4, 15; Jean-Noël Luc, *La statistique de l'enseignement primaire, 19e-20e siècles* (Paris: INRP, 1985), 182 and *passim*.

43. Bordeaux. 27 September 1837; Mayor's report, 4 September 1833, copy in 5T 1 A.D.G.; 1832 report, copy in 5T 1 A.D.G.; Mayor to Minister of interior, 12 August 1816, F^{6}II Loire 16, A.N.; Paul Masson, ed., *Les Bouches-du-Rhône. Encyclopédie départementale*, 11 (Marseille: Archives départementales des Bouches-du-Rhône, 1913), 15. The evidence in these cities underscores the observations of Grew and Harrigan—made in general about French schooling—namely, that demand was ahead of supply. Raymond Grew, Patrick J. Harrigan, with James Whitney, "The Availability," 35-36; Grew and Harrigan, *School*, 31-53.

44. Toulouse. November 16, 1832; Daumas, "L'enseignement primaire," 23; Gaillard, "L'enseignement primaire," 25. This was slightly higher than the national average, which was 61 percent; Raymond Grew, P.J. Harrigan and J.B. Whitney, "La scolarisation," 118.

45. The contrasts in enrollment reflected the general phenomenon noted by Furet and Ozouf that old traditional cities had higher literacy and schooling than industrializing cities. François Furet and Jacques Ozouf, "L'alphabétisation," *Annales, économies, sociétés, civilisations*, 32 (1977), 488-502. The same trend was noted in the comparative study of schooling in industrializing and agricultural regions in the département of the Nord: Maryvonne Leblond, "La scolarisation dans le département du Nord au xixe siècle," *Revue du nord*, 52 (1970), 39-42. In Marseille, migrants were more literate than the city-born inhabitants: William H. Sewell, Jr., *Structure and Mobility—The Men and Women of Marseille, 1820-1870* (New York: Cambridge University Press, 1985), 169.

46. Inspector Report, Bouches-du-Rhône, June 1859, F^{17}9322, A.N.; Durousset, "La vie ouvrière," 73; Report on *arrondissement* of Toulouse, 1855-1856, F^{17}9325, A.N.

47. Marseille. 17 June 1831; Délégation cantonale, May 1854, 4R2, A.M.M.; 1833 inspection report, F^{17*} 89, A.N.; Marseille. 5 March 1857.

48. Délégation cantonale d'instruction primaire, 30 January 1862, 4R4, AMM; Vicomte de Pelleport, *Historique des écoles populaires de Bordeaux* (Bordeaux: Métreau, 1866), 13; same author, *Etudes municipales sur la charité bourgeoise*, 1ere partie (Paris: Librairie académie, 1870), 182; Marie-Bernadette Bédry, "L'instruction primaire dans l'arrondissement de Toulouse sous le second empire," *Annales du midi*, 91 (1979), 488-89; Marseille. 19 December, 20 December 1865; Pierre Chevallier, "L'évolution de l'enseignement primaire en France de 1850 à 1963," Pierre Chevallier, ed. *La scolarisation en France depuis un siècle* (Paris: Mouton, 1974), 36.

Chapter 5: Public Schools

49. 1866 reports, q. in Gaillard, "L'enseignement primaire," 30.

50. Inspection report of 1881, F¹⁷9264, A.N.; "Situation scolaire à Lyon en 1888-89," R 18, A.M.L.; Félix Ponteil, *Histoire de l'enseignement en France* (Paris: Sirey, 1966), 290.

51. H.C. Rulon, *Un siècle de pédagogie dans les écoles primaires (1820-1940)* (Paris: Librairie philosophique, 1962), 28.

52. Letter from Frère Floride to Mayor, 23 May 1833, 1R10, A.M.T.; Toulouse. 23 December 1869; H. Devun, "La politique scolaire," 17.

53. "Etat des locaux, 7 May 1880, Instruction publique 127, A.M.T.; Inspector general to Minister of education, 11 March 1883, F¹⁷9255, A.N.; Saint-Etienne. 16 April 1874; 1880 inspection report, F¹⁷9272, A.N.; Lyon, *Documents divers 1893* (Lyon: 1892), 477.

54. "Rapport sur les écoles primaires communales," by Barckhausen, adjoint maire, 15 November 1883, 102 R 2, A.M.B.; "Rapport à M. le Ministre de l'instruction publique sur le résumé des états de situation de l'enseignement primaire pour l'année scolaire, 1886-1887," (Paris: Delagrave, 1888); Prefect report, "Dettes et travaux," Lyon. 19 March 1874, bound in Lyon. July-November 1874; J. Janicot, *Monographie des écoles communales de Lyon depuis 1828 jusqu'en 1891* (Lyon: Joseph Chanard, 1891), 58; R38, A.M.L.; Délégation cantonale, procès verbal, 23 May 1887, 19 December 1887, 26 March 1888, 10 July 1890, R 20, A.M. L.

55. Délégation cantonale de Saint-Etienne, 19 November 1873, 1R1, A.M.S.E.

56. Exposition de Philadelphie, "Rapport de M. Deschamps sur l'organisation générale de l'instruction publique en Amérique," (n.d., 1876), copy in 102 R11, A.M.B.; Bordeaux. 15 February 1884.

57. F¹⁷*67, A.N.; Bordeaux. 5 October 1835; Comité communal d'instruction, séance 11 August 1834, 4R 1 A.M.M.; Comité d'instruction publique, 14 September 1858, 4R12, A.M.M.; Marseille. 3 January 1848; Inspecteur d'académie to mayor, 27 May 1857, 8T2, A.D.G.; Bordeaux. 31 January 1868; "Rapport sur les écoles de filles," 4 April 1856, 102R2, A.M.B.; "Statistique sur la situation des écoles primaires publiques en 1884," F¹⁷* 3043, A.N.; Letter from Bureau municipal d'hygiène, 27 May 1895, R38, A.M.L.

58. Inspector of Académie to Mayor, 8 November 1881, R 33, A.M.L.; Maurice Saurat, "Les institutrices et les instituteurs à Lyon de 1870 à 1914," (Unpublished D.E.S., University of Lyon, 1968), 28.

59. Grew and Harrigan, *School,* 304; Emile Levasseur, *l'enseignement primaire dans les pays civilisés* (Paris: Berger-Levrault, 1897), 562.

60. Sylvie Daumas, "L'enseignement primaire à Bordeaux de 1816 à 1833,"(Unpublished T.E.R., Université de Bordeaux III, 1986), 108; Comité de surveillance sur les écoles primaires, séance 31 August 1850, Instruction publique, 250, A.M.T.; Report of 1907, Instruction publique, 133, A.M.T.

61. Marseille. 5 July, 5 December 1883; Jacqueline Félician-Le Corre, "Action sociale de la municipalité de Marseille, 1892-1939," I (Unpublished Thesis, 3ème cycle, University Aix-Marseille, I, 1987) 112; Idem; "L'action sociale de la municipalité de

Marseille en faveur des mères sous la IIIe république," Yvonne Knibiehler et al., eds., *Marseillaises—les femmes et la ville* (Paris: Côté femmes, 1993), 256; Anon. *Lyon et la région lyonnaise en 1906* ,I (Lyon: A. Rey et Cie., 1906), 208, 211.

62. Marseille, Délégation cantonale, 18 November 1862, 4R13, A.M.M.; Toulouse. 10 September 1869; Grew and Harrigan, *School*, 279.

63. Devun, "La politique scolaire," 20-21.

64. Jean-Noël Luc, *La statistique de l'enseignement primaire, 19e -20 e siècles* (Paris: INRP, 1985), 22-23; Devun, "La politique scolaire," 33-36.

65. Bordeaux. 14 August 1868; City council, q. in H. Devun, "La politique scolaire de la ville de Saint-Etienne," *Actes du 89e congrès national des sociétés savantes,Lyon 1964*, II (Paris: Imprimerie nationale, 1965), 563-588; idem, "La politique scolaire de la ville de Saint-Etienne du prémier empire à la IIIe République," (DES, Université de Lyon, n.d.), 34.

66. Devun, "La politique scolaire," 20-21; Toulouse. 6 October 1848; Marseille. 12 November 1869.

67. Devun, "La politique scolaire," *Actes*, 2: 585; idem, "La politique scolaire," 35-36; Marseille, 7 May 1872; M. Gontard, "Une bataille scolaire au xixe siècle: l'affaire des écoles primaires laïques de Lyon (1869-1873)," *Cahiers d'histoire*, 3 (1958), 269-94; Prefect to Mayor, 14 March 1872, R 39, A.M.L.; Lyon. 8 March 1873, 16 September 1873, 14 October 1873.

68. Marseille. 13 November 1869; Lyon. 3 December 1872; Toulouse, 13 December 1872.

69. Bordeaux. 20 December 1872, 1 December 1873.

70. Grew and Harrigan, *School*, 279; Toulouse. 10 June 1874; Vcmte Pelleport, *Etudes municipales*, 182; Bordeaux. 11 November 1874.

71. Marseille. 21 September 1874; "Rapport sur la substitution d'instituteurs laïques aux instituteurs congréganistes," by L. Liard to Bordeaux conseil municipal, 28 July 1880, 102 R2, A.M.B.

72. Grew and Harrigan, *School*, 280; Inspector of Académie to Prefect, Lyon, 12 February 1875, R 14, A.M.L.; "Situation à Lyon en 1888-1889," R 18, A.M.L.; Inspector general to Minister of Education, Paris, 11 March 1883, F[17]9255. A.N.; Marseille. 5 December 1883. Inspector general to Minister of education, Paris, 11 March 1883, F[17]9255, A.N.; "Etats de situation, écoles publiques, 1902-1903," F[17]10691, A.N.; "Rapport sur la substitution d'instituteurs laïques aux instituteurs congréganistes," by L. Liard to conseil municipal, 28 July 1880, 102 R2, A.M.B.

73. Luc, *La statistique*, 103; 27 brumaire, Year XI, F[6] II Loire 16, A.N.; Circular of 29 February 1816, 4 November 1820, 1 June 1828, France, Ministère de l'instruction publique et des cultes, *Circulaires et instructions officielles*, 334-37, 396, 587-89.

74. 1819 instruction, q. in Daumas, "L'enseignement primaire," 99; Speech of 29 August 1840, 4R7, A.M.M.; Comité de surveillance sur les écoles primaires, 11 Janaury 1846, Instruction publique, 200 A.M.T.; Speech, 27 September 1839, 4R6, A.M.M.;

A. Lafourcade, "L'enseignement primaire à Toulouse," in *Ville de Toulouse, Documents sur Toulouse et sa région,* I (Toulouse: Privat, 1910), 108; Jean Bousquet, *Améliorations à faire à la ville de Toulouse* (Toulouse: Vve. Dieulafoy, 1859); Toulouse. 9 February 1872. The Revolution did not inaugurate new attitudes towards female education; on the persistence of a traditional attitude that viewed women's educational needs as minimal, see Geneviève Fraisse, *Muse de la raison—la démocratie exclusive et la différence des sexes* (Paris: Alinea, 1989).

75. Michelet, q. in Auspitz, *Radical,* 39; Toulouse. 16 May 1881; also q. in Cavaye, "Question scolaire," 8.

76. Marseille. 2 November 1839; Toulouse. 16 November 1832; Bordeaux. 27 September 1837; Report on 1855-56, F[17]9325, A.N.; A. Lafourcade, "Etat de l'enseignement primaire à Toulouse," in Association française pour l'avancement des sciences, *Toulouse* (Toulouse: E. Privat, 1887), 818; "Rapport sur l'instruction primaire du département du Rhône," June 1855, F[17] 9332, A.N.; "Etat de situation des écoles de garçons, 1860," F[17]10417, A.N. (changes in the method of establishing the statistics may explain this sudden change: Luc, *La statistique,* passim); Délégation cantonale d'instruction primaire, 30 January 1862, 4R4, A.M.M.; Devun, "La politique scolaire," 36; "Etat de situation des écoles publiques et libres," 1875, F[17]10524, A.N.; "Etat de situation des écoles publiques et libres, 1875", F[17]10522, A.N.; Chevallier, *La scolarisation,* 46-47.

77. "L'instruction primaire à Toulouse sous le rapport de la gratuité et de la rétribution scolaire," Académie inspection, 1861, Instruction Publique 127, A.M.T.; Département de la Gironde, *Bulletin statistique de l'instruction primaire, année 1875* (Bordeaux: Lanefranque, 1874).

78. Letter, Prefect to Mayor, 28 July 1856; Mayor to Prefect, 30 July 1856; Prefect to Mayor, 2 August 1856, 8T2, A.D.G.

79. Comité d'instruction publique, 14 September 1858, 4R 12,A.M,M.; Farrington, *The Public Primary School,* 40; Inspection report of 1881, F[17]9264, A.N.

80. Giolitto, *Histoire de l'enseignement,* 48-54; Eugéne Brouard and Charles Defodon, *Inspection des écoles primaires* (Paris: Hachette, 1887), vi.

81. Inspector General to Minister of Education, 11 March 1883, F[17]9255, A.N.; E. Cazes, "Enseignement," Association francaise pour l'avancement des sciences," *Marseille* (Marseille: Barlatier, 1891), 271; Prefect to Mayor, 26 June 1901, R 18, A.M.L.; Commission scolaire, 21 June 1902, 4R1, A.M.B.

CHAPTER 6

1. The complaints of the lack of culture are summarized in Philippe Poirier, et al., "Introduction," Philippe Poirier, *et.al,* eds. *Jalons pour l'histoire des politiques culturelles locales* (Paris: Documentation française, 1995), 15-17.

2. For the importance of municipal museums, see Daniel Sherman, *Worthy Monuments: Art Museums and the Politics of Culture in Nineteenth Century France* (Cambridge, MA: Harvard University Press, 1989); and for scientific societies, Mary Joe Nye, *Sciences in the Provinces: Scientific Communities and Provincial Leadership in France, 1860-1930* (Berkeley: University of California Press, 1986). Still in the contemporary period, theater and music constitute the largest proportion of cultural expenditures; in 1966, municipalities with populations over 100,000 spent 55 percent of their cultural affairs budgets in these twin fields. M. Raclot, *Les municipalités et la culture en 1966* (Paris: F.N.C.C.C., n.d), 68.

3. These figures represent regular annual expenditures and do not take into account the large outlays on theatre buildings.

4. Marseille. 28 February 1876; Toulouse. 17 July 1876.

5. Max Fuchs, *La vie théâtrale en province au xviiiè siècle* (Paris: Droz, 1933), 68.

6. Report of Prefect to City Council, Lyon. 28 September 1855.

7. *Album du voyageur à Bordeaux* (Bordeaux: J.B. Constant, n.d. [1840s]), 1.

8. Emile Isnard, "Opéra," *Marseille* (February 1937), 3-15; Marie-Pierre Debbane, "L'architecture des salles de spectacles à Marseille, 1787-1924," (Unpublished Mémoire de Maitrise d'histoire de l'art, Universite de Provence, Aix-en-Provence, 1980); Isabelle Bonnot, *Divines Divas . . . et vivat l'opéra* (Marseille: Archives de la ville, 1987), 57.

9. Danielle Teil and Roger Heyraud, *Saint-Etienne et le théâtre* (Saint-Etienne: Xavier Lejeune, 1990), 10-13; Q. from an 1849 journal, in Barthélemy Braud, *Histoire anecdotique du théâtre de Saint-Etienne de 1764 à 1853* (Saint-Etienne: Loire républicaire, 1899), 129.

10. Paul Ronin, *Le théâtre à Saint-Etienne—de Molière à nos jours* (Saint-Etienne: Paul Ronin, 1961), 51; Teil and Heyraud, *Saint-Etienne et le théâtre*, 46-48; Jean Lorcin, "Economie et comportements sociaux et politiques—La région de Saint-Etienne de la grande dépression à la seconde guerre mondiale," (Unpublished Thesis, Dr. d'état, University of Paris, 1987), 1583.

11. Jacky Meaudre, "La poussée urbaine à Saint-Etienne (1815-1872)," (Unpublished Diplôme d'études supérieures, University of Lyon, 1967), 150.

12. Toulouse. 21 November 1808; Auguste Rivière and Alain Jouffray, *Le Théâtre du capitole, 1547-1977* (Toulouse: Privat, 1978), 20, 27.

13. "Observations sur le projet d'achèvement du Capitole et de construction d'un théâtre définitif," 30 May 1864, 6D195, 208, A.M.T.

14. Riviére and Jouffray, *Le Théâtre*, 38-39.

15. Toulouse. 16 May 1878, 25 November 1879, 19 February 1880, 20 May 1882.

16. Barère q. in Gérard Corneloup, *Trois siècles d'opéra à Lyon* (Lyon: Bibliothèque municipale de Lyon, 1982), 77; Decree of National Convention, 14 August 1793, repr.

Chapter 6: "The Primary Schools of Enlightened Men"

in Claudine Roubaud, *L'Opéra de Marseille* (Marseille: Service educatif des Archives municipales, 1987), 31.

17. Q. in Pierre Bossuet, *Histoire des théâtres nationaux* (Paris: E. Jorel, n.d. [1910?]), 20.

18. Minister of interior to prefects, 18 March 1816, *Récueil des circulaires et instructions* (Paris: Imprimerie nationale, 1851), 68.

19. Victor Cousin, *Sur le fondement des idées absolues du vrai, du beau et de bien* (Paris: Hachette, 1836), 284; Marseille. 12 December 1840, 16 September 1840, 14 October 1844, 2 May 1853; L. Lamothe, *Le Théâtre de Bordeaux* (Bordeaux: Chaumas, 1853), 104-105.

20. Marseille. 26 January 1866, 8 March 1867, 13 November 1867.

21. Marseille. 14 February 1877; Bordeaux. 2 March 1880.

22. Minister of interior to Prefect of Bouches-du-Rhône, 18 March 1816, q. in Roger Klotz, "Une faillite aux theâtres priviligiés de Marseille en 1859," *Marseille*, no. 108 (1977), 34; similar wording in Memorandum, 16 March 1832, F^{21}1210., A.N.

23. Prefect of Haute-Garonne to Conseiller d'état chargé de l'instruction primaire, Toulouse, 13 Brumaire, an XI, F^{21}1185, A.N.; Bordeaux. 23 March 1831; similar terms used in Bordeaux. 8 November 1823.

24. Marseille. 24 July 1822; similar argument in Mayor of Bordeaux to Prefect, 9 February 1842, F^6 II Gironde 23, A.N; Lyon. 16 May 1831; Toulouse. 15 September 1855.

25. Marseille. 24 July 1822; similar ideas in 14 July 1831; Préfet of Haute-Garonne, Toulouse, 26 October 1838, F^{21}1186, A.N.; Toulouse. 15 September 1855; Antoine Baton, *Le théâtre des Célestins de Lyon* (Lyon: Joseph Buscoz, 1936), 29.

26. Fuchs, *La vie théâtrale*, 170; Charles Tilly, "Charivaris, Repertoires and Urban politics," in John Merriman, ed. *French Cities in the Nineteenth Century* (New York: Holmes and Meier, 1981), 73-91.

27. Commissaire to Mayor, 26 March 1822, 2R 19, A.M.T.; Haute-Garonne. Prefectural arrêté 28 March 1822; André Ségond, *L'Opéra de Marseille, 1787-1987* (Marseille: Jeanne Laffitte, 1987), 66.

28. V. Combarnous, *L'Histoire du Grand théâtre de Marseille, 31 octobre 1787-13 novembre 1919* (Paris: Imprimerie méridionale, n.d), 127-129; Pierre Echinard, "L'Opéra de Marseille en 1900," *Marseille*, no. 149 (November 1987), 42-53.

29. Edmond and Jules De Goncourt, *Journal*, ed. by Robert Ricatte (Paris: Flammarion, 1956), q. in Harold Hobson, *French Theater since 1830* (Dallas: Riverrun Press, 1978), 3-4.

30. Bordeaux. 9 June 1833, 16 February 1849; Marseille, 18 February 1847; Marseille. 8 March 1878, 8 January 1905; Toulouse. 25 June 1892.

31. Bordeaux. 12 January 1877, 13 January 1877.

32. Lyon. 12 December 1910.

33. Toulouse. 25 June 1892, 15 September 1892.

34. Lyon. 23 January 1873; Marseille. 14 December 1844; Toulouse, 13 April 1850, 15 September 1855, 15 February 1864, 19 February 1880; Bordeaux. 26 January 1874.

35. Letter, 25 February 1817, 77R4, A.M.M., also q. in Bonnot, ed. *Divines*, 16; Marseille. 12 December 1840.

36. Such a rivalry still exists today: Françoise Taliano-des Garets, "Deux villes et leur orchestre: Bordeaux et Toulouse, deux politiques de la musique depuis 1945," Poirier, et al., *Jalons*, 105-21.

37. Prefect report of 1818, q. in Pierre Guiral, "Quelques notes sur la politique des milieux d'affaires Marseillais," *Provence historique* (1957), 157; Stendhal, q. in Félix Tavernier, "Les Marseillais au Théâtre," *Marseille*, 3rd. ser., no. 29 (May-July 1956), 25; Eugéne Guinot, *Voyage pittoresque en Provence*, (1833), q. in Tavernier, *Vie quotidienne*, 126-127; Hélène Echinard, "Julie Pellissone (1768-1837) ou les Mémoires d'une Marseillaise," Yvonne Knibiehler et al., eds., *Marseillaises—les femmes et la ville* (Paris: Côté femmes, 1993), 223.

38. *Le Temps*, 1 Jan 1883, q. in Jacqueline de Jomaron, ed., *Le théâtre en France*, 2 (Paris: Armand Colin, 1989), 126.

39. James H. Johnson, *Listening in Paris* (Berkeley: University of California Press, 1995).

40. Arrêté du maire, 10 November 1837, Bonnot, *Divines Divas*, 19.

41. Henrica Françoise Rees van Tets-Gevaets, *Voyage d'une hollandaise en France*, ed. by Maurice Garçon (Paris: Pauvert, 1966), 54; Tavernier, "Les Marseillais au Théâtre," 22-25.

42. J. Chatelus, *Souvenirs d'un Stéphanois*, 46-47, q. in J. Lorcin," Du théâtre municipal à la maison de la culture: le cas particulier de Saint-Etienne," *Actes du colloque du centre méridional d'histoire sociale, des mentalités et de cultures*, (1978), 597-98.

43. "Rapport," Commissaire de police, 28 November 1817, 2 R 19, A.M.T.

44. Teil & Heyraud, *Saint-Etienne et le théâtre*, 30.

45. *France méridionale*, 21-22 September 1845; Letter Mayor to Prefect, 24 November 1842, A.M.L.

46. Jacques Boisgontier, *Toulouse* (Paris: Christine Bonneton, 1990), 201; Marseille. Arrêté du maire, 10 November 1837; Mayor Circular, 2 November 1842, A.M.L.

47. Armand Victorin, *L'ancienne place des Célestins* (Lyon: Dizain et Richard, 1887), 83; Corneloup, *Trois siècles*, 131.

48. Corneloup, *Trois siècles*, 87; Tets-Gevaets, *Voyage d'une hollandaise*, 60.

49. Jacques Boulo, q. in Rivière and Jouffray, *Le Théâtre du capitole*, 195.

50. Combarnous, *Histoire*, 146.

51. *Ibid.*, 181-82, 255-56; Ségond, *L'opéra de Marseille*, 70.

Chapter 6: "The Primary Schools of Enlightened Men"

52. William Crosten, *French Grand Opera—An Art and a Business* (New York: Da Capo Press, 1972) [Reprint of 1948 ed.], 45; Marvin Carlson, *The French Stage in the Nineteenth Century* (Metuchen, NJ: The Scarecrow Press, 1972), 64-65; Maurice Descotes, *Le public de théâtre et son histoire* (Paris: Presses universitaires de France, 1964), 249.

53. Corneloup, *Trois siècles*, 128; Bonnot, ed. *Divines divas*, 15; Marseille. 23 December 1865; all these examples disprove the claim that *claques* were limited to Paris, as stated in F.W.J. Hemmings, *The Theatre Industry in Nineteenth-Century France* (New York: Cambridge University Press, 1993), 101, 115.

54. Prefect to Mayor, 24 April 1823, R 18, A.M.T.; M. Lépine, *Répertoire de police administrative et judiciaire*, 2 (Paris: Berger Levrault, 1899), 2258; Commission Report, April 1842, R 2, Théâtre, A.M.L.; Lyon. 25 January 1873.

55. Teil and Heyraud, *Saint-Etienne et le théâtre*, 21; Commissaire spéciale pour les débuts des artistes," 1854, 6 D394, A.M.T.; Bordeaux. Arrêté, 20 May 1863; "Débuts des artistes du Capitole (année 1884-1885)," Instruction publique, 118, A.M.T.

56. Teil and Heyraud, *Saint-Etienne et le théâtre*, 22.

57. Marseille. 15 January 1877; Lyon. 25 January 1873, 6 February 1874; Lyon. 7 November 1844; Mayoral Report to Municipal Council, 1847, R 2, Directions, 1841-1861, A.M.L; Bordeaux. 28 June 1867; Marseille. 7 February 1885, 12 December 1840, 16 September 1840, 14 October 1844.

58. Q. in René Merle, "Fonction sociale du théâtre francais et du théâtre dialectal dans le sud-est de la fin de l'ancien régime à 1840," *Provence historique* 40 (April-June 1990), 160.

59. Director to Mayor, 19 February 1831, 2R 18, A.M.T; Marseille. 4 March 1864; Teil & Heyraud, *Saint-Etienne et le théâtre*, 32; Félix Martin-Doisy, *Dictionnaire d'économie charitable ou exposé historique, théorique et pratique*, 3 (Paris: Migne 1855), 503.

60. Maurice Descotes, *Le public de théâtre*, 242-43; Hemmings, *The Theatre Industry* , ch. 8.

61. Hemmings, *The Theatre Industry*, 32; André Spies, "French Opera During the Belle époque: A Study in the Social History of Ideas," (Unpublished Ph.D. Dissertation, University of North Carolina, 1986), 130; Jane F. Fulcher, *The Nation's Image— French Grand Opera as Politics and Politicized Art* (New York: Cambridge University Press, 1987), 167.

62. R 2 Directions, 1841-1861, A.M.L.; *Revue municipale*, 16-31 December 1908; "Cahiers de charges," 1856, "Cahiers de Charges," 1886-1889, 6D 355, A.M.T.; *Revue municipale*, 2 July 1898.

63. Marcel Roncayolo, *L'imaginaire de Marseille, Port, ville, pôle* (Marseille: Chambre de commerce et d'industrie de Marseille, 1990), 153.

64. Teil & Heyraud, *Saint-Etienne*, 56.

65. Dominique Leroy, *Histoire des arts du spectacle en France* (Paris: Harmattan, 1990), 81.

66. Jean Gargon, "L'exploitation du grand théâtre," (Mimeographed copy, 1938), 3.

67. Bordeaux. 8 November 1823; Emile Spiteri, "La permanence de l'Opéra à Marseille," *Marseille*, no. 149 (November 1987), 30; Combarnous, *L'histoire*, 43, 49; Marseille. 24 July 1822; Toulouse. 19 January 1828; Fulcher, *The Nation's Image*, 56.

68. Bordeaux. 1 February 1847; Ronin, *Le théâtre à Saint-Etienne*, 21; Teil & Heyraud, *Saint-Etienne*, 50.

69. L. Lamothe, *Le Théâtre de Bordeaux* (Bordeaux: Chaumas, 1853), 102; Joseph Méry, *Marseille et les Marseillais*, new edition, (Paris: Calmann-Lévy, 1884), 41.

70. Ronin, *Le théâtre à Saint-Etienne*, 20; Combarnous, *L'Histoire*, 50; Corneloup, *Trois siècles*, 132; Prefect to Minister of interior, 7 November 1852, F^{21}1186, A.N; Letter to Mayor, 5 May 1914, Instruction publique, 101, A.M.T.

71. Mayor to Prefect, Bordeaux, 2 June 1862, F^{21}1190, A.N.; Méry, *Marseille*, 43-44.

72. Bordeaux. 9 December 1884; Maurice Reuchsel, *La musique à Lyon*, 2nd. ed. (Lyon: Legendre, 1903), 105; for Saint-Etienne, Armand Audiganne, *Les populations ouvrières et les industries de la France dans le mouvement social du xixe siècle*, 2 (Paris: Capelle, 1900), 80, 85; Toulouse. 17 July 1876; *Petite Gironde*, 1 October 1900; Letter from adjoint delegué aux beaux arts of Lille to Mayor of Lyon, Lille, 6 January 1900, R 2, A.M.L.

73. Marseille. 30 January 1840; Toulouse. 10 August 1857; Jules Ward, "Des théâtres subventionnés de la province, de leur état présent et de leur avenir," *Mémoires de l'académie impériale des sciences, belles lettres et arts de Lyon* , 13 (1866-1868), 100-110.

74. Pierre Echinard, "Une tentative de cirque permanent vers 1830: le cirque olympique de Marseille," *Provence historique*, 40 (April-June 1990), 189-209; Charles Rearick, *Pleasures of the Belle Epoque* (New Haven, CT: Yale University Press, 1985), 94.

75. Teil & Heyraud, *Saint-Etienne et le théâtre*, 32, 44; Prefect of Haute-Garonne to Minister of Instruction, Toulouse, 4 February 1911, F^{21}4687, A.N.; *La Rapide* (Toulouse), 11 December 1910.

76. Leroy, *Histoire des arts* , 256, 263, 307.

77. J.B. Duchon-Doris, Junior, "Observations du Grand Théâtre , exposition d'un projet de réunion commerciale," (Bordeaux: P. Coudert, 1831), 2.

78. Lyon. 7 November 1844; Mayoral Report to Municipal Council, 1847, R 2, Directions, 1841-1861, A.M.L.; Marseille. 14 December 1844; Bordeaux. 1 February 1847; Bonnot, *Divines divas*, 32.

79. Crosten, *French Grand Opera*, ch. 5; Leroy, *Histoire des arts*, 52-58; Duchon-Doris, "Observations," 2.

80. Charles Baret, *Le théâtre en province* (Paris: Renaissance du livre, 1918), 225; Albert Dachin, *L'exploitation théâtrale et la municipalité* (Lille: Camille Robbe, 1911), 104; Bordeaux. 6 September 1869.

81. Toulouse. 15 January 1866; Alphonse Brémond, *Histoire de l'élection municipale de 1865—documents officiels et autres* (Toulouse: Philippe Montaubin, 1867), 333-334; Marseille. 7 March 1850, 12 January 1877.

82. Toulouse. 12 January 1911; Prefect of Haute-Garonne to Minister of interior, Toulouse, 9 December 1852, F 21. 1186; Prefect of Haute-Garonne to Minister of interior, Toulouse, 4 February 1911, F^{21}4687, A.N.

83. Letter from adjoint délégué aux beaux arts of Lille to Mayor of Lyon, Lille, 6 January 1900, R 2, A.M.L.; Dachin, *L'exploitation*, 187-88; on the founding of the Réunion des théâtres lyriques municipaux, Taliano-des Garets, "Deux villes et leur orchestre," 109.

84. Marseille. 22 March 1867, 19 March 1877.

85. Mayoral Report to Municipal Council, 1847, R 2, Directions, 1841-1861, A.M.L.; Marseille. 13 January 1877, 14 February 1877.

86. Q. in *Revue municipale*, 16-31 October 1905.

87. Lyon. 2 August 1848; Anon., "Mémoire sur la question des théâtres par un membre de la commission des théâtres," [1848], printed leaflet in Directions, 1841-1861, R 2, A.M.L.; Marseille. 2 February 1866; Anon., "Lettres à Messieurs les membres du conseil municipal de Marseille," (Marseille: A. Arnaud, 1867), 7-8; Bordeaux. 16 August 1869; Commission Report, Lyon. 4 October 1873.

88. Georges Bureau, *Le Théâtre et sa législation* (Paris: Paul Ollendorff, 1898), 78.

89. Bordeaux. 11 August 1835; Alexandre Vivien,"Etudes administratives—les théâtres," *Revue des deux mondes*, n.s. 6 (1844), 377; Bordeaux. 7 May 1860; Toulouse. 25 June 1892.

90. Corneloup, *Trois siècles*, 131.

91. Anon., "La victoire de la bourgeoisie," (Lyon: Beau jeune, 1881), 7.

92. Madeleine Réberioux,"Jean Jaurès, élu municipal de Toulouse (1890-1893)," *Cahiers internationaux*, no. 107 (1959), 69-75; Toulouse. 30 December 1890, 25 June 1892, 18 November 1892.

93. Marseille. 27, 28 January 1893.

94. Combarnous, *L'histoire*, 210-11, 229-32; Marseille. 14 November 1897; *Revue municipale*, 20 November 1897; Marseille. 15 January, 19 June 1898; *Le Temps*, 17 February 1898.

95. Saint-Etienne. 17 March 1905, 27 December 1907; Lorcin, "Economie et comportements," 1583-94.

CHAPTER 7

1. Ann F. La Berge, *Mission and Method—The Early Nineteenth Century French Public Health Movement* (New York: Cambridge University Press, 1992), 245; William Coleman,

Death is a Social Disease—Public Health and Political Economy in Early Industrial France (Madison: University of Wisconsin Press, 1982).

2. "Rapport du comité de salubrité du 1er arrondissement," 20 April 1832, 3D 143, A.M.T.; and similar views in A. Couvière, *Rapport de la commission médicale envoyée à Paris, par l'administration municipale de Marseille pour étudier le choléra-morbus* (Marseille: Feissat, 1832); Piorry. "Rapport sur les épidemies qui ont regnés en France de 1830 à 1836," *Mémoires de l'académie royale de médecine,* 6 (9 August 1836).

3. La Berge, *Mission and Method;* similar argument for Europe in general is made in Richard J. Evans, "Epidemics and Revolutions: Cholera in Nineteenth Century Europe," *Past and Present,* 120 (August 1988), 123-46.

4. J.B. Monfalcon and A.P.I. de Polinière, *Traité de la salubrité dans les grandes villes suivi de l'hygiène de Lyon* (Paris: J.B. Baillière, 1846), 19.

5. Ann Fowler La Berge, "The Paris Health Council, 1802-1848," *Bulletin of the History of Medecine,* 49 (1975), 339-52; Jules Rochard, *Traité d'hygiène sociale* (Paris: Delahaye et Lecrosnier, 1888), 9, fn.1; Dr. A. Dassier, *Travaux du conseil de salubrité de la ville de Toulouse du 21 juin au 31 décembre 1847* (Toulouse: A. Chauvin, 1848), x.; Lyon Conseil de salubrité, " Rapport," (1824), I^1. 267, A.M.L.

6. Gironde, *Rapport général des travaux du conseil central de salubrité du département de la Gironde pour les années 1833 et 1834* (Bordeaux: Trechney, 1835), 1, 4, 12; Dr. G. Drouineau, "Le budget de l'hygiène publique," *Revue d'hygiène et de police sanitaire* [henceforth abbreviated as RHPS] (1879), 788-90; Dr. Charles Levieux, *Que faut-il penser de nos institutions d'hygiène publique et de salubrité?* (Bordeaux: Duverdier, 1872), 4, 16.

7. Chabaud," L'hygiène dans la ville de Toulouse," Ville de Toulouse, *Documents sur Toulouse et sa région,* 2 (Toulouse: Privat, 1910), 17; Etienne Ginestous, *Les services d'hygiène de la ville de Bordeaux. Le bureau municipal d'hygiène, étude historique* (Bordeaux: Delmas, 1940); Lion Murard and Patrick Zylberman, "Experts et notables— les bureaux municipaux d'hygiène en France (1879-1914)," *Génèses,* 10 (January 1993), 69.

8. Bezault, "Législation française," 167; Dr. Loir," Enquête sur les conditions sanitaires du Havre," *RHPS,* 32 (1910), 1366-71; R. Delperie, "Toulouse et sa municipalité, 1900-1910, politique financière, économique et sociale," (Unpublished, D.E.S, University of Toulouse, 1967), 89; M. Bousquet, *Hygiène des villes* (Paris: Masson et Cie., 1912), 10.

9. Georges Vigarello, *Le propre et le sale—l'hygiène du corps depuis le moyen age* (Paris: Seuil, 1985), 155-67; William Coleman, *Death is a Social Disease.*

10. Renaux and Mathieu, "Projet de constructions de fontaines publiques," (Lyon: Louis Perrin, 1834), 1; Lyon. 23 January 1834.

11. Edmond de Planet, *Les fontaines publiques de Toulouse* (Toulouse: Privat, 1889), 34.

12. Roger Girard, *L'alimentation en eau de Lyon* (Strasbourg, n.d. [1935]), 34; Charles Guillemain, *Histoire des eaux publiques de Lyon* (Lyon: Provincia, 1934), iii.

13. Bernadette Lacroix-Spacenska, "Recherches sur les fontaines publiques de Bordeaux dans la première moitié du xixème siècle," (Maitrise, History of Art, Université de Bordeaux, III, 1985), 29; André Lagarde, *Les épidémies à Bordeaux au xixe siècle* (Bordeaux: Castera, 1970), 35; Société linéenne de Bordeaux, "Examen de la question rélatif à la reprise des travaux du recherche des eaux artésiennes," (Bordeaux, 1841).

14. Q. in Anon., *L'eau à Marseille* (Marseille: Imprimerie municipale, 1984), 93; "A MM. les membres de la chambre des pairs et de la chambre des députés, observations sur le projet du canal de Marseille," (Marseille, undated [1835?]).

15. Jacques Schnetzler, "Saint-Etienne et ses problèmes urbains," *Etudes foréziennes*, II, *La vie urbaine dans le département de la Loire et ses abords*, 2nd. ed. (Saint-Etienne: 1972) 253, fn.38; A. Martourey, "Formation et gestion d'une agglomération industrielle au xixème siècle, Saint-Etienne de 1815 à 1870," (Unpublished Doctorat d'état, University of Lyon, II, 1984), 624.

16. Girard, *L'alimentation*, 20-21.

17. Bordeaux. 23 October 1816.

18. Guillemain, *Histoire des eaux*, 51-54.

19. Dr. W. Manès, *Des eaux publiques en général et de celles de Bordeaux en particulier* (Bordeaux: Gounouilhou, 1866), 68-72; Anon., "Quelques réflexions soumises à M. le maire et à mm. les membres du conseil municipal," (Lyon: 1832), 4; M. Chalumeau, "Notice historique sur l'alimentation en eau de la ville de Lyon," *La technique sanitaire et municipale*, 15 (March-April 1914), 2; "Exposé 1827," F^{6}II Loire 18, A.N.

20. Lyon. 4 May 1846; J.B. Monfalcon and A.P.I. Polinière, *Hygiène de la ville de Lyon, ou opinions et rapports de l'ancien conseil de salubrité du département du Rhône, 1845-1849* (Lyon: Nigon, 1851), 69-71.

21. Paul Masson, ed., *Les Bouches-du-Rhône. Encyclopédie départementale*, 8 (Marseille: Archives départementales des Bouches-du-Rhône, 1926), 89; Jean-Pierre Goubert, *La conquête de l'eau* (Paris: Pierre Laffont, 1986), 56-57; Jean-Pierre Goubert and André Guillermé, "La Génèse des réseaux de distribution d'eau dans la France contemporaine," *Les réseaux techniques urbains. Séminaire* (Paris: Ecole nationale des ponts et chaussées (12-15 December, 1983), 18.

22. Q. in Gérard Martel-Reison, "Les eaux publiques à Marseille avant le canal de la Durance," (Unpublished Dr. en droit, Aix-Marseille, 1960), 286; Bordeaux. 7 February 1842; "Rapport de la commission spéciale du canal de Provence au conseil municipal de la ville de Marseille," (Marseille: Feissat and Demmoncly, 1834), 17; Mary to city, 14 December 1841, 419 O:1, A.M.B.

23. J.F. Terme, *Les eaux potables à distribuer pour l'usage des particuliers et le service public* (Lyon: Nigon, 1843); Bordeaux. 28 September 1843.

24. La Berge, *Mission and Method*, 24.

25. A. Arban, *Les eaux de Toulouse* (Toulouse: ISPA, 1891), 3; Vigarello, *Le propre et le sale*, 196; Guillermé and Goubert," "Génèse," 5; La Berge, *Mission and Method*, 192.

26. A. Dumont, *Note sur un projet ayant pour but d'approvisionner Lyon et ses faubourgs* (Lyon: Dumoulin, 1843), 9-11, 81; *Revue britannique, I (1850)*, 284, q. in Goubert and Guillermé, "La Génèse," 5.

27. Girard, *L'alimentation*, 40-47; Charlene Marie Leonard, *Lyon Transformed—Public Works of the Second Empire, 1853-1864* (Berkeley: University of California Press, 1961), 87-89.

28. Marie-France Brive, "La politique économique de la ville de Toulouse de 1870 à 1880" (Unpublished Diplôme d'études superieures, University of Toulouse, 1967), 29; *Journal de Toulouse*, 16 July 1852.

29. Bordeaux. 29 July 1879; Association française pour l'avancement des sciences, *Saint-Etienne*, 3 (Saint-Etienne: Théolier, 1897), 266; Comité consultatif d'hygiène publique, 3 December 1894, F^{8}201, A.N.; Seance 5 May 1890, Comité consultatif d'hygiène publique, F^{8}191, A.N.; *Dépêche de Toulouse*, 3 August 1890; Marseille. 9 December 1894; E.J. Letallec, "L'alimentation en eau de Marseille," *Marseille*, 125 (1981), 34; Emile Camau, *Marseille au xxe siècle* (Paris: Guillaumin, 1905), 39-43.

30. Bordeaux. 8 August 1890; A. Debauve & Edouard Imbeaux, *Assainissement des villes—distributions d'eau*, II (Paris: H. Dunod & E. Pinat, 1906), 9; Jules Rochard, "Les eaux potables," *Revue des deux mondes*, 4h ser., 136 (1 August 1896), 599; Paul Brouardel and J. Ogier, "Alimentation en eau de la ville de Toulouse," *Annales d'hygiène publique et de la médecine légale* [henceforth abbreviated as *AHPML*], 3rd. ser. XXIV (1890), 388; A. Arban, *Les eaux de Toulouse* (Toulouse: ISPA, 1891), 5-6.

31. Bordeaux. 29 July 1879; J. Lidy, "Les eaux de Bordeaux," *Revue philomathique* (1903), 483; "Rapport, 1884-1888," 11 O:4, A.M.B.; Pierre Guillaume, *La population de Bordeaux au xixe siècle* (Paris: Armand Colin, 1972), 17.

32. Guillemain, *Histoire*, 3.

33. Jean Lorcin, "Le projet du Lignon: une tentative d'application de la doctrine du 'socialisme municipal' à Saint-Etienne en 1900," *Bulletin du centre d'histoire économique et sociale de la région lyonnaise*, no. 4 (1973), 63-76.

34. Lidy, "Les eaux," 491, 499.

35. Henri Monod, *La santé publique (législation sanitaire de la France)* (Paris: Hachette, 1904), 300; Richard J. Evans, *Death in Hamburg* (New York: Oxford University Press, 1987)

36. M. Bechman, "Enquête statistique sur l'hygiène urbaine dans les villes françaises," *RHPS*, 14 (1892), 509-15, 1062-1109; Samuel H. Preston and Etienne Van de Walle, "Urban French Mortality in the Nineteenth Century," *Population Studies*, 32 (1978), 275-97.

37. Goubert, *La conquête de l'eau*, 213; Goubert and Guillermé, "La Génèse," 1; *Dépêche de Toulouse*, 24 August 1898.

38. M. Bechmann, "Enquête statistique sur l'hygiène urbaine dans les villes françaises," *RHPS*, 14 (1892), 510.

Chapter 7: Public Health

39. A. Armengaud, "Quelques aspects de l'hygiène publique à Toulouse au début du xxe siècle," *Annales de démographie historique* (1975), 134-35.

40. Marseille. 19 May 1912.

41. Note by Bordeaux city engineer, 25 September 1867, 441 O 2, A.M.B.; Goubert and Guillermé, "Génèse des réseaux," 28.

42. De Voisins D'Aubuisson, "Histoire de l'etablissement des fontaines à Toulouse," *Histoire et mémoires de l'académie royale des sciences, inscriptions et belles-lettres de Toulouse* (1825), 187-92, 261-63, 316; Bernadette Lacroix-Spacenska, *Aqueducs et fontaines-Bordeaux, xixe siècle* (Bordeaux: Office du tourisme de Bordeaux, 1987), 60; Edouard Féret, *Statistique générale topographique, scientifique, administrative, industrielle, commerciale, agricole etc.* I (Bordeaux: Féret, 1878), 326; Martourey, "Formation et gestion," 627; Saint-Etienne. 10 June 1851.

43. Dr. Rougier and Dr. Glenard, *Hygiène de Lyon—comptes rendus des travaux du conseil d'hygiène publique et de salubrité du département de Rhône* (Lyon: Aimé Vingtrinier, 1860), 69.

44. M. Bechmann, "Enquête statistique sur l'hygiène urbaine dans les villes françaises," *RHPS*, 14 (1892), 1068; Roger-Henri Guerrand, *Les lieux. Histoire des commodités* (Paris: La Découverte, 1985), 119; Lagarde, *Les epidémies à Bordeaux au xixe siècle* (Bordeaux: Castera, 1970), 362; Marc Guyez, *Alimentation de Lyon en eau potable* (Lyon: Léon Delaroche, 1886), 3; "Rapport sur les vidangeurs automatiques," 28 May 1890, 5148 I:1, A.M.B.; Petrus Sambardier, *La vie à Lyon* (Lyon: no publisher, 1939 [?]), 28; Association française pour l'avancement des sciences, *Lyon 1906*, 2 (Lyon: A. Rey & cie, 1906), 45; Lyon *Documents rélatifs au budget de 1907* (1906), 208; "Exposé du nouveau projet . . . par M. Villard père," 10 September 1895, 63 O:93, A.M.M.

45. Etienne Fournial, et al., *Saint-Etienne—Histoire de la ville et de ses habitants* (Paris: Horvath, 1976), 258.

46. Q. in Lacroix-Spacenska, *Aqueducs*, 73.

47. André Guillermé, *Les temps de l'eau. La cité, l'eau et les techniques* (Seyssel: Champ Vallon, 1983), 167, 170, 179, 200-201.

48. Bernard P. Lécuyer," "L'hygiène en France avant Pasteur," in Claire Salomon-Bayet, *Pasteur et la révolution pastorienne* (Paris: Payot, 1986), 67-139; Coleman, *Death is a Social Disease*.

49. Alain Corbin, *Le miasme et la jonquille—l'odorat et l'imaginaire social, xviiie-xixe siècles* (Paris: Aubier Montaigne, 1982); Mayor to prefect, 4 October 1832, 5I2; Letter, Member to Comité de salubrité du second arrondissement, 24 May 1832, 3D 143, A.M.T.

50. "Rapport du conseil central de salubrité à M. le préfet, Toulouse, 10 April 1832, 3D 143; Séance 6 April 1832 of conseil central de salubrité du département de la Haute-Garonne, posted notice, in 2D 17, A.M.T; Bordeaux, 1 April 1832; Marseille, 5 April 1832; Marseille. Arrêté of Mayor, 11 April 1832; Erwin Ackerknecht, "Anticontagionism between 1821 and 1867," *Bulletin of the History of Medecine*, 22, no. 5 (1948),

562-93; Dr. J. Mabit, "Rapport sur le choléra morbus asiatique qui a été observé à Bordeaux depuis le 4 août 1832 jusqu'à ce jour . . ." (12 September 1832), 45.

51.   P. Bourdelais, P. and J.Y. Raulot, *Une peur bleue. Histoire du choléra en France, 1832-1854* (Paris: Payot, 1987), 238.

52.   Anon., "L'eau de Marseille," 94; Guerrard, *Les lieux*, 81; Henri Gintrac, *Relation de l'épidémie cholérique qui a régné dans l'arrondissement de Bordeaux pendant l'année 1855* (Bordeaux: Ragot, 1855), 49; Dr. J. Rousset, "Les épidémies à Lyon aux xviiiè et xixè siècles et les mésures de prévention médical qui leur furent opposées," *Actes du 89ème congrès national des sociétés savantes, Lyon 1964* (Paris: Imprimerie nationale, 1965), 179.

53.   Mayor Report to Council, pluviose Year XIII, 1 L 17, A.M.T.; similar description in Bordeaux at the same time, Jean Coste, *Le maire et l'empereur—Bordeaux sous le premier empire* (Bordeaux: Société archéologique et historique de Lignan et du canton de Créon, 1993), 168.

54.   Marseille. 10 August 1840; Camau, *Marseille au xxe siècle*, 96.

55.   12 messidor, Year X, reprinted in *Bulletin officiel municipal de Lyon* (18 October 1908), 379; Mayor to Prefect, Lyon, 15 January 1829, 4M 3, A.R.; Marseille. 27 November 1829.

56.   Lyon, 1 May 1819. Budget reports, 1811, 1819, 1826, F^6. II Loire, 16-18, A.N.; Martourey, "Formation et gestion," 617; Marseille. 11 July 1848; 11 August 1853; Toulouse. 24 December 1878.

57.   O. Du Mesnil, "Nettoiement de la voie publique," *AHPML*, 3rd. ser, XII (1884), 314; Saint-Etienne, Arrêté 27 August 1901; Ville de Saint-Etienne, *Règlement sanitaire* (Saint-Etienne: Tribune, 1906), 14-15; Arrêté 6 April 1878, Ville de Lyon, *Receuil des arrêtés et règlements de police* (Lyon: J. Gallet, 1880), 83-86; Lyon, *Documents rélatifs au projet de budget de 1887*, 345; Du Mesnil, "Nettoiement;" 305-27; Jeanne-Hélène Jugie, *Poubelle-Paris* (Paris: Découvrir, 1993), 57-59, 213; Letter Director of Service Municipal to Mayor, Toulouse, 28 December 1906, Ingénieur 293, A.M.T.

58.   Marseille. 11 March 1906, 4 April 1913.

59.   Bourdelais and Raulot, *Peur bleue*, 240; Mayor to Prefect, 21 March 1865, Archives voirie, section 76, vol. 1; "Rapport de l'ingénieur adjoint, 11 January 1873, Archives voirie, 76, vol. 2, A.M.L.; Lyon. 6 June 1871.

60.   Martourey, "Formation et gestion," 618; Marseille. 28 February 1872; Dr. Fontagnères, "Hygiène publique de la ville de Toulouse," *Revue médicale de Toulouse*, 7 (1873), 305-17; Toulouse. 31 August 1904.

61.   Conseil de salubrité, "Rapport à M. le maire sur l'état des boucheries et des triperies dans la ville," 20 July 1844. 5 I:3, A.M.S.E.

62.   Arrêté rélatif au nettoiement à la salubrité et la bonne tenue des voies publiques de la ville (Marseille: Jules Barieur, 1853), 10; Emile Isnard, *Recueil des arrêtés et règlements municipaux (1806-1934)* (Marseille: Imprimerie municipale, 1935), 6, 23, 31.

63. *Le Temps*, 10 September 1884; Bordeaux, *Bordeaux, aperçu historique, sol, population, industrie, commerce, administration*, 2 (Paris: Hachette, 1892), 444; Conseil central d'hygiène publique et de salubrité de Saint-Etienne, *Compte rendu des travaux des conseils d'hygiène publique et de salubrité du département de la Loire pendant les années 1899 et 1900.* (Saint-Etienne: Théolier, 1901), 10; Ville de Saint-Etienne, *Règlement sanitaire* (Saint-Etienne: Tribune, 1906), 53-55.

64. Ghislaine Bouchet, *Le cheval à Paris de 1850 à 1914* (Geneva; Droz, 1993), 3, 45; Camau, *Marseille au xxe siècle*, 54.

65. Isidore Hedde, "Saint-Etienne, ancien et moderne," *Revue du lyonnais*, 14 (1841), 454; Roger Chartier, *Histoire urbaine*, 3 (Paris: Seuil, 1981), 155, 450.

66. Bourdelais and Raulot, *Peur bleue*, 241; Louis de Courbettes-Labourdie, *Souvenirs d'un étudiant—Toulouse en 183 . . .* (Toulouse: Chauvin, 1870), 239.

67. Association française pour l'avancement des sciences, *Bordeaux, métropole du sud-ouest* (Bordeaux: Gounouilhou, 1923), 133-34; Michel-Luc-Gabriel Gaudin, *Histoire et vie des égouts de Bordeaux* (Bordeaux: E. Drouillard, 1958), 22-30; Bordeaux, *Aperçu historique*, 2: 262-264; Bordeaux. 11 August 1890; Michel-Luc-Gabriel Gaudin, *Histoire et vie des égouts de Bordeaux* (Bordeaux: E. Drouillard,1958), 31; Rochard, *Traité*, 54; "Des différents projets de distribution des eaux à Lyon, rapport au conseil municipal par M. le maire de Lyon," (Lyon Association typographique, 1883); Marseille. 22 August 1873; Dr. H. Mireur, *La question des vidanges à Marseille* (Paris: G. Masson, 1888), 65; Franck Scherrer, "L'égout, patrimoine urbain, l'évolution dans la longue durée du réseau d'assainissement de Lyon" (Unpublished thèse doctorat, nouveau régime, Université de Paris, Val-de-Marne, 1992), 143.

68. Guerrand, *Les lieux*, 27, 79; Masson, ed., *Les Bouches-du-Rhône* 14:44; Arrêté rélatif au nettoiement, à la salubrité et la bonne tenue des voies publiques de la ville," (Marseille: Jules Barieur, 1853), 8.

69. "Rapport au comité de salubrité du 10e arrondissement," 17 April 1832, 3D 143; Rapport du comité de salubrité du 1er arrondissement," 20 April 1832, 3D 143; Comite de salubrité to a property owner, 21 April 1832. 5 I:2, A.M.T.; Dr. J. Mabit, "Rapport sur le cholera morbus asiatique qui a été observé à Bordeaux depuis le 4 août 1832 jusqu'à ce jour . . ." (Bordeaux, 12 September 1832), 45; similar information in "Instructions sur les moyens à employer pour prévenir le développement du choléra morbus par le conseil central de salubrité du département de la Gironde, 31 March 1832, 5 M 51, A.D.G.

70. Ville de Saint-Etienne. "Rapports du commission au conseil municipal, 1867"; *Petit marseillais*, 28 June 1900.

71. *Précurseur*, 5 May 1829; Lyon. Arrêté, 28 June 1860, 28 February 1862.

72. Inspecteur de salubrité to Mayor, 8 January 1846, 151 O:1, A.M.B.; Toulouse. Arrête, 6 February 1827, 8 December 1830, copy in 2D17, A.M.T; *Dépêche de Toulouse*, 19 October 1892, 16 June 1895.

73. Edouard Billioud, "La voie publique à Marseille jusqu'à la monarchie de juillet" (Thesis, Dr. en droit, University of Marseille, 1957), 163; "Rapport général sur les travaux du conseil de salubrité du département des Bouches-du-Rhône pendant

les années 1826 et 1827," (Marseille: Antoine Ricard, 1828), 12; Masson, ed., *Les Bouches-du-Rhône* 9: 435; Charles Dickens, *The Uncommercial Traveller*, 2 (Boston: Estes and Lauriat, 1895), 179; H.A. Taine, *Journeys through France* (New York: Henry Holt, 1897), 105.

74. "Rapport du conseil de salubrité de la ville de Lyon sur l'assainissement, du curage des fosses d'aisance, n.d.[1838?] I[1] 267, A.M.L.; Arrêté, 12 September 1839, Pionin, *Code de police municipale de la ville de Lyon* (Lyon: Dumoulin, Ronet and Sibouet, 1840), 29; similar precautions were taken in Toulouse, "Cahier de charges concernant le service des vidanges des lieux d'aisance de la ville de Toulouse," 29 September 1813, copy in F[6]II Haute-Garonne 7, A.N.

75. Dr. M. Ségaud, "De l'assainissement et du nettoiement des rues de Marseille et de son port" (Marseille: Dreissat ainé and Demonchy, 1832), 16-17; Registres de permissions, I[1] 267, A.M.L.

76. Barrie M. Ratcliffe, "Cities and Environmental Decline: Elites and the Sewage Problem in Paris from the Mid-Eighteenth to the Mid-Nineteenth Century," (Unpublished paper, Society for French Historical Studies, May 1989) 17; Pionin, *Code*, Arrêté 2 May 1872, 19 October 1876, 25 August 1880; Dr. P. Bézy, "Statistique démographie et hygiène," in Association française pour l'avancement des sciences, *Toulouse* (Toulouse: Privat, 1887), 1050, 1061.

77. Toulouse. 27 June 1829; Marseille, Arrêté 22 March 1836; Marseille. 19 February 1839; 1841 Budget, F[6]II Gironde 31, A.N.; Asistant mayor to Commandant, garde municipal, 2 July 1847, 236 I:5, A.M.B.

78. On the Paris tubs, see Ratcliffe, "Cities and Environmental Decline," 20; Horace Bertin, *Les heures Marseillaises* (Marseille: Laveirarie, 1878), 142.

79. Comité médical des Bouches-du-Rhône," Réponse du comité médical aux habitants d'Arenc sur cette question—les dépôts d'engrais accumulés sur un point du quartier d'Arenc ne sont-ils pas une cause d'insalubrité," (Marseille: Jules Barile, 1867), 16; Emile Camau, *Marseille au xxème siécle*, 48.

80. Kiendi, "Service général de salubrité publique de la ville de Marseille," [1867?]. Report, repr. in Dr. Charles Levieux, *Etudes sur l'assistance hospitalière dans la ville de Bordeaux et sur diverses questions d'hygiène publique.* 2nd. ser. (Bordeaux: Ragot, 1882), 345; Lyon, *Documents administratifs et statistiques* (1882), 162; *Dépêche de Toulouse,* 14 July 1897; Louis Masson, "Conférence sur les villes assainies," *Compte rendu, ive congrès provincial des architectes* (Toulouse: Joseph Fournier, 1888), 8; Scherrer," L'égout," 146-48, 158.

81. Dr. Jules Arnould, "Les controverses récentes au sujet de l'assainissement des villes," *AHPML*, 3rd. ser. VIII (1882), 12; Scherrer," L'égout," 161-162.

82. *Dépêche de Toulouse,* 6 October 1898.

83. *Petite Gironde,* 20 October 1904.

84. Conseil central d'hygiène publique et de salubrité de la Gironde, Séance 29 July 1885, 5148 I[1], A.M.B., Commission des logements, *Délibérations,* Séance 3 May 1892, 5106 I[3], A.M.B.

Chapter 7: Public Health

85. *Petite Gironde*, 6 October 1904; Dr. Julien, "Tout à l'égout," *RHPS*, 28 (1906), 869.

86. *Petite Gironde*, 20 October 1904.

87. Conseil d'hygiène publique et de salubrité du département de la Loire, "Des infections des vidanges," séance 24 April 1866; Martourey, "Formation et gestion," 633; Ville de Saint-Etienne, "Rapports du commission au conseil municipal," 1867; André Lagarde, *Les epidémies à Bordeaux au xixe siècle* (Bordeaux: Castera, 1970), 37; Dr Prunelle, city councillor and future mayor in Lyon. 4 May 1846; Michel Jules Marmy and Ferdinand Quesnoy, *Topographie et statistique médicale du département du Rhône et de la ville de Lyon* (Lyon: Aimé Vingtrinier, 1866), 326, 338-41; I[1] 268, A.M.L.

88. Philippe Béroud, *Etude sur l'hygiène et la topographie médicale de la ville de Saint-Etienne* (Saint-Etienne: J. Pichon, 1862), 62; Saint-Etienne. 29 April 1898; Association française, *Saint-Etienne*, 3: 121.

89. One historian has mistakenly written that Paris's unitary system "was established relatively early" and served as a model for provincial cities and the rest of Europe. Gabriel Dupuy, *Urbanisme et technique* (Paris: Centre de recherche d'urbanisme, 1978), 170-71; Gabriel Dupuy and Georges Knaebel, *Assainir la ville hier et aujourd'hui* (Paris: Dunod, 1982), 4. In a general discussion of city services, Jean-Pierre Gaudin claims that foreign models influenced city services in France only after World War I; this neglects the nineteenth-century record: Jean-Pierre Gaudin, *L'avenir en plan-technique et politique dans la prévision urbaine, 1900-1930* (Paris: Champ Vallon, 1985), 70.

90. Dr. H. Mireur, *Le mouvement comparé de la population à Marseille, en France et dans les états d'Europe* (Paris: G. Masson, 1889), 126-28, 331.

91. Mireur, *Mouvement*, 240-43, 249.

92. Félix Baret, "Rapport." Marseille. 16 September 1890; Masson, ed., *Les Bouches-du-Rhône* 8: 173.

93. Frédéric Charavel, "Projet d'assainissement de la ville de Marseille, Rapport" (Marseille, 1885), 5; Dr. A. Proust, Report to Comité consultatif d'hygiène publique de France, q. in Félix Baret, "Rapport," Marseille. 16 September 1890; *Le Temps*, 8 May 1886.

94. J. Charles-Roux, *Vingt ans de vie politique* (Paris: Guillaumin, 1892), 121-35.

95. Ingénieur de la voirie," Projet d'une canalisation," August 1883, 31 O:13, A.M.M. For Parisian opposition to the unitary system on medical grounds, see Gérard Jacquemet, "Urbanisme Parisien: La Bataille du tout à l'égout à la fin du xixè siècle," *Revue d'histoire moderne et contemporaine*, 26 (1979) 512-14; Guerrand, *Les lieux*, 148-49; Alfred des Cilleuls, *L'administration parisienne sous la 3ème république* (Paris: Picard, 1910), 413.

96. Dupuy, *Urbanisme*, 168; *Le Temps*, 13 June, 23 November 1886; Marseille. 4 June 1886. A more balanced description of the system than Dupuy can be found in Paul Wéry, *Assainissement des villes et égouts de Paris* (Paris: Charles Dunod, 1898), 34-46. 102; Edouard Imbeaux, *L'alimentation en eau et l'assainissement des villes*, vol. II (Paris:

C. Bernard & Cie., 1902), 391-92; Gabriel Dupuy, *Urbanisme,* 166-67; *Le Temps,* 8 February 1887.

97. G. Bechmann, "Quels sont les résultats techniques des canalisations," *Comptes rendus et mémoires, huitiéme congrès international d'hygiène et de démographie,* 4 (Budapest: Pesti Konyunyomda-Reszventyarasag, 1896), 280; Dominique Barjot, "Contraintes et stratégies: les débuts de la société des grands travaux de Marseille (1891-1914), *Provence historique,* 40 (October-December 1990), 381-401.

98. Some commentators on the elections saw at the time and subsequently Flaissières's opposition as a demagogic appeal to public fears of what in France was a relatively unknown and untried system. But given the scientific controversy at the time, it is likely that the Socialists were sincere in their convictions. They joined in their views the scientific opinion of the German Max von Pettenkofer, holder of the chair of hygiene at Munich University, who believed that the climate and soil were the sources of cholera; Patrick Zylberman, "L'Hygiène dans la république, 1877-1916," (Unpublished doctorat d'état ès lettres, 1994), 153; Frank M. Snowden, *Naples in the Time of Cholera, 1884-1914* (New York: Cambridge University Press, 1995), 67-69. Pettenkofer's idea won a wide hearing through the writings of the Paul Brouardel, the dean of the Paris Faculty of Medicine. The great Pasteur had opposed the Paris unitary sewer also for fear it would lead to the spread in the subsoil of diseases; Jacquemet, "Urbanisme Parisien," 512-14.

99. Dominique Barjot, "La Société des grands travaux de Marseille," *Provence historique,* 40 (1990), 388.

100. Jacqueline Félician-Le Core, "Action sociale de la municipalité de Marseille, 1892-1939," 1 (Unpublished Thesis, 3ème cycle, University Aix-Marseille, I, 1987), 109; Masson, ed. *Les Bouches-du-Rhône* 10: 96; "Situation sanitaire des communes de plus de 5,000 habitants et des communes saisonnières, résultats de l'enquête pour le département des Bouches-du-Rhône, 5 December 1913, F^{7}216, A.N.

101. Dominique Angles, "Le *Journal de Marseille* de 1895 à 1900," (Unpublished Maitrise, University of Aix-en-Provence, n.d.), 35-42.

102. Coppolani, *Toulouse au xxe siècle,* 315; A. Armengaud, "Quelques aspects de l'hygiène publique à Toulouse au début du xxe siècle," *Annales de démographie historique* (1975), 134-35; Scherrer, "L'égout," 171-72.

103. Louis Genis, "Conférénce sur les travaux d'assainissement de cette ville," (Marseille: Barthelet et cie., 1895), 26-27.

104. A. Debauve, *Distributions d'eau—égouts,* 2 (Paris: Vve. Dunod, 1897), 447; E. Mondon, *Assainissements des villes et de petites collectivités* (Paris: 1934) q. in Dupuy, *Urbanisme,* 175.

105. Anne Thalamy, "Réflexions sur la notion d'habitat au XVIII et XIXe siècles," in J.M. Alliaume, et al., *Politiques de l'habitat (1800-1850)* (Paris: COPEDITH, 1977), 42-51; Ann La Berge, *Mission and Method;* Jean-Baptiste Monfalcon & Polinière, *Traité de la salubrité dans les grandes villes suivi de l'hygiène de Lyon* (Paris: J.B. Baillière, 1846), 115.

106. Louis Villermé, *Tableau de l'état physique et moral des ouvriers employés dans les manufactures de coton, de laine et de soie* (Paris: J. Renouard, 1835), 168-171; Conseil d'hygiène de Rhône, *Hygiène de la ville de Lyon* (Paris: Baillière, 1851), 13; in 1910, that figure was 10 percent, Laurent Bonnevay, *Les habitations à bon marché* (Paris: Dunod, 1912), 106.

107. "Rapport fait à l'intendance," 25 May 1832, 5M48, A.D.G.; Bordeaux, *Aperçu historique historique, sol, population, industrie, commerce, administration*, 2 (Paris: Hachette, 1892), 444.

108. David S. Barnes, *The Making of a Social Disease—Tuberculosis in Nineteenth-Century France* (Berkeley: University of California Press, 1995), 31-37.

109. In *L'alliance d'hygiène sociale*, (January 1904), q. in Colette Bec, *Assistance république—le recherche d'un nouveau contrat social sous la IIIe république* (Paris: Editions ouvrières, 1994), 193; André Alfred Dumont, *Les habitations ouvrières dans les grands centres industriels* (Lille: A. Masson, 1905), 23; Henry Duret, *De l'intervention des municipalités en matières d'habitations ouvrières* (Paris: Arthur Rousseau, 1910), 5.

110. Anon., *Tableau des améliorations dont la ville de Bordeaux est susceptible relativement à la salubrité* (Bordeaux: Lavalle, 1817), 57.

111. Martin-Doisy, *Dictionnaire d'économie*, 459; Louis Chevallier, *Laboring Classes and Dangerous Classes in Paris During the First Half of the Nineteenth Century*, Frank Jellinek, transl. (Princeton: Princeton University Press, 1973), 411-31, summarizes some of this fear of degeneration.

112. Alfred de Foville, "Enquête sur les conditions de l'habitation en France," *Bulletin de la société française d'habitations à bon marché* [henceforth abbreviated as BSFHBM], 5 (1894), 189; Laws of 19 January, 7 March, and 13 April 1850; copy in F⁸210, A.N.; Philippe Passot, *Aperçu sur les travaux de la commission des logements insalubres de Lyon* (Lyon: Aimé Vingtrinier, 1870), 5.

113. Jules Challamel, "Rapport sur les modifications à introduire dans la législation concernant les logements insalubres," *BSHBM* (1901), 442; E. Macé & Edouard Imbeaux, *Hygiène générale des villes et des agglomérations communales* (Paris: J.B. Baillière, 1910), 175; Q. in Meaudre, "La Poussée urbaine à Saint-Etienne (1815-1872)," (Unpublished Diplôme d'études supérieures, University of Lyon, 1967), 172; A. Martourey, "Formation et gestion d'une agglomération industrielle au xixème siècle, Saint-Etienne de 1815 à 1870," (Unpublished Doctorat d'état, Université of Lyon, II, 1984), 643; Prefect of Loire to Minister of interior, 21 May 1879, F⁸211, A.N.; Prefect of Haute-Garonne to Minister of Commerce, 28 April 1879, F⁸ 211, A.N.; Marseille. 21 October 1861; Prefect of Bouches-du-Rhône to Minister of Commerce, 16 September 1878, F⁸211, A.N; Eugène Rostand, "Conférence sur la coopération appliquée à la construction des habitations à bon marché," *BSFHBM* (1890), 329; Bordeaux. 20 November 1854.

114. "Rapport sur l'exécution de la loi des logements insalubres," 18 October 1858, F⁸210, A.N.; Commission des logements insalubres, *Délibérations*, séance 23 May 1856, 5106 I:1, A.M.B.; Bordeaux. 4 August 1856.

115. Dr. P.H. Millas, *Des droits de l'hygiène vis à vis de la propriété bâtie* (Toulouse: M. Cleder, 1898), 17; Emile Camau, *Les institutions de bienfaisance, de charité et de prévoyance à Marseille* (Marseille: Assistance par le travail, n.d.) [1891?], 320; Francois Burdeau, "Propriété privée et santé publique-étude sur la loi du 15 février 1902," Jean-Louis Harouel, ed. *Histoire du droit social—mélanges en hommage à Jean Imbert* (Paris: Presses universitaires de France, 1989), 125.

116. Bordeaux. 4 August 1856; Commission des logements insalubres, *Délibérations*, 12 November 1858; 30 March 1859, 5106, I:1, A.M.B.; Séance 4 September 1885, Conseil général, Bouches-du-Rhône; Dr. Brouardel, "Sur l'apparition d'une nouvelle épidémie cholérique à Marseille," *AHPML*, 3rd. ser. XIV (1885), 231.

117. Commission des logements insalubres, *Délibérations*, 2 April 1889, 5106, I:3, A.M.B.; Mauriac, *Hygiène urbaine*, 10.

118. Henri Monod, *La santé publique (législation sanitaire de la France)* (Paris: Hachette, 1904), 28; *Le Temps*, 16 May 1898; Burdeau, "Propriété privée," 125-33.

119. Henri Monod, *De l'administration de l'hygiène publique* (Caen: F. Leblanc-Hardel, 1884), 5, 12.

120. Léon Le Baron, *Le problème du logement ouvrier* (Paris: M. Giard & E. Briére, 1917), 28-29; Ann-Louise Shapiro, *Housing the Poor of Paris, 1850-1902* (Madison: University of Wisconsin Press, 1985), 150-58; Bezault, "Législation française rélative à l'hygiène publique," *Compte rendus des travaux, association française pour le développement des travaux publics* (1912), 167; M. Bousquet, "Les municipalités et l'hygiène urbaine," *Congrès international et exposition comparée des villes*, ser II (1913), 229; Henri Turot and H. Bellamy, *Le surpeuplement et les habitation à bon marché* (Paris: F. Alcan, 1907), 62; Clemenceau, q. in Jean Humbert, *Du rôle de l'administration en matière de prophylaxie des maladies épidémiques* (Paris: Jouve, 1911), 53; and in Zylberman, "L'Hygiène," 102.

121. Antonin and Maurice Péhu,"Les logements insalubres à Lyon de 1891 à 1904," *AHPML*, 4th ser., III (1905), 127; Lyon, *Documents rélatifs au budget de 1913* (1912), 320; Lyon. 1 August 1910; Complaint by the national director of hygiene, (Léon Mirman, 29 November 1909, q. in Murard and Zylberman, "Experts et notables," 67.

122. Mazodier, a lawyer and member of the housing section of the Congrès de l'hygiène social in 1903, q. in L.J. Gras, *Histoire du commerce local et des industries qui se rattachent dans la region stéphanoise et forézienne* (Saint-Etienne: J. Thomas, 1910), 416.

123. *Death in Hamburg—Society and Politics in the Cholera Years, 1830-1910* (New York: Oxford University Press, 1987).

124. La Berge, *Mission and Method*, 306, 313, 317; Goubert and Guillermé, "La Génèse," 1.

125. Zylberman, "L'Hygiène," 189.

CHAPTER 8

1. For the argument that the welfare projects of the Revolution mirrored the views of the reformers in the 50 years or so preceding the Revolution, see Catherine Duprat, *"Pour l'amour de l'humanité"—le temps des philanthropes*, vol. 1 (Paris: C.T.H.S., 1993). For the Revolution and subsequent developments, see Alan Forrest, *The French Revolution and the Poor* (New York: St. Martin's Press, 1981); Colin Jones, *Charity and Bienfaisance—The Treatment of the Poor in the Montpellier Region, 1740-1815* (London: Cambridge University Press, 1982); Robert M. Schwartz, *Policing the Poor in Eighteenth—Century France* (Chapel Hill: University of North Carolina Press, 1988).

2. Philip Nord, "The Welfare State in France, 1870-1914," *French Historical Studies*, 18, 3 (Spring 1994), 821-38, argues that initiatives taken by the national government in the first four decades of the Third Republic laid the foundations of the modern welfare state. This fine review, however, neglects the varied and prolonged activities of French municipalities on behalf of the poor.

3. Frances Fox Piven and Richard A. Cloward, *Regulating the Poor—The Functions of Public Welfare* (New York: Pantheon: 1971), ch. 1; Timothy B. Smith, "Public Assistance and Labor Supply in Nineteenth-Century Lyon," *Journal of Modern History*, 68 (March 1996), 1-30. The model has been seriously attacked by American historians: Walter I. Trattner, ed., *Social Welfare or Social Control—Some Historical Reflections on Regulating the Poor* (Knoxville: University of Tennesee Press, 1983).

4. Gaston V. Rimlinger, *Welfare Policy and Industrialization in Europe, America, and Russia* (New York: John Wiley and Sons, 1971) 41; Fleury Ravarin *De l'assistance communale en France* (Paris: E. Larose, 1885), 8-9; François Ewald, *L'état providentiel* (Paris: Grasset, 1986), Book I.

5. Q. in A. Martourey, "Formation et gestion d'une agglomération industrielle au xixème siècle, Saint-Etienne de 1815 à 1870," (Unpublished Doctorat d'état, Université de Lyon, II, 1984), 949.

6. Q. in Olivier Faure, "La médicalisation de la société dans la région lyonnaise au xixe siècle, 1800-1914. (Unpublished Thèse Dr d'état, University of Lyon II, 1989), 49.

7. *Le Courrier de Lyon*, 5 October 1844; Georges Ribe, *L'opinion publique et la vie politique à Lyon lors des premières années de la seconde restauration* (Paris: Sirey, 1957), 59; "Extinction de la mendicité," Report of 1843 commission, 1 Q2, A.M.T.; Q in J.C. Paul Rougier, *L'économie politique à Lyon, 1750-1890* (Paris: Guillaumin, 1890), 138. (The copy I have consulted at the University of Chicago was inscribed by the author to the liberal economist Paul Leroy-Beaulieu).

8. Q. Olivier Faure, "La médicalisation," (Thesis), 346; Société de charité maternelle, q. in Annie Flacassier, "L'Hospice de maternité de Bordeaux sous la révolution et l'empire (1794-1815)," *Colloque sur l'histoire de la sécurité sociale—Actes du 106e congrès des sociétés savantes* (Paris: Association pour l'étude de l'histoire de la sécurité sociale, 1982), 51; Eliane Richard, "Bienfaisance et charité à Marseille entre 1850 et 1880," *Colloque sur l'histoire de la sécurité sociale-Actes du 106e congrès des sociétés savantes*

(Paris: Association pour l'étude de l'histoire de la sécurité sociale, 1982), 280; Thomas R. Christofferson, "Les conceptions sociales des notables de Marseille sous la seconde république," *Annales du midi*, 85 (1973), 424.

9.   Alexis de Tocqueville, *Mémoire sur le paupérisme* (Paris: n.p., 1835); Vcomte. Alban de Villeneuve-Bargemont, *Economie politique chrétienne ou recherches sur la nature et les causes du paupérisme en France et en Europe*, I (Paris: Paulin, 1834), 79-80, 379; François Ewald, *L'état providence* (Paris: Bernard Grasset, 1986), 91-92; Henri Hatzfeld, *Du paupérisme à la sécurité sociale* (Paris: Armand Colin, 1971), 6-10; Joseph De Gérando, *De la bienfaisance publique*, 1 (Paris: J. Renouard, 1839), 205; Philippe Sassier, *Du bon usage des pauvres—histoire d'un thème politique, xvi-xxe siècle* (Paris: Fayard, 1990), 181; Lyon welfare board, q. in Timothy B. Smith, "The Politics of Public Assistance in Lyon, France, 1815-1920," (Unpublished Ph.D. Dissertation, Columbia University, 1994), 125-26.

10. Roger Chartier, "La pauvreté à l'age moderne (xvi-xviiie siècles). Définitions, représentations, institutions," A. Fracassi, et al., eds., *La pauvreté, une approche plurielle* (Paris: Editions ESF, 1985), 28-29; Jean-Pierre Gutton, *La société et les pauvres en Europe: xvie-xviiie siècle* (Paris: Presses universitaires de France, 1978); Daniel Puymèges, "Introduction," Jean Baptiste Martin, *La fin des mauvais pauvres* (Paris: Champ Vallon, 1983). The Comité de mendicité during the Revolution had worried a lot about how to differentiate between the deserving poor and others, the handicapped and the physically able: Duprat, *"Pour l'amour de l'humanité,"* 1: 296, 315, 317.

11. Rougier, *L'économie politique*, 92.

12. Katherine Lynch, *Family, Class, and Ideology in Early Industrial France* (Madison: University of Wisconsin Press, 1988), 72; Cathérine Pélissier, "Les sociabilités patriciennes à Lyon du milieu du dix-neuvième siècle à 1914," (Doctorat de l'université, Lyon II, 1993) 1093; the historiographical debate regarding 1830 as a turning point is dealt with in Smith, "The Politics of Public Assistance," 119-20.

13. Q. in Faure, *Génèse de l'hôpital moderne. Les hospices civils de Lyon de 1802 à 1845* (Lyon: Presses universitaires de Lyon, 1982), 178; Lyon. 22 April 1874; Bureau de bienfaisance to Mayor, 12 January 1871, 25Q2, A.M.B.; Q. in Jacqueline Félician-Le Corre, "Action sociale de la municipalité de Marseille, 1892-1939," 1 (Unpublished Thesis, 3ème cycle, University Aix-Marseille, I, 1987), 54.

14. On this development, see Louis Chevalier, *Laboring Classes and Dangerous Classes in Paris During the First Half of the Nineteenth Century*, Fran Jellinek transl. (Princeton: Princeton University Press, 1973).

15. *De la charité dans ses rapports avec l'état moral et les bien être des classes inférieures de la société* (Paris: Mesnier, 1829), 26, q. in Sassier, *Du bon usage*, 256; de Gérando, *De la bienfaisance*, 1: 2; Jules Siegfried, *La misère, son histoire, ses causes, ses remèdes* (Le Havre: Ponsignon, 1877), 11, q. in Sassier, *Du bon usage*, 257.

16. Bordeaux. 20, 26, 28 October 1830; Saint-Etienne. 18 October 1830; Martourey, "Formation et gestion," 758; Maurice Durousset, "La vie ouvrière dans la région stéphanoise," (Unpublished D.E.S., University of Lyon, 1960) 200; Max Consolat, *Rapport sur la situation financière de la ville de Marseille, présenté au conseil municipal le 9*

Chapter 8: Municipal Welfare

juillet 1840 (Marseille: Hoirs Freissat ainé et Demonchy, 1840), 19; Roquelaine, q. in David Mason Mindock, "Poverty and Public Assistance in Toulouse, France, 1830-1870," (Unpublished Ph.D. Dissertation, Northwestern University, 1987), 67; and for others in Toulouse with similar goals, see Ronald Aminzade, *Class, Politics, and Early Industrial Capitalism—A Study of Mid-Nineteenth Century Toulouse, France* (Albany: State University of New York Press, 1981), 161.

17. Albert Charles, *La révolution de 1848 et la seconde république à Bordeaux et dans le département de la Gironde* (Bordeaux: Delmas, 1945) 19; Mayor in letter to prefect, repr. in *Dépêche de Toulouse*, 22 August 1896.

18. Philippe Wolff and Jean Dieuzaide, *Voix et images de Toulouse* (Toulouse: Privat, 1962); Prefect to Mayor, 2 June 1824, I[1], 746, A.M.M.; Prefect to Mayor, 23 June 1826, I[1]749, A.M.M.; Mayor to Prefect, 2 January 1832, I[1]750, A.M.M.

19. Marseille. 17 December 1846; Col. Duhamel, "De la mendicité," Lyon 1 August 1854; *Dépêche de Toulouse*, 5 January 1897; Smith, "Public Assistance."

20. Ordonnance 10 December 1831, copy in 1Q 2, A.M.T.; Toulouse. 1807 budget report, F[6]II, Haute-Garonne, 13, A.N.; "Observations du maire de Toulouse," 1806, F[6]II, Haute-Garonne, 13, A.N.; Mayor to Police Commissioner, 26 September 1828, 12 December 1829, I[1]749; Mayor of Marseille to Mayor of Bordeaux, Undated [1829?], copy in I[1]179, A.M.M.; on Bordeaux, F.M. Naville, *De la charité légale, de ses effets, de ses causes, et spécialement des maisons de travail,* 2 (Paris: Dufart, 1836), 22, 27-28.

21. Ordonnance 6 June 1818, Arrêté, 24 September 1834, 2D 17, A.M.T.; "Nombre de mendiants existants dans la commune de Marseille," 1808. I[1]744, A.M.M.; "Etat des mendiants domiciliés dans la ville de Marseille," 31 December 1827, I[1]749, A.M.M; Commissaire to Mayor, 5 September 1842, 1 Q 2, A.M.T.

22. Mayor to Commissioner, 24 March 1848, 1Q2, A.M.T.; a poster dated 9 September 1844, 1 I 57, A.M.T.; Claude Chatelard, *Crime et criminalité dans l'arrondissement de Saint-Etienne au xixème siècle* (Saint-Etienne: Centre d'études foréziennes, 1981), 111, 115; Jean-Paul Courbon, "Délinquence et population mouvante à Toulouse au milieu du xixe siècle," *Annales du midi,* 86 (October-December 1974), 453; William H. Sewell, Jr., *Structure and Mobility—The Men and Women of Marseille, 1820-1870* (New York: Cambridge University Press, 1985), 214.

23. Marseille. 8 February 1865, 10 May 1867; Bordeaux. 5 August 1872; Toulouse. 23 February 1872; Smith, "Public Assistance," 23; *Dépêche de Toulouse*, 20 August 1903.

24. Colette Bec, *Assistance république-le recherche d'un nouveau contrat social sous la IIIe république* (Paris: Editions ouvrières, 1994), 56.

25. For the origins of the *dépôts*, see Schwartz, *Policing the Poor.*

26. Jones, *Charity*, 134, 240; Flavie Leniaud-Dallard, "L'assistance sous le consulat et l'empire (an VIII à 1815)," *Colloque sur l'histoire de la sécurité sociale—Actes du 107e congrès national des sociétés savantes (Brest, 1982)* (Paris: Association pour l'étude de l'histoire de la sécurité sociale, 1983), 109.

27. Arrêté 1 December 1810; Inspecteur et agents de police to Mayor, 15 June 1811, I^{1}745, A.M.M.; Letter Director of Dépôt, Aix, to Mayor of Marseille, 30 December 1814, I^{1}746, A.M.M.; Mindock, "Poverty and Public Assistance," 168.

28. Q. in Ewald, *L'état providence* 75; "Tableau composition et situation de la population du dépôt de mendicité des Bouches-du- Rhône ou plutôt l'Hôpital général de ce département au 23 mars 1816," I^{1}747, A.M.M.; Association française pour l'avancement des sciences, *Lyon 1906*, 1 (Lyon: A. Rey & Cie., 1906), 865; Baron D'Haussez, "Rapport à l'assemblée générale de la société pour l'extinction de la mendicité," (Bordeaux: Lanefranque, 1828), 10; David Higgs, "Le dépôt de mendicité de Toulouse (1811-1818)," *Annales du midi*, 86 (October-December 1974), 403-17; Martin-Doisy, *Dictionnaire d'économie charitable ou exposé historique, théorique et pratique* (Paris: Migne 1855), 1293; Louis Mathurine Moreau-Christophe, *Du problème de la misère*, 3 (Paris: Guillaumin, 1851) 434-35.

29. E. Durieu and Germain Roche, *Répertoire de l'administration de la comptabilité des établissements de bienfaisance*, 2 (Paris: Mémorial des précepteurs, 1842) 419; Q. in Paul Masson, *Les Bouches-du-Rhône. Encyclopédie départementale*, 10 (Marseille: Archives départementales des Bouches-du-Rhône, 1923), 386; Léopold Ménard,"Etude statistique sur la mendicité," *Revue de Marseille* 7 (1861), 464; D'Haussez, "Rapport," 7; Higgs, "Le dépôt," 403-17; Mindock, "Poverty and Public Assistance," 168.

30. Léopold Ménard, "Des effets de la répression de la mendicité," *Répertoire des travaux de la société de statistique de Marseille*, 18 (1855), 65; Marseille. 10 May 1867; Jacqueline Félician, "L'action sociale à Marseille vers 1900," *Colloque sur l'histoire de la sécurité sociale—Actes du 106e congrès national des sociétés savantes* (Perpignan, 1981) (Paris: Association pour l'étude de l'histoire de la sécurité sociale, 1982), 298.

31. "Note et statistique sur le dépôt de mendicité, [undated, 1847?]," 1 Q 2, A.M.T.; Letter from Commission member pour l'extinction de la mendicité to Mayor, 25 August 1847, 1 Q 2, A.M.T.; Martin and Fauroux, "L'assistance à Toulouse," Association française pour l'avancement des sciences, *Documents sur Toulouse* (Toulouse: E. Privat, 1887), 53.

32. Bordeaux. 19 November 1833; d'Haussez, "Rapport," 8; Bordeaux, *Aperçu historique*, 3 (Paris: Hachette, 1892), 446-47.

33. Huré, jeune, *Revue et critique sur l'hôtel Dieu, la Charité , l'Antiquaille* (Lyon: Ayne, 1829), 196; Lyon. 12 August 1859; Anon., *Lyon, 1906-1926 [50e congres de l'association francaise pour l'avancement des sciences]*, 1 (Paris: Masson, 1926), 865.

34. Toulouse. 2 March 1841; D'Haussez, "Rapport," 7; Prefect to Mayor, q. in Marseille. 26 July 1883; Q. in Smith, "Politics of Public Assistance," 308.

35. Moreau-Christophe, *Du problème de la misère*, 3: 434-35; D'Haussez, "Rapport," 2; Bordeaux. 19 November 1833; Naville, *De la charité* 2: 22, 27-28.

36. Jean Imbert, ed., *Histoire des hopitaux en France* (Toulouse: Privat, 1982), 9; such a division was recognized by the minister of interior in a circular of 1840, q. in Fleury Ravarin, *De l'assistance communale en France* (Paris: E. Larose, 1885), 37; Olivier Faure, "L'hôpital et la médicalisation au début du xixè siécle: l'exemple lyonnais (1800-1830), *Annales de Brest*, 86 (1979), 277-90.

37. Olivier Faure, *Genèse de l'hôpital moderne. Les hospices civils de Lyon de 1802 à 1845* (Lyon: Presses universitaires de Lyon, 1982), 175.

38. Maurice Garden, "Le patrimoine immobilier des hospices civils de Lyon (1800-1914)," *Cahiers d'histoire,* 29 (1984), 119-34.

39. Jean-Pierre Gutton, *La société et les pauvres en Europe, XVIe-XVIIIe siècle* (Paris: Presses universitaires de France, 1974), 295-303; Schwartz, *Policing the Poor,* ch.3.

40. Martin-Doisy, *Dictionnaire,* vol. 4: 1400; Faure, "La médicalisation," 789; Dr. W. Manès, *Notice sur l'Hopital Saint-André* (Bordeaux: Gounouilhou, 1865), 5; Imbert, *Histoire des hôpitaux,* 342.

41. Marseille. 9 November 1838; De Polinière, *Considérations sur la salubrité de l'Hôtel Dieu et de l'Hospice la Charité à Lyon* (Lyon: Louis Perrin, 1853), 120, 123; A. Bouchet, "La fin d'un grand hopital lyonnais: La Charité," *Conférences d'histoire de la médecine, cycle 1981-1982,* 123; Faure, "La médicalisation," 789.

42. Bordeaux. 6 July 1835; Gellis, "Rapport relatif au projet de création d'un hospice général sur le domaine Pellegrin," (Bordeaux: Ragot, 1864); *La Gironde,* 31 October 1877; Dr. Charles Levieux, *Etudes sur l'assistance hospitalière dans la ville de Bordeaux* (Bordeaux: Ragot, 1882), 90, 104-105, 114, 143.

43. Levieux, *Etudes,* 233; Toulouse. 7 February 1859; Dr. E. Solles, *L'emprunt municipal et l'assistance hospitalière à Bordeaux en 1890* (Bordeaux: G. Gounouilhou, 1890), 18-19; Dr. Gérard Marchant, *Rapport presenté à la commission administrative. Hospices civils de Toulouse* (Toulouse: J.M. Douladoure, 1846), 5; Toulouse. 30 December 1872; Timothy B. Smith, "The Politics of Public Assistance," 69-72.

44. Association française pour l'avancement des sciences, *Saint-Etienne,* 3: 148; Pralong, *La charité,* 72-78.

45. J. Charles-Roux, *Vingt ans de vie politique* (Paris: Guillaumin, 1892), 3; Charles Lassère, "Depuis longtemps oublié, . . . l'hôpital de la manufacture et des enfants trouvés de Bordeaux, (1658-1881)," *Bordeaux médical* (1968), 82; Polinière, *Considérations sur la salubrité de l'Hôtel Dieu et de l'Hospice la Charité à Lyon* (Lyon: Louis Perrin, 1853), 139; Smith, "Politics of Public Assistance," 371.

46. Henri Napias, "Budgets municipaux et budgets hospitaliers," *Revue générale d'administration* (1896), 272-73; Martin and Fauroux, "L'assistance à Toulouse," Association française pour l'avancement des sciences, *Documents sur Toulouse,* 2: 41.

47. Ministère de l'intérieur. Direction de l'assistance. *Statistique des dépenses publiques d'assistance . . . 1885.*

48. Michel Foucault, *Madness and Civilization: A History of Insanity in the Age of Reason,* Transl. Richard Howard, (New York: Mentor Books, 1967), 54-61; idem., *Discipline and Punish: The Birth of the Prison* (New York: Random House, 1979).

49. Forrest, *The French Revolution and the Poor,* 75-98; Duprat, *"Pour l'amour de l'humanité,"* vol 1, 362-63.

50. Frances Gouda, "Poverty, Society, and Public Assistance in the Netherlands and France, 1815-1855" (Unpublished, Dissertation, University of Washington, 1980),

112; Dr. Paul Rougier, "L'assistance à domicile," *Compte rendu de la société d'économie politique et d'économie sociale de Lyon* (1881), 284.

51. Bordeaux. 9 December 1884.

52. Thomas R. Christofferson, "Urbanization and Political Change: The Political Transformation of Marseille under the Second Republic," *Historian*, 36 (February 1974), 190; the historian of Marseille, Busquet, describes 40,000 as indigent, but 30,000-or a third the population—as receiving aid. Raoul Busquet, *Histoire de Marseille* (Paris: Laffont, 1945), 378; Alfred de Cilleuls, *Histoire de l'administration Parisienne au xix siècle*, 1 (Paris: Champion, 1900), 321; Bordeaux. 13 June 1820; Bureau central de charité. Circular, 11 December 1827, 26Q1, AMM; Desgraves and Dupeux, *Bordeaux au xixe siècle*, 67; Joelle Dusseau, "L'indigence Bordelaise et les bureaux de bienfaisance," (Unpublished T.E.R., University of Bordeaux, 1968), 19, 111; André Steyert, *Nouvelle histoire de Lyon*, 4 (Montbrison: Louis Pelardy, 1939), 72-73.

53. Roger Price, "Poor Relief and Social Crisis. Mid-Nineteenth-Century France, *European Studies Review*, 13, 4 (October 1983), 433; David Higgs, "Politics and Charity at Toulouse, 1750-1850," J.F. Bosher, ed. *French Government and Society, 1500-1850* (London: Athlone Press, 1973), 206; Paul Bucquet, *Enquête sur les bureaux de bienfaisance* (Paris: Imprimerie nationale, 1874), 20; Dusseau, "L'indigence."

54. Gouda, "Poverty, Society, and Public Assistance," 39-40; Bec, *Assistance république*, 50. In 1888, of roughly 36,000 communes in the country, 19,111 had bureaux of some sort: Henri Monod, "L'assistance publique en France en 1889," (Paris: Imprimerie nouvelle, 1889), 25.

55. Fleury Ravarin, *De l'assistance communale*, 233; John Weiss, "Origins of the French Welfare State: Poor Relief in the Third Republic, 1871-1914," *French Historical Studies* (Fall 1984), 50; Compte moral de l'exercice de 1889. (Lyon: Association typographique, 1890); F[20] 282/2 and 4, A.N.; Bordeaux, *Aperçu historique*, 3 (Paris: Hachette, 1892), 404; Anatole Weber, *L'assistance aux miséraux en France*, 1 (Paris: Marcel Rivière, 1914) 106.

56. F[20]282/2, A.N.; Bucquet, *Enquête*, 120, 132, 282, 410; Weiss, "Origins," 50.

57. Smith, "Public Assistance," 24-25.

58. Weiss, "Origins," 72-73; Ville de Lyon. Bureau de bienfaisance. *Année 1893* (Lyon: Delmas, 1894); Martin and Fauroux, "L'assistance à Toulouse," Association française pour l'avancement des sciences, *Documents sur Toulouse*, 43; Patrick Garcia, "De la charité à la dignité—Aspects des relations entre les pauvres, le bureau de bienfaisance et le pouvoir municipal à Toulouse à la fin du xixe siècle" (Toulouse: Maitrise, Histoire, 1982), 20; Claude Chatelard, *Crime et criminalité dans l'arrondissement de Saint-Etienne* (Saint-Etienne: Centre d'études foréziennes, 1981), 54, 207; Emile Camau, *Marseille au xxe siècle* (Paris: Guillaumin, 1900), 171. Smith sees the introduction of heavier industry as making unnecessary reservoirs of labor and hence leading to a decline in concern for the poor. He chose to base his argument on the decreasing number of people on welfare; that criteria does not hold as an explanatory variable, for as many of our cities became more industrial, they put more people on the dole.

59. Chatelard, *Crime*, 149; Toulouse. 14 December 1867, 3 April 1868; Ministère de l'intérieur. Direction de l'assistance. *Statistique des dépenses publiques d'assistance . . . 1885*; Toulouse. 17 November 1892; Pradelle, q. in Garcia, "De la charité," 131; Henri Lerner, *La Dépêche de Toulouse—Journal de la démocratie* 1 (Toulouse: Université de Toulouse, 1978), 416; Félician, "Action sociale (Thesis)," 1: 55; Saint-Girons, "Le paupérisme," *Réforme sociale*, 4 (1882) 165; Henri Monod, "L'oeuvre assistance de la Troisième république," *Revue philanthropique*, 26 (1909-1910) 276; for a similar view in a legal treatise, Paul Blanc, *La vie mendiante-vagabondage* (Avalon: Paul Grand, 1911), 73.

60. This evidence contradicts the conclusions in Joan Scott, "Mayors versus Police Chiefs: Socialist Municipalities Confront the French State," John Merriman, ed., *French Cities in the Nineteenth Century* (New York: Holmes and Meier, 1981). Scott also points out that Socialists attempted to change welfare from a form of charity to a worker's right. The provision of services was not an act of beneficence, but an obligation to the victims of an exploitive economic system. Such views are not strongly represented in our municipalities, even when they were under Socialist control: Scott, "Mayors versus Police Chiefs," 241.

61. Price, "Poor Relief," 423-54; Saint-Girons," Le paupérisme," 165; *Dépêche de Toulouse*, 2 September 1902.

62. Brunot Théret, "Les dépenses d'enseignement et d'assistance en France au xixe siècle: une réevaluation de la rupture républicaine," *Annales, économies, sociétés, civilisations*, no. 6 (November-December 1991), 1406.

63. Emile Camau, *Les institutions de bienfaisance, de charité et de prévoyance à Marseille* (Marseille: Assistance par le travail, n.d. [1891?]), xii-xiv; Association française pour l'avancement des sciences, *Saint-Etienne*, 3 (Saint-Etienne: Théolier, 1897), 172; Moreau-Christophe, *Du problème de la misère*, 3: 464-65; Maurice Beaufreton, *Assistance publique et charité privée* (Paris: E. Giard, 1911), x; Cathérine Pélissier, "Les sociabilités patriciennes à Lyon du milieu du dix-neuvième siècle à 1914," (Doctorat de l'université, Lyon II, 1993), 1088; Association pour l'avancement des sciences, *Lyon et le région lyonnaise en 1906*, 1: 876; Eliane Richard, "Bienfaisance et charité à Marseille entre 1850 et 1880," *Colloque sur l'histoire de la sécurité sociale—Actes du 106e congrès des sociétés savantes* (Paris: Association pour l'étude de l'histoire de la sécurité sociale, 1982), 288, 292; Smith, "The Politics of Public Assistance," 20.

64. Administrator of Hospice to Mayor, 27 November 1810; Préfet to Mayor, 2 April 1812, 1Q 2, A.M.T.; q. in Georges Ribe, *L'opinion publique et la vie politique à Lyon lors des premières années de la seconde restauration* (Paris: Sirey, 1957), 59; Toulouse. 12 March 1844; Jean Pralong and Yves Delomier, *La charité-de l'hospice à l'hôpital gériatrique* (Saint-Etienne: Le Hénaff, 1983), 69; Toulouse. 16 November 1853, 14 December 1867, 3 April 1868.

65. Saint-Etienne. 5 May 1857, 19 December 1868.

66. Ville de Lyon, "Secours aux ouvriers sans travail. Compte rendu des opérations faites par la commission supérieure et par les comités," (Lyon: 1877); Letter to Mayor, 24 September 1884, Ouvriers sans travail, 1877-1889, Q2, A.M.L.

67. Bordeaux. 20 June 1816, 13 June 1820; P. Truchon, "La vie ouvrière sous la restauration," *Revue d'histoire de Lyon*, 11 (1912), 208-209; Saint-Etienne. 18 October 1830; Bordeaux. 20, 26, 28 October 1830; Bordeaux. 27 January 1832.

68. Paul Ronin, *Saint-Etienne à ciel ouvert* (Saint-Etienne: Paul Ronin, 1959), 95; "Extinction de la mendicité," Report of 1843 commission, 1Q2, A.M.T.

69. Charles, *La révolution*, 125; François Dutacq, *Histoire politique de Lyon pendant la révolution de 1848* (Paris: Edouard Cornely, 1910), 208-209; Lyon. 14, 17 July 1848, 14 November 1848; Christofferson, "The Revolution of 1848," 75, 149; Marseille. 3 June 1848; Norbert Rouland, *Le conseil municipal Marseillais et sa politique de la II à la IIIe république (1848-1875)* (Aix-en-Provence: Edisud, 1974), 98-99; Mary Lynn McDougall, "After the Insurrections: The Workers' Movement in Lyon, 1834-1852," (Ph.D. Thesis, Columbia University, 1974), 111, 277; Lyon. 14 November 1848; Ronin, *Saint-Etienne*, 95.

70. Etienne Ginestous, *La Rousselle* (Bordeaux: Biere, 1942), 8; Adjoint mayor to Mayor, 19 March 1879, 25 O 1, A.M.B.; "Rapport du directeur des travaux publics, " 31 January 1910, Ingénieur 293, A.M.T.

71. Thierry Halay, *Le mont-de piété des origines à nos jours* (Paris: Harmattan, 1994), ch. 1.

72. Arrêté of prefect, 15 fructidor, Year IX; Toulouse. 22 November 1817; Q. in Bordeaux, *Aperçu*, 3: 507.

73. Toulouse. 10 October 1866.

74. Bordeaux, *Aperçu*, 3: 495; Marseille. 3 September 1840; Moreau-Christophe, *Du problème*, 3: 447; Adolphe De Wattevile, "De Monts-de piété," *Annales de la Charité* (1845), 237; city budgets.

75. De Watteville, "Des Monts-de-Piété," 226; Balzac, q. in Halay, *Le mont-de-piété*, 86.

76. F^{20}282/54, A.N.; *Revue municipale*, 28 July 1900.

77. Jean-Marie Benaben, "L'action sociale de la municipalité Bordelaise à travers les budgets de 1850 et 1880," *Actes du 105e congrès national des sociétés savantes, Caen 1980* (Paris: Association pour l'étude de la sécurité sociale, 1981), 17; Toulouse. 19 December 1879, 10 February 1881.

78. Calculations based on Camau, *Marseille*, 173-74; Mont de Piété de Toulouse, *Compte rendu des opérations, execice 1901* (Toulouse: Adolphe Trinchant, 1901); Mont de Piété de Bordeaux, *Compte rendu statistique des opérations* (Bordeaux: F. Pech, 1912); Félician-Le Corre, "Action sociale," 1, 56.

79. J. Soviche, "De l'établissement d'un mont de piété à Saint-Etienne," *Bulletin de la société d'industrie et d'agriculture de Saint-Etienne* (28 August 1850), 20; Bordeaux. 22 January 1849; Ange Blaize, *De monts-de piété et de banque de prêt sur gage*, 1 (Paris: Pagnerre, 1856), 495; Petition to Mayor, 25 November 1896, 2 Q52, A.M.S.E.

80. Halay, *Le mont-de-piété*, 132-136.

81. Private groups in Lyon did argue in terms of pronatalism and patriotism: Smith, "The Politics of Public Assistance," 300, 347-48. The issue of welfare, pronatalism,

and a new policy empowering women is mentioned among others in: Ann F. La Berge, *Mission and Method—The Early Nineteenth Century French Public Health Movement* (New York: Cambridge University Press, 1992), 317, 326; Rachel Fuchs, *Poor and Pregnant in Paris: Strategies for Survival in the Nineteenth Century* (New Brunswick, NJ: Rutgers University Press, 1992); Nord, "The Welfare State in France," 831; Bec, *Assistance*, 215-18; Mary Lynn Stewart, *Women, Work, and the French State: Labour Protection and Social Patriarchy, 1879-1919* (Kingston: McGill-Queen's University Press, 1989); Elinor A. Accampo, Rachel G. Fuchs, and Mary Lynn Stewart, eds. *Gender and the Politics of Social Reform in France, 1870-1914* (Baltimore, MD: Johns Hopkins University Press, 1995).

82. Pierre Rosanvallon, *L'état en France de 1789 à nos jours* (Paris: Plon, 1990), 148.

83. Saint-Etienne. 13 February 1911; Jacques Cremadeills, "La politique financière, économique et sociale de la municipalité Toulousaine de 1910 à 1920," (Unpublished D.E.S., University of Toulouse, 1967), 163; Raphael Milliès-Lacroix, "le budget national et l'assistance publique," *Revue philantropique*, 29 (1911), 129-38; Weiss, "Origins," 72-73.

CHAPTER 9

1. Jean-Claude Perrot, *Genèse d'une ville moderne—Caen au xviiième siècle*, 1 (Paris: Mouton, 1975), 12-13; Jean-Louis Harouel, "Les fonctions de l'alignement dans l'organisme urbain," *Dix-huitième siecle*, 9 (1977), 13; Richard Etlin, "L'air dans l'urbanisme des lumières," *Dix huitième siècle*, 9 (1977), 123-34.

2. J. P. Poussou, "Le développement urbain de Bordeaux au XVIIIe siècle," P. Butel and L.M. Cullen, eds. *Cities and Merchants, French and Irish Perspectives on Urban Development, 1500-1900* (Dublin: Trinity University, 1986), 75-95; Xavier Emmanuelli, *Un mythe de l'absolutisme bourbonnier: L'intendance, du milieu du xviième siècle à la fin du xviiie siècle* (Aix-en-Provence: Université de Provence, 1981), 139-43; Roger Chartier, *Histoire de la France urbaine*, 3 (Paris: Seuil, 1981) 480-81.

3. Bernard Lepetit, "Pouvoir municipal et urbanisme," Gustav Livet et Bernard Vogler, eds. *Pouvoir, ville et société en Europe, 1650-1750* (Paris: Ophrys, 1983), 40; idem. "Armatures urbaines et organisation de l'espace dans la France préindustrielle" (University of Paris, Dr. d'état, 1987)," 186; Paul Mesple, "L'Urbanisme à Toulouse au xviie siècle," *Auta*, n.s. no. 241 (August 1954), 82-86; M. Lespinasse, "Les Origines de la Place Wilson," *Mémoires de l'académie des sciences, inscriptions, et belles lettres* (1932), 235-73.

4. A. Kleinclausz, *Lyon des origines à nos jours* (Lyon: Pierre Masson, 1925), 64, 243.

5. Lyon. 4 July 1806; "Mémoire de l'ingénieur de la voierie," 27 January 1806, 11 0 3, A.M.B.; A. Martourey, "Formation et gestion d'une agglomération industrielle au xixème siècle, Saint-Etienne de 1815 à 1870," (Unpublished Doctorat d'état, Université of Lyon, II, 1984), 601.

6. Lyon. 14 September 1808; 6 O 2, A.M.M.; Institut français d'architecture, *Toulouse, 1810-1860* (Brussels: Mardaga, 1985), 71; Jacky Meaudre, Les débuts de l'aménagement urbain de Saint-Etienne (1820-1872), *Etudes foréziennes*, 4 (1971), 81.

7. Roncayolo paper at Society for French Historical Studies, May 5, 1989 and commentary by John Merriman.

8. L. Desgraves and G. Dupeux, *Bordeaux au xixe siècle* (Bordeaux: Fédération historique du sud-ouest, 1969), 95; Institut français d'architecture, *Toulouse* 152-57; Stendhal, entry of 28 March 1838, *Dans le midi—de Bordeaux à Marseille* (Paris: Encre, 1984), 71; M. Descreux, *Notices biographiques stéphanoises* (Saint-Etienne: Constantine, 1868), 304-306; Paul Ronin, *Saint-Etienne à ciel ouvert* (Saint-Etienne: Paul Ronin, 1959), 86.

9. R. Chartier, et al., *Histoire de la France urbaine*, 3: 574.

10. Lyon. 26 March 1846, 23 April 1846, 2 August 1836.

11. Jal, "Lyon par notre compatriote M. Jal, Extraits de Paris à Naples," *Revue du Lyonnais*, III (1836), 19; Jules Michelet, *Tableau de la France*, Lucien Refort ed. (Paris: Société des Belles Lettres, 1934), 64.

12. Ambroise Gravejat, *La rente, le profit et la ville—analyse de la constitution de la ville romaine antique et de la ville de Lyon du 6e au 19e siècle* (Paris: Anthropos, 1980), 201.

13. Joseph Bard, "Tableau de Lyon," *Revue du Lyonnais*, n.s. I (1850), 167.

14. Toulouse. 20 March 1837, 6 May 1839, 5 May 1846; Institut français d'architecture, *Toulouse*, 61-62.

15. Stendhal, entry of 1 June 1837, *Mémoires d'un touriste*, 1 (Paris: Calmann-Lévy, 1854), 151; Dumont-Reuwer, "De Saint-Etienne et ses habitants," *Revue du lyonnais* (1840), 193-215, q. in André Vant, *Imagerie et urbanisation-recherches sur l'exemple stephanois* (Saint-Etienne: Centre d'études Foréziennes, 1981), 158-59; Théodore Ogier, *La France par les cantons et par communes—le département de la Loire-Lyon* (1849), II:10. q. in Jacky Meaudre, "La Poussée urbaine à Saint-Etienne (1815-1872)," (Unpublished Diplôme d'études supérieures, University of Lyon, 1967), 118; Martourey, "Formation et gestions," 670.

16. Paul Courteault, "Le centenaire du Port de Bordeaux," *Actes de l'académie nationale des sciences, belles lettres et arts de Bordeaux*, 5 (1922), 77-101; Saint-Etienne. 12 January 1819, 1 August 1839.

17. Ted Margadant, *Urban Rivalries in the French Revolution* (Princeton: Princeton University Press, 1992), 279; Meaudre, "Les débuts," 79; Martourey, "Formation et gestion," 623; Etienne Fournial, *et al. Saint-Etienne—Histoire de la ville et de ses habitants* (Paris: Horvath, 1976), 242.

18. Dr. Fonteret, *Hygiène des cimetières* (Lyon: Aimé Vingtrinier, 1874), 3; Régis Bertrand, "Les Marseillais et leurs tombeaux: cimetières et architecture funéraire à Marseille," *Bulletin de la société d'histoire moderne*, 16th ser, 36, 4 (1987), 16; Michel Vovelle and Régis Bertrand, *La ville des morts* (Paris: CNRS, 1983), 24.

19. Théophile Lagrange, *Port de Marseille* (Paris: Garnier frères, 1842); also q. in Masson, ed. *Bouches-du-Rhône*, 9: 439; Joseph Bousquet, *Améliorations à faire a la ville de Toulouse* (Toulouse: Vve. Dieulafory, 1839), ii; Bordeaux. 22 December 1837.

20. Jacques Schnetzler, "Saint-Etienne et ses problèmes urbains," *Etudes foréziennes*, 2, *La vie urbaine dans le département de la Loire et ses abords*, 2nd. ed. (Saint-Etienne, 1972), 252; Marcel Roncayolo, "Croissance et division sociale de l'espace urbain. Essai sur la genèse des structures urbaines de Marseille." Unpublished Dr. d'état, University of Paris, 1981. vol. 2.

21. Yves Janvier, "L'industrie des batiments à Marseille de 1815 a 1851," (Diplôme d'études supérieures, Aix-en-Provence: 1964), 43-44; Marseille. 16 November 1846, 19 April 1847; Institut français d'architecture, *Toulouse*, 71.

22. On developments in the capital, see François Loyer, *Paris au xixe siècle—l'immeuble et la rue* (Paris: Hazan, 1987), 106.

23. Report of Mayor to council on Budget, Year 13, 1217, A.M.T.; Lyon. 27 January 1806.

24. "Rapport à M. le Maire sur le compte administratif, 1820," F^6 II, Rhône 20, A.N.; A. Hodieu, *Essais de nomenclatures lyonnaises municipales et autres de 1800 à 1865* (Lyon: Thibaudier and Boin, 1866), 13.

25. Poster, 12 February 1825, copy in 32 M1, A.M.M.

26. Bordeaux. 14 June 1831, 12 November 1832.

27. Alexis Bailleux de Marisy, *Transformation des grandes villes de France* (Paris: Hachette, 1867), 119; Lyon. 1, 6 April 1831; Kleinclausz, *Lyon des origines*, 180-85.

28. Toulouse. 10 August 1837, 15 December 1841; 21 October 1848, 9 August 1849; 5 May 1846.

29. Circular of 12 August 1840.

30. "Rapport de la commission spéciale du canal de Provence au conseil municipal de la ville de Marseille," (Marseille: Freissat ainé et Demonchy, 1834), 33-34; Max Consolat,"Rapport 1840" 19-20; idem, "Rapport sur la situation financière de la ville de Marseille presenté au conseil municipal le 10 juillet 1843," (Marseille: Hoirs Feissat ainé et Demonchy, 1843), 10.

31. Prefect to Minister of interior 25 March 1821, F^{6}II Rhône 20, A.N.; Lyon. 29 September 1826; J.B. Dupuch, *Quelques observations* (1828), 103; Bordeaux. 27 December 1842, 3 April 1843; 24 August 1842.

32. Marseille. 12 February 1857; S. Berteaut, "Un vote Marseillais," *Revue de Marseille*, 5 (1859), 61; Marius Chaumelin, *Marseille en 1962* (Marseille: Camoin frères, 1862), 7; "Examen de l'opinion de M. Peyret-Lallier sur l'emprunt proposé pour la ville de Saint-Etienne," (Lyon: 1838), 30-32; Marseille. 5 January 1854.

33. Marseille. 24 August 1865; Régis Bertrand, "Les Marseillais et leurs tombeaux: cimetières et architecture funéraire à Marseille," *Bulletin de la société d'histoire moderne*, 16th ser, no. 36 (1987), no. 4 , 16; Vovelle and Bertrand, *La ville des morts*, 68;

Martin, *Le cimetière Saint-Pierre, historique, guide et plan* (Marseille: Barlatier, 1898), 10-13; Mémoire de l'ingénieur en chef de la ville, "Aggrandissement du cimetière de Loyasse," (Lyon: Bellon, 1872), 6; Madeleine Lasserre,"La création du cimetière de Terre-Cabade à Toulouse au xixe siècle," *Annales du midi*, 106 (Jan.-March 1994), 79-96.

34. Bordeaux. 19 November 1860; Edmond About, *Rome contemporaine* (1860), q. in Félix Tavernier, *Marseille et la Provence, 1789-1871* (Marseille: Centre national de documentation pédagogique, 1988), 99; "Examen de l'opinion de M. Peyret-Lallier sur l'emprunt proposé pour la ville de Saint-Etienne," (Lyon, 1838), 30-32; Lyon. 27 November 1857.

35. Saint-Etienne. 17 October, 1851; "Projet de traité pour l'exécution de divers travaux d'utilité générale, rapport de M le sénateur," 1855. Similar arguments in Dr. Rougier and Dr. Glenard, *Hygiène de Lyon—comptes rendus des travaux du conseil d'hygiène publique et de salubrité du département de Rhône* (Lyon: Aimé Vingtrinier, 1860), 278; and by Marseille publicist, S. Bertaut, "Un vote Marseillais," *Revue de Marseille*, 5 (1859), 60.

36. A. Charles, "Mouvement démographique de la Gironde," *Annales du midi*, 69 (1957), 140-41; A. Hodieu, *Essais de nomenclatures lyonnaises municipales et autres de 1800 à 1865* (Lyon: Thibaudier and Boin, 1866), 13; Jean-Pierre Alline, "Le Crédit foncier de France, 1852-1920—De l'affaire à l'institution." (Unpublished Thèse Universitaire de Droit, 1978), 134.

37. Jean-Pierre Gaudin, *L'avenir en plan—technique et politique dans la prévision urbaine, 1900-1930* (Paris: Champ Vallon, 1985), 37-38.

38. Marseille. 12 February 1857; M. Cazes, fils, propriétaire, "De la rue impériale proposée au conseil municipal de Toulouse," (Toulouse: 1857), 2; Ville de Bordeaux, *Compte rendu de la délégation du conseil municipal* (January-March 1853), 22; Bordeaux. 14 March 1853; Bordeaux. 21 December 1857; Pierre Honoré Thomas, *Lyon en 1860* (Lyon: Aimé Vingtrinier, 1860), 47.

39. C. de Saulnier "A propos des intérêts de Bordeaux," (Bordeaux: Durand, 1857), 479; Bordeaux. 19 November 1860; Dr. T. Desmartis, *Lettre à M. le maire* (Bordeaux: Vve. Justin Dupuy, 1861), 2; Mayor's report, 1859, copy in 1 L 17, A.M.T.; Toulouse. 19 November 1864, 6 March 1860.

40. Bordeaux. 14 March 1853; 1871-72 questionnaire sent to these cities, 5M58, A.D.G.; Marseille. 10 September 1858.

41. Louis Desgraves and Georges Dupeux, *Bordeaux au 19e siècle* (Bordeaux: Fédération historique du sud-ouest, 1969), 174; Bordeaux. 14 March 1853; A. Charles, "Mouvement demographique de la Gironde," 143-44.

42. Maryvonne Deler, "Le Jardin public de Bordeaux (xviii-xixe siècles)," (Unpublished DES, Université de Bordeaux, 1960).

43. Desgraves and Dupeux, *Bordeaux*, 274.

44. Françoise Bayard and Pierre Cayez, *Histoire de Lyon*, 2 (Le Coteau: Horvath, 1990), 291-92; Charlene Marie Leonard, *Lyon Transformed. Public Works of the Second Empire, 1853-1864* (Berkeley: University of California Press, 1961), 14.

45. Military Governor Castelanne, q. in Pierre Lavedan, *Les villes françaises* (Paris: Vincent et Fréal, 1960), 209; Gravejat, *La rente*, 261; Dutacq, "La politique," 41.

46. Lyon. 7 January 1853; Q. in Gravejat, *La rente*, 259-61; Marisy, *Transformation*, 110-11.

47. Germaine Vieux, "Les premières années du Parc de la Tête d'or," *Rive gauche*, no. 68 (March 1979), 5.

48. Leonard, *Lyon Transformed*, 118.

49. James K. Pringle, "Augustin Fabre's Imperial Road: The Urban Geography of Citizenship in the Second Empire," *History of European Ideas*, 7, 4 (1986), 389-400.

50. Louis Girard,*La politique des travaux publics du second empire* (Paris: A. Colin, 1952).

51. Marcel Roncayolo, *L'imaginaire de Marseille, Port, ville, pôle* (Marseille: Chambre de commerce et d'industrie de Marseille, 1990), 183.

52. Marisy, *Transformations des grandes villes*, 158-59; H.A. Taine, *Journeys through France* (New York: Henry Holt, 1897), 174.

53. Toulouse. 26 January 1856; Mayor's report, 1859, copy in 1 L 17, A.M.T.

54. Mayor's report, 1859, 1 L 17, A.M.T.; Toulouse. 27 September 1866.

55. J. Meyer, "Quelques vues sur l'histoire des villes à l'époque moderne," *Annales, économies, sociétés, civilisations*, 29 (1974), 1559-1564, gives complete credit to the central government for the rebuilding of nineteenth-century French cities.

56. Jean Coppolani, "Une opération d'urbanisme à Toulouse-les rues nouvelles de la fin du xixème siècle," *Mémoires de l'académie des sciences, inscriptions et belles lettres de Toulouse*, 15 th. series. Vol. VII (1976), 209-17; Michael Darin, "Les grandes percées urbaines du xixe siècle: quatre villes de province," *Annales, économies, sociétés, civilisations*, 43, 2 (March-April 1988), 477-505.

57. While the prefect, Thuillier, helped in facilitating these accomplishments, the most recent study of the municipality credits it with providing the main impetus for these transformations. Martourey, "Formation et gestion," 940-43.

58. Meaudre, "La poussée urbaine," 134; Maxime Perrin, *Saint-Etienne et sa région économique—un type de la vie industrielle en France* (Tours: Arrault, 1937), 415.

59. Martourey, "Formation et gestion," 862-87.

60. Meaudre, "Les débuts," 81.

61. Martourey, "Formation et gestion," 1117-21.

62. Louis Gras, *Histoire du commerce local de Saint-Etienne et des industries qui se rattachent dans la région stéphanoise et forézienne* (Saint-Etienne: J. Thomas, 1910), 618.

63. *Le Temps*, 30 July 1867.

64. *Le Temps*, 5 October 1865.

65. Toulouse. 23 December 1869.

66. Anon., "Triomphe de l'opposition de Marseille," (Marseille: 1865), 41.

67. "Rapport. Arrondissement de Bordeaux. 1er trimestre," 14 January 1862, 1M369, A.D.G.

68. M. J. L. Hénon, "Discours, 12 April, 1869," (Paris: L. Poupart-Davyl, 1869); Marseille. 12 August 1869.

69. Toulouse. 11 February 1870, 22 March 1870; Marseille. 22 April 1871.

70. Anon., "Triomphe de l'opposition," (1865).; Toulouse. 11 February 1870, 22 March 1870; Hénon, "Discours, 12 April, 1869."

71. Marseille. 15 June 1878; Baret's remarks were actually not about public works, but rather public festivals. Also Conseil municipal de la ville de Lyon, "Rapport du budget de 1873," (bound in Lyon, Procès verbaux, January-April, 1873); *Le Temps*, 26 October 1879; "Elections municipales lyonnaises. La victoire de la bourgeoisie-ses causes," (Lyon: Beau jeune, 1881); Toulouse. 19 February 1872; "A MM. les électeurs de Toulouse," (Toulouse: n.d. [early 1870s]); *Petite Gironde*, 22 December 1900.

72. "Rapport adressé au ministre de l'intérieur et des cultes sur la situation financière des communes en 1877," (Paris: Imprimerie nationale, 1881).

73. In Lyon, the yearly regular city income was in the mid-1870s ll million, and the debt payments were 5 million; in Marseille, the yearly income was 14.4 million, and the debt payments 7.8 million; Lyon, "Statistique financière de la ville de Lyon," 1900; Marseille. 11 October 1875.

74. Marie-France Brive, "La politique économique de la ville de Toulouse de 1870 à 1880." (Unpublished Diplôme d'études supérieures, University of Toulouse, 1967), 44.

75. Ournac, March 1891 statement, q. in François Cavaignac "La Politique budgétaire de la municipalité de Toulouse de 1888 à 1900," (Unpublished Maitrise, University of Toulouse, 1973), 201; *Dépêche de Toulouse*, 16 December 1898, 20 February 1900.

76. *Dépêche de Toulouse*, 8 January 1895, 10 January 1895.

77. Toulouse. 7 May 1857, 11 May 1857; *Dépêche de Toulouse*, 6 October 1892.

78. Jean Coppolani, *Connaissances de Toulouse* (Toulouse: Privat, 1974), 7.

79. Bordeaux. 17 February 1880; "Rapports," 1884-1888, 11 O 4, A.M.B.; *Petite Gironde*, 30 April 1896.

80. Desgraves & Dupeux, *Bordeaux au xixe siècle*, 397, 403-404; Dr. Charles Levieux, *Rapport sur les causes d'insalubrité de la ville de Bordeaux* (Bordeaux: Ragot, 1871), 36; Bordeaux. 21 October 1898.

81. Bordeaux. 21 October 1898; Etienne Ginestous, *L'assainissement du vieux Bordeaux*. *Les grands travaux de voirie* (Bordeaux: Bière, 1941), 18-19; J. Darriet, "A propos de la grande voie devant relier le centre de la ville à la gare du midi," (Bordeaux: G. Delmas, 1896).

82. *Le Journal de Bordeaux,* [Bonapartist] 16 April 1896; *Nouvelliste, 3 April 1897* [Royalist, Orléanist] *La France,* [Radical] 2 May 1896.

83. Q. in *Petite Gironde,* 25 November 1902.

84. Desgraves & Dupeux, *Bordeaux,* 409.

85. Debts in 1912: Bordeaux, 38 million frs; Toulouse, 32 million; Saint-Etienne, 40 million. Pierre Léris, "Les dettes comparées des villes de France," *Journal des économistes* (1912), 24.

86. Félix Rivet, *Une réalisation d'urbanisme à Lyon à la fin du xixe siècle. L'aménagement du quartier Grolée (1887-1908). [Institut des études Rhodaniennes de l'Université de Lyon, Mémoires et documents, no. 10]* (Trevoux: J. Patissier, 1955) 13-15.

87. Gogoluenhe, "Les abbatoirs de la mouche," *Rive gauche*, no. 74 (September 1980), 3-6.

88. Alain Charre, "L'organisation esthétique des villes et les projets d'urbanisme à Lyon, 1905-1914," 1 (Unpublished Thèse, Histoire de l'art, Lyon Université II, 1983), 211.

89. A. Kleinclausz, *Lyon des origines à nos jours* (Lyon: Pierre Masson, 1925), 412-14.

90. Marseille. 17 February 1901, 3 March 1901; Gaston Rambert, "Esquisse de géographie urbaine—l'agglomération Marseillaise," *Vie urbaine,* 3 (1921), 247; H.L. "La rénovation," *Marseille,* (December 1937), 28-30.

91. Marcel Roncayolo, "Marseille: plan de la ville et spéculation," *Actes du 83ᵉ congrès national des sociétés savantes, Aix–Marseille, section de géographie* (Paris: Editions du comités des travaux historiques et scientifiques, 1958), 245-263.

92. Léris, "Les dettes comparées des villes," 13.

93. Edouard Baratier, *Histoire de Marseille* (Toulouse: Privat 1987), 389-90.

94. Jean Lorcin, "Economie et comportements sociaux et politiques—La région de Saint-Etienne de la grande dépression à la seconde guerre mondiale." (Unpublished Thesis, Dr. d'état, University of Paris, 1987), 938, 942, 1533.

95. J.B. Piolet, q. in Lorcin, "Economie et comportement," 936, 1525.

96. *Guide de Saint-Etienne* (1908), q. in Lorcin, "Economie et comportement," 1524; Leguet q. in Lorcin, "Economie et comportement," 936.

97. L.J. Gras, "Les transformations de Saint-Etienne," *Les amitiés Foréziennes et vellaves,* ser II, no. 7 (June 1924), 304.

98. Léris, "Les dettes," 24; If the Socialists in Limoges favored urban renewal, it was probably because so little had been done during the Second Empire and hence the

city was not as heavily mortgaged—ambitious plans could be envisioned. John M. Merriman, *The Red City—Limoges and the French Nineteenth Century* (New York: Oxford University Press, 1985), 249.

99. Jean Gohier, "L'evolution de l'urbanisme en France," *Centre de recherche d'urbanisme* (Paris: 1965), 6.

100. Georges Risler, "Les plans d'aménagement et d'extension des villes," *Musée social. Mémoires et documents* (1912), 301-13; Kern, "Comments," *Compte rendu des travaux, association française pour le développement des travaux publics* (Paris: Ingénieurs civils, 1912), 153; André Bénard,"Les exposants—français et étrangers," *Exposition internationale des industries* (Turin, 1912) 106-7.

101. M. Bechmann, "Causerie sur les plans d'extension et d'aménagement des villes," *Techniques et sciences municipales,* 8 (February 1913), 37-41; Anthony Sutcliffe, *Towards the Planned City—Germany, Britain, the United States, France, 1780-1914* (New York: St. Martin's Press, 1981), 126-27.

102. Sutcliffe, *Towards the Planned City,* 152-53.

103. Jean-Paul Brunet, *Un demi siècle de gestion municipale à Saint-Denis la Rouge, 1890-1939* (Paris: Cujas, 1981).

CHAPTER *10*

1. Maurice Félix, *L'activité économique de la commune.* I (Paris: Sirey, 1932), 13.

2. Marseille. 21 April 1832, 25 June 1836, 6 August 1838, 27 June 1839, 11 August 1853, 28 August 1865; Bordeaux. 18 October 1881.

3. Marseille. 10 November 1841; Bordeaux. 7 February 1848; "Renseignements sur la distribution d'eau de la ville de Bordeaux," 1861, 421 O:1, A.M.B.

4. Lyon. 19 November 1846, 12 February 1846.

5. 1837 budget, F^{6}II Loire 20, A.N.; Bordeaux. 16 December 1884; Toulouse. 5 January 1905; *Revue municipale,* 16-30 June 1905; "Rapport du directeur des travaux publics," 31 January 1910, Ingénieur 293, A.M.T.

6. Bordeaux. 11 November 1878; *Petite Gironde,* 5 December 1905; Bordeaux. 8 June 1906.

7. *Peuple,* 17 October 1895.

8. Philippe Delas, "Les transports en commun dans l'agglomération Bordelaise," (Unpublished mémoire, Université de Bordeaux III, 1970), 36; *Petite Gironde,* 23 Dec 1903; Lyon. 14 March 1910; Claude Schmit, "Les transports en commun à Lyon, 1830-1914," (D.E.S., University of Lyon, 1969), 116, 129; Lyon. 28 June 1909; Peusner," Saint-Etienne de 1856 à 1914," (Maîtrise thesis, University of Lyon, n.d.)

Chapter 10: Municipalization

100; Jean Robert, *Histoire des transports dans les villes de France* (Paris: Jean Robert, 1974), 416-18.

9. Henri Carvin, "La Marseille de Mirès," *Marseille*, no. 156 (April 1990), 30; the city's experience is summarized in Marseille. 1 June 1870, 2 June 1871.

10. *Dépêche de Toulouse*, 25 November 1898; Philippe Delahaye, "Introduction" in Léon Garnier and Paul Dauvert, *Les concessions de gaz et de l'électricité* (Paris: Journal des usines à gaz, 1894), 153-59; Saint-Etienne. 27 December 1907; Alain Beltran, "Les pouvoirs publics face à une innovation," *Histoire, économie, et société*, 6 (1987), 160.

11. *Bulletin des usines électriques*,(December 1897); *Petite Gironde*, 17 February 1900; "Note pour MM les experts sur le préjudice causé à la compagnie par la concurrence de l'éclairage électrique, 1904, 457 O 2, A.M.B.; "Résumé des conditions économiques des cahiers des charges d'éclairage des principales villes de France," 1902, 445 O 1, A.M.B.; Alexandre Fernandez, "Electricité et politique locale à Bordeaux, 1887-1956," (Thèse pour le doctorat, Université de Bordeaux, II, 1994), 65-69; *Journal des usines à gaz*, 16 (20 January 1892), 30-35.

12. Lyon. 12 February 1846; "Exposé des questions en litige entre la compagnie de gaz et la ville de Bordeaux," 1884[?], 443 O 9, A.M.B.

13. E Trénit, *Questions en suspens entre la ville et la compagnie française des tramways electriques et omnibus de Bordeaux* (Bordeaux: G. Delmas, 1909), 6-7.

14. Commissariat report, 9 March 1904, F 17. 12547, A.N.; *Petite Gironde*, 20 December 1905; Bordeaux. 8 June 1907; Bordeaux. Arrêté, 18 July 1898, 442 O 32, 14 D 85, 104, A.M.B.; Toulouse. 29 December 1905, 8 May 1907; R. Delperie, "Toulouse et sa municipalité, 1900-1910, politique financière, économique et sociale," (Unpublished, D.E.S, University of Toulouse, 1967), 101.

15. Marseille. 21 April 1832; Bordeaux. 18 October 1881, 16 December 1884; *Petite Gironde*, 30 October 1905.

16. *Echo du Rhône*, 28 November 1892; Marseille. 10 April 1904.

17. *Revue municipale*, 16-31 January, 1904; E. Herriot, "La mise en régie du service des eaux de Lyon et ses résultats," *Annales de la régie directe*, I (November-December 1908), 39-42; slightly different figures, but same trend in Lyon. 20 January 1908.

18. Marcel Galibert, *La régie municipale des distributions d'énergie électrique* (Toulouse: Sud-ouest, 1924), 12, 18; Emile Bouvier, *Les régies municipales* (Paris: O. Doin, 1910), 1; Louis Roger, *Le domaine industriel des municipalités* (Paris: A. Rousseau, 1901), 7, 12.

19. Bordeaux. 29 September 1871; "Gaz de Bordeaux. Rapport de l'adjoint et de l'ingénieur de la ville sur leur mission en Prusse et en Angleterre," 29 November 1871, 42 O 11, A.M.B.; Eustache Pilon, *Monopoles communaux. Eclairage au gaz et à l'électricité* (Paris: V. Giard, 1899), 251-56.

20. Ville de Bordeaux, *Aperçu historique, sol, population, industrie, commerce, administration*, 1 (Paris: Hachette, 1892), 92; André Mater, *Le socialisme conservateur ou municipal* (Paris: V. Giard, 1909), 583; Lyon. 1 December 1913; Victor Augagneur, "La régie directe des services publics par les municipalités," Paul Pic and Justin Godart,

329

Le mouvement économique et social dans la région lyonnaise, 2 (Lyon: Stock, 1905) 84-86; *Documents rélatifs au projet du budget de 1904* (1903), 74.

21. Saint-Etienne. 1 March, 27 December 1907; E. Solles, "L'emprunt municipal," (1890), 32-33; *Petite Gironde,* 22 May 1901, 24 May 1901; Lyon, *Documents rélatifs au projet... 1904* (1903), 74; Lyon. 28 December 1908; Saint-Etienne. 1 March 1907; Alfred de Cilleuls, *Le socialisme municipal à travers les siècles* (Paris: A. Picard, 1905), 145.

22. Toulouse. 6 September 1899; Henri Duret, *De l'intervention des municipalités en matières d'habitations ouvrières* (Paris: Arthur Rousseau, 1910), 342.

23. Galibert, *La régie municipale,* 16-17.

24. Bouvier, *Régies,* 18; Jean-Louis Lartigue, *Les tramways—étude pratique de droit administratif* (Toulouse: Marquès, 1904), 201.

25. See the trilogy, Alan Mitchell, *The German Influence on France after 1870: The Formation of the French Republic* (Chapel Hill: University of North Carolina Press, 1979; *Victors and Vanquished: The German Influence on Army and Church in France after 1870* (Chapel Hill: University of North Carolina Press, 1984); *The Divided Path—The German Influence on Social Reform in France after 1870* (Chapel Hill: University of North Carolina Press, 1991).

26. Bordeaux. 29 September 1871; "Gaz de Bordeaux. Rapport de l'adjoint et de l'ingénieur de la ville sur leur mission en Prusse et en Angleterre," 29 November 1871, 42 O 11, A.M.B.; the report was reprinted in *Petite Gironde,* 22, 24 April, 1901.

27. Saint-Etienne. 1 March, 27 December 1907, 17 February 1911; Lyon. 28 December 1908; Pilon, *Monopoles communaux.,* 5.

28. Jean-Jacques Bienvenu and Laurent Richer, "Le socialisme municipal a-t-il-existé?," *Revue historique de droit français et étranger* (1984), 207.

29. Jules Guesde, *Services publics et socialisme* (Bordeaux: E. Forastié, 1883), 30; also q. in Michael John Mcquillen, "The Development of Municipal Socialism in France, 1880-1914," (Unpublished Ph.D. Dissertation, University of Virginia, 1973), 41-42; Pierre Mimin, *Le socialisme municipal devant le conseil d'état* (Paris: Sirey, 1911), 12-14, 124-33.

30. L. Stehelin, *Essais de socialisme municipal* (Paris: Larose, 1901), 12-14; Débats, 20 November 1894, Assemblée nationale.; *Le socialiste,* 26 December 1891, q. in Maurice Moissonnier, "Les Guesdistes et la bataille municipale (1891-1900), *Cahiers d'histoire de l'institut Maurice Thorez,* 19 (1976); Bienvenu & Richer, "Le socialisme municipal a-t-il existé?," 211.

31. Benoît Mâlon, *Le socialisme intégral,* 2 (Paris: F. Alcan, 1891), 35; Geneviève Prosche, "La 'dérive' réformiste du socialisme municipal ou 'possibiliste,'" *Revue historique,* 577 (January-March 1991), 121-32.

32. Adrien Veber, *Le socialisme municipal* (Paris: V. Giard and E. Brière, 1908), 5-7; Joseph Odelin, *L'évangile du parfait candidat* (Paris; Jouve & cie., 1913), 22.

33. Jean-Paul Brunet, *Un demi siècle d'action municipale à Saint-Denis—la ville rouge, 1890-1939* (Paris: Hachette, 1980), 7; McQuillen, "The Development of Municipal Socialism," 77-80, 110; Marseille. 29 April 1892, 23 June 1901.

Chapter 10: Municipalization

34. J. Lorcin, "Le socialisme municipal à Saint-Etienne en 1900," in *Mélanges offerts à M. le doyen André Latreille* (Lyon: Audin, 1972), 569. In his thesis, Lorcin provides a milder rendition of this quote: they are like beautiful girls "who take time ceding, but in the end do." Jean Lorcin, "Economie et comportements sociaux et politiques—La région de Saint-Etienne de la grande dépression à la seconde guerre mondiale." (Unpublished Thesis, Dr. d'état, University of Paris, 1987), 1382; Jean Lorcin, "Le projet du Lignon: une tentative d'application de la doctrine du 'socialisme municipal' à Saint-Etienne en 1900," *Bulletin du centre d'histoire économique et sociale de la region lyonnaise*, no. 4 (1973), 63-76; idem., "Houille blanche contre houille verte: le projet du Lignon à l'interconnexions entre 'Loire et centre' et les Alpes du Dauphiné," *Actes du Ve colloque sur le patrimoine industriel* (Arles: 19-21 October 1983), 100-102.

35. Marseille. 20 January 1901; V. Combarnous, *L'histoire du Grand théâtre de Marseille, 31 octobre 1787-13 novembre 1919* (Paris: Imprimerie méridionale, n.d), 249-65; Pierre Echinard, "L'Opéra de Marseille en 1900," *Marseille*, no. 149 (November 1987), 46-50.

36. Lyon. 6 February 1902; *Revue municipale*, 15-29 February 1904; Lyon. 12 December 1905; Gérard Corneloup, *Trois siècles d'opéra à Lyon* (Lyon: Bibliothèque municipale de Lyon, 1982), 164.

37. Judith F. Stone, *Search for Social Peace: Reform Legislation in France, 1890-1914* (Albany: State University of New York Press, 1985), 87-88; R.D. Anderson, *France, 1870-1914. Politics and Society* (London: Routledge and Kegan, 1977), 99.

38. Toulouse. 6 September 1899, 21 February 1905; Lyon. 13 April 1908.

39. Paul Leroy-Beaulieu, "L'état moderne et ses fonctions—les grands travaux publics, l'état central et les municipalités," *Revue des deux mondes* 3rd. ser, 90 (15 November 1888), 363-67; idem, *L'état moderne et ses fonctions* (Paris: Guillaumin, 1891), 88.

40. Lyon. 26 April 1911; Alfred de Cilleuls, *Le socialisme municipal à travers les siècles* (Paris: A. Picard, 1905), 2, 145.

41. L. Paul-Dubois, "Le socialisme municipal en Angleterre," *Revue des deux mondes*, ser. 5, 44 (1 March 1908), 135-58; Yves Guyot, *La gestion par l'état et les municipalités* (Paris: Alcan, 1913); Saint-Etienne. 8 December 1911.

42. For instance, the chief administrator of the privately run Lyon transportation company, Joseph Petit, "Municipalisation des services publics," *Exposition internationale de Turin* (1911), 61-62.

43. "Rapport du directeur des travaux publics," 31 January 1910, Ingénieur 293, A.M.T.

44. Bouvier, *Régies*, 20; Félix, *L'activité économique*, 1: 22, fn.2; Frédéric Ogereau, *Le développement des services municipaux particulièrement dans les grandes villes de France* (Paris: Arthur Rousseau, 1905), 112; Pilon, *Monopoles*, 201; Bouvier, *Régies*, 25-26; Henry Taudière, "La cherté de vivres et les autorités municipales," *Réforme sociale*, 7th. ser., 3 (1912), 760.

45. Lartigue, *Les tramways*, 195; *Le Temps*, 5 August 1894; Mimin, *Le socialisme municipal*, 29-47; "Vidange des fosses," Maurice Block, ed. *Dictionnaire de l'administration*, 2 (Paris: Berger-Levrault, 1905), 2634; Bouvier, *Régies*, 25.

46. Joan Scott, "Mayors versus Police Chiefs: Socialist Municipalities Confront the French State," John Merriman, ed., *French Cities in the Nineteenth Century* (New York: Holmes and Meier, 1981), 230-45; Mcquillen, "The Development of Municipal Socialism," 32.

47. Saint-Etienne. 30 January 1903.

48. Pierre Machelon, "L'idée de nationalisation en France de 1840 à 1914," Michel Brugière, et al., *Administration et contrôle de l'économie, 1800-1914* (Genève: Droz, 1985), 9-27; Claire Andrieu, et al., *Les nationalisations de la libération* (Paris: Presses de la fondation nationale des sciences politiques, 1987).

AFTERWORD

1. *Le Temps*, 27 July 1889; 16, 17, 20 August 1889.

2. On local statues, see William B. Cohen, "Symbols of Power: Statues in Nineteenth Century Provincial France," *Comparative Studies in Society and History*, 31, 3 (July 1989), 491-513.

3. Hippolyte Adolphe Taine, *Les origines de la France contemporaine*, 5 (Paris: Hachette, 1891), 369; the 44,000 figure refers to the highest number of communes existing and does not reflect a lower number, around 37,000, present at the time Taine wrote.

4. Robert Delorme and Christine André, *L'état et l'économie* (Paris: Seuil, 1983), 50, 73; Thomas Köster, *Die Entwicklung kommunaler Finanzsysteme am Beispiel Grossbritanniens, Frankreichs und Deutschlands, 1790-1980* (Berlin: Duncker & Humblot, 1984), 113-14.

5. On the garbage issue, Jeanne-Hélène Jugie, *Poubelle-Paris* (Paris: Découvrir, 1993), 212-13.

6. Marjatta Hietala, *Services and Urbanization at the turn of the Century—The Diffusion of Innovations* (Helsinki: Finnish Historical Society: 1987). Between 1838 and 1840, for instance, Toulouse corresponded with the following municipalities regarding their lighting policies: Arras, Avignon, Belleville, Bordeaux, Dijon, Guillotière, Lyon, Marseille, Montpellier, Orléans, Saint-Etienne, Strasbourg, and Valenciennes, 6D398, A.M.T.; L214 [provisional call number], Archives municipales de Bourges (information kindly supplied by Jean-François Babouin); 944WP, A.M.L. The information and archival reference regarding Lyon comes from Pierre-Yves Saunier.

7. Vivian A. Schmidt, *Democratizing France—The Political and Administrative History of Decentralization* (New York: Cambridge University Press, 1990); Douglas E. Ashford, *British Dogmatism and French Pragmatism: Central-Local Policy-Making in the Welfare State* (Boston: G. Allen and Unwin, 1981).

Index

Index